War, Politics and Jus

Essays 2003 - 2014

Lansana Gberie

Sierra Leonean Writers Series

War, Politics and Justice in West Africa
Essays 2003 - 2014
Copyright © 2015 by Lansana Gberie

ISBN: 978-9991-0-9218-8

First published 2015

Sierra Leonean Writers Series
Warima/Freetown/Accra
120 Kissy Road, Freetown, Sierra Leone
Publisher: Osman Sankoh (Mallam O.)
publisher@sl-writers-series.org

Dedication

For late Chief Hinga Norman and his comrades in the staunchly pro-democracy Civil Defence Force, Moinina Fofana and Alieu Kondewa to whom Sierra Leone owes everything.

Praises for another book by Lansana Gberie
A Dirty War in West Africa: the RUF and the Destruction of Sierra Leone

"…should be compulsory reading for anyone interested in Sierra Leone's 1991-2001 war… combines the skills of his career as a journalist and then a scholar and analyst. This book sets the standard for analysing Sierra Leone's war. This book should attract readers beyond Sierra Leone or West Africa specialists, since Gberie offers such a useful framework for explaining the behaviour of armed groups in wars in other corrupt states."
William Reno, Professor of Political Science, Northwestern University, in Journal of Modern African Studies / Volume 46 / Issue 02 / June 2008, pp 329-330

'…an even handed and perceptive account of the country's tragic civil war during the 1990s…Gberie's analysis is consistently readable, and he does a fine job of disentangling the complexities of the civil war, the international peacekeeping efforts, and the reemergence of reasonably stable constitutional rule….'
Foreign Affairs, January/February 2007 issue

"Gberie's writing offers an authoritative narrative, much of the strength of which derives from the detail that he provides. For those unfamiliar with Sierra Leone, this book is an invaluable introduction to and examination of the war."
Zoe Marriage in Africa Today Volume 54, Number 2, Winter 2007

"A Dirty War's great advantage is that Gberie is a journalist who was on the ground at the time…The result is lively history… Gberie is able to add a much more complete map of the nihilistic progress of the RUF and the abortive efforts to combat it."
Suanne Kelman, in Literary Review of Canada, June 2006

"…by far the most detailed and insightful yet about the conflict, and in one sense at least path-breaking: It covers the entire war years, and it can claim to be have been written by someone who was, in many ways, truly an insider…a very lucid and engaging account of Sierra Leone's implosion into violence and state collapse."
Foday Bockarie Fofana, in Awareness Times (Sierra Leone), 1 January 2006.

"The book is a valuable addition to the literature on the Sierra Leone war, written by a well-informed Sierra Leonean intellectual."
Mark Doyle, BBC, 12 January 2006.

Contents

Part IV: WAR AND MEMORY

Part V: WAR ON TRIAL

Part VI: A WAR ON SCREEN

Part VII: ELECTIONS AND THE POLITICAL FUTURE IN SIERRA LEONE, LIBERIA, IVORY COAST AND NIGERIA

Part VIII: OTHER WARS

PART IX: OTHER WRITINGS: PEOPLE AND BOOKS

Foreword

Before trying to resolve a conflict, one must first try to understand it. One must investigate its origins, study the context and background in which the conflict is taking place, and get into the mind-set of the individuals involved. If one adopts this approach, one soon realises that no two conflicts are the same and therefore there is no one blue-print for resolving every conflict. This may all sound blindingly obvious but sadly and all-too-often, attempts are made to resolve conflicts without following these simple rules, especially by outsiders who are not directly involved.

To assist us in this cause it is vital to have a catalogue of well-written and well-researched material of past and present conflicts. I therefore applaud the Sierra Leone Writers Series for publishing this collection of articles and book reviews written by Lans Gberie over the period 2002 to 2014. 'War, Politics and Justice in West Africa' is, an informed snapshot of events in West Africa and in particular of the conflict in Sierra Leone and Liberia, unsurpassed.

As he says in his introduction, the defining issue in Dr. Gberie's adult life was the rebel war in Sierra Leone and Liberia. He is well placed to write about these events. Others have done so; but by combining his journalistic and academic backgrounds he is able to both report vividly and analyse meaningfully. Few others have ventured into the field of conflict to meet the protagonists and also spend endless hours studying the reams of documentation deriving from it. Few others have interviewed Foday Sankoh in Sierra Leone and Joshua Blahyi (aka General Butt Naked) in Liberia and studied in detail the voluminous reports of the Truth and Reconciliation Commissions and the Sierra Leone Special Court.

Several of the articles are merely Dr. Gberie's reviews of what others have written, or filmed, but by bringing them all together in one publication the book provides a useful routemap to guide those wanting to learn more about events in West Africa.

But one is also able to discern what Dr. Gberie himself feels. Thomas Sankara, the late lamented leader of Burkino Faso, had noted that the ultimate challenge facing Africa was 'a just peace, dignity and genuine independence' and one can discern these threads running through Dr. Gberie's writings.

Sierra Leone is of particular interest to me having served as British High Commissioner during the latter stages of the conflict. Lans Gberie's book, 'A Dirty War in West Africa' remains, in my view, the best account of the RUF's war. I would like to think that if it had been available earlier, it might have prevented some of the mistakes made in trying to resolve that conflict and its aftermath, especially with reference to the antics of the Sierra Leone Special Court – the war crimes court set up to try those most responsible for the terrible atrocities in the Sierra Leone rebel war. Dr. Gberie's own views probably come across more clearly in the articles he has written about this expensive piece of international judicial machinery than in much of his other writings.

Like me, he condemns the indictment of Chief Sam Hinga Norman and his two fellow CDF members, Moinina Fofana and Alieu Kondewa. Indeed he dedicates this book to them, a dedication I warmly applaud.

Supporters of the Sierra Leone Special Court cite the indictment and conviction of Charles Taylor, the former President of Liberia, as evidence of the success of the Court but the indictment and subsequent death in detention of Sam Hinga Norman remains a stain on the legacy of the Court and by its actions, the Court has made it more difficult to resolve conflicts peacefully elsewhere in Africa. Who else will come forward to fight for peace and democracy if they find themselves indicted as war criminals? Tellingly Gberie quotes Justice Thompson, the dissenting Sierra Leonean judge of the Court, who expressed 'serious doubts whether a tribunal should hold liable persons who volunteered to take up arms and risk their lives and those of their families to prevent anarchy and tyranny from taking a firm hold in their society.' It is interesting to note how in recent times Western countries who have engaged in conflicts have actively supported 'civil militias'!

In his writings Dr. Gberie often focuses upon the individuals involved which adds flesh and colour to the stories told. In my experience nondescript officials sitting in their bureaucratic offices in Western capitals often find it difficult to accept the power and influence that individuals can have on situations and events in Africa. The role of Sam Hinga Norman has already been commented upon. I much enjoyed Gberie's profile of Desmond Luke, another unsung hero of Sierra Leone whom I much admire.

This collection of articles is brought right up to date with a couple of articles about the latest scourge to affect Sierra Leone, Liberia and Guinea – Ebola. There are some interesting parallels between the present Ebola crisis and the earlier conflicts, not least how meaningless national borders can be sometimes. On the topic of borders, I much enjoyed the account of Dr. Gberie's road trip from Accra to Lagos via Togo and Benin, which will bring a smile to all those who attempt to drive across from one African country to another!

Dr. Gberie's writings are immensely readable. He draws heavily upon other writers. Robert Kaplan's defining article, 'The Coming Anarchy', clearly had a big impact on him and there is no doubt that two of his favourite authors are Joseph Conrad and Charles Dickens. But as a modern observer and analyst he sets his own standard to which others should aspire.

Readers of this book will be better informed and thus better placed to offer their own opinions on war, politics and justice in Africa.

Peter Penfold
Former UK High Commissioner to Sierra Leone

Chief Komrabai Peter Penfold is the author of *Atrocities, Diamonds and Diplomacy – the inside story of the conflict in Sierra Leone*

Introduction and Acknowledgements

This book collects articles and book reviews I wrote for various publications, academic and journalistic, over the past 14 years. They are not arranged in chronological order, but there is a consistent underlying theme: my reaction to war, politics and transitional justice in Africa, with a particular focus on Sierra Leone and Liberia. Although I have studied these two countries more intimately than all others, this book includes articles on Ivory Coast, Nigeria and the Democratic Republic of Congo, all of which I visited for the purpose of writing the articles, among others.

The defining issue of my adult life to date was the 'rebel' wars in Liberia and Sierra Leone in 1990s. I had just entered university when the war broke out in Sierra Leone in 1991, and it profoundly shaped my stay there – the convulsions the war caused interrupted study; some colleagues on holiday were abducted and forcefully recruited by the Revolutionary United Front (RUF) rebels; and by the time I finished university in 1994, the war had engulfed the country with a destructive force. Deadly ambushes on highways prevented normal travel from Freetown to other parts of the country. My intense interest in the war influenced my becoming a journalist – I studied history in university – and I became fully engaged in reporting the war partly as a way of understanding it; comprehension as social inquiry, as much as journalistic vocation and earning a living, was a key motivation for me.

I was one of the first journalists to meet and interview the RUF leader, Foday Saybanah Sankoh, in early 1996; before then he was more or less a disembodied voice on the BBC. I also covered the war in neighbouring Liberia for Inter Press Service. In late 1996 I decided to undertake postgraduate studies with the aim of writing a thesis on the war, which I completed in Canada in 1997. After that I wrote a book length study, *A Dirty War in West Africa: the RUF and the Destruction of Sierra Leone* (London, 2005). I have travelled extensively in Africa, trying to understand political conflict. Some of the articles I wrote as a result are collected in this book.

The book is offered as a personal testimony. It is by no means a definitive or exhaustive study of those situations, each one of which deserves book-length accounts. It is offered to the general reader mostly without the academic apparatuses of footnotes and endnotes – the more curious reader may go to the original articles for those. Many of the shorter articles, which were originally published outside of West Africa, were republished in Sierra Leonean newspapers, the *Concord Times* (for which I was Features Editor in 1994) and the *Global Times*. I am grateful to the editors and publishers of these papers – Kingsley Lington and Sorie Fofana – for their enduring friendship and interest in my views and reporting.

The idea of putting this book together was persistently encouraged by Dr. Osman Sankoh, the amiable publisher of the Sierra Leonean Writers Series (SLWS), an old friend and compatriot. My wife, Karima, assisted with making the selection of articles for the book. Her enthusiasm for the project kept it on track. My friends Ian Smillie and Kingsley Lington read through the collection, liked them, and made some very helpful comments. I am grateful to them all, and to all those who – in various ways – stimulated my interest or added depth to my understanding of the countries represented in this collection. In this regard, I am especially thankful to my friend and former colleague Aaron Weah in Liberia, Jeddi Mowbray Armah (also in Liberia); my brother Vandi, my mother Haja Hawa Kallon, and Smart Kokofele in Sierra Leone; and Sam Turay formerly based in Ivory Coast. In Canada, Dr. Sarjoh Bah, Abu Samu, Monty Domingo, Lekan Akinsolo, Elikplim Dornor and Matilda Cole were immensely supportive. I am very grateful to Professor Miriam Conteh-Morgan of the Fourah Bay College, University of Sierra Leone, for her editorial guidance and assistance.

Part I

Contested Spaces

1.

Africa: The Troubled Continent[1]

'We're not "half-made" people[s], we're a very old people. We've seen lots of problems in the past. We've dealt with these problems in Africa, and we're older than the problems. Drought, famine, disease, this is not the first time that we're dealing with these things in Africa' - Chinua Achebe.

INWILLIAM BOYD'S NOVEL *A GOOD MAN IN AFRICA*, which is set amidst the putrefactions of a post-colonial West African state, Fanshawe, a smug British diplomatic official who is 'given to lyrical outbursts', reflects sardonically on a continent he now finds himself in after long service in the Far East. Africa, he says, gave him 'culture shock'. 'And the African, well, what can I say?' he blurts out, mordantly. 'A beautiful, elegant person . . . Harmony, you know, that's at the back of it all.' He is being sarcastic, of course, and he really means to refer to the 'Oriental'. But this idea of 'harmony', of the essential placidity of Africa, was once one of the fantasies of some Europeans about the continent. Clearly, it was mere fantasy. For 400 years the continent was ravaged by slave traders, and tin-pot despots and mercenary warlords were spawned as a result, continuing their depredations into the twentieth century. European colonial rule imposed its own form of order, but this was largely artificial; colonialism, by definition, is inherently unstable. In the postcolonial era, the continent's great contradictions and apparent unwieldiness, in the absence of a superimposing imperial force, have been given full vent. Much of Africa has since suffered violent political struggles, civil wars and now, in some places, normative collapse.

Scholars as well as policy-makers and journalists continue to argue about what, exactly, went wrong. There may never be any agreement, but it is idle to pretend that the continent's long history of exploitation, predation and despotic rule plays no role in its present decrepitude. It also does not help, however, to see the continent's predicament as a deterministic

---

[1] First published in *African Affairs* (Oxford University Press, London) (2005) 104 (415): 337-342

process flowing from this history. This is no place to consider the spurious, if tantalizing, debate about 'internalism' versus 'externalism'; but some of the issues the debate throws up are pertinent: Africa's condition, even its deadly civil wars and predatory insurgencies, are shaped by both internal and external factors, and any real solution must take this fact into consideration.

Peter Schwab's *Africa: A continent self-destructs* is a breezy catalogue of woes and failures, which, on the whole, creates the impression of a hopeless continent whose very survival, not to mention development, can no longer be assured.

The continent — he refers specifically to 'Africa south of the Sahara' — has been since 1991 'in the throes of a capacious and more permanent destructive cycle that [is] not idiosyncratic'. This clumsy sentence, appearing in the introduction to this little book, sets the tone for a less than careful and sensitive stock-taking of some of the continent's trouble spots. Schwab lumps together conflicts as different as those in Sudan, Ethiopia and Eritrea, Angola, Liberia and Sierra Leone, and gives the impression that all are the result of the failure of governance and postcolonial mismanagement and greed. True, he does take note of the historical problems of slavery and exploitative colonial rule, of the imbalances of global trade and the burdens of debt-servicing, but this appears largely as a ritual bow to intellectual rigour.

The problem is that, like so many of his contemporaries and 'fellow travellers' of the 1960s, Schwab, a political scientist, seems overwhelmed by the frustrations and disappointments of independent Africa. As a young man, he was idealistic enough to join the Peace Corps and became a volunteer teacher in Liberia (one of his students was Amos Sawyer, the former Liberian interim president and the country's best-known intellectual, who provides an enthusiastic endorsement for this slim book). The other, probably more important, problem is that which Paul Nugent, in his important study of Africa since independence, has identified: the difficulty of assessing the recent past, especially recent or ongoing conflict situations. There is, Nugent writes, 'an enormous outpouring of writing about contemporary Africa, but a lot of it is unreflective and does not seek to place the material in any kind of historical context'. Nugent adds that journalists 'seek to make sense out of the jumble of information, which they gather at some speed, but it is by no means sure that they make the best sense of it. Often, their noses are pressed up too close to the events for them to be able to properly explain them.'

Much journalistic writing—and not just journalistic writing, as Schwab's book demonstrates—on African conflicts is similar. But in this general outpouring of mediocrity, a gem sometimes appears which sets a new tone, adds significantly to knowledge, and becomes a reference point for years to come. Howard W. French's *A Continent for the Taking* could be such a gem.

I first encountered French in the *New York Times* — for which he was the West Africa bureau chief — in 1996. It was by way of an excellent portrait of Foday Saybanah Sankoh, the mysterious and nihilistic guerrilla leader who was causing havoc in Sierra Leone, including crudely amputating peasants' limbs and laying waste to the countryside. The article, which appeared in the paper's Sunday edition in April 1996, was charmingly entitled "African rebel with room service". I still have a cutting of this piece in my drawer, and I have referred to it in some of my writings on Sankoh's Revolutionary United Front (RUF). In the piece, French goes beyond the simplistic and sensational image of Sankoh and the RUF as barbarous thugs who were doing sensational things, to trace his background in the British colonial army, his imprisonment by the corrupt postcolonial government of Siaka Stevens, and his utter confusion arising from all kinds of influences, all of which made him quite neurotic. I had just met and interviewed Sankoh myself, and I couldn't help concluding, after reading French's portrait, that this American reporter had got it so much more accurately than anyone before him. I later learnt that French makes a lot of background inquiries, including email inquiries to H-Net Africa, the electronic forum for scholars of Africa, before setting out to write on issues he does not himself know a lot about. Needless to say, this is an invaluable methodology.

A Continent for the Taking is French's distillation of his many years of extensive travel in Africa and his reporting on the continent for various publications, most notably the *New York Times*. French is particularly interested in the Congo, which is a by-word for dysfunction—as well as a monument to greed and cruelty—to which he returns again and again; but his reflections on the ravages of Charles Taylor in Liberia and the allure of poor but dignified Mali can hardly be bettered. Africa for French is not simply a passing subject; it is a passion. "The personal reportage contained in these pages ranges from my earliest travels on the continent to the end of the century, " he writes. Those travels gave him, in his words: "a growing intimacy with the continent, where I discovered that questions of identity were usually far more complex than the stark black-white divide that I had grown up facing as an African-American in Washington, D.C., in the 1960s . . ." Questions of identity, French's acute awareness of Africa as ancestral home, and also as the object of exploitation and racist slurs, could be said to constitute the philosophical drift of this book, so to speak. "Africa is the stage of mankind's greatest tragedies . . . We awaken to the place mostly in fits of coarse self-interest and outright greed," French writes. "Once upon a time, these brief awakenings involved a need for rubber or cotton, gold or diamonds, not to mention the millions of slaves, branded and ferried like cattle across the Atlantic, whose contributions to the wealth of Europe and its coveted New World are scarcely acknowledged."

In less capable and sensitive hands, such an approach can easily descend to crude narcissism. But French, who writes that he accepted the *Times'* West Africa bureau in 1994 'as a personal challenge', manages to portray contemporary Africa in terms of both its strengths and weaknesses. When he took up the job, he was determined not to become a 'fireman' or voyeur, following the continent's many disasters merely to satisfy 'the world media's insatiable market in images of horror'. His elegant account stands in sharp contrast to the absurdities of Keith Richburg's *Out of America: A black man confronts Africa* (1997) or the solipsistic if sometimes insightful and admirably sympathetic *Mandela, Mobutu and Me* (2003) by Lynne Duke, both African-American journalists who also covered Africa as correspondents for major American newspapers.

5

French is no doubt well-versed in African history, and the first chapter of this book moves quickly through the continent's precolonial empires to the slave trade and colonialism. French somewhat inaccurately describes this period as 'prehistory', which provides an interesting context for the account of dereliction, violence, state failure and decay which dominates the book, in spite of the author's own wish. He balances this bleak picture — of the "Leviathan" Nigeria, so wealthy yet so poor and decadent, of Liberia and its warlord insurgency, of the wretched kleptocracy of Mobutu's Zaire, which finally implodes to become, once again, the Congo that attracts external pillagers — with his almost romantic reflections on Mali, so rich in history and culture and dignified in its steady adherence to democratic values and respect for human rights.

Africa, however, is a place of such chronic recidivism — crime mutating into worse crime, state embezzlers becoming warlords — that it is hard not to think of its bright spots as freakish. The real challenge, it seems to me, is not merely to describe its troubles and its hopes, which French does very well, but to seek a deeper comprehension of them. What forces, internal or external, physical or spiritual, philosophical or banal, are keeping the continent down? French shows very well the destructive nature of Western policies, including the hypocrisy of even the apparently well-meaning Bill Clinton. ' "The Clinton administration, actually, is no more than a representative sample, because the deplorable fact is that the United States has never had a sound Africa policy," French writes, noting that "starting from the height of the independence era, when the Central Intelligence Agency helped engineer the overthrow of Patrice Lumumba... [a coup which became] the first of dozens that would contribute to making Africa the world's least stable and arguably most corrupt continent."

The most emblematic problem of this problem-plagued continent has been civil wars or violent insurgencies. Until recently, about a third of Africa's states were embroiled in localized or regional warfare (or both), and weapons proliferated among private citizens, including children, whose participation in such conflicts has become a metaphor for the continent's underdevelopment and the lunacy that passes for much of its social functioning. A large number of these conflicts — excluding the

6

very significant ones in Angola and Sudan — began after the end of the Cold War, and are low-intensity. They became so widespread in Africa that Michael Ignatieff, a prominent liberal writer on conflict issues, could find it convenient to make this evident exaggeration: "War, like a virus, has worked its way into the very tissue of the Great Lakes regions, part of West Africa . . . It is the major employer, the chief economic activity. All power comes from the barrel of an AK-47." An earlier assessment by another liberal writer, Victoria Brittain of Britain's *Guardian* newspaper, put it in even more apocalyptic terms, speculating on a future for the continent in which "Conrad's *Heart of Darkness* will be read as straightforward description." The Congo was the exact setting for Conrad's famous short novel, and it is still a grim place. But West Africa, which Conrad never wrote about, has been only marginally better. As the editors of *West Africa's Security Challenges: Building peace in a troubled region* note, the sub-region "is among the world's most unstable regions."

In the last decade alone, Liberia, Sierra Leone, Guinea, Ivory Coast, Guinea-Bissau and Senegal have, in the words of West African security analyst Adekeye Adebajo, one of the editors, "been embroiled in an interconnected web of conflicts that have seen refugees, rebels, and arms spill across porous borders." This collection of essays, which he edits with Ismail Rashid, a historian at Vassar College in the US, trenchantly analyses these conflicts, providing insights into efforts at resolving them, with a focus on the role of the West African regional body ECOWAS. There are sixteen chapters in this collection, including the introduction (written by Adebajo) and a conclusion (written by Rashid), and as the editors note, most of these are written by African scholars and practitioners. The ECOWAS' Secretary General, Mohamed Ibn Chambas, provides the Foreword. The book is the product of a series of seminars organized by the New York-based International Peace Academy in 2002 and 2003.

It is an invaluable collection. Collaborative work of this nature is usually of an uneven quality, and it is almost trite to make this observation in reviews. This book is, in my view, an exception. Still, I find the chapters by James O. C. Jonah, a former UN Under-Secretary General (as well as a former senior cabinet minister in Sierra Leone), and Amos Sawyer, referred to earlier in this review, singularly insightful, and that is partly because they both offer the perspectives of practitioners who have been intimately involved in trying to resolve some of the conflicts in the region, while avoiding unnecessary polemics. Jonah's chapter evaluates the role of the UN, and particularly its often strained relationship with the regional body ECOWAS during the peace operations of ECOMOG, the regional peacekeeping force. Sawyer's chapter argues that issues of governance and democratisation are not only linked to security, but are 'central element[s] in the attainment of human security'. The point cannot be better put.

This short review cannot do justice to this rich collection of essays, but the quote from former Burkinabe President Thomas Sankara, with which the editors preface the book, is a good summary — and, one hopes, an apt conclusion for this essay. 'Our struggle will in no way be a limited struggle characterised by narrow nationalism. Our struggle is that of all peoples aspiring to peace and freedom. That is why we must never lose sight of the qualities and the just aspiration toward peace — a just peace, dignity, and genuine independence . . .'

A 'just peace, dignity, and genuine independence': this, it seems to me, is the ultimate challenge facing Africa and Africans around the world.

2.
West Africa: The Curse of Borders[2]

At the start of VS Naipaul's acerbic novel *A Bend in the River*, set in a disrupted post-colonial Central African state, the narrator, an Indian trader on the move, comments waspishly about "all that business at the frontier posts, all that haggling in the forest outside wooden huts that flew strange flags." Salim is clearly voicing the feelings of the deeply cynical and Afro-pessimist Naipaul himself, and the comment can be read as a yearning for the supposedly bucolic and ordered European-ruled Africa which so suited the fantasies of the likes of Evelyn Waugh and Graham Greene—a world so accessible and safe for non-Africans. But it nonetheless carries a particularly important truth. African borders are for the most part less places for customs or immigration regulation than for extortion and harassment of travellers and businesspeople by petty officials acting with impunity. And the cost, in the disruption of regular and legitimate trade, in travellers' time and vehicles fares, and in the accumulated frustrations and small terrors, is enormous.

To travel by road through West Africa is to arrive at this conclusion: For the sake of meaningful integration, Ecowas must devise a more rational, integrated and coherent frontier policy, one that would probably do away with more than 50 per cent of the officials and resources devoted by individual countries apparently to patrol their borders.

It was in November 2004 that I was starkly confronted with the problem when I made a road trip from Accra, Ghana, to Lagos, Nigeria, passing through Togo and Benin, all on the so-called Gulf of Guinea coast, and all proud members of the regional integration body Ecowas. The trip, which should take about seven hours, actually had me spend a sleepless night in Cotonou, at the craggy bedlam which passes for the border post supposedly separating Benin from Nigeria. And what an experience!

---

[2] First published by Znet, 19 January 2005

In the fourteenth century, Ibn Battuta, travelling "alone, having neither fellow-traveller in whose companionship I might cheer," observed after a long journey in West Africa that a traveller in the region would have no need to travel with companions because of the safety of [the] roads there. That was during the pre-colonial period, and Ibn Battuta's sojourn took him through the fabled empire of Mali, which was a model of functionality and coherence at the time. Not long after, however, the empire collapsed, partly the result of external predation, and the whole region was soon after ravaged by slave traders, and then, still later, partitioned into small colonies by European imperialists. The current Africa, the Africa of small states and shabby borders and strange flags, is the result. And in this Africa, the road is certainly not as safe as during Battuta's time, to put it no stronger.

I started the journey in Accra, in a vehicle provided by the British Council there (I was going to Abuja to speak at a conference on 'Strengthening African Democracies', organised by the British Council and Chatham House in London). The driver, a mild-mannered man with an anodyne face and clean hair-cut, claimed to have made the journey to Lagos before, which turned out to be a lie—and a huge problem. It turned out also that the vehicle itself had never made the journey—a worse problem.

Accra is experiencing something of a boom, with new buildings and new roads being constructed daily, a healthy economy. So it comes as a slight shock to be confronted, a few miles outside of it, evidence of the antique squalor still pervading rural Africa: the unpaved road, villages built of thatched huts that perish after a few seasons, the topless, sweating men working on their dug-outs, stunted little peasant farms. It took us about three hours to get to the border with Togo. It is the Aflao border station, and on the other side is the charming little beachside city of Lome, Togo's capital. This border area has been described colourfully, but not inaccurately, by the American journalist Robert Kaplan as 'chaotic: a rustic and clanging gate, charred and corrugated barrack houses, dirt, sand, flies amid piles of mangoes hawked by a small crowd of women, and lots of teenage boys armed with wads of cedis, the Ghanaian currency, which they were selling in exchange for CFA francs,' the currency used in Togo.

There are numerous customs and immigration officials, and one is required to pay an exit fee (for which, at least, a receipt is provided on the Ghanaian side); and immediately after crossing the imposing gate, one is again made to pay money to enter Togo. I did not need to get out of the car in either case, just handing my passport—an Ecowas passport—and some money to the driver to handle the eager—and, one might add, incurious—officials. But the transaction took time, and of course money. I noticed that the dozens of young people on either side of the border would walk from one side to the other with no one bothering them: the border controls, in other words, were not really for immigration or customs purposes but were instruments designed to make money out of travellers and businesspeople.

It was at this border post, on the Togolese side, that the decent and down-to-earth President Sylvanus Olympio, Togo's first president, was gunned down by his own soldiers in 1963. The man who led that utterly self-serving coup, a thuggish young officer named Gnassingbe Eyadema, took over after the assassination, and has since not ceased to be president. Today, the area is a bustling market town, with thousands of people in both countries doing cross-border trade which is made a little more expensive and needlessly formal by border restrictions. Both Togo and Ghana are peopled largely by the Akan-speaking group, drawing upon the same tradition and cosmology. The European colonisers, Britain (which ruled Ghana until 1957) and France (which ruled Togo until 1960) separated these peoples into different political units, gave them English and French as official languages respectively, and the result is that tiny Togo, which should really be a province of Ghana, is an impoverished backwater subsisting largely on underground trade (the result of the foolish border restrictions) with its neighbours.

Lome is a small city that seems to clutter about its beautiful Atlantic Ocean beachfront with its excellent auto road, with well-groomed coconut trees lining its side. This road leads straight to Cotonou, capital of Benin, about four hours away. The coastline, which you see almost throughout the journey, and which goes on to Lagos, constitutes the area known as the Gulf of Guinea. Long ago it was called the Slave Coast, the most important entrepot for the Atlantic slave trade which saw millions of Africans shipped to the Americas, a continent ravaged and neutered.

11

Just before one gets to Cotonou there is Ouidah, a small town in Benin which was one of the most important slave ports in West Africa. The port was the point of departure for 1.5 million slaves; the area is now a UNESCO cultural site. Ouidah's notorious history, partly popularised by Bruce Chatwin in The Last Viceroy of Ouidah, is the source of its celebrity status: the town is home of voodoo, from which Toussaint L'Overture got inspiration to lead the world's most successful slave rebellion, in Haiti in the eighteenth century; and it may have been the departure point for more enslaved African who peopled the Americas than any other.

An hour or so after Ouidah, we got to Cotonou, a dishevelled and bustling little city (population: 200,000) sporting more motor bikes—the speed and energy of these toys, men and women packed tight on top of them—than cars. But this was not my first or most striking impression of the place. As our car made its way through the packed but well-maintained asphalt road to the end of town where the border post (with Nigeria) is situated (there is an imposing toll gate just before it), one was struck by the hundreds of little street-side tables with jerry-cans full of petrol which are peddled to passing vehicles and motor bikes. These are smuggled petrol from Nigeria, sold openly on the streets, making redundant the few petrol stations that this little city sports. They also make nonsense of the frantic and overcrowded border post at the edge of the city. It was now almost 7:00 pm—we started the journey at about 1:00 pm—and the rush of energy in Cotonou, the speeding cars and motor bikes, thousands of people crowding the streets from work or just simply idling about, market women packing their wares, was simply overwhelming.

The desperate-looking Togolese border official in flowing, drab gown, his dusty feet in matching slippers, asked to see our papers, which we produced. He pretended to inspect them, and handed them quickly back. Then he asked to see papers for the car. The driver produced them. The official looked at the papers for about five minutes inside his shed, came back, and asked for papers showing that the car had made the journey to Nigeria before. He spoke in perfect Nigerian broken English (or patois) rather than French, the official language of Togo. It was then that I knew that neither the car nor the driver had travelled to Nigeria before. The official said that the car would have to be registered, which would take a whole day to arrange. After over 20 minutes of haggling, he decided that we would have to pay the equivalent of $20 in lieu of that, and warned us that we will face greater difficulties with the Nigerian border officials anxiously waiting a few meters away. "People take cars across the border into Nigeria to sell them, and there have been a lot of car thefts lately," he said. Since our car had never made the journey, it would be assumed that we are taking it to Nigeria to sell. The driver paid the $20—the two of us had by now paid more than $50 to an assortment of officials since we started the journey.

Benin and the huge area of Nigeria bordering it are peopled mainly by the Yoruba, a famously talented and enterprising people whose culture dominates the African diaspora, from Brazil to Cuba to the US and Haiti. But by colonial fiat, Benin was carved out of the disintegrating Yoruba empire of Oyo—attacked and looted of its marvellous bronze art by the British in the nineteenth century—by an encroaching French army. On maps, both Benin and Togo look almost like manic anomalies, cadaverous pieces of real estate sandwiched between Ghana and Nigeria. The impression of anomaly is only enhanced by the very circumstance of a place like Cotonou—depressed and almost chaotic, subsisting mainly on foreign aid and goods smuggled from its vastly bigger and richer neighbour, Nigeria, of which it should be a province. In fact, in spite of the lugubrious name and even more lugubrious politics, Cotonou seems like one sprawling suburb of Lagos, only an hour or so drive away.

The bored Nigerian border officials seated on hard wooden chairs in the corridors of an imposing structure built by Ecowas years back, apparently forgotten government civil servants who make bearable their often dreary vacancies by petty graft, are the first to make this suggestion to you. "They are prickly lot, these Benin people," one of them volunteered, apropos of nothing, as I handed over my passport. 'They have nothing. The day we closed this border to them, the whole country screamed."He was referring to an incident in 2004 when the Nigerian authorities, concerned about car thefts and smuggling from Nigeria into Benin, temporarily closed down the border. But the irony of the situation, since the whole point is that it borders (no pun intended) on his livelihood, appears lost on him. He was Yoruba, and he said although he felt "an ancestral connection" to the people of Benin," he had "a job to do." There lay the pathos of the situation: muddled ideas of sovereignty, the starveling patriotism, petty graft as policy.

This border post, on the Nigerian side, must count as one of the world's most bizarre, irrational and corrupt. The official eyed my passport as one would do some exotic object, clumsily turned the pages, and, ignoring it, asked whether I had my yellow fever vaccination papers. I said I didn't, and didn't need it anyway. He said that that was for him to decide. And his decision was that I must pay the equivalent of $15 for not having it. At the far end of the border post, in a dusty and cluttered room that passed for the Customs Section, the driver was being quizzed about the car. It was now past 8:00 pm, and the place was dark.

The official wanted to know who owed the car. When that was confirmed, he asked whether the car had previously made the journey to Nigeria. There was no record of that. The official smiled covetously and announced that in that case the driver must put a bond of $1000 for him to allow the car to cross the border. Meanwhile, I had negotiated down what I was to pay for the lack of yellow fever immunization papers, and given the official $10. I asked for a receipt. He smiled at me sardonically, as at a clueless foreigner and a fool, and waved me off, telling his colleagues—who were seated in a row after him—to inspect my papers further. It was now clear that we were going to spend a long time at this border post.

In fact, refusing to pay the $1000 bond, we spent the night there. I wanted to go across and have a drink in Badagry only a few miles away, on the Nigerian side. Badagry, like Ouidah, was a famous slave entrepot, and hundreds of thousands of enslaved Africans were shipped through there to the Americas. Badagry—the poetic name was alluring. It was now about 10:00 pm. A kindly woman at the post advised me against going. There were, she said, dozens of little roadblocks along the way, and in spite of these—she perhaps meant because of these—the road wasn't safe at night.

I bought beer by the roadside, and sat down with the border people, who had now become suddenly friendly. By about mid-night, dozens of young men arrived at the vast, open space before the post and were spreading mats to sleep on. On inquiry, I was told by a Nigerian border guard that they were 'touts' from all over West Africa, and that an enterprising woman rents out mats to them at night. Touts!

I walked to a group of the men, young people from different parts of West Africa: there were Ghanaians, Sierra Leoneans, Nigerians, Togolese, others. They all spoke broken English and appeared at home in their harsh world. There are millions of such young people all over the region, the vast, overwhelming world of lumpen West Africa. In *This House has Fallen*, the journalist Karl Maier quotes a figure of between 60-70 million young people in Nigeria alone, many of them unemployed—in effect touts. These young men, denizens of the streets and the border areas and the city slums, make a mockery of almost every conception of identity based on nationality or borders: they move across borders with little awareness that they are moving into a different country: it is simply a vast lumpen world for them.

Robert Kaplan, travelling through West Africa mainly by road in the early 1990s, his imagination overwhelmed by these unemployed young people, thought that he was at 'the frontiers of anarchy.' I didn't see anarchy. Yes, I saw wasted energy, a great dereliction. But I also saw in it all a new, creative signal, of pointless West African borders finally withering away, of the region integrating more fully in spite of its pedestrian political class. This process, so inevitable, needs a little guidance, a form of political oversight. Ecowas, founded in the 1970s as an instrument for regional economic integration but now overwhelmed by internal conflicts, should provide such an oversight. In the absence of such an effort, the energy of these young people, as we now know, gets sucked into endeavours entirely destructive, like mercenary warfare. We think of these wars as rebel wars. But they are rebellion only in so far as nihilism is rebellion. These young people are not the ones rebelling—they are simply co-opted into enterprising warfare by utterly predatory elements: whether these despairing and poor young people know it, they are essentially mercenaries. This is the new bane of the continent, and borders are contributing immensely to it. They should go.

15

A POSTSCRIPT: I spent the night at the border post, smoking through it and counting the hours. Early the next morning, I hired a car, and went through the border to Badagry. The car from the British Council went back to Accra. Badagry: I was now in Nigeria, in this old Yoruba port city, a Dickensian creation. I was happy I did not make it to the place the previous night. For here, "You groped your way for an hour through lanes and bye-ways and court-yards and passages; and you never once emerged upon anything that might be reasonably called a street. A kind of resigned distraction came over the stranger as he trod those devious mazes, and, giving himself up for lost, went in and out and round about and quietly turned back again when he came to a dead wall; and felt that the means of escape might possibly present themselves in their own good time, but to anticipate them was hopeless. Gables, housetops, garret-windows, wilderness upon wilderness, smoke and noise enough for all the world at once." The passage is from Charles Dickens Martin Chuzzlewit, and it describes Todger's section of London. But the passage captures best the jumbled nature of Badagry, giving a good notice of what parts of Lagos, a much bigger and richer city, would be like.

I got to Lagos by road and then flew to Abuja, Nigeria's modern administrative capital (what a contrast from Badagry, Lagos, and the wretched border post!) A week later, I flew to Geneva, Switzerland. From there, I went by road through France to Mont Blanc in Italy. The journey took about one hour and thirty minutes. A journey through three countries, and there wasn't a single border post. And these are countries with a history of bloody wars and tribal rivalries.

I started by saying that the innumerable West African borders are bad for business, bad for travel, and a mockery of Ecowas' avowed aim to integrate West African economies. I have even suggested that they may be complicit in the region's perennial instability. I am restating these points for emphasis: the borders must go.

3.
Guinea: on the brink?[3]

There is something almost freakish about Guinea, a West African nation of deceptive size (it is as big as the UK but with a population of only about 8 million) and a heroic history. It seems to have remained on the brink, but never falling off the precipice, since it gallantly wrested its independence from France in 1958. Its young and charismatic and radiant leader at the time, Shekou Toure, a former trade unionist and a descendant of the great nineteenth century West African resister of European colonialism, Samori Toure. Toure first caught the attention of the world when he rejected De Gaulle's offer of a wider union with France – something that Toure, with good reasons, saw as a neo-colonialist ploy – and opted for immediate and complete independence with the words: "We, for our part, have a first and indispensable need, that of our dignity. Now, there is no dignity without freedom. We prefer freedom in poverty to riches in slavery."

High, powerful, resonant words – and the French, angry at the defiance, reacted with extraordinary malevolence and vandalism. They withdrew immediately from the former colony, taking with them everything from colonial archives and development plans to light bulbs, dishes from the governor's mansion and telephone receivers, and even emptied pharmacies of their medication, which they burned. They then launched a campaign to isolate the newly-independent African nation. Toure was unfazed; and with crucial help from Kwame Nkrumah's Ghana – a handy loan of 10 million pounds as well as some technical support – Guinea survived, albeit falteringly. Momentarily, it held a strong, romantic fascination for many (In 1971, many around the world cheered when Toure repelled a nasty mercenary invasion from Portuguese-controlled Guinea Bissau, with which his country shares borders). For

---

[3] Znet, 15 September 2006.

Guineans, however, stalked by technical and economic disabilities – soon to be compounded by demented policies of repression which the naturally paranoia Toure enacted to maintain power – they never came to enjoy either freedom or riches.

I first went to Guinea in 1983, shortly before Toure's rule was ended by his death in a hospital in Morocco and a coup that brought to power Lansana Conte, the head of the army. Though barely in my teens then, I could sense the tenseness of the atmosphere in Guinea (compared to its neighbours), the palpable fear, the feeling that state security was an ever-menacing presence. Shops opened and closed at a time set by the government, and there were local party officials and gendarmes everywhere to enforce even such mundane orders of the state. Toure's party, in his own words, directed "the life of the nation; the political, judicial, administrative, economic and technical" structures of Guinea. It was totalitarianism of sort, anchored on pretend socialism, and its deformities were felt widely in Guinean society. Guinean intellectuals who expressed any scepticism towards Toure's government were either forced into exile (like the famous novelist Camara Laye) or jailed (the fate of dozens). And jail, in Guinea then, meant death: prisoners were fed on what the regime ominously called 'black diet', locked up in tight cells with no light, and only occasionally food or water, where they simply wasted away.

When Conte took over the bankrupt state in 1984, he tried to liberalise both the economy and politics, inviting exiled Guineans to return, and giving impetus to a bourgeoning private sector. There were limits, however. When Conte organised nation-wide elections in 1993, he rigged them brutally. In 1996, he crushed an army pay mutiny, and condemned some of the mutineers to die and allowed others to die in jail. In September 2000, 'rebels' attacked a number of Guinean border towns immediately south of the capital, Conakry. The area had become home to tens of thousands of Sierra Leonean refugees fleeing RUF attacks on civilians inside Sierra Leone. Not long afterwards, similar groups attacked Guinean towns and villages in the 'Parrot's Beak' area of the country, emerging from Sierra Leone and from points along the Liberian border, causing great destruction and dislocation, driving Guineans out of their homes along with as many as 75,000 Sierra Leonean refugees who had been living on the Guinean side of the border for several years. The rhetoric of the 'rebels' notwithstanding – the carefully-choreographed impression was that Commandant Gbago Zoumanigui, one of the officers behind the failed army mutiny, was leading the incursions – it was clear that the attacks were inspired by Charles Taylor. Conteh organised a brutal counter-attack (with his overzealous and sometimes ill-disciplined soldiers attacking refugees, raping and killing some of them), which succeeded in repulsing the incursions.

I visited Guinea again at the height of the tension, in 2001. The country was less tense than it was under Toure, but it was hardly less paranoid. The shops were far better stocked, but Conakry, the capital, had become more, not less, chaotic; where under Toure people feared the gendarme acting on the orders of the state, now the ordinary fear was of soldiers and armed police acting in collaboration with armed robbers to steal from the hapless, impoverished population. "In the towns," Conte had declared, "the population has developed the habit of living off the crumbs of society, pilfering and trafficking of all sorts. Production is abandoned. Theft and corruption rule." Meanwhile, the country's jails, symbolically emptied when Conte first came to power, were becoming full again, and becoming just as ghastly.

Human Rights Watch issued a seriously disturbing report on the prison conditions in the country. Entitled "The Perverse side of Things," the 32-page report documents excessive police brutality in the country, including the torture of men and boys held in police custody. The victims, the report notes, are individuals suspected of common crimes as well as those perceived to be government opponents. Once transferred from police custody to prison, many of these are "left to languish for years awaiting trial in cramped, dimly lit cells where they face hunger, disease and sometimes death." In other words, the "black diet" has returned. The grisly report, which includes shocking photographs of police victims of torture, can be found at: http://hrw.org/reports/2006/guinea0806/.

For anyone remotely interested in the West African sub-region, or for that matter in issues relating to repression, political stability and human rights, the report is a must read, as is an earlier one published by the International Crisis Group (ICG), "Guinea in Transition" (April 2006). Human Rights Watch gives a hint of the urgency of the situation in the statements opening the report: "With its president, Lansana Conte, rumored to be gravely ill, its economy in a tailspin, and its military thought to be deeply divided, Guinea is a country teetering on the edge of a political transition. But while Guinea's political future may be uncertain, the fact that ordinary Guineans are regularly brutalized by the very security forces responsible for protecting them is not. Immediate measures to combat this culture of violent law enforcement are critical, and could boost Guinea's stability at an uncertain time of impending political transition."

Both reports speak sedately of an impending "political transition." Of course the chain-smoking, diabetic Conteh, once regarded as a national hero for leading Guinean forces in repelling the Portuguese-supported mercenary invasion of 1971, will probably die soon. What will happen next, however, is far more unclear. Conteh has ruled Guinea as his personal fiefdom, and there is no clear, constitutional line of succession. Guinea stands out in the region for its almost complete lack of a viable civil society: there is none of the vibrant semi-political groupings one finds in surplus in places like Liberia and Sierra Leone, groups that helped these states to maintain a level of democratic consensus even when governments collapsed and praetorian terror reigned. Should Conteh die without establishing a successor, the army, which is highly corrupt but still largely coherent, will take over, but there might be serious convulsions within the body politic: Guinea, after-all, has been experimenting with elections, and there are disgruntled political parties, however enfeebled, and they have their support bases (in ethnic groupings and regions, for example). The problem is that it doesn't have to be like this. Guinea is a highly resource-endowed country, and unlike its neighbours Liberia and Sierra Leone, it has a strong tradition of patriotism and a strong sense of self-worth. These are partly the legacy of Toure's rule and his defiance of powerful countries. Guinea certainly takes its independence very seriously. Many Guineans have seen the nihilistic violence which gripped their neighbours and are wary of violent struggles for power. Guinea played a positive role during the wars that ravaged the region, playing host to thousands of refugees from Sierra Leone and Liberia, and contributing troops to enforce peace in both countries. In fact, it was largely as a result of Guinea's determination that Charles Taylor was forced out of power – and is now convicted war criminal.

That Guinea itself now faces the prospect of unraveling in an impending power struggle – which would inevitably throw the region once again into a spiral of violence and refugee movement – is highly unsettling. It calls for the most urgent and creative conflict-prevention strategy at the highest levels of the international system, from the West African body Ecowas, the African Union (AU), and the UN Security Council. Powerful governments with huge economic investments in Guinea (like the US, which mines the lucrative bauxite deposits, of which Guinea holds 30 per cent of the world's supplies), and those with significant military and diplomatic interests (like Britain, which its continuing commitment in Sierra Leone), should play a more proactive role in nudging the sclerotic Conte administration towards setting a timetable for political transition. Multilateral institutions like the World Bank and the IMF suspended cooperation with Guinea in 2003, partly as a result of Conte's rigging of elections and his brusque, inept and corrupt style of leadership. This suspension needs to be reviewed: for all their faults and cruelty, these multilateral institutions have a powerful influence in much of Africa.

If the hard-won peace in Sierra Leone and Liberia are to be sustained, and if the region is to be spared another round of violence and displacement, the world should focus more constructively on Guinea now.

4.

The Yenga Affair: Guinea–Sierra Leone border dispute[4]

A necessary and mutually applauded security measure taken by Guinean forces during Sierra Leone's brutal rebel war has escalated into a border dispute which threatens the stability of both states. But while the issue – the Yenga dispute – is often cast in romantic and highly inflammatory terms by Sierra Leonean poets, so-called civil society activists and journalists, the entire story is steeped in bathos. Before the war, Yenga was a tiny impoverished fishing village of fewer than 100 people and 10 old shacks. But it is strategically placed among a system (albeit largely undeveloped) of inter-connected waterways tied to the large Moa river and formed by the convergence of three other rivers emanating from Guinea, the Mellacourie, Fourecaria and Bereira. Much of this area, extending far into northern Sierra Leone and including Rio Pongas and Rio Nunez in Guinea, was once known collectively as Mellacourie.

Until its recent notoriety, hardly anyone emerging into Yenga from the humungous grassed and potholed road would take any particular notice; the more important places were Kailahun, Koindu, Bomaru and Sienga on the Sierra Leonean side and Guekecdou and Forecariah on the Guinean side. It was a sleepy fishing hamlet, separated from Guinea by the Moa River. However, this cartographic factor was purely fictive for the people living on both sides of the river: movement from Sierra Leone into Guinea and vice versa was unrestrained by border guards, and people on either side of the river maintained families on both sides.

Believe it or not, this was exactly the vision of the colonial powers, Britain and France, when they demarcated the area between the two competing empires. The new political and geographical reality was only expressed in the two dozen or so beacons planted by the Europeans, over them flying two flags at the close of the 19th century. They rudely

---

[4] *Pambazuka, 2009-09-03, Issue 446.*

separated the Kissi people and even separated families living in the area, forcing them into states they never bargained for. The border demarcation wasn't exactly as perfunctory as the carving out of Uganda, which, as legend has it, was given as a birthday gift to Britain's Queen Victoria by an English adventurer marauding through East Africa, but the logic was the same: there was scant consideration for the Africans living in these places and of course no concern about the future viability of the hastily created states. It is mainly for this reason that Amos Sawyer has made the important suggestion, as of yet not taken up elsewhere, that more concrete steps should be taken towards a political union of all three Mano river basin states (Sierra Leone, Guinea and Liberia).

So why do people in the poverty-stricken and militarily disabled Sierra Leone and Guinea, who just recently emerged from brutal wars (with Guinea still crippled by political instability) speak about this strip of land as though they want to ignite another violent conflict in the region? There is obviously a need for a serious reality check.

I spent a grim afternoon with a very senior Sierra Leonean army officer who told me rather blithely and against all available evidence that all the Sierra Leonean military needed was the order from 'the civilians' and Yenga would be recaptured from the Guineans promptly. And as I write, there is a virtual movement in Sierra Leone quaintly named 'Save Yenga Save Salone', a campaign that has attracted media activists, poets, 'civil society' and some politicians. One such politician, Musa Tamba Sam, belonging to the opposition Sierra Leone Peoples Party (SLPP) recently tried to get Yenga debated in parliament, but the effort was wisely rebuffed by the speaker. The issue, the speaker said, was being handled diplomatically by the government. The honourable Sam is from Yenga, born at a time when the village was still part of the Kissi-Teng Chiefdom in Kailuhun District in the Eastern Province of Sierra Leone.

The (uncharacteristic) restraint of the Ernest Koroma government on the Yenga issue, which mirrors that of the previous Kabbah's, is admirable. If every serious national issue since Koroma came to power would have been approached the same way, calmly and deliberately, then a lot of the serious errors of judgment – the churlish sacking of civil officials believed to be supporters of the opposition, attacks on

24

opposition infrastructure and many other acts of venality and peevishness that his government has committed – would have been avoided.

The Yenga issue is, as hinted above, the legacy of two searing historical factors: European colonialism and a brutal post-colonial civil war. Surprisingly, both now carry equal resonance. However, for all the right reasons the emphasis should be on the more recent past. For Guinea entered Yenga not as an enemy but as a friend in pursuit of a common enemy, a "rebel" force of medieval barbarity. Guinea, in fact, has been a very good neighbour of Sierra Leone, on countless occasions coming to the aid of the desperately inept Sierra Leonean army as well as taking in tens of thousands of Sierra Leoneans fleeing the depredations of the rebels, as refugees. I will return to this point, but first to the colonial provenance.

Ian Brownlie's *African Boundaries: A Legal and Diplomatic Encyclopaedia*, published by Hurst (London) for the Royal Institute of International Affairs in 1979, at 1355 pages long is the invaluable guide to the historical basis of African borders. The book reproduces a number of documents, including agreements and letters and memoranda from British and French officials which formed the basis of the Sierra Leone–Guinea border. The first was the Anglo-French Convention of 28 June 1882 (preceding the Berlin Conference which officially partitioned the African continent among the Europeans, by two years). The British recognised French claims to Mellacourie (of which, as I noted earlier, Yenga would have formed a part) which now meant French control of the entire Futa Jallon region, the basis of their colony of Guinea. Article 11 of the convention stated that the 'Island of Yelboyah and all islands claimed or possessed by Great Britain on the West Coast of Africa lying to the south ... as far as the southern limit of the ... colony of Sierra Leone' shall henceforth be recognised by France as belonging to Great Britain and the 'Matacong and all islands claimed or possessed by France on the West Coast of Africa to the north ... as far as Rio Nunez' shall be recognised by Great Britain as belonging to France.

This document is rather imprecise with respect to important details and successive agreements between the two European powers would modify it considerably. In fact, the present border was only firmly agreed on in 1912–13. The original agreement, for example, placed Pamalap and a large part of Kabala District under French jurisdiction. However, pressure from British merchants (the area was lucrative in the groundnut trade) forced the British authorities to renegotiate with the French. Consequently, these places were ceded to the British. Then British Foreign Secretary Sir Edward Grey, who never visited West Africa, proposed the final adjustments in January 1911. The new agreement defined the Moa or Makona River as the physical boundary dividing the two entities; none of the documents – which are exact about place names and physical conditions ("ruined villages", etc: this was during the era of frequent slave raids by Sofa warriors from what is now Guinea.) – mention Yenga. It almost certainly did not exist at the time. But the final protocol delimiting the boundary is precise: "the frontier … follows the thalweg [a line connecting the lowest points of successive cross-sections of a valley] of the River Meli [from Guinea] to its meeting with the Moa, or Makona, on the understanding that the islands marked by Letters A and B on the attached map belong to France and that the island marked C belongs to Great Britain." The protocol, signed at Pendembu on 1 July 1912, accepted Grey's proposal that within six months of the signing of the agreement "the natives in the transferred territories shall be permitted to cross the frontier to settle on the other side and to carry with them their portable property and harvested crops."

Grey had also proposed – and this was accepted – that where 'a river forms the boundary, the populations on both banks shall have equal rights of fishing'. And there's the rub. What if something more valuable than fish, oil or diamonds say, are found in the river? How would this agreement work? The agreement simply said that the use of "hydraulic power" in the river would only be authorised by agreement between the two states. Furthermore, using a river as a boundary is problematic, since rivers can dry up (there is the greenhouse effect, which no one knew about then) and damming can change the course of any river.

In fact, it all worked well until the recent war in Sierra Leone and with it, the Revolutionary United Front's (RUF) discovery of diamonds in the Moa and subsequent Guinean occupation, initialised by RUF incursions into Guinea. It worked rather too well, in fact. Graham Greene, idling for a day or so at that border area in the early 1930s, walked from Kailahun into Guinea (then French Guinea), but of course he does not mention Yenga in his classic travel book of this West African trip, *Journey without Maps,* as almost certainly, he wouldn't have taken notice. The border between the two colonies, Greene wrote, "is the Moa River, about twice the width of Thames at Westminster." Then Greene makes a very sapient observation: "The curious thing about these boundaries, a line of river in a waste of bush, no passports, no Customs, no barriers to wandering tribesmen, is that they are as distinct as a European boundary; stepping out of a canoe one was in a different country. Even nature had changed; instead of forest … a narrow path ran straight forward for mile after mile through tall treeless elephant grass."

I have visited the area. The lush rainforest on the Sierra Leonean side that so impressed Greene has been largely denuded by unrestrained logging activity, and there is generally no husbandry. One now sees the same humungous or elephant grass that Greene saw on the Guinean side harassing the tiny motor road leading to Yenga. Guinean troops are now firmly in control and recently forced a Sierra Leone political contingent to disarm its security before entering the place.

A bad sign, but in fact it was not always like that. The problem began in September 2000 when the RUF attacked a number of Guinean border towns south of the capital, Conakry. The area had become home to tens of thousands of Sierra Leonean refugees fleeing attacks on civilians inside Sierra Leone, part of the RUF's 10-year campaign of terror and destruction in that country. Not long afterwards, the RUF attacked Guinean towns and villages in the 'Parrot's Beak' area of the country, emerging from Sierra Leone and from points along the Liberian border. Here they caused much greater destruction and dislocation, driving Guineans out of their homes along with as many as 75,000 Sierra Leonean refugees who had been living on the Guinean side of the border for several years.

The RUF attacks attracted little attention, except as a humanitarian footnote to the more notorious conflict in Sierra Leone. I spent two weeks in Guinea at the time researching a report for Partnership Africa Canada and I reported then that Guineans themselves appeared to be

27

confused. Following rebel attacks on Forecariah, less than 100km from the capital Conakry and home to tens of thousands of refugees from Sierra Leone and Liberia, in early September 2000 the Guinean President Lansana Conté broadcast an inflammatory statement on state radio and television. He blamed the incursions on the refugees, provoking widespread attacks by Guinean police, soldiers and civilian militias on the already traumatised refugees.

The attacks on Forecariah, by RUF rebels operating from Kabala, a Sierra Leonean town close to the Guinean border, were diversionary and the rebels withdrew without much resistance after Guinean forces counter-attacked. However, better planned and more coordinated incursions were soon to follow. In January 2001 the RUF moved from Sierra Leone, along with Charles Taylor's forces into the diamond-rich areas around Macenta (in the so-called Forest Region), Madina Oula (near Kindia) and the important trading city of Guéckedou, which like Forecariah, was home to tens of thousands of refugees. The attacks on Macenta and the destruction of Guéckedou alerted Guineans to the seriousness of the crisis. The attacks quickly spread, threatening to engulf the districts around Bonankoro.

Then finally Guinea responded proportionately. With crucial help from the United States (which maintained an annual C-JET training program with the Guinean army) and France, Guinea acquired some armoured helicopters and some old MiG fighter bombers which were used to pound rebel bases in both Sierra Leone and Liberia. Guinea also helped to train over 1,000 Donsos (the Kono name for Kamajors or the Civil Defence Forces) made up of Konos and Kissis from the Yenga area and Kono District, all along the Guinea–Sierra Leone border, deploying them against the RUF. I saw about a thousand of them during my visit and also saw British officers who had an open-ended military commitment to Sierra Leone, helping to train the Guineans and the Donsos militia. Guinea routed the RUF, helping to accelerate the disarmament process in Sierra Leone; in effect, Guinea defeated the RUF. It then occupied the Sierra Leonean side of the border, including Yenga.

After the war ended, Kabbah negotiated the withdrawal of most of the Guinean forces but renegade officers, now engaged in lucrative mining at

Yenga, refused to move and the ailing Guinean leader was simply a hostage of the military. An agreement was signed on 15 November 2002, months after the war officially ended by Sierra Leone's internal affairs minister the late Hinga Norman and his Guinean counterpart, El-Haj Moussa Solano, affirming the colonial-era border agreement. But the agreement was not conclusive; it called for the setting-up of a committee to work towards a resolution that would restore Yenga to Sierra Leone but assure Guinean border security – a very legitimate issue obviously. But the talks have become open-ended and there is no assurance that Yenga will be restored to Sierra Leone soon, or perhaps ever at the current pace.

Personally, I see little problem with the Guinean presence at Yenga, but clearly it is a volatile issue, what with the attempt to politicise it. But all loose talk about reclaiming the village by force should be discouraged. Inflammatory steps by some NGOs like World Vision's (a notoriously vulgar group which is in the habit of showing poor and sick black and brown kids on TV to raise money) which a couple of years ago claimed that it was prevented from building a school at Yenga by Guinean troops, should be firmly suppressed. Many of the impoverished villages on both sides of the border do not have functioning schools, so why pick on beleaguered Yenga?

The flamboyant Sierra Leonean Defence Minister Palo Conteh has been quoted saying that there is no point in negotiating with the Guinean junta since it has not been recognised by either the Economic Community of West African States (ECOWAS) or the African Union (AU). He has a point, though it is utterly impolitic of him to have gone public with such a statement; street corner talk has its place, but it should be allowed in the Defence Ministry or State House.

While President Koroma can make his very loud votaries and supporters feel good by declaring that Sierra Leone and Guinea are sister countries who are working together to resolve the Yenga issue without resort to international mediating bodies, the overheated rhetoric elsewhere is not reassuring. I think it is time that ECOWAS takes tentative steps to engage both nations on the issue. There is a clear early warning signal here...

5.

Is Democracy under threat in West Africa?[5]

In May 2012, Said Djinnit, head of the UN Office for West Africa (UNOWA), briefed Security Council members on what he saw as a disquieting trend in West Africa. During the preceding two months, Mr. Djinnit told council members, military coups had aborted preparations for democratic elections in Mali and Guinea-Bissau. Senegal, where his office is based, just managed to escape a violent turn. Electoral violence in Nigeria in April 2011 caused the deaths of more than a thousand people, while terrorist violence — led by an Islamist group called Boko Haram — has since escalated, leading to many more deaths and destruction in the country. Also in 2011, a simmering civil war in Côte d'Ivoire was reignited after the incumbent president, Laurent Gbagbo, refused to honour an electoral verdict against him. In fact, over that past year, Africa has experienced eight such unconstitutional or extra-constitutional attempts to change governments or to hold on to power, and some have been successful. Something must be done to tamp down this trend, Mr. Djinnit told council members.

The Norm

Because of West Africa's past experience with coups and civil wars, it was inevitable that the latest developments would induce strong anxieties. Yet for the past 10 years, elections and peaceful changes of government were becoming more the norm. Some of the region's long-lasting wars, like those in Sierra Leone and Liberia, were ended, and democratic elections brought in more capable governments. That Africa as a whole is becoming more democratic, stable and prosperous as a result of frequent elections was celebrated even by the mildly "Afro-pessimist" London magazine The Economist. In July 2010 it commented, "Only a decade ago countries such as Sierra Leone and Liberia were bywords for anarchy and bloodshed. Now their people vote enthusiastically. It will be hard even for dictators to take that right away

---

[5] *African Renewal*, 18 August 2012

altogether, for the experience of elections, even flawed ones, seem to help embed democracy."

In February 2009, following coups in Mauritania and Guinea and an attempted coup in Guinea-Bissau, the African Union (AU) enunciated a policy of zero tolerance for all coups. It condemned the "resurgence of the scourge of coups d'état in Africa" and declared that it will never recognise a government that comes to power unconstitutionally, a position later endorsed by the UN Security Council. Mr. Djinnit's alarm and the swift condemnation of the coups in Mali and Guinea-Bissau — first by the Economic Community of West African States (ECOWAS), then by the AU and the Security Council — were therefore predictable.

Yet the manner in which these developments have played out suggests a complicated picture. Guinea-Bissau has been an exception to the overall trend of democratisation in West Africa: the country has experienced five military coups in the past decade, and no elected president has served out his term. So when soldiers seized power on 12 April and imprisoned interim President Raimundo Pereira, Prime Minister Carlos Gomes Junior and several other senior officials, aborting preparations for a run-off presidential election, the move did not come as a particular shock.

Setback in Mali

Mali, however, was a celebrated case of democratic awakening in West Africa, so the events there did take many by surprise. On 22 March, soldiers led by a young officer named Amadou Sanogo abandoned a faltering campaign against Tuareg rebels in the north of the country and seized power from President Amadou Toumani Touré. ECOWAS promptly condemned the coup and imposed financial and other sanctions on Mali. This was not simply a case of the military going awry: external factors clearly played a decisive role in the turn of events. The problem partly had to do with the resulting return to Mali of tens of thousands of migrants, including a few thousand heavily armed and battle-hardened Tuareg fighters who had fled Libya following the overthrow of the dictator Muammar al-Qaddafi. These fighters gave new potency to the few and largely contained Tuareg separatists in northern Mali, leading to the rebels' capture of the three northern regions of Gao,

Kidal and Timbuktu and a proclamation of secession from southern Mali. There are wider implications for the region, beyond Mali itself. A report by a UN inter-agency mission to the Sahel in January to assess the impact of the return of about 420,000 migrant workers to Mali, Niger and Mauritania predicted broader instability. The mission found that Libyan small arms, explosives, rocket-propelled grenades and small-calibre anti-aircraft cannons mounted on pick-ups were finding their way into the hands of diverse separatists and other rebels. Groups like Al-Qaeda in the Islamic Maghreb (AQIM) and Nigeria's Boko Haram were already flocking to Mali in mid-2011. Many parts of Mali, Niger, Mauritania and Chad have been overwhelmed by the returnees from Libya, 95 per cent of who are male, poorly educated, aged 20-40 and embittered. AQIM was providing relief for some of the returnees, facilitating potential recruitment and popular support, the mission was told. According to the mission, the most advanced of the measures adopted to deal with these problems were probably those taken under Mali's Special Programme for Peace, Security and Development in the North, a pet project of President Touré, although there were local concerns about poor management. Barely two months after the report was issued, the coup took place, and Mr. Touré later fled to Senegal.

Averting crisis in Senegal

When Mr. Touré arrived in Senegal in April as a refugee, the scene was steeped in pathos. Less than two months earlier, Mali, with the dignified Mr. Touré presiding over an electoral process in which he was not participating, seemed to stand taller than Senegal, which was then deep in a morass created by its fumbling president. Senegal has been a constitutional democracy since it gained independence from France in 1960, and has suffered no coup or serious political upheaval. This would suggest that elections had become routine. However, President Abdoulaye Wade, who came to power in 2000 and was already in his eighties, introduced a new constitution. The Constitutional Court issued a curious legal judgment permitting Mr. Wade to run for a third term, maintaining that since the constitution was new, his first term could not be counted. The argument had a narrowly legalistic logic that was lost on most Senegalese. All they knew was that the constitution said the president should not serve more than two terms, and Mr. Wade had already served two.

There were mass protests, leading to burned public buildings and several deaths. Senegalese — and the world — prepared for the worst. But when the elections finally came in February, Mr. Wade secured only 34.8 per cent in the first round. In the run-off the following month, he was crushed by 51-year old Macky Sall, who had previously served as his prime minister. Following his humiliating rebuff, Mr. Wade handed power over to Mr. Sall.

What accounted for the different outcomes in Mali and Senegal? First, of course, was the spreading rebellion in Mali, bolstered by Libyan arms. Also important is that the two countries have rather different historical experiences, with electoral institutions and a democratic culture much stronger in Senegal than in Mali. In fact, the four communes of the French colony of Senegal enjoyed a remarkable democratic franchise dating back to the 19th century. History does matter.

Election triggers

Yet Senegal's democratic traditions did not prevent pre-election tensions and violence, suggesting that even reasonably strong democratic systems in the region are vulnerable. Vulnerable to what? In all the cases cited, elections were either taking place or approaching. Are elections becoming, as the UK political scientist and Africa expert Dennis Austin suggests, a "spur to violence" in the fragile democracies of West Africa? Competitive politics, while attractive, clearly add depth to the sense of division in diverse societies, since there is a strong temptation for rogue leaders to exploit ethnic and other fault lines. The problem is that there seems to be no better alternative. A June [2012?] report by the New York–based International Peace Institute on "Elections and Stability in West Africa" recommends a creative approach to electoral assistance. It suggests that external electoral assistance be integrated within a broader conflict-prevention strategy that gives attention to the political aspects of the electoral process, as well as the technical ones. Safeguarding elections, in other words, should be seen as just one component of a longer-term commitment to building democracy. Also important are the growing calls on the international community to stand firm in not recognising any coup, as espoused by the African Union.

Part II

This is War!

1.
The 'Rebel' Wars of Africa: From Political Contest to Criminal Violence?[6]

I spent a grim afternoon in January 2008 with Joshua Blahyi, a notorious factional leader during Liberia's civil war. Blahyi, also known as General Butt Naked, had a few days earlier told his country's South African-style Truth and Reconciliation Commission (TRC) that he killed 20,000 people during Liberia's civil wars. He had started as a boy soldier for the United Liberation Movement of *Liberia* for Democracy–Johnson faction (*ULIMO-J*), an ethnic militia group, and later formed the Butt Naked Brigade, a band of naked child fighters who believed that nudity made their bodies impervious to bullets. This faction fought in the very destructive battles of Monrovia in April 1996; claims that the group committed ritual cannibalism were widespread at the time.

We met in downtown Monrovia, Liberia's capital. Blahyi, appearing eager to be interviewed, confirmed to me the claims that his group committed ritual cannibalism. But he regretted that this happened; he was now a born-again Christian and wanted to send a message of contrition to his fellow citizens. Curiously, though, he was insistent on the sensational point that he did indeed kill 20,000 people during the war. Why was he so certain about this large detail, I asked? Did he count his victims? As a good Christian, Blahyi said, he did not want to lie. Why, I asked, did he fight? What was the point of the Butt Naked Brigade? Here, Blahyi was far less certain. He said simply that there was a war, and fighting was all that mattered at the time. He didn't want to be a victim; that wasn't the manly way to go. As a former 'tribal priest', he said, he knew how to protect himself and his people, and this was what he was doing. He was happy now that it was all over, and he was asking for forgiveness from all Liberians.

---

[6] Published in *The Journal of Modern Africa Studies* (Cambridge University Press) Volume 52 / Issue 01 / March 2014, pp 151-157

What accounted for a group like the Butt Naked Brigade? Was it a 'rebel' movement? What was it rebelling against? Did he have an idea of Liberia as a political and social community when he led those naked boys to inflict unspeakable violence on mainly defenceless people? What, in any case, constitutes rebellion in this context?

Blahyi, like many of those he recruited, belonged to the Krahn ethnic group in Liberia. Master Sergeant Samuel Doe, the dictator who exercised tomcatting powers over Liberia from 1980 to its descent into civil war in late 1989, belonged to that group. Charles Taylor's National Patriotic Front of Liberia (NPFL), which started the war against Doe, was made up largely of rivals of the Krahn, whose primary motivation was to wreak vengeance against the Krahn for past outrages under Doe. It was in that atmosphere that Blahyi and his Butt Naked Brigade emerged: more or less as an entrepreneurial ethnic militia. Violence, in other words, had merely begotten more violence; and warfare was more or less a correlate of state collapse. It was Hobbes' fantasy realised. In important ways, in other words, the state, in all its fissiparous complexity, was central to the widespread violence, even as a now-neutered agent. In neighbouring Sierra Leone at the same time, the Revolutionary United Front (RUF) was having the bodies of its child recruits crudely tattooed with the words R-U-F and then sending them – flagellant and immensely lethal machines – to inflict a regime of terror and rapine on defenceless people, much like the écorcheurs who desolated parts of Europe in its period of deranged transition several centuries ago.

William Reno's *Warfare in Independent Africa*, probably the most penetrating and comprehensive account of the many wars, petty and large, postcolonial Africa has suffered, gives an extended treatment to the RUF but does not mention Blahyi and his colourful gang. This is partly because the RUF was far more significant than the short-lived and puny Butt Naked Brigade; and also because Reno has devoted more time to the study of Sierra Leone (the subject of his first, profoundly illuminating, book, *Corruption and State Politics in Sierra Leone*) than any other country in Africa. But the choice underlies a difficulty this book attempts to grapple with: why call all these diverse armed groups rebels? Why lump together the exalted anti-colonial guerrillas in the Portuguese colonies of Guinea-Bissau and Angola, the armed vigilante groups in

Nigeria, anarchic gangs in Somalia, and the largely criminal outfits like Taylor's NPFL and its sidekick, the RUF, about which there was absolutely nothing enobling? "Whatever these armed groups are called," Reno writes, "they share the feature of challenging the authority of Africa's state regimes over the last half century, and for that purpose they will be called 'rebels' in this book" (p.3).

One can quibble: many of the groups discussed in the book did indeed challenge state authority, but some others emerged precisely because such an authority no longer existed. In his introductory overview Reno discusses the evolving nature of warfare in Africa over several decades, sketching a depressing trajectory which accurately mirrors the changed fortunes of the African state, from the great hopes of independence to the great meltdown of the 1980s and 1990s. Guinea-Bissau, the tiny West African state whose inspiring liberation struggle under the great Amilcar Cabral has now been completely forgotten as it degenerates into Africa's first narco-state, emblematises this journey more than every other; and Reno rightly begins his book with a reference to its exalted beginnings and the pathos of its current condition.

Reno writes of the "changing fields of leverage" in which "rebels" have operated in Africa over the decades, and he identifies five categories of rebels who have reflected these circumstances or in some cases shaped them. The first were the anti-colonial rebels who took on their repressive European overlords: they systematically liberated their territories from the Europeans, building up alternative regimes and providing coherent visions for the future. These were followed by "majority-rule" rebels, groups rather similar to the former in modus operandi and who fought mainly against racist European settler minority regimes in South Africa, Rhodesia (now Zimbabwe), and Namibia. A third set of rebels to have emerged in Africa, more or less chronologically, have been "reform rebels" who, in the 1980s, launched what they consciously felt were 'second liberation' struggles against regimes as hopelessly repressive to the vast majority of their citizens as the European colonial regimes they had replaced. Yoweri Museveni of Uganda best exemplifies this category. The 1990s, probably the worst period of regression in postcolonial Africa, saw the emergence of a category that Reno well-delineated in a

previous book,[7] "warlord rebels". Their successors or contemporaries –
but certainly their inferior in organization and capacity to wield political
influence – Reno calls 'parochial rebels'. These are groups often in the
pay of sociopathic political entrepreneurs or acting on their own. Their
aims are mostly limited to criminal appropriation and carrying out
assassinations and limited violence or thuggery. Reno insists on calling
them 'rebels'; United Nations reports often refer to such groups, not at
all inaccurately, as 'militias'; the media and many ordinary people may see
them merely as gangsters. Young fighters in all these categories were
similar, Reno writes, but the aims of the leaders of the groups in the
1990s "were more parochial: to grab power in the existing political
system instead of creating a new one, or to defend a particular ethnic
group" (p.1)

Reno elaborates that the leaders of warlord and parochial rebels are often
insiders holding important positions in the pre-war patrimonial political
order, and their aim is merely to capture the political order for
themselves once that order starts to hollow out or they find themselves
out of favour, but not to change the system. Ideologically-driven rebels
do not emerge in such a degraded political system because "the regimes
in Africa that base their authority most thoroughly on the manipulation
of access to patronage opportunities, have been very effective in
disrupting the organizing strategies of ideologues, and have made
deployment of rebel commissars considerably more difficult than under
colonial or apartheid regimes". These categories, he writes, "do not fit
easily into a simple scheme of state collapse and ungoverned spaces." (p.
246).

There is much truth in this observation. Liberia's prolonged civil wars
had rebel leaders like Charles Taylor, Alhaji Kromah and George Boley,
all of them former senior government officials. In Côte d'Ivoire,
Alassane Ouattara, a former Prime Minister, emerged as the "godfather"
for the so-called Forces Nouvelles de Côte d'Ivoire (New Forces: FNCI
or FN), who led a successful rebellion against Laurent Gbagbo. But
Sierra Leone's Foday Sankoh and his colleagues were entirely different:
they were totally alien from the governing elite, and completely lacked

---

[7] *Warlord Politics and African States* (Boulder, Colo: Lynne Rienner, 1998)

political instinct, never mind sophistication. The evidence collected by the Special Court for Sierra Leone, which Reno makes no use of, exhaustively shows that the RUF survived and became powerful largely because it was a (sort of) sub-warlord force tied to Taylor in Liberia, fighting a near-collapsed patronage state in Sierra Leone. Reno remarks of Joseph Kony, the demented, sex-crazed leader of the Lord's Resistance Army (which began its depredations in northern Uganda, but now operates in parts of the Democratic Republic of Congo and Central Africa Republic), that his group largely reflects his ideas, style and initiatives, but this is entirely true of almost every rebel group in all the categories Reno delineates. Surely, as Brian Crozier noted in *The Rebels: a Study of Post-war Insurrections* (Boston, 1960), the objective conditions notwithstanding, without the emergence of a *rebel*, there can be no rebellion. All rebellions are inevitably shaped by the character of their charismatic leadership, and this remains a very important point about rebels and rebellions anywhere and at any time but particularly, I suggest, about warlord and parochial rebels.

Another important point is that the earlier categories of rebels faced exclusionary and powerful regimes, and their leaders had to be men (always men) of character and vision. They were, therefore, able to provide alternative systems that were both more humane and more effective than those they sought to destroy. Moreover, they were operating during the Cold War and politics mattered then: rebel leaders were perforce to demonstrate some sophistication in international affairs; had to be able to speak the language of one or the other of the superpowers.

Must one repine, therefore, at the absence of ideological commitment of the so-called warlord or parochial rebels? There are, in fact, immensely well-organised and ideologically sophisticated rebels operating in Africa, but they are as depressing as the warlord and parochial types: Nigeria's Boko Haram and Somalia's Al Shabaab, Islamist terrorist groups whose outrages against the civilian populace compares rather favourably with the depredations of the likes of Taylor.

Towards the end of this important book, Reno reflects mordantly on the nature of the African state, which, despite the destructive warfare and

internal contestations, its fissiparous vulnerability, has remained
sacrosanct so far as its international borders are concerned even to those
forces whose activities are profoundly inimical to its very survival.
African countries have supported rebel groups operating in neighbouring
states, but even powerful states in Africa have not tried to remake the
map of Africa. Reno writes that this is a "fortunate outcome" of the
Cold War (p. 243). This is probably true to a point; but far greater credit
must be given to African regional organisations and, most importantly,
the United Nations, that very influential factor in African decolonisation.
In recent years, the United Nations has contrived the concept of 'peace
building' (and fashioned the Peace building Commission) precisely to
make sure that failing or collapsing states which it has helped bring into
existence are put back together and protected.

Jennifer Hazen's *What Rebels Want* begins by challenging the view that
recent conflicts in West Africa have been purely civil or intrastate wars;
and with great acuity she explores both the motivation and the reasons
for the significant durability of the category that Reno calls "warlord
rebels" in Liberia, Sierra Leone and Côte d'Ivoire.

Hazen examines seven "rebel" groups in the three countries, and sheds
important new light on particularly three – the Liberians United for
Reconciliation and Development (LURD), the Movement for
Democracy in Liberia (MODEL), and the Front Populaire Ivorien.
These groups, never particularly well-organised or integrated, had
nonetheless immense impact due largely to the support they got from
outside.   A rebel group's capacity to fight, Hazen found, "is the
measurement of the group's access to resources" (p. ix). As a resourceful
investigator for the International Crisis Group, Hazen saw firsthand
Guinean government and military support for the LURD, which almost
overwhelmingly accounted for its strength, leading her to conclude that
intrastate conflicts "are rarely purely intrastate in nature; most involve
transnational dimensions of some kind" (p. 1).

The theory of "greed versus grievance" –which seeks to explain, or to
explain away, recent African civil wars, depoliticising them and
dismissing them as criminal, rather than examining them as political–has
been one of the seductive academic fads since Paul Collier published a

paper for the World Bank with the title in 2000. Hazen rightly rejects this argument, noting that 'greed' plays only a 'minor role' in conflict (p.175). This is debatable; generalisations such as this are unwise, particularly regarding intangible factors like greed and grievance. But it serves Hazen's purpose well. There is often a presumption, she writes, "of [sic] access to resources rather than an assessment of access," leading to "a focus on certain lucrative gems and minerals or drugs as primary sources of income." This overwhelming focus, she argues cogently, "detracts attention from the wide range of support groups receive and the numerous ways in which they obtain resources that enable them to continue fighting." And this leads "to an overestimation of groups resources and capacity to fight and the assignment of certain motives (i.e., greed) to a group, all of which are less evident on closer scrutiny" (p. 171-172).

This is Hazen's original – and important – thesis. From this, the picture she paints of the various rebel groups is a messy one which cannot fit any single theoretical frame. How does, she asks, having access to economic resources lead to enhanced military capacity? Or does it really? What economic resources are easily fungible into military resources? Hazen's careful examination of the rebel groups' decision-making processes, and how factors like resources, ethnic support, charisma of rebel leadership, and, most important, external interventions help to prolong civil wars, or ultimately end them, is an important contribution to the debate about how to end these petty wars quickly. On average, she writes, external interventions "prolong rather than end civil wars" (p.45). This is because such intervention "alters the dynamics of civil war by changing the resources available to warring factions" (p.46). This is both true and important; but from the evidence *Why Rebels fight*, all the civil wars in West Africa, that vortex of instability, were ultimately ended by external, mainly United Nations, interventions.

It is surprising that Hazen does not use the very copious and indispensable data from the trials of the Special Court for Sierra Leone, for they would have helped to both strengthen and to modify her arguments in parts. The 2493-page trial judgment involving Charles Taylor (including annexes of maps, sources, and a long table of authorities) detailed how "beyond reasonable doubt" Liberian president

Taylor's support and mentoring of the RUF helped prolonged the war in Sierra Leone and make it so deadly. The judgment noted that diamonds mined or stolen at gunpoint by the RUF in Sierra Leone were taken to Taylor in Liberia for "safekeeping" – or in exchange for weapons. The trial Chamber unanimously found that Taylor's support for the RUF was driven by pillage not politics.

I have drawn attention to this very careful, deliberative judgment to show that while Hazen's thesis can largely stand up to scrutiny it may not always be true. The RUF and some of the other groups she writes about in *Why Rebels Fight* may have started out with genuine grievances, but they more or less went septic, and warfare became little more than organised theft. This dynamic, it is important to note, was often driven by external interest. It is a small variation on Hazen's thesis.

That so-called rebel wars in Africa have become messier and in some cases anarchic, and rebel leadership less admirable, there can be no doubt. These two very valuable books tell us why this is so, and they tell us a lot about Africa's current state and prospects of its future stability.

2.

Why 'A Dirty War in West Africa': An Interview by Znet[8]

Can you tell ZNet, please, what your new book, *A Dirty War in West Africa* is about? What is it trying to communicate?

Gberie: The book is about the conflict that ravaged the small West African state of Sierra Leone for a decade, beginning in 1991. When I started writing it I had the idea of simply recounting what I saw and heard and experienced as a journalist writing about the war in the 1990s. I didn't have grand theories or ideas; I simply had my notes and very vivid memories. I wanted to tell a story…But then I was writing my MA thesis on the war. So I had to grapple with a lot of misconceptions about the war. There was in particular Robert Kaplan's highly influential article, "The Coming Anarchy," which appeared in the *Atlantic Monthly* magazine in 1994. The article, one of those breezy and impressionistic accounts favoured by some Western journalists with a taste for lofty pronouncements, depicted the war as an anarchic – rather than political – meltdown due to environmental problems, unchecked population growth, the spread of disease and crime, and, in his words, "the rise of tribal or regional domains." I was a journalist based in Sierra Leone when this article appeared, and I didn't see any of these things that Kaplan was describing. Yet this foolish article was faxed by the Clinton administration to all of its embassies around the world as a warning about so-called "failed states!"

A number of scholars quickly challenged Kaplan's views. Paul Richards, a British anthropologist who has worked for a long time on Sierra Leone, wrote a book-length essay disputing Kaplan, and some Sierra Leonean scholars also wrote dismissing Kaplan's highly damaging views. I am thinking about people like the historian Ibrahim Abdullah, Yusuf

---

[8] Znet, 7December 2005

Bangura, Ismail Rashid, Patrick Muana, and a few others. I was greatly influenced by their views, and I communicated with them extensively while writing my MA thesis on the war. That was finished in 1997-98.

After that I got involved with Partnership Africa Canada an Ottawa-based group which was doing work around natural resource predation and violent conflict in Africa. I worked with a team – including Ian Smillie and Ralph Hazleton – doing a study of the Sierra Leone war which focused on the role of diamonds in the conflict. That study, published as "The Heart of the Matter: Sierra Leone, Diamonds and Human Security" (2000) became one of the most influential documents about the war; it was extremely well-publicised, and was adopted as a policy document by many organisations and governments.

I thought then that it was time to put all of my findings, my reflections, and my journalism into one consolidated document. The present book is the result.

As I note in the preface, the book combines journalistic reportage and historical analysis. It does not pretend to be an aloof academic work. I wanted to write for a general readership, simply, accessibly, and without polemics. Tell a factual, unsentimental account about the travails of a country blighted by misgovernment, the cruelties of the international capitalist system, and demented geopolitics…

ZNet: Can you tell ZNet something about writing the book? Where does the content come from? What went into making the book what it is?

Gberie: The book, as I said, is really more or less a personal account. It is written largely from my notes taken in the course of many years. Of course I also relied on the work of others. Some academics and journalists and non-academic researchers have written, over the past few years, quite incisively about the war. One has to acknowledge their contribution, and this I do in the text. But I'll be appalled if this book is

45

read as an academic text; it is not and it is not meant to be. I hope it'll be seen as some kind of elevated journalism, the reflections of one man who saw some of the horrors associated with the war, who relied on his instincts in understanding them, but who also relied on the insights of others.

Quite a lot of passion but also restraint went into writing the book. One has to be affected by some of the outrages and violations – the hacking off of hands, the burning down of villages, towns and parts of the capital city, the murder of thousands of people and the associated injustices of it – one has to be affected by these, and this comes out in the text. But I aimed very much at comprehension, not just the recounting of horrors and the condemning the perpetrators as "evil". I do no such thing. The commitment was to understand, and to explain in an intelligent, reasonable way what happened in Sierra Leone during the wars years.

ZNet: What are your hopes for *A Dirty War in West Africa*? What do you hope it will contribute or achieve, politically? Given the effort and aspirations you have for the book, what will you deem to be a success?

Gberie: The book is aimed at Sierra Leoneans generally, and all those people who have an interest in Africa, and those who make decisions that profoundly affect Africans. When you read through the book, you'll see how apparently playful or irresponsible decisions sometimes have extremely profound impacts. Millions of human lives are at stake. People who fantasise about revolutions, about regime change etc, should reflect very carefully on how their fantasies will eventually play out. The fate of nations and human beings cannot be abstract; they are real. And any action aimed at that fate will have real impacts on lives and whole societies. That is one way to look at it.

There is, of course, the issue of misgovernment by successive leaders of Sierra Leone. There was that long reign by the despotic and very corrupt All Peoples Congress (APC) party, and then the depredations of the military regimes which succeeded it. So, good governance is a very real issue, in more ways than one. The absence of it made the country so vulnerable, unprepared; the country atrophied in the face of assaults by a petty army armed sent into country by   foreign interests. I am thinking of the machinations of Liberia's Charles Taylor and various arms dealers and diamond merchants. When you study the war carefully, you'll realise that the whole threat of the so-called Revolutionary United Front (RUF), the rebel army which spearheaded the war, could have been easily contained by a reasonably functioning state with a decent police force. The country was in the throes of collapse when the RUF invaded in 1991; and mercenary though the RUF undoubtedly was, it was able to recruit support among the country's disenchanted youth population, sometimes quite easily. What people forget is that it is very easy to provide causes for poor people. The opportunity for looting quite easily becomes a political cause: it could look like taking aim at the corrupt elite.

I note in the book that Sierra Leone's rulers have no alternative but to build up an effective bureaucratic state that functions at the social level – provides jobs, social services, that is responsive to the needs of its populace, avoid extravagant corruption etc. The war should be seen as a hard lesson for the negation of this basic requirement, this compact between citizens and the state.

But there are wider lessons. The war was undoubtedly funded to a large extent, particularly in its mid to final stages, by proceeds from the illicit trade in diamonds, of which the country abounds. It was as a result of our work at Partnership Africa Canada (and the work of others, including Global Witness, the UN, some major governments, the UK, Canada and South Africa in particular) that the Kimberley Process was initiated to control the flow of diamonds into the international market. The Kimberley Process was an important step forward. Now, as a direct spin-off from it, some NGOs and the diamond industry itself have started a Development Diamond Intiative (DDI), with the aim of making the conditions of work of diamond miners and mining communities in

Africa decent and more rewarding. It is outrageous that while the global rough diamond trade is worth about $7 billion a year (this translates to nearly $70 billion when the diamonds are made into jewelry), the average diamond digger in Africa subsist on less than a dollar a day. This has to change – if poverty is to be reduced, and if the nihilism that we saw exhibited in Sierra Leone is to be avoided in similar situations.

[ZNet?]: What would leave you happy about the whole undertaking? What would leave you wondering if it was worth all the time and effort?

Gberie: I would be happy if the book actually gets read in Africa, especially in Sierra Leone. I highlighted a number of lessons to be learnt: regarding governance, resource management, the business of war and peace, the sacrifices of ordinary people, the efforts at local civil defence. I was particularly fascinated by the work of the Civil Defence Force, especially the Kamajors. These are ordinary men and women who, abandoned by a failing state and a criminal army, mobilised to defend their villages and towns. They are the true heroes of the war. It is unfortunate that their spiritual leader, so to speak, Hinga Norman, is in detention of a rather very misguided foreign-imposed judicial system, the UN-Sierra Leone Special Court. It is an outrage, really.

I also note the role of foreign intervention forces, from the West African ECOMOG to the UN and the British forces. A lot of lessons to be learnt from these as well…

3.
Reflections on Liberia[9]

I arrived in Liberia, not for the first time, in January 2008, and lived in the country for nearly two years. Like many outsiders who had been following the Liberian crisis for years, I was enthusiastic. It was two years into the rule of President Ellen Johnson-Sirleaf, Africa's first female president.

All the reports from the country seemed to indicate the right trajectory: Ma Ellen, as the President was affectionately called, had been an inspired choice. She was robust, a Harvard-educated economist who said all the right things, and was working hard. Roads were being constructed, the airport, long in a battered, shambolic state, was being renovated, and for once in a lifetime, Liberians appeared optimistic.

There was, as expected after years of civil war, no running water or mains electricity (despite a previous fanfare about street lights), but few of us expatriates minded this. The country had just emerged from a bloodbath, and was now gallantly--under a passionate leader who knew how to talk about "absorptive capacity," "capacity building," "pro-poor changes" etc--moving forward.

Besides, the homes of expatriates--in not-so-exclusive places like Mamba Point, Sinkor and Congo Town, and rented for tens of thousands of US dollars from mainly Lebanese landlords who had bought up the crumbling structures for peanuts during the war and had them rebuilt just in time--were well-supplied with electricity from generators, and water in tanks driven in every day or so.

One could, in other words, afford to be philosophical about these things. Monrovia, in fact, was rather well-spruced for these kinds of residents: it even had sushi restaurants, a pastry shop, and supermarkets that sold excellent French and South African wine at bargain prices.

---

[9] *New African*, 1 October 2010.

So, for some people at least, the country was doing well, and these are the people whose views and reports about Liberia one reads or hears in the ubiquitous international media. The lives of ordinary Liberians were automatically reckoned to be improving: surely they now had peace, costing the international community, in the form of the UN mission called UNMIL, over $600m a year. In fact, in 2008, the country was reckoned by international financial institutions as the fastest improving African nation.

It did not matter much, in still other words, that for the vast majority of its citizens, Liberia was completely bottomed-out, ordinary subsistence a near-miracle; and the country was seething with a special, almost mysterious (to an outsider), rage. I think now, reflecting on the great dissonance in the country's new reputation and the grim reality of its daily life, that at least for some expatriates, life in the country provided a form of liberation, and idle self-cherishing – the kind of people who go to poor countries to celebrate the security or licence provided by the passport they carry, and the money they possess.

Liberians, sadly, have lived this lie for most of the country's existence. Fashioned in its modern form as a settlement for freed American slaves in the 19th century, it had as its motto "The love of liberty brought us here," and prides itself on being Africa's first Republic. It was all, of course, a hoax.

Far from being liberating, the Republic became a place of depressing consumer squalor burdened by usurious loans from Western governments, and was soon enmeshed in slaving scandals. A visiting African-American journalist--who got to the country at about the same time as Graham Greene in the early 1930s, and not long after a League of Nations report into Liberian slave trading recommended European colonisation of the country--wrote that to the motto "The love of liberty brought us here", should be added "And the lack of money keepsushere."

A cruel self-flattering American joke; but the reality of the country was no joke to indigenous Liberians. Still, there was a pathos about a country which, established by the American Colonisation Society (ACS) in 1827 as a colony for freed blacks, could come to regard the indigenous Africans as a people fit only for subservience, in the process degrading itself so completely that a bunch of European powers, former slave traders through and through, could lecture convincingly about the baseness of the Liberian enterprise. (One needs only to read the reams of pages constituting the League of Nations report, as I did at the Rhodes Library at Oxford many years back, to experience the rawness of its appeal nearly a century after its publication.)

Time magazine at the time wrote a damning story based on the League of Nations report, depicting Liberia, in an ironic twist of phrase--for it was playing on the exact words of Liberia's defenders, who were referring to its white critics--as "brutal, arrogant, prejudiced."

This jolted Liberia's defenders into action. Writing in the exalted pages of *Foreign Affairs*--the US foreign establishment house organ--W.E.B. Dubois, that great pan-Africanist, journalist and scholar, wrote in defence of Liberia amidst the scandal: "The record of peace, efficiency and [encouraging] ability made by this poverty-stricken settlement of the rejected and despised, sitting on the edge of Africa and fighting the world in order to be left alone, is, despite querulous criticism, one of the most heartening efforts in human history."

So, not much was changed after the League of Nations' findings: Liberia continued its deformed trajectory, the settlers continued suppressing the indigenous population, the country serving an elite class of about a dozen (initially mainly half-caste) families for decades until it imploded into a destructive coup in 1980, and subsequently collapsed into bloody anarchy in the 1990s.

The end of the brutal war, it was generally hoped, was an opportunity to refashion Liberia in a more viable way; it provided an opportunity to create a more just and coherent country out of the ruins of nihilistic warfare.

Sincere well-wishers imagined that as a result of the destruction wrought by the war, Liberia had become something plastic, ready to be moulded into whatever configuration donors wished.

The destruction wrought by the war had indeed been immense. It killed tens of thousands of Liberians, and wounded or maimed hundreds of thousands more. About 1.8 million citizens were displaced at several points during its span, mostly internally--this from an overall population of three million.

Grim statistics; but they do not tell the full story. Liberia existed long before the war, and certainly life in the country did not start with the arrival of international well-wishers in 2003.

And as it happens, the first practical step that would have laid the foundations for refashioning Liberia--a call for a national conference before the elections of 2005 made by Amos Sawyer, Liberia's foremost intellectual and statesman--was ignored. The Comprehensive Peace Accord (CPA), signed in Ghana, which ended Liberia's civil war in 2003, called for the restructuring of the Armed Forces of Liberia (AFL) and the Liberia National Police (LNP). But these institutions had been utterly degraded or destroyed, and there was no money set aside to build a new police force.

The UN police (UNPOL) began a programme of assisting what remained of the LNP to maintain law and order, and also recruited and vetted new officers. The LNP reached its targeted strength of 3,000 by 2006/7, and a 500-strong elite special force, the Emergency Response Unit (meant to combat armed robbery and mob violence), has was set up. Training is being done by DynCorp, an American security company.

But 3,500 police officers is obviously a very small number for a country of three million, falling way below the UN's stipulated police-citizens ratio of 1:400. It is also seriously logistically impaired.

In the rural areas, the police remain largely absent, and the lack of basic equipment has meant that the UN continues its policing duties. Over 70 police personnel were summarily dismissed in 2008 for alleged collusion in crimes, including armed robbery. During the public hearings of the Truth and Reconciliation Commission (TRC), war victims identified serving police officers as former militia fighters who had committed gross atrocities. Serious incidents concerning rights violations and the use of excessive force by the police are reported regularly, and instances of detention without charge and beatings of civilians remain commonplace.

The result is that police-citizens relations are so poor that often, enraged community people will physically attack police officers, suspecting them of collusion in criminal activity, at crime scenes, and in a few instances outside of Monrovia, citizens have burnt down police posts and badly assaulted police officers.

The creation of an army has been even more fraught. DynCorp and PAE, also an American company, were given the contract by the American government--which had pledged $210m for creating a new AFL on the signing of the CPA--to recruit and train a new army of 2,000 men and women. DynCorp was tasked to "recruit and make soldiers," and PAE to "mentor and develop them into an operational force." Not surprisingly, the DynCorp process has been expensive and slow. By August 2007, only 105 soldiers had gone through basic training.

Recruitment accelerated after that, and close to 2,000 soldiers have by2010 been trained. But command and control of an army built from scratch remains an issue, as is sustainability. A Nigerian officer still commands the army, and the attrition rate has been perplexingly high: by the end of last year, about 90 soldiers had left.

I thought I knew a lot about Liberia after five previous visits there, beginning in the 1980s when Samuel Doe--the sub-literate army Sergeant who murdered President William Tolbert in his bedroom and seized the Executive Mansion--was still in power. But I was wrong. The first eye-opener happened when I started attending the public hearings of the TRC, one of the Liberian institutions I had been tasked to support.

The TRC, made up of largely inexperienced people--including two described as "housewives"--was chaired by Jerome Verdier. It was tasked with creating "a clear picture of the past" in order to facilitate reconciliation in the suffering country. It collected about 20,000 statements, and in early January 2008, began its public hearings. Two dramatic testimonies were given in the first week of the hearings, which was attended by President Johnson-Sirleaf and her cabinet. The first witness, David Saweh, identified a prominent musician and close aide to the president, Marcus Davies, otherwise known as Sun-daygar Dearboy, as a former rebel fighter who caused the gang-rape and killing of his sister. Saweh claimed chat his father was also killed in the attack by Dearboy. It was an extraordinary moment.

The other sensational testimony was that of Joshua Blahyi, a former fighter for the Krahn-dominated ULIMO-K faction headed by Roosevelt Johnson and later leader of the "Butt Naked Brigade," a band of naked child fighters who believed that nudity protected them from bullets. This faction fought in the very destructive battles of Monrovia in April 1996, in which Blahyi was said to have played a leading role. Shortly after this, Blahyi became a born-again Christian, and established a popular church in Monrovia.

In his testimony, Blahyi claimed that he was responsible for the death of thousands of people during the war, and he made clear that his confession was a form of contrition, calling on other factional leaders to come forward and confess to the TRC. In fact, the testimony looked suspiciously histrionic, and Blahyi--preening and evidently proud of himself--behaved less like a contrite sinner than a hero seeking a national platform.

I met him a week after his testimony. As we walked to a nearby restaurant, he was embraced by passers-by, and the 37-year-old saluted everyone who recognised him in triumph. I was stumped.

I was to see this same attitude on display when I attended the TRC hearings that week. None of the alleged perpetrators who appeared asked for amnesty before they gave their testimonies, and all of them behaved as though what they did--gang-raping women, participating in mass killings, or leading gangs of fighters to invade neighbouring countries where they exported their brand of cruelty--was unusual but not particularly despicable.

Often even the TRC commissioners, looking un-shocked, would smile or laugh, the early solemnity of the proceedings abandoned. Worse, onlookers would giggle when victims narrated unusual forms of atrocities, including particularly creative forms of rape. These regrettable but telling episodes can be read as something of a variation on the phenomenon observed by Frantz Fanon during the Algerian War of Independence in the 1950s: the congruent abasement of victim and victimisers, of oppressors and the society they oppress.

It is as though, after over a decade of near-universal experience of distress and pain, the sense of a moral universe had been obliterated in the country; and as though, because of a long history of injustice and casual violence, notions of justice are no longer contemplated or easily grasped; and as though ideas of truth and memory are simply meaningless. Cruelty, of course, had long ceased to have any meaning; it had been a part of life for so long.

Thus, I was not at all surprised when the TRC produced, in July last year, a very badly written and poorly-argued report which caught attention only because of the outrageousness of its recommendations--including two lists calling for prosecutions and the banning of people from holding public office.

Reaction to the report was predictably swift and brutal. A group of former warlords called a press conference in Monrovia and warned, not-too-subtly, that the report would undermine the country's fragile peace and possibly return it to war.

The report remained the key issue of public debate for months, but the embarrassment it caused to the international community--which had been enthusiastic in its support for Johnson-Sirleaf--was such that when the US secretary of state, Hillary Clinton, visited Monrovia in August 2009, she carefully avoided any mention of it. Hillary Clinton appeared at a press conference with President Johnson-Sirleaf and declared: "President Sirleaf has been a very effective leader of the new Liberia. The US officially supports what this government is doing. We think that Liberia is on the right path, as difficult as that path may be."

4.
Liberia: the more things Change[10]

There is a poignant moment in Howard French's excellent book, *A Continent for the Taking: the Tragedy and Hope of Africa* (2004) that, in its intensity and suspense, has the quality to stay forever in one's mind. French, a former New York Times West African Bureau chief, encounters the murderous Liberian warlord Charles Taylor in Monrovia. Amidst the general distress, Taylor, "impeccably coiffed, manicured and groomed," is "dressed in a finely tailored two-piece African-style suit," and exuded of "haughty self-contentment." He is seated "in a high-backed rattan chair reminiscent of the one of the famous pictures of Black Panther leader Huey Newton," and he is holding, for good measure, "an elaborately carved wooden scepter." It is a triumphant Taylor -- this is after the 1996 Abuja Accord which would finally pave his way to becoming President of Liberia—and, for all intents and purposes, the warlord must look presidential.

Taylor is holding a press conference, and French takes his chance. "Isn't it outrageous," he asks Taylor, who had just described his predatory insurgency as "God's war, " for someone who has drugged small boys, given them arms and trained them to kill to call this God's war? How dare you call the destruction of your country in this manner and the killing of two hundred thousand people God's war?" Ever wily and articulate, Taylor did not miss a beat. "I just believe in the destiny of man being controlled by God, and wars, whether man-made or what, are directed by a force," he said. "And so when I say it is God's war, God has his own way of restoring the land, and he will restore it after the war."

This statement was made in 1996. A year later, after rigged elections, Taylor became President. Seven years later, however, God has still not restored much in Liberia. A visitor to the country is immediately struck

[10] Znet, 4 August 2004

by its decrepitude. The Roberts International Airport is a ramshackle outfit looking very much like a makeshift trading outpost. One of its terminal buildings was burnt down during the early phases of the war, in early 1990, and has not been rebuilt. And developments that should be hopeful are marred by the country's unique complications.

A large UN force, 15,000 strong, has now been deployed throughout the country, and is desperately trying to disarm the demented combatants who ravaged the country for over a decade. The disarmament should have been easy: many of the Liberian militias have gone through such a process before, some of them twice (ahead of the 1997 elections, and during Sierra Leone disarmament process, in which some of current Liberian fighters were active). But nearly a year after the UN mission in the country, UNMIL, deployed, officials still do not have an accurate estimate of combatants to be disarmed. Before the start of disarmament in December last year, UNMIL had a "working figure" of 38,000 combatants to be disarmed. The first attempted demobilisation that month quickly turned into chaos, after the militias, desperate for the cash incentive to hand in their weapons (an initial $150 per combatant to be followed by another $150 several months later) before Christmas, stormed Monrovia, the capital. At least 8 people were killed in the ensuing violence. In the event, the UN paid 12,000 soldiers but received only 8,000 weapons.

Disarmament restarted in April this year, with the setting up of four cantonment sites where the various militias would hand in weapons. At that point, the UN estimated that 45,000 combatants would be disarmed. By mid-July, however, the UN had already taken weapons from 54,000, and there were more turning up each day. A UN official I spoke to in Monrovia in July calmly explained how, after a 2-hour long meeting with "48 Generals", he was still unable to tell how many militias remained to be disarmed. Forty-eight Generals? 'Yes, they are rebel generals, bush generals, and they are jealous of their ranks!' He was not facetious, this bright, diligent bureaucrat; he was deadpan. And that, in a way, sums up the pathos of the Liberian situation: the corrosive audacity of its militias, the sense of entitlement of a people steeped into neurosis.

At the start of the disarmament in April, I traveled with one of the UN teams to Gbarnga, once the headquarters of Taylor's National Patriotic Front of Liberia (NPFL) militias. Formerly a fairly prosperous town, with abandoned gas stations and bullet-riddled villas to show for it, Gbarnga is now, after years of fighting, a sullen outpost, its residents sucked into a brooding, almost hermetical mode. A very long line of militias had already been formed by 10:00 am, waiting at the cantonment site to hand in old AK 47 rifles and collect their money. At first glance, there was nothing in their stupefying, red-eyed vacancies to indicate the vicious murderers they have been. Things were proceeding smoothly until, suddenly, a scrawny militia with bandana around the head jumped ahead of the queue, raised his old rifle and started shouting abuses at the UN officers. "Jacques Klein is a mother-fucker, you are all shit! Give us our money now or we'll go to Sierra Leone, to Guinea, to Ivory Coast, and start fighting all over again. We'll go!"

Liberia is obviously a highly traumatised country, but outbursts like this still have the capacity to unsettle. Founded by ex-American slaves in the nineteenth century, and misused as a client state by successive US governments during the Cold War—only to brutally abandon it when the awful dictatorship they had been bankrolling imploded with disastrous humanitarian consequences—Liberia confronts the international community with undaunted challenges. The country's politics have always found expression either as brutal hysteria or bathos: anything that can go wrong will go wrong.

Fortunately, the UN mission in the country appears to be finally gaining traction. It began on a false footing. The American marines who landed as back-up to Nigerian troops on pre-UN deployment immediately after Charles Taylor was forced to relinquish power in September last year quietly melted away even before the mission would get underway. Their main gripe, it was reported, was that there were too many mosquitoes in the country (all of them were no doubt quickly sent to Iraq—the real reason for their Liberian withdrawal). The new head of the UN mission, Jacques Klein, is an abrasive ex-American soldier who distinguished himself in the Balkans as a UN official but who had little knowledge of West Africa, and even less, interest to learn. On arrival in Liberia, Klein is said to have suggested separating the Muslims from the Christians to avoid 'ethnic cleansing'—a Quixotic mindset from the Balkans. I heard that Klein's relationship with the UN force commander, the highly respected Kenyan General Daniel Opande—who oversaw the disarmament process in Sierra Leone—was bad to the point of hostility. The two men simply were not on speaking terms. Morale among the UN staff, cowered by Klein's often boorish behavior, was very low. The Liberian press, ever vociferous and often more vocal than reasoning, was uniformly hostile to the mission.

Things have much improved now, and there is real hope that the country, Africa's first republic, will make the transition from interminable, low-level criminal warfare to real peace. A successful disarmament, of course, will be the key to this. This is why greater effort should be made to vet ex-combatants submitting themselves to the process. But beyond a successful disarmament is the challenge of reintegrating the ex-combatants in a society impoverished and degraded by war. A promised American reintegration package, worth millions of dollars and said to be aimed at providing employment for 10,000 ex-combatants, has still not arrived. Inundating the country, on the other hand, are hundreds of North American Baptist missionaries holding conferences and seminars almost monthly. More churches have been rebuilt or renovated than schools, and there is still no electricity or running water in the country.

There is also the dismal fragmentation of the political class. General and presidential elections are set for October this year, and already 19 aspirants have emerged as possible presidential contestants—this in a nation of slightly more than 3 million people, more than half of them displaced by warfare. 'Liberian politics,' Graham Greene once wrote, 'were like a crap game played with loaded dice.' Greene was writing in the 1930s, and then the legendary corruption of Liberia's politics had set rules that were universally acknowledged. Today, that tidy, antique corruption has a quaintness that can only be imagined. The country's fiercely competitive diversity has foreclosed that. The stakes are much higher now. And judging by the occasional rowdiness of the ex-combatants, it is hard to say whether they, hired guns of one sociopathic entrepreneur or another in the past, will not make themselves available to some disgruntled politician-turn-warlord. And there is that wild card Charles Taylor, who should be turned over to the UN-mandated Special Court for Sierra Leone if only to make the atmosphere look less foggy.

The International Community, in short, needs to continue to actively engage in the region. Among the UN staff in Liberia today, the talk is that Guinea is the next flashpoint, and some opportunistic staffers are already learning French for a future posting to Guinea. Peacekeeping in West Africa, in other words, is becoming a growth industry. This should not be allowed to happen.

5.

On Politics and the Diamond Economy of Sierra Leone[11]

The author makes three large claims in this beautifully-jacketed book about an important economic and geopolitical subject. They are: that diamonds, commercially exploited in Sierra Leone since the 1930s, have stifled the country's economic growth and made it a basket case; that Sierra Leone has suffered neocolonial exploitation as a result, leading to a brutal civil war in 1990s; and finally that international criminal and, more disturbing, the al-Qaeda terrorist networks have in recent years joined this exploitation, with profoundly sinister results. The author is Diane Frost, an academic at the University of Liverpool in England. No armchair pundit, she arrived at these conclusions through impressive research. In 2003, Frost made a field trip to Sierra Leone where she found that activist groups trying to get their "message of injustice and inequality across" saw her, a "white Westerner," as a very good conduit to the outside world. She therefore hopes that the resulting research would become "a tool to further the cause of injustice [sic] by those subjects being studied" [sic]. This is in the note on methodology at the end of the book (p.197).

The preceding pages recount the history of diamond mining in the country, carefully and appropriately grounding it into the broader political and economic history of the country from the 1930s through the end of a brutal civil war in the early 2000s. Using colonial-era documents, including the records of proceedings of the Sierra Leone Legislative Council and the records of the colonial office in London – as well as well-known published sources like van der Laan's pioneering work (1965) – the author builds a compelling picture of the chequered history of the industry. She shows how the British colonial authorities facilitated the creation of a monopoly, the Sierra Leone Selection trust (SLST), which was given control of the entire industry for 99 years, in 1934; and

---

[11] Review of Diane Frost's *From the Pit to the Market: Politics and the Diamond Economy of Sierra Leone* (James Currey, Oxford 2012); published by *International Development Planning Study* (Vol. 36 No.3 2014).

how agitation by local politicians as the decolonisation process set in in the 1950s forced the British to scale back this monopoly and allow indigenous participation in the industry. The legislative debates during this period, which shows the depth of feelings of local politicians towards what was a plainly exploitative colonial regime, is refreshing in view of the almost complete lack of popular debate of recent mineral deals and legislations (including the Petroleum Act 2011) passed in Sierra Leone.

This is the best part of the book, but it is – like all other parts – marred by egregious errors of facts which keep one alert to any claim in the book. On page 39 Frost introduces two mysterious characters who headed the Diamond Corporation of Sierra Leone (DCSL), a branch of the Diamond Corporation of London (which was buying almost all of the world's rough diamonds), in the early 1960s: Joseph Momoh ("chairman of the public service commission who went on to become President") and Dr. D.S.H.W. Nicol, who was formerly principal of the University of Sierra Leone. Momoh was a 24-year-old army cadet in 1961 when Frost has him as director of DCSL (he never worked for it), and the knowledgeable reader may tentatively identify 'Nicole' as Dr. Davidson Nicol, who indeed was director of the DCSL and was a former principal of Fourah Bay College (not yet constituted as part of the University of Sierra Leone). She writes that De Beers borrowed its legendary advertising slogan, "A diamond is forever," from a novel by Ian Fleming (p.5), which was published in 1956, when in fact the slogan was designed by an American advertising firm for De Beers 14 years earlier, in 1948. Her ponderous research unearths the truly significant fact that the 2006 Ed Zwik-directed movie *Blood Diamond* (she makes this plural) was actually the work of Steven Spielberg (p. xvii).

Needless to say, Frost didn't need to have traveled all the way to Sierra Leone to get these facts right, or even to get access to the materials on which the section is built: the key primary materials she uses are all stacked in London, and the works of van der Laan, Greenhalgh (1985) and Zack-Williams (1995), which she copiously cite, covered all the important grounds that she so falteringly treads, and much more elegantly, too.

In Sierra Leone, she spoke to two officials of the Ministry of Mineral Resources in Freetown and spent a lot of time with the members of the putative Movement of Concerned Kono Youth (MOCKY) in Kono, the main theatre of diamond mining in the country. She was clearly enamoured of MOCKY, whose members must have flattered her earnest sense of justice for the world's disadvantaged. She writes feelingly about it, though the group, whose activities sometimes verged on the criminal (in 2002 it abducted a Lebanese businessman and only released him after his family paid a ransom), had long ceased to be any factor by the time the book was published. That makes the book feel dated. She writes about Branch Energy, which was at the time exploring for kimberlite in Kono, as one of 'multinational companies' that might be considered a neocolonial venture in the country. The company was actually far from being a multinational, and had ceased to exist in Sierra Leone by the time Frost's book was published. There is, sadly, no justice in this world.

The book is perfunctory about the important claim that transnational organised crime and al-Qaeda have infiltrated the industry, citing only news reports and a report by the British NGO Global Witness which have made the tentative connection on the latter point. Frost writes: "The criminality involved in the diamond trade has to be seen as part of a wider pattern of organised crime in West Africa that often transits this area rather than originates here" on the former (p. 187). A more penetrating insight she gives in conclusion to the book is that artisanal/small-scale mining "such as that which exists in Sierra Leone is driven by poverty"(p.191). Indeed, who might have guessed?

Over-all, this is a disappointing though immensely well-intentioned book.

6.
A Liberia Journal: the UN at Work in 2005[12]

The flight from Ghana began almost four hours late. It was the SLOK Airline, a new company. About seven months ago when the airline owned, I am told, by a Nigerian politician who had it tactfully registered in the Gambia, started operations it was different. It arrived and flew on time, or almost. Now it had settled into normality, and in this region that means that it must miss schedules by several hours.

I had booked a seat in it a week earlier. I wanted to visit Liberia once again. Once again because I had been there three times before since a massive UN intervention in October 2004 signaled that the ravaged republic was finally getting peace; and once again because my trip was unplanned, and in that sense almost purposeless. One felt intensely drawn to the place, the result of a long and intimate interest in the country and its very unhappy recent history.

The weather was wretched (it had been raining all day), the in-flight food bad, and the passengers, having spent such a long time at the small Kotoko Airport, were sulky. I tried to read a book but was distracted. Liberia, for anyone familiar with the republic, induces strong anxieties. Will there be surprises this time? What will be different in this trip? In spite of myself - I am thoroughly familiar with situations almost exactly like Liberia's and very much with Liberia itself – I was full of nerves.

Mercifully, the flight was brief – lasting for about two hours. The Robertsfield International airport of Monrovia was just the way I had left it six months earlier: the white UN helicopters, a couple of planes, airport officials looking oddly busy, a withered and degraded landscape, the main terminal building still a shell without roof as though to give one notice of greater ruins lying ahead. But a difference soon emerged. A neat, almost new, bus arrived close to the airport exit, and we all boarded it to the immigration area. I saw a similar bus parked confidently as we got close. A small sigh of relief: there is a little change.

12 Znet, 11 July 2005

When it was built by the Americans years back, Robertsfield was a near-elegant, imposing structure. It was at the height of the Cold War, and the Americans, eager to keep the volatile region under close watch, had reinforced their traditional presence in Liberia, which was founded as a settlement for freed American slaves in the nineteenth century, using it as a CIA listening post as well as setting up the VOA relay station for the entire region there (much the same thing). Liberia was then in the blood-stained grip of President (formerly Master-Sergeant) Samuel Kanyon Doe, who came to power by staging a coup in 1980. The US gave hundreds of millions of dollars to Doe, and urged their Israeli allies to beef up Doe's murderous security forces. So impressed were the Americans with Doe's performance that President Ronald Reagan invited the almost illiterate dictator to the White House, and there referred to him, one could only sense affectionately, as 'Chairman Moe.'

On Christmas Eve in 1989, a group of about 150 armed dissidents invaded Liberia's Nimba County from Ivory Coast. They were led by Charles Taylor, formerly a senior official in Doe's government. A colourful speaker with an even more colourful past, Taylor, who studied in the US, had escaped detention from a Massachusetts jail, where he had been held pending his possible extradition to Liberia for allegedly stealing $900,000 from Doe's government. Now, he claimed he wanted to free the country of the depredations of Doe.

I happened to have visited Liberia shortly before Taylor's armed incursions. The country was then, unlike some of its neighbours, reasonably well-functioning: Monrovia had electricity and running water, its shops were full, civil servants received their salaries on time, and Monrovia's nightlife, so seedy, had a faintly American echo, with its brawly bars and bad beers and the anxiously bohemian feel. But it was also a grim place. Doe, a paranoid and near-psychotic, had brutally rigged elections in 1985, carried out ethnic massacres against perceived supporters of his regime's opponents, murdered political opponents, and was gearing up for yet another nasty assault on the democratic aspirations of Liberians in the form of elections to be held in 1990, elections in which he would run and which he would undoubtedly rig. Drunken gun-toting soldiers roamed about the streets of Monrovia – a city that was, in spite of its vibrancy, so bare and lacking in grandeur –

terrorising people in bars and other public places, and there were reports of "disappearances." Although this may sound absurd, given the background, the atmosphere of Monrovia sometimes felt as though a chapter from Kafka was being enacted in this crummy little republic.

UNMIL'S LIBERIA

That menacing feel, so visceral then, is no longer palpable: from the ramshackle airport on, Liberia seems to be dominated by UN soldiers and police officers, giving the place a reassuring atmosphere. Reflecting the ambient anxiety, however, the infrequent visitor will inevitably ask: how long will this last?

I put this question a few days after I arrived in Monrovia to Major General Joseph Owonibi, the Nigerian commander of the UN force (UNMIL) in the country. General Owonibi is an articulate officer, one of those with whom one feels comfortable discussing military strategy as well as politics. I had a copy of a paper on the UN mission in Liberia he had presented at the Kofi Annan International Peacekeeping Training Centre in Ghana, where I had been Senior Research Fellow, months back. The paper, entitled 'Translating policy planning into on-the-ground realities,' gave an insight into the enormous challenges that the mission faced, particularly in dealing with the unrealistic hopes and expectations of ex-combatants, most of whom were opting to be trained for professions that the Liberian economy would simply not support even in the medium term.

'This is difficult to say,' General Owonibi said in answer to my question. 'Putting this country together, building up a functioning system, is not going to be easy. The destruction was immense. We have completed the disarmament process, with over 100,000 militia people going through it. We had earlier thought we will be dealing with slightly over 30,000. That is what this mission planned for. This has impacted immensely on the reintegration process, which is not going on well. There is a lack of funds, and the ex-fighters are restive. They occasionally riot, and this is a bad sign.'

How bad it all is can be easily gleaned from the statistics. Of the more than 100,000 disarmed, 40,000 were targeted for reintegration. Of these, 20,000, all teenagers or pre-teenagers, were sent to school, and the other 20,000 are now undergoing different kinds of vocational training (tailoring, carpentry etc.) What about the 60,000 not targeted? General Owonibi said that some of them have formed themselves into co-operative societies with the aim of starting self-help enterprises. The danger with that, however, is that the command structures of the various militias will then be kept intact, because ex-militia commanders control these co-operative societies, the General added. "The challenge is to infiltrate them and diffuse the command structures, and the NCDRR (the UNMIL-related National Committee for Disarmament, Reintegration and Reconstruction) is well-placed to do this," he said. It is not hard to connect the budding co-operative societies to the series of occasional riots by ex-combatants in recent weeks.

Abdullah Dukuly, the editor of *The Analyst*, one of Liberia's better papers, sees it in more dramatic terms. The day I met him for lunch at a fine Monrovian restaurant, the briskness of Liberian restaurant staffers contrasts sharply with the studied clumsiness of their cousins in places like Accra and Freetown. His paper had carried a page one story grimly warning that LURD's Death Squad Lives On. The LURD was one of the factional militias that had been supposedly disarmed, and some of its leaders are now in the National Transitional Government of Liberia (NTGL) headed by slick businessman Gyude Bryant. *The Analyst* was reporting that a 'death squad' within the Lurd was out to eliminate one of the LURD's ex-military commanders, Sekou Conneh. "Will UNMIL and NTGL act in time to prevent bloodshed and loss of life in â€˜peace time," the paper asked, unctuously.

Was this alarmist, as so many of the country's papers normally are? No, Dukuly responded. "We are in fact being very restrained. We know that the disarmament process was largely a sham. Many of those disarmed were not even fighters, and some of the real fighters are out in the forests regrouping. There are still armed militias, loyal to Charles Taylor, in Gbapolu, and they are terrorizing people in those areas. There may be over 500 armed men in the rubber plantations in western Liberia, stealing and terrorizing civilians. They include Kamajors from Sierra Leone. But of course all Unmil now wants to talk about is the elections in October! The country is simply not prepared for elections."

Unmil's head of Civil Affairs Peter Tingwa suavely dismisses such reports. I met him two days after I arrived in Monrovia. Tingwa is a genial civil servant who also worked in the UN's Sierra Leone mission UNAMSIL. "The disarmament process here was very well done," he said. "You are never going to have a complete, 100 per cent disarmament anywhere. People were saying the same things about the Sierra Leone process, but where are the RUF [Sierra Leone's arm-chopping Revolutionary United Front] arms now? In the last major riots, the ex-militias used machetes, knives and sticks. There were no guns. Armed robbery is minimal. The process here was as comprehensive as can be possible in the circumstances." □

Not all the 100,000 disarmed were fighters, Tingwa conceded. Some of them were camp followers or "wives" of the militia fighters: this innovation is a potential UN "best practice," the result of "lessons learnt" from the Sierra Leone process where only the armed fighters were targeted, leading to criticism by rights groups that abducted women and children were ignored by the UN.

With over 1000 civilian staff (local and international) and 15,000 troops, UNMIL is the UN's biggest and most expensive peace mission, costing over half a billion dollars per annum. The mission began full deployment in September 2003 after the country's corrupt and destructive despot, Charles Taylor, was forced out by agreement and went into self-exile in Nigeria. By end of 2004, UNMIL declared that it had completed disarming the various factions, and announced that it will now restructure the Liberian national army by demobilising a large number of the soldiers. The 14,000-strong army is made up of 9,000 hastily recruited conscripts and 5,000 regulars (that is, supposedly professional soldiers who have been serving in the decrepit force for years). The plan is to demobilise the 9,000 and retrain and equip the remaining 5,000, but this process is seven months behind schedule. The US, which should spearhead the process (as the UK did in Sierra Leone) is largely lukewarm about it, preferring indirect involvement (providing some cash and hiring private security companies to do the job.) In such a delicate nation-building effort, it simply cannot get messier than that.

ELECTIONS BLUES

The tragedy is that in Liberia today, some of these fundamental issues are overlooked. The talk is about the forthcoming elections in October, the milestone of the UN's involvement in the country. Both the UN officials and Liberian politicians appear desperate for the elections. This is partly a reflection of the poor esteem in which the National Transitional Government (NTLG) is generally held. Made up of recidivist warlords and a sprinkling of respectable civil society leaders, the deformities of NTLG were evident from the start, but no one can say that the Bryant-led government has made much of what little they had to start with. The government has already been accused of entering into shady deals with mining corporations and of embezzling public funds; and Bryant is in the habit of frequently traveling abroad with large delegations at state's cost. There has been no attempt to rehabilitate any of Liberia's many war-damaged public buildings and basic infrastructure (there is still no treated water supply, let alone electricity).

Apparently the government's only saving grace is its legislature: or, if truth be told, a lone Senator representing civil society, Conmany Wesseh. A longtime political activist, Wesseh returned from exile in Ivory Coast in 2003 (where he had been living for years after Taylor's thugs raided the offices of Centre for Democratic Empowerment (CEDE), which he co-founded with the well known academic and politician Amos Sawyer, beating both men up and threatening to kill them), and became a member of a revamped Senate as nominee of Liberia's fledging civil society movement. Against great opposition, Wesseh introduced and helped pass the elections bill (some of the NTGL members were opposed to it because they preferred a deferment of the polls), and, in June, finally convinced his colleagues to pass the Truth and Reconciliation Commission (TRC) Act, and Bryant to sign it into law. "It was a struggle," said, talking about the TRC Act. He was laconic. I later learnt that many of Wesseh's colleagues, formerly members of militia factions, had bitterly opposed the bill for obvious, and understandable, reasons.

I first met Conmany Wesseh at a conference in Canada in 2000, and was in touch with him during the difficult struggle to get Taylor out of power and to face justice for his many crimes. During this trip, however, Wesseh, usually ebullient, appeared very reticent. He delicately did not find time to grant me an interview about his legislative work or about Liberia's coming elections, although he took me around to meet other people. One such meeting we went to was that of the Young Men's Christian Association (YMCA) in downtown Monrovia. The keynote speaker at the meeting was Medina Wesseh, his wife.

Mrs. Wesseh, an elegant and articulate woman who was a lecturer at Ghana's Institute of Journalism, spoke about the future of Liberia's youth. Liberia's youth (between 15-35 years of age), she said, constituted the core of the militias; a staggering seven per cent of them fought in the war (to put this into perspective: the figure was less than one percent in the case of Sierra Leone). During the war, she said, there was "a breakdown of family structures; fear and mistrust created, and the usurpation of traditional authority by wayward and vagrant youth." This is why, she said, the "past should guide us on the way forward, although we must not dwell on it."

From the look of things, Mrs. Wesseh is being understandably optimistic. For the outsider, Liberia (not the US) could seem like what James Baldwin had in mind when he spoke about history being a nightmare from which no one can awaken. People are trapped in history and history is trapped in them. Just how badly trapped Liberians are trapped in their history could be seen from the way the electoral process has been unfolding.

The process effectively started with registration of voters, which was completed in June. According to Ray Kennedy, an American who is in charge of UNMIL's elections wing (in effect running Liberia's National Electoral Commission), the process, which started in April, registered 1.34 million voters, of which 671,519 were women and 671,379 were men. The average age of voters is 35 years, but those 27 years and younger constitute 40 per cent of the total. The internally displaced Liberians constitute 59,671 or 4 per cent of the total, and of that 70 per cent chose to register for county of their origin, Kennedy, who had arrived in country from Afghanistan (where he helped organise that country's elections) three weeks before I met him, told me with some emphasis.

I thought the number of internally displaced voters too small, and I thought the 70 per cent bit a little creepy. The point is that the whole issue is of potentially momentous political importance in Liberia. The voter-registration was not based on a national census: there has been no national census in Liberia for the past 20 years or so, and no election in the country has been based on a national census. The war caused huge displacement of particularly the rural population, and Monrovia's population may have more than doubled during the war years. This demographic shift, likely to be altered slightly as the country becomes more stable, has potent political implications.

Liberia's traditional fault-line has been the divide between rural residents (so-called natives) and those in the coastal city of Monrovia and adjacent towns (mainly Americo-Liberians, as descendant of the freed American slaves who colonised the West African state in the nineteenth century are called.) The coup of 1980, which marked the beginning of Liberia's descent into anarchy, was spearheaded by "native" NCOs promising to put an end to the more than century-old Americo-Liberian hegemony, but it very soon went septic. The bloodthirsty Doe junta employed much the same reactionary and divisive tactics as the old discredited elite he had overthrown, demonstrating in bold relief the congruent corruptions of oppressor and oppressed which is such a marked feature of Third World politics. The destructive war may have helped, in some measure, to wipe out any vestigial privileges that the old elite held; and educated Liberians are quick to play down the old divide, rather like their cousins in Sierra Leone more convincingly do. But there is no doubt that this is a factor.

Why all this? Liberian has 15 counties, and representation in the National Legislature is determined on the basis of the registered voters in each county. There is, however, a threshold of two senators for each county. But there are 64 seats to be filled, and the mandatory two seats for each county add up to only thirty seats. The rest will have to be filled on the basis of the number of registered voters in each county. It is representation based on electoral district, and it is hugely confusing. On the electoral map, Montserrado County, which includes Monrovia and is the traditional domain of the America-Liberians, has by far the largest number of registered voters, 471,657. This is partly because of the massive movement of people from places like Lofa (which has only 85,659 registered voters) into Monrovia during the war years; and partly because many people in that county, as well as in others like Nimba, were unable to vote because of the sheer logistical constraints (bad roads, inaccessible villages, poor security).

True, there was a lot enthusiasm among Liberians for the voter-registration exercise; indeed, in some cases, over-enthusiasm. (*New Democrat* newspaper, 23 May 2005: "Voter registration in the once-mining enclave of Bong Mines ended in chaos Saturday, forcing elections workers to flee cutlass-wielding youthsstormed the registration centre demanding to register.") But these were mainly in relatively accessible areas. The logistical nightmare will be compounded by the time of elections in October, the end of the rainy seasons, when the decrepit roads, where they exist, would have been washed away by the torrential rains; and this will adversely affect the polls. (UNMIL has put in place an elaborate community outreach, spearheaded by its ever-resourceful Public Information Unit, which includes the performance arts, media releases, and debates in high schools. I attended one of such debates, at the Len Millar High School, and was somewhat amazed at the articulateness of Liberia's young people.) After the elections, which will cost the UN mission $18 million, Liberians will likely be surprised to find that places like Montserrado has by far the largest number of representatives (about 20 senators). Thoughtful politicians like Ellen Johnson-Sirleaf, a presidential candidate, are demanding air-transport facilities from UNMIL for the candidates during the campaign period.

Johnson-Sirleaf, so capable and experienced and elegant, is put ahead of eleven other leading presidential hopefuls (there are at the moment nearly 30 hopefuls) by a recent poll by the Liberian Institute of Public Administration. (Full disclosure: I first met Johnson-Sirleaf in Ivory Coast, where she had fled to escape Taylor's depredations, in 2001, and have followed and admired her work ever since. I interviewed her for this report.) The other contestants include an inarticulate football star, several lawyers and businessmen and bankers. There is something a little unnerving about a place, Graham Greene wrote about Liberia in the 1930s, "where every other man is a lawyer, and the next a banker." □

BY WAY OF AN EPILOGUE

For obvious reasons, UNMIL officials are quick to play down the importance of the forthcoming elections in October, claiming that they will merely be transitional. But for that very reason, they are hugely important. The UN has to get this right; and in Liberia, the plain fact is that anything that can go wrong will go wrong.

It is easy to make fun of the earnest UN officials in Monrovia; of the former political head of the mission, Jacques Klein, who would respond to any criticism of his frantic leadership style by stating that his mission was busy feeding thousands of Liberians each day. But then one remembers the sheer sacrifices and heroism of serving in a country so bare and potentially dangerous, where over 50 UN staffers have died of preventable or utterly curable diseases since the mission started because of the lack of basic health care or the infrastructure that could sustain the minimum standards of modern comfort. And looking at it more closely, the Liberian mission, so high-minded and difficult, could seem genuinely inspiring, in spite of the haphazard reintegration process and the pedestrian politics and the dollars, always the dollars. Liberia is very expensive. Although there is the Liberian dollar (a picture of the thuggish dictator Doe adorning the 50 dollar note) the US greenback is preferred, even by beggars. A decent meal costs at least twice as much in Monrovia as in Accra, and ditto accommodation.

To think about current Liberia, the heroisms and the pathos, is confront a mystery: how come such a fun-loving, God-fearing (many Liberians are conspicuously Christian), and friendly people would carry out such destruction on themselves? The Liberian war was not short-lived. It went on for over a decade. The violence and destruction was sustained for many years, and there were dedicated people and organizations, all Liberian, carrying them out. There was a whiff of anarchy about the war's early and late manifestations, but it was madness with method. Clearly, then, to understand the Liberian problem one has to confront something much more than mercenary violence and corrupt leadership: one has to look at the way the state was founded, how it progressed over the years to the point that by the 1980s it had become overtaken by scum politics, where people would think that serious structural problems would be solved by simply eliminating the 'right' people.

James Youboty, a Liberian journalist, has provided his own, unique insight. The Liberian problem, he writes *in A Nation in Terror: The True Story of the Liberian Civil War* (2004), could be partly blamed on the segregational way in which the ex-slaves from America founded the country and kept the majority of the native population benighted for more than a hundred years. All these disparities in the society set the stage for Satan to take advantage in brutally turning brothers against brothers.☐ Even Taylor, Youboty writes, is like most Liberians among the "most generous people on the face of the earth. But Satan, the devil, came from hell and corrupted the minds of the peace-loving Liberian people to start killing one another for no good reason."

As I rushed to the airport to catch the plane that would be late, I thought about these words; and, in spite of myself, I still feel unable to disagree with Youboty.

7.
Sierra Leone Civil War: a Fresh Perspective[13]

The Sierra Leone "rebel" war (1991-2002) has over the years attracted huge scholarly attention: a debate about the origin and nature of the war still rage among academics and, before the Special Court for Sierra Leone (SCSL), jurists. This is somewhat curious, since the conflict, though devastating, was puny. A hundred or so well-trained soldiers with perhaps two combat helicopters would have snuffed out Foday Saybanah Sankoh and the petty army he called Revolutionary United Front (RUF) in March 1991, and no one would have remembered either after a year or two. In the event, the Sierra Leonean state, denuded after decades of misrule, incompetence and corruption under the All Peoples Congress (APC), not only failed to contain the RUF but later became somewhat complicit in its depredations. The so-called rebellion festered, violence engulfed the country, thousands of civilians were killed, about half the population of the country displaced, and only with the insertion of thousands of foreign troops – who enforced a peace agreement by disarming combatants – was stability realised.

It is entirely possible that a hundred years from now this traumatic period will be treated as a not-so-significant episode in the history of Sierra Leone, if indeed the country survives to that point and prospers. The point is that the war resolved nothing: nothing fundamentally changed as a result of the war: the postwar settlement ensured that Ahmad Tejan Kabbah and his Sierra Leone Peoples Party, which managed the transition from war to peace, were re-elected in a landslide in 2002. The SLPP had led Sierra Leone to independence from Britain in April 1961. Its chief opponent at the time was the APC, the same as in 2002 when the war ended. The entire postwar reconfiguration of the state – sponsored, with exquisite fitness, by the British – was anchored

---

[13] A critique of *Epistemologies of African Conflicts: Violence, Evolutionism and the War in Sierra Leone* (New York: Palgrave, 2012), by Zubaru Wai published by *Journal of Sierra Leone Studies* Vol.II (January 2013).

75

on restoring colonial era institutions that had been neutered by the APC; and a former colonial District Commissioner was hired, from his retirement in the UK, to help with a Paramount Chieftaincy restoration scheme. A report by the Truth and Reconciliation Commission (TRC) in 2004 found that some of the conditions which led to the 'rebel war' of the 1990s were still very much present at the time the report was published. In 2007, the APC once again gained power by defeating the SLPP. It was re-elected in 2012. Since independence, in other words, the two parties remain the only ones capable of winning national elections and running the country in a democratic setting.

The disturbing question that issued out of the war, therefore, was: why was it that the RUF, which many agree was a largely criminal group perpetuating near-mercenary violence, was able to recruit support in the country and survived for so long while the state and its agents appeared so ineffective in meeting that challenge? Thanks to Paul Richards – who must be credited as the first scholar to study the war with industry and seriousness – the state or rather its "patrimonial" nature was a focus of the early analyses of the war but this was soon overtaken by other, more tantalizing aspects of the war. This turned on the basic character of the RUF: its neurotic brutality, its reliance on foreign fighters at the initial stages, and on child soldiers throughout the war, and its enigmatic and somewhat cult-like leader, Sankoh. The analyses that followed – which more or less took as its starting point Robert Kaplan's feverish but highly influential "The Coming Anarchy" article in the *Atlantic Monthly* magazine in 1994 – congealed into a depiction of the war as part of a wider narrative of youth nihilism, state collapse, and mercenarism in West Africa. The war, in other words, had major geopolitical significance.

Wai's Purpose and Method

Zubairu Wai, a young Sierra Leonean scholar who lived in the country throughout the war period, is not impressed with much of what has been written about the war, or about similar wars in Africa. In *Epistemologies of Conflict: Violence, Evolutionism and War in Sierra Leone* (2012), he makes a refreshing and provocative critique of the ways in which the war has been analysed or depicted. His targets are wide. Wai is not much interested, in this book, in giving an account of the war from his own perspective; he gives only 19 of the book's 263 pages to a chronological narrative of the war, and this account, though largely accurate, is bland. (He has informed me that he is writing another volume dedicated to the war.) The book comes alive when Wai is demolishing the various interpretations – or, as he prefers, "discourses" – of the war's meanings and character. He does this with forensic acuity and brilliance, laying out his opponents' arguments often scrupulously fairly, and then destroying them with relentless cruelty, leaving no room for appeal. (By way of full disclosure, I must report that I am myself a small victim of Dr. Wai's scalpel, though I come off largely intact.)

"The themes and questions that animate this book emerged from my frustration with the way contemporary African conflicts have come to be understood," Wai writes in the introduction. The causes and nature of the Sierra Leone civil war had been puzzling enough for him, but once he started to study what others have written about the war, "I started to detect a disconnect between my experiences, having lived through the war, and the accounts that were purporting to explain it" (p.2). The anxiety is deeply felt; and it is part of the originality and rightness of Wai's purpose and method that he has placed the alleged distortions of the published accounts of the war in Sierra Leone within the larger context of the debasement of the African past and present condition by conventional Western scholarship.

Wai is interested, in other words, in epistemology – which is the philosophy underpinning the production of knowledge – with respect to Africa. Here he relies particularly on the work of the Duke University scholar VY Mudimbe (who provides an enthusiastic but characteristically bombastic preface) as a theoretical framework for his own understanding of the "problematique." Mudimbe is a notoriously difficult and opaque writer, a trait which his admirers perhaps see as evidence of his profundity; Wai, clearly much better at the use of the English language, tries strenuously to emulate this trait. Mudimbe both fires and limits Wai's vision – as someone who prefers clarity in writing above all else, I think that this reliance on Mudimbe somewhat obscures the originality of Wai's purpose and method. (In the preface, for example, Mudimbe applauds Wai for having "ontological seniorship" or "anteriority" –

which means, I later found out, only something like "native interpreter," in other words that Wai's work stands above others for this reason. But other works that Wai so convincingly argues against are also produced by "natives." Wai's nuanced justification for his rejection of some of the scholarly reflections on the war by other Sierra Leoneans is that though their work may disagree with those of Western scholars "in remaining within the frames of Africanism and in their fidelity to the conceptualities of colonial library, they may not be very different epistemologically from the perspectives of Western discourses." I find this argument unanswerable: only Wai, one presumes, has managed to escape this invidious colonial trap!)

This approach to knowledge – which derives from the work of Michel Foucault, Edward Said and many others, mainly from France's Ecole Normale Superieure – takes it as a matter of course that the production of knowledge is not neutral or innocent; it is a calculated part of the power matrix. It emphasizes deconstruction, poststructuralism, and postmodernism.

This approach can be taken too far (to justify crude nativism, for example); when applied in moderation it contains very important elements of truth. Wai attempts to pursue the following questions, among others: who produces knowledge of these African conflicts and why? What are the "modalities of the dominant and dominating" perspectives? What are the "epistemological structures" within which the knowledge is produced? What is the nature of these structures that make the knowledge production and the "particular interpretive dispositions" that they foreground possible? Above all, what is the role of the knowledge production in "defining Africa's position in the world, its relationship with the West, and the articulation of international policy toward Africa as a result of these conflicts?"

The anxiety suffusing these loaded questions suggests the very large claim that there is an overarching agenda driving the production of this knowledge of African conflict. But is this always the case? And who controls this agenda? "It does mean something," Wai writes, "when conflicts are interpreted or understood as cultural ('ethnic' or 'tribal') or economic ('greed' and the struggle over economic resources). For whom or for what the discourse is produced then becomes an important question." Of this one might ask: more important than the fact that the interpretation is true? Surely, virulent ethnicity or 'tribalism' exists in parts of Africa? Surely, also, there was nothing ennobling about the campaigns of the likes of Charles Taylor, and he seemed more interested in primitive accumulation than in building the state or its sources of wealth? Truth, however, is disputed or denied within this framework; it is a subjective concept, as Foucault and Derrida made us to understand. I need not state here that I am unsympathetic to this approach, but I shall lay out carefully Wai's arguments.

Power and Truth

I understand Wai's book to be concerned with showing how power, which seems to reside solely in that omniscient entity called the West, manufactures realities or "truths: in Africa by interpreting the African condition, especially its many crises, and then, through its many powerful agencies, contriving "solutions: for the crises that justifies those manufactured realities. The book, in Wai's words, is about the "discursive production of African realities and how the continent is constructed as an object of knowledge and power" (p.13). But aren't some realities independent of "discourses?" This approach draws from Mudimbe's seminal work *The Invention of Africa* (published in 1988; Said's *Orientalism,* published 10 years earlier, is the intellectual path-breaker for these brave insights.)

Narrowing on the Sierra Leone rebel war, Wai, like other analysts, begins his critique by tearing apart Robert Kaplan's notorious "Coming Anarchy," which uneasily welded together the thesis of Martin van Creveld about post-Cold War wars by non-state actors, Thomas Homer-Dixon's pessimistic environmental prognosis and Samuel Huntington's thesis about the unavoidable "clash of civilizations" to describe the war as anarchic and criminal (as opposed to political) violence that would lead to a Hobbesian state of nullity and terror. Wai then confronts Kaplan's critics, in particular Paul Richards, a British anthropologist with very intimate knowledge of Sierra Leone, whose *Fighting for the Rainforest: War, Resources and Youth* (1996) was the first serious study of the war. Richards had analysed the RUF as a 'group of embittered pedagogues' fighting to replace the corrupt patrimonial state with a 'revolutionary egalitarian one' and appealing "directly to deracinated youths with blighted educational prospects." Wai isn't impressed by Richards' efforts either. He notes the extended criticisms of Richards' book by Yusuf Bangura and Ibrahim Abdullah, finding the interpretations of both, however, only marginally preferably to Richards' because though "Richards and his Sierra Leonean critics may be separated by their theoretical and methodological formulations, but insofar as they are witnessing to the 'truth' of Africanism, are epistemologically bound by its condition of knowledge, and are immersed in the context of its epistemological region of possibility, the differences between them might in fact be exaggerated"(p.126). He gives short shrift to the luminous work of William Reno (from which, Wai writes, Richards derived his ideas of patrimonialism and state collapse in Sierra Leone).

Wai credits Bangura's critique of Richards with setting the analytical template and research agenda for other Sierra Leonean intellectuals, Abdullah and Ismail Rashid in particular. The result does not please him. He is particularly concerned about Abdullah's "lumpen thesis": the interpretation of the war as driven by "lumpen youth," which Abdullah defines as socially uprooted and criminally disposed young people among whom had emerged, after decades of a corrupt and ultimately failed one-party system, a "lumpen youth culture" - a despairing anti-social movement of drug addicts, petty thieves and gamblers, growing up mostly in the slums of Freetown. This group, Abdullah contended, formed the core leadership of the RUF, which is why the group was pathologically disposed to criminal violence and terror. The war, in other words, was a kind of rootless urban youth revolt. The "mutilation, murder and rape of innocent women and children by the RUF are acts that are incompatible with a revolutionary project," Abdullah argues. "The 'revolutionary' acts…were committed again and again precisely because of the social composition (of the RUF)…A lumpen social movement breeds a lumpen revolution."

Wai makes an extended discussion of this thesis, laying out Abdullah's argument carefully and accurately, noting that the substantial narrative reconstructing the origins of the RUF "really did clarify a lot of misconceptions about the war and provided information on exactly what the rebels were" (p.210). The influence of Abdullah's article on the historiography of the war remains profound; when it was first published, in 1996 or 1997, its impact was almost revolutionary, and its immediate adherents, including the present reviewer, were many. Wai states, correctly, that I later "ditched" the lumpen theory in favour of emphasing the mercenary character of the RUF, but I still flinch at his demolishing the theory for its "totalilising conceptual simplicity" and as a "disparaging and condescending elitist slur" that does not provide a "useful conceptual and analytical category" (p.224). The problem Wai finds with Abdullah's lumpen thesis is that it is a catch-all term which "fails to disaggregate [the] disparate groups of insurgents by grouping them under a label that suggests their homogenous and fixed essences" (p.219). If, as Abdullah sees it, lumpens were unemployed or unemployable youths, how does Foday Sankoh, a middle aged photographer, fit that description?

This line of inquiry leads Wai to a number of very astute comments about the nature of the war. Though few Sierra Leoneans became combatants during the war, he writes, "we were all caught up in the same pattern of violence and warfare", which is why "ordinary civilians would easily hack to death or burn those accused of being rebels or rebel collaborators alike" (p.21). There was "no wholesale predilection" towards violence among any group or class of Sierra Leoneans, and violence is never "psychobiological; it is always social and political."

It also leads him towards stating his own tentative position on the origins of the war, which – in its present form – is, however, far from being convincing.

Wai's Will to Truth

Wai states three "interrelated series of violence" out of which the RUF insurgency issued. They are: firstly, "the structural and systemic violence exerted by the global political and economic order" which reduced Sierra Leone to an impoverished backwater; secondly, the fact that Sierra Leone was founded through violence and this foundational neurosis, so to speak, infected its very nature, making it instinctively violent politically; and finally, the creation of "an atmosphere of violence" in the course of the country's history (p.223-4). It is worth quoting his exact words here: "we were," he writes, "caught up in a...pattern of victimhood or victimization, so that even those culpable for perpetrating the most disturbing atrocities were themselves victims of the political violence of the state informed by the culture of violence it had been founded on...In short, the war in Sierra Leone was a collective indictment of the very idea of Sierra Leone" (p.221).

This is Wai's astounding thesis. Forget about the odd phrase "collective indictment;" forget also the fact that the provocative thesis suggests a sullen strain of fatalism: it cannot be glibly dismissed; it demands proper interrogation.

Wai foregrounds the thesis in the very interesting Chapter 2, an idiosyncratic retelling of the story of the Sierra Leone colony – it is entitled, with a bow to Mudimbe, "The Idea of Sierra Leone." In it he identifies two events in the country's history "which have become so central" in the way it is "imagined and narrated" -- its 'discovery' by Pedro da Cintra in 1462 and the resettlement of freed slaves in the new colony in 1787. The events, he writes, "were not neutral encounters or natural historical occurrences and accidents; they were political and violent acts signifying, and making possible, the imposition of new cultural models and new political and economic orders" (p.68). But how violent and linked were these events? Da Cintra certainly did not set out to discover" Sierra Leone, and there was clearly nothing violent about his purpose. Over 300 years separate his visit and the establishment of Freetown. Wai introduces the buccaneering trips of the English slaver John Hawkins and the ensuing trans-Atlantic slave trade to fill in the gap, but this suggests new questions. Hawkins first raided the coast in 1562, exactly 100 years after da Contra's visits. During much of the 100 years, Europe appeared to have been in turmoil, gripped by forebodings that it was in irreversible decline, and certainly no one there seriously considered the possibility of building an empire in West Africa. Europe revived; the slave trade and the American colonies helped in this revival, but by the time the Sierra Leone colony was founded, new ideas and new sensibilities had taken hold on its most powerful nation, Britain.

Wai roundly rejects the humanitarian motives of the British in establishing the colony of Sierra Leone for freed slaves, depicting it as a racist and violent enterprise. In one extraordinary endnote, he writes of the Liberated Africans: "They were known as 'Liberated Africans' because they were thought to have been 'liberated' by the British Navy from slave ships. I prefer 'Recaptives', however, which suggests that these kidnapped Africans remained in captivity, even after the British rescued them from slave ships; indeed it was very easy to identify where these captives came from, but because of the British desire to civilize and Christianize, they were not returned to their original native lands but were brought to Freetown for those purposes, and so they remained in captivity of another kind" (p.232).

Of course, it was not at all easy to have known where the motley collection of Africans in any slave ship originated from; it certainly would have been either impossible or profoundly cruel to have returned them to such places (in all likelihood they would have been easily re-enslaved or perhaps killed). In any case, Sierra Leone was not the only place where the Liberated Africans were resettled by the British – some were sent to Brazil, Luanda and a few other places. The anti-slavery issue at the time was the great foreign and domestic issue for the British – who spent an enormous amount of capital and the lives of hundreds of their sailors pursuing it – and Sierra Leone might be said to have been only a collateral outcome of that venture. I find the humanitarian motive entirely plausible. The British anti-slavery effort was the first ever such effort in history; no other slave-owning nation had bothered to give the issue any moral consideration before, from the classical world to that point. "We have seen something unprecedented in history," the great French humanist Alexis de Tocqueville wrote of the British abolition of slavery at the time, "slavery abolished, not by the desperate effort of the slave, but by the enlightened will of the master…Open the annals of all peoples, and I doubt whether you will find anything finer or more extraordinary."

Sierra Leone's foundational principles, then, were not at all based on violence: they were based on enlightened and humane principles, though in practice those principles were from time to time betrayed or compromised.

In making the claim about Sierra Leone's foundational deformity and violence as the origin of the RUF's nihilism of the 1990s, Wai writes about "the nature of the state and the structures of violence that are constitutive of the state of Sierra Leone from its very moment of conception as a colonial project, and how the nature and pattern of that violence continues to structure everyday power relations and exercise of power in that country." This broad statement may be applicable to any country that has had a colonial experience, which is almost any modern country, including Britain, and it therefore cannot provide a valid explanatory framework.

I have gone at length to critique Wai's book because, though I disagree with its key thesis about the origins of the so-called rebel war, I find it a very important contribution to the debate on Sierra Leone's recent past. I take it very seriously. I think it should be read very widely, and should provoke debate among the country's intellectuals. I offer this critique as a starting point for that debate.

Part III

Pawns and Players in Sierra Leone's War

1.
Who were the Kamajors of Sierra Leone?[14]

In August 2011, I visited Hoggard Bockarie at his home in Bo, Sierra Leone's second largest city. Bockarie is a former Kamajor leader. I had got to know him during the disarmament programme in 2000-2001. Educated and articulate, he was then one of those facilitating the process by getting the younger Kamajors to the disarmament camps in Bo District.

On his cluttered desk, atop all other documents and a few books, was the CDF Calendar 2001. The CDF – Civil Defence Force – was the umbrella organisation of all the pro-government militia fighters, including, most prominently, the Kamajors. It was called into being by the exiled government of Ahmad Tejan Kabbah in Guinea in 1997 (following the disastrous Armed Forces Ruling Council, AFRC, coup of May that year); though the name itself, Danny Hoffman tells us in *The War Machines: Young Men and Violence in Sierra Leone and Liberia*, had been confected by exiled pro-democracy Sierra Leoneans earlier that year, in Monrovia, Liberia.

For Bockarie, the calendar was obviously a precious possession, a memento that must be preserved. He proudly took me through its pages. On the cover are two pictures: one, of a triumphant Ahmad Tejan Kabbah, Sierra Leone's former President, and the other, of his Vice, Albert Joe Demby. Kabbah's official title – President and Commander-in-Chief – is appropriately stated under the picture. On the inside of the cover page is the visage of Samuel Hinga Norman, hair greying, the expansive face exuding great charisma and determination. Norman is described, again appropriately formally, as "Deputy Minister of Defence and Regent Chief of Jaiama-Bongor Chiefdom." The language gets more

---

[14] (Review of Danny Hoffman *The War Machines: Young Men and Violence in Sierra Leone and Liberia* (Duke University Press 2011) published in *The Journal of Sierra Leone Studies* Vol.I, January 2012.

florid on page 3: here, there is a picture of a youthful and handsome Moinina Fofanah, who did not hold any formal national position. The calendar makes up for this lack with an ingenious literary contrivance: Fofana is described as National Director of War – and one, moreover, whose primacy was unchallenged: "As far as the Sierra Leone Civil defence Forces are concerned," the encomium under the picture reads, "they don't say war unless he says they say war...popularly known within the CDF as Director, [Fofana] is the man who oversees [sic] the mobilisation and deployment of the volunteer fighters of the CDF. When his men are not engaged in combat against the rebels, Fofanah refers to himself as Director of Peace." Two pages later there is a very striking picture of Kundewa (or Kondowa, on the calendar), extravagantly turned up in his "ceremonial attire" as High Priest, the sartorial choice and intense look at first suggesting that he was posing for the cameras but actually, on second look, he is in what looks like a formal meeting (there is, prominent behind him, Sierra Leone's Coat of Arms). He is described as "Hon. Alieu Kondowa, the Chief Initiator of the Kamajors and allied militia forces...the embodiment of the legend and mystery of the Kamajors."

Reverend Alfred Samforay, the indefatigable champion of the CDF who produced the calendar on behalf of the Sierra Leone Action Movement (SLAM) in the US, has assured me in a recent telephone conversation that neither Fofana nor Kondowa, who are completely unlettered anyway, had suggested the extravagant description of their roles during the war in the calendar. The whole enterprise, Samforay told me, was meant to be a celebratory bookend to the gallant efforts of the CDF in saving Sierra Leone's democracy from the ravages of The Peoples' Army (the coalition of so-called Revolutionary United Front, RUF, and the rogue soldiers constituting the AFRC.) Instead, the calendar was used by prosecutors of the Special Court for Sierra Leone (SCSL) to advance their view that the CDF was a coherent military organisation with a functioning chain of command – and that, therefore, its leaders, Norman, Fofanah and Kondowa, should be held responsible for violations committed by all its members. When shown the calendar in court by the prosecutors, Norman was understandably puzzled; it was a foolish foreigner's fuss.

A Militia or an Army?

Hoffman, a resourceful and energetic American scholar, has been studying the various militias, in particular the Kamajors, in Sierra Leone and Liberia for the past seven years, in the course of which he met and interviewed hundreds of kamajors as well as countless other people involved in the war. He is also a photo-journalist, and the wonderful pictures he reproduces in this book merit a review on their own. Hoffman's standing as the indisputable expert on the subject was underlined when he was invited, in 2006, as an expert witness for the defence. The brief he prepared, later modified and published by the journal *African Affairs*, comprehensively rubbished a report prepared for the prosecution on the CDF by a British colonel with the unimprovably thudding name Iron – Richard Iron.

Reading Iron's report is still excruciating: prepared after a two-week visit to Sierra Leone, the report used the Hanging Judge's methodology. Iron was commissioned to produce a report that would show the CDF as an organised military force with a coherent hierarchy, which he did with un-ironical enthusiasm, throwing about such meaningless generalities as "the *nature* of conflict is regardless of the *type* of conflict. General war and insurgency, whether today or two thousand years ago, have more in common with each other than any other kind of non-warlike activity. It should be no surprise, therefore, that military organizations tend to have recognisable hierarchies and structures." When he took the witness stand on 14 June 2005, Iron repeated the same points, calling the CDF a proper military organization – though, he added loftily, "not a very good one."

In his brief, Hoffman noted that the CDF is better understood as "the militarization of a web of social relations", and not a military outfit to begin with. This was not simply a matter of awkward linguistic parsing; the characterisation goes to the heart of the Special Court's indictment of Norman, Fofana and Kondewa, who were deemed to have 'individual criminal responsibility' as leaders of a military organization in which they "exercised authority, command, and control over all subordinate members of the CDF." "The Kamajors' very identity is predicated on the

88

protection of [their} villages" rather than as a military force with capacity for both offensive and defensive actions, Hoffman noted.

I was in the court on 3 June 2004 when David Crane, the court's very theatrical chief prosecutor at the time, unveiled the indictments. In the trial of these men, Crane promised, his voice rising to the pitch of pathos, the path of justice "will be strewn with the bones of the dead, the moans of the mutilated, the cries of agony of the tortured, echoing down into the valley of death below." Specific acts of war crimes in the indictment were all limited to about the end of 1997 to about April 1998: that was exactly when the CDF fought to unseat the AFRC and reinstate the legitimate elected government of President Kabbah. This point needs to be properly underscored. For much of this period – one must underline this fact as well – Norman was in Liberia as guest of the Nigerian-led ECOMOG force coordinating support for the disparate groups of pro-Kabbah militias who had, by fiat in Conakry, been tagged as Civil Defence Force. When, on 25 January 2006, Norman was questioned in court about his activities at the time by his lead counsel Bubuakei Jabbi, the Special Court's transcripts[15] recorded these exchanges:

Jabbi: Your own interaction with ECOMOG?
Norman: Well, I have called that interaction co-ordination.
Jabbi: Yes.
Norman: My task was to receive whatever that was a support, whether in the form of arms, ammunition, food, medicine, transport, from ECOMOG and then have it delivered to the men on the ground through their commanders and this was done between myself and the one appointment that had been made in the person of Mr. M.S. Kallon as administrator. He received and then delivered to the commanders. Sometimes I went there and made sure these deliveries were actually done so they could not be deceived, like especially arms and ammunition and food.
Jabbi: What about the interaction between the hunters and ECOMOG?
Norman: That was strictly between themselves and the commanders of hunters. I linked up with the chief of staff. The chief of staff had his

---

[15] The trial transcripts, as well as the judgments, can be found on the Special Court for Sierra Leone's website at http://www.sc-sl.org/; they run to tens of thousands of pages.

various officers in the field who were to link up with the commanders of the hunters as they went further into the hinterland of Sierra Leone.

Jabbi: Was that interaction under your personal purview?

Norman: The interaction between myself and ECOMOG --

Jabbi: No.

Norman: Was the interaction between the hunters and commanders and commanders were in their own area of command.

Jabbi: That was outside your own responsibility?

Norman: That was definitely, My Lord.

I spent an hour with Norman in his cell, a room in a small house with a curiously domestic atmosphere, at the Special Court a day before his testimony. He seemed untroubled by the charges against him – he spoke in sadness, more than in anger, about the cruel turn of events that got him into the cell. In Crane's indictment, Norman is described as the principal force in establishing, organising, providing logistical support, and promoting the CDF. What the indictment does not say is that Norman had been appointed to this putative position by Kabbah in Guinea, and in the presence – and with the endorsement – of the diplomatic representatives of the US (Ambassador John Hirsch), UK (High Commissioner Peter Penfold), Nigeria (High Commissioner Alhaji Abu Bakar), and the UN (Berkhanu Dinka.) The four diplomats had made clear to Norman that this was the only way to sustain the resistance against the AFRC and reinstate the democratically elected government.

Of the four, only Penfold, retired by his government a few years before, testified on behalf of Norman. He called Norman "a true hero" who should never have been charged by the court. Probably through Penfold's encouragement – I had lunch with Penfold at which he mentioned the possibility a month before – General David Richards, the British commander (he later headed the NATO forces in Afghanistan) whose intervention helped save the faltering UN mission in 2000, also took the witness stand in favour of Norman. General Richards had observed the CDF in action in Freetown in 1999, and thereafter interacted intimately with Norman for about three months in Sierra Leone. On 21 February 2006, he took the witness stand. He spoke warmly of Norman ("He had military acumen. He was very determined... But I suppose I had already formed the opinion on my first visit that he was a very effective minister. He was dynamic. He took decisions and had the courage of his convictions, if you like.") On the crucial matter whether the CDF was an organized, hierarchical military force, General Richards said that he had spent a total of 14 days observing the CDF prepare for battle, "watching how the overall command and control of government forces functioned."

General Richards: So although I take the point about only observing a battle once, of course I'm forming, as a professional soldier, a view of them all the time from all the other activities that an army of any kind manifests. My view remains that... they were a very brave and, at a low level, effective fighting force. They exhibited what to me could best be described as a militia force. Some were well trained, others came along for a few weeks and then would go away again, which I know frustrated their commanders... there were those that were, if you like, mainstream CDF and those that appeared to me to be on the periphery of the organisation that, nevertheless, were described as CDF and I never really could quite -- I never really knew which was which except some clearly were more cohesive in their approach. What I do know is that they were vital to the defence of Freetown in January '99. I observed very little fighting in February '99, but we already discussed with the President [Tejan Kabbah] the idea that they ought to be brought into the mainstream of government defence forces, which of course happened, I think, in 2000 - some time later. But there was a clear desire to bring them in to the mainstream to ensure they acted in line with the government's intentions and could be part of a coherent defence force. I think that's probably enough.

Norman's defence cleverly tried to push this line, which appears to completely undermine the Special Court's expert testimony – a highly significant development, since Colonel Iron was entirely inferior in every respect (rank and knowledge of the CDF and of Sierra Leone) to the distinguished General Richards.

Jabbi: Thank you very much. Finally, General, do you know one Colonel Iron?
General Richards: I do.
Jabbi: Would it surprise you to learn that he depicted the –

At this point, prosecutor Desmond de Silva, a friend and former senior colleague of Tejan Kabbah who had been seconded to the court by the Sierra Leone government, sensing the danger, intervened and stopped the questioning. The grounds of his objection are as absurd as the trial itself: "Colonel Iron was an expert witness whose expert report was laid before the Court," de Silva said, the parody of the moment so appositive of the entire trial. "What my learned friend Mr Jabbi is now trying to do is to get this very distinguished senior officer, General Richard, to comment on an expert whom the Court has already heard about. This was the very thing that I have been trying to avoid. In our respectful submission, it is quite wrong that expert evidence should be dealt with in this..." It is a testament to the awe that this very experienced lawyer held over the defence team that even Jabbi meekly submitted to his bullying on every substantive point throughout the trial. Needless to say, there was an awful mismatch – in experience, talent and resources – between the prosecution and the defence, making our ordinary conception of justice unlikely from the very start.

As it happened, on 22 February 2007, Norman died after a botched operation on his hips while in the detention of the court, so there was no verdict in his case. But the judgment convicting Fofana and Kondewa on 2 August 2007 made clear that had he not died, Norman would also have been convicted. Justice Thompson, the only Sierra Leonean on the bench, disagreed with the judgment, writing in his dissenting opinion the following: "The safety of the State of Sierra Leone, as the supreme law, became for the CDF and the Kamajors the categorical imperative and paramount obligation in their military efforts to restore democracy to the country. I entertain more than serious doubts whether in the context...a tribunal should hold liable persons who volunteered to take up arms and risk their lives and those of their families to prevent anarchy and tyranny from taking a firm hold in their society..."

The travesty of the trial knew no bounds. The two CDF leaders, who had fought to return an exiled government to power, were flown out of the country, to Rwanda, to be jailed – grotesquely reminiscent of the exile and detention, in the Gold Coast (now Ghana), of Bai Bureh and

Nyagua by the British colonial authorities after the Hut Tax War in the late 1890s.

How did it come to this? How was it that we allowed perhaps the most successful civil defence effort in post-colonial West Africa to be so grossly profaned by people who have never shown any sincere interest in our affairs?

Four Plateaus

Hoffman does not directly address this issue: indeed he does not examine the trial itself, though he makes clear both in his testimony and in this very important book that the three CDF leaders should never have been charged by the Special Court. *The War Machines* focuses on the origins and trajectory of the CDF and the Liberians United for Reconciliation and Democracy (LURD) through to 2007, by which time both groups had ceased to exist in an organised form. Even so, Hoffman writes, "the forces and pressures that assembled these young men and deployed their violence in war were still very much in evidence in the region's diamond mines, rubber plantations, city streets, and political party offices." This observation is both true and important, and I shall return to it in due course.

Hoffman notes Norman's unease during the trial when Jabbi, his chief counsel, first used the term 'War Machine' to describe the 'Kamajor system'. Jabbi, a literary scholar perhaps more than a lawyer, is rather given to convolution, but here Hoffman defends the use of the term – for it captures, in his view, the militarisation of what was essentially a social movement. Hoffman relies here on the work of French philosophers Gilles Deleuze and *Félix* Guattari. I think I understand why Hoffman has to mobilise these European authorities of arcane philosophy, but the great value of this book lies in its careful and sensitive interviews with many of the actors in Sierra Leone and Liberia, and its sophisticated understanding of the region's recent history and politics. To begin with, it is the first serious study to integrate fully the wars in the two contiguous countries, showing convincingly that the conflicts that ravaged the two were a single, continuous war that "exceeds our timeframes normally cited for these conflicts." He calls them, appropriately, the Mano River Wars. We encounter characters here who fought as militia fighters in Sierra Leone, and later (once the CDF had effective been disbanded in Sierra Leone) just as enthusiastically, as LURD. There has been much anxiety within the UN Security Council about an estimated 4,500 Liberian mercenaries "hired and deployed" by former Côte d'Ivoire President Laurent Gbagbo – as well as over reports that Ibrahim Bah, a notorious Burkina Faso-based Senegalese and former associate of the Revolutionary United Front of Sierra Leone, had attempted to recruit ex-fighters in Sierra Leone for similar purpose – during the conflict in that country. Hoffman's book makes clear why this problem exists in the first place, and why it remains a standing threat in the region.

I concentrate in this essay on the Kamajors, who are more fully realised and interesting in this book. Here, the important question is: how did a phenomenon that started purely as community defence networks come to be caught up in the global drama of "humanitarian justice" as liberal peace?

The War Machines, while a sympathetic study, does not romanticise the militias: it charts four plateaus in the trajectory, or evolving character, of the Kamajors. The first plateau examines the "mythopoetic" origins of the term Kamajors, the popular idea, rooted in Kamajor self-image, that the phenomenon has antecedents in some kind of antiquity. Hoffman is rightly sceptical: "...the desire to find explanations for what the Kamajors became by looking to the ethnographic details of village *Kamajoisia,* early colonial mercenaries, or even to revolutionary youth culture in the postcolony is, I think, misplaced. The kamajors' historical antecedents are not explanatory in the ways we might like them to be." I would put it in stronger terms: looking for a "primordial" provenance or antecedents for the Kamajors, a move to suggest that some kind of atavism is at work (as the Special Court prosecutors and judges strongly implied), is a serious mistake. The Kamajor phenomenon was a product of the war in 1990s. While there was among the pre-colonial Mende a putative hunter guild, this was hardly a war instrument.

I have read through the substantive Chalmers' report on the Hut War of 1898 (which runs to 175 pages) and the transcripts of interviews and other appendixes (running to over 600 pages). Though many people who actively participated in the conflict – Mende chiefs, warriors, British officers, colonial administrators, and Creole traders – were extensively interviewed, I found no reference to Kamajoi or Hunter-warrior guild; the references are to "Mende Warboys." Poro is mentioned, but a key factor appeared to have been a new contrivance called "Gepelondo" ('Keep Silent' in Mende), which was said to be more exclusive and powerful than even Poro in the mobilization of the Mende against the tax as well as against everything that the British colonialists stood for. There are references to warriors "painting" their bodies, but these are few, and clearly this wasn't a dominant feature of the war – few of the warriors actually painted their bodies. This history of war mobilisation among the Mende in the face of outside aggression – as well as the various repertoires associated with such mobilization – was, however, important in the growth of a powerful Kamajor movement.

This brings us to Hoffman's second plateau, 'mobilisation' into citizens' militia, beginning as early as April 1991 (a month after the war started): the pioneering effort being Captain Prince Benjamin Hirsch's in Segbwema. The idea spread after Hirsch was killed in suspicious circumstances: "Fearing the military as much as the rebels," Hoffman writes, "many communities organized civil defense committees or civil defense units, mostly groups of local youth manning roadblocks, interrogating strangers, or conducting defensive patrols." These early efforts "lacked a central command and fixed organizational structure." This started to change as the war spread, and as it became clear after the National Provisional Ruling Council (NPRC) coup that some army officers who remained loyal to the overthrown All Peoples Congress (APC) government were actively sabotaging the NPRC's war efforts by collaborating with the RUF at various levels (the Sobel phenomenon). Dr. Alpha Lavalie organised EREDCOM in Kenema, which was "one of the largest and most successful of these civil defense efforts." Lavalie, too, was murdered, doubtless by Sobels. In his testimony, Norman explained how he started community defence mobilisation at Telu, where he was Regent Chief, and how he encouraged other traditional authorities to do the same. He put together about 75 young men to be trained; one night in 1995, 'rebels' descended on the village and killed many of them. Norman escaped miraculously. The massacre, almost certainly by Sobels, did not kill the idea; in fact it exponentially grew after that.

Patrick Muana's pioneering article (1997) on the phenomenon noted how the growth of these civilian initiatives was associated with the "politics of displacement". This is true, but these early recruitments, as Hoffman notes, were "intimately connected not only to the *kamajoisia* mythos but also to the logic of Mende chieftaincy and elite patronage."

Hoffman's third plateau, 'institutionalisation', is the stage at which Kamajors were co-opted as something close to a "de facto army" by the new Sierra Leone Peoples Party (SLPP) government after it gained power in 1996. The new government understandably loathed and feared the national army, and with Norman as Deputy Minister of Defence, began encouraging the spread of civilian defence militias. In early May 1997, Sierra Leone's Parliament gazetted a bill formally granting state support to the CDF. Almost immediately, the Sobel AFRC coup of 1997 happened: the coup-makers listed the bill as one of their grievances, but clearly the coup itself had been planned long before. The coup-makers' apparent close ties to the RUF, in any case, considerably made the case for such an arrangement for state support for the CDF. Hoffman writes that a large number of the youths who joined the Kamajors and groups like Gbenthis, Kapras, and Hunting Societies – collectively constituting the CDF – may not have cared much for the SLPP, but "faced with a regime like the AFRC/RUF junta, for which violent profiteering was so nakedly its sole purpose, the political fantasy of a well-functioning, democratic polity was salient indeed. The CDF responded to the necropolitics of the junta with a vague but powerful narrative of fighting for the ideal government that might replace it."

> Later, when the SLPP had been restored to power, the conflation of the party with the political fantasy of ideal government would be challenged repeatedly. But with the SLPP forced out of power and sitting in exile, it was possible for youth affiliated with the CDF to live – and fight for – a political project that was both material *and* idealistic.

The upshot, however, was that the political imaginary of the CDF movement was organized according to the categories of the state. Whatever experiments or unforeseen consequences might have come from the grassroots mobilization of the kamajors were curtailed by the AFRC coup because the militia took its sole new task to be the recapture of the Sierra Leonean capital and hence the state (and, subsequently, the overthrow of Charles Taylor in Liberia). What had begun as a decentralized community defense effort, as a creative war machine, was in the end captured by the logic of the state. Its revolutionary possibilities were curtailed by the fantasy of a democratic polity that could only be imagined in the form of a reinstated SLPP.

The actual restoration of the SLPP revealed the fantasy. Hinga Norman retained his post as Deputy Minister of Defense, and Joe Demby the post of Vice-President. But the preponderance of CDF fighters felt that they went unrecognized and unsupported after their integral role in re-establishing the government.

That feeling only heightened when Kabbah dropped Demby as Vice-President, and ignominiously handed over Norman to the Special Court. The indictment of the CDF derived from the pathos of their changed role: "the CDF moved from defending rural communities to fighting to reinstate an elected government, and to protecting that government from a military that had proven itself to be uncooperative, it grew much harder to construe the force as a grassroots mobilization of society against the state. The Black December operation and the other efforts by the CDF to restore the SLPP shifted the "defensive" role of the militia from one of defending rural communities to defending the state – albeit in the form of the SLPP party and a certain fantasy of democratic governance. The militia grew more predatory and more abusive toward the population it was ostensibly meant to defend (though it never approached the thoroughly paranoid, necropolitical mode of violent authority exercised by the AFRC and RUF). Equally important, the movement grew less creative. It ceased to experiment, to open up new ideas or envision new possibilities for a future in Sierra Leone." [Note that the Truth and Reconciliation Commission of 2004 stated that overall the RUF committed 60.5% of the atrocities committed during the war in Sierra Leone; the Armed Forces Ruling Council (AFRC) 9.8%; the Sierra Leone Army 6.8%; the Civil Defence Force (mainly Kamajors) 6%; and ECOMOG, the Nigerian-led West African intervention force, 1%.]

Now that they were aligned to a government, the impression would be that the CDF was well-organised as a military force, though this was clearly not the case. Still, if it made any sense to indict Norman, why wasn't Kabbah indicted?

Hoffman's fourth and last plateau – 'Capital's axiomatic', the pre-dominance of mercenary tendencies – resulted from the third plateau, and particularly the feeling of neglect by the CDF after the reinstatement of Kabbah. During this phase, members of the CDF got involved in harassments at checkpoints and other serious abuses; Kondewa became more and more ingenious in his initiations, creating fictive categories to make money and in the process commit various kinds of abuses; and a large number of Kamajors took their skills elsewhere, to the LURD, say. This phase is still regnant: young men, militarised by brutal conflict, having no other skills, are now arranging their lives, Hoffman warns, "according to contemporary capital's global axiomatics." UN reports, like the 7 December 2011 Panel of Experts on Liberia report which details the activities of Liberian mercenaries returning from fighting Côte d'Ivoire, don't quite capture this nuance.

Conclusion

Hoggard Bockarie, long past his prime, still with a sentimental attachment to the ideal of civilian mobilisation for the defence of democracy – holding on to that ideal despite the Special Court's attempt to criminalise that mobilisation, and now planning to write an insider's history of the Kamajors for posterity – Hoggard Bockarie is far from being representative of the vast majority of the fighters who constituted the Kamajors. Neither, in fact, were Norman, Kundewa and Fofana, persecuted, because of their national prominence and reputation, as the leaders of the disparate group. These were only the people who were able to channel, through their charismatic, otiose guidance, the great energy of the youthful volunteers towards an overwhelmingly worthy goal.

Kundewa, in spite of his compelling necromantic appeal, is not representative of the overwhelmingly youthful Kamajor fighters. Indeed, in what other war crimes dock can you find the likeness of this man?

> I was born in Sierra Leone. No one sent me to school. No one taught me a trade. I simply lived in my village in Yawbeko Chiefdom, Bonthe District, until the war came.
>
> Many people died when the war reached Yawbeko. My father was killed. My brother Kafu was killed. My mother was killed. My wife…was injured, and our child starved when we were in the bush running from the rebels…
>
> It was there in the bush that I had my dream. I saw my father and my mother. They came to me with three people I did not know. "Alieu," my father said, "we have come to see you." We have come with them so that you will not be afraid."
>
> The first of the three figures was a man, and he spoke to me about his death and the death of his wife and children. "We have come," he explained, "so that you…can stop the killing. We have come to bring you an herb [tifa] that you can use to stop this violence."

The speaker is Kundewa, narrating his story to Hoffman, who finds Kundewa's presence in the court singularly incongruous, completely out of place.

In December 2009, I spent an hour with the reclusive former Liberian President Gyude Bryant in Monrovia. He had been my neighbour for over a year, but I hadn't known that till much later. He told me that thousands of former Kamajor fighters now resident in Liberia had mobilised when Norman was arrested, and that he had to work quickly with the UN forces to diffuse the situation by bringing together their leaders at a meeting during which they were told it was Norman's wish for them to keep calm and respect the judicial process; later some of the ex-fighters were arrested and deported to Sierra Leone. I can't help thinking about many of those who remained there while reading the 7

December 2011 Panel of Experts on Liberia report which referred to mercenaries fighting in the recent conflict in Côte d'Ivoire who "do not share an ideology, although they commonly recalled their previous participation in former rebel groups."

Perhaps more important may be Hoffman's penetrating observation in a chapter for a book I edited in 2009:

> The Court's approach to the CDF leaves no room to envision an acceptable mode of civilian defensive mobilization. This is a legacy that would have to be on the minds of regional or local authorities (governmental or non-governmental) organizing against future excesses by the military or by the ruling party. Certainly any political party in power in Sierra Leone will be able to draw upon the precedent set by the Court to crack down on what it perceives to be (or simply labels as) mobilizations of community defence bodies.
> And it seems increasingly likely that such circumstances will arise. There are two key reasons. First, such violent mobilizations are woven into the logic of postcolonial African democracies. And second, there is an ever greater push on the part of external forces, notably the United States, to militarize social networks as a form of community defence.

Hoffman adds: "the possibility that communities, particularly in the rural areas, will be required to mobilize themselves for their own security against the forces of the State or against forces the State is in no position to defeat [remains immense]. Such mobilizations may be as limited as gathering intelligence or as expansive as violent, armed resistance. Whatever form such community defence initiatives take, they will no doubt be part of a more general conversation about the rights and responsibilities of citizenship in Africa today; and...that is a project made vastly more complex in the aftermath of Sierra Leone's Special Court."

The Special Court, needless to say, wouldn't care. Trial Chamber I, which passed judgment on the CDF defendants, readily admitted that "there is nothing in the evidence which demonstrates that either Fofana or Kondewa joined the conflict in Sierra Leone for selfish reasons. In fact, we have found that both Fofana and Kondewa were among those who stepped forward in the efforts to restore democracy to Sierra Leone, and, for the main part, they acted from a sense of civic duty rather than for personal aggrandizement or gain." The robbed judges, like the 'outraged justice' from the high seas descending onto the Congo bush in Conrad's Heart of Darkness, were merely keen on punishing Kondewa and Fofana for violations that they had committed in serving what the judges admitted was a noble cause. Was there a defence of "necessity" in international law for those violations? they asked. Certainly "validating the defence of Necessity in International Criminal Law would create a justification for what offenders may term and plead as a 'just cause' or a 'just war' even though serious violations of International Humanitarian Law would have been committed," they copiously argued. But to do so in the CDF cases would "negate the resolve and determination of the International Community to combat" the "heinous, gruesome or degrading" crimes against innocent victims which international humanitarian law intends to protect.

2.
ECOMOG: The Story of an Heroic Failure[16]

IN APRIL 1998, UN SECRETARY GENERAL KOFI ANNAN ISSUED an extraordinary document. Entitled *The Causes of Conflict and the Promotion of Durable Peace and Sustainable Development in Africa*, it emphasized the need to develop and reinforce the capabilities of African states to undertake peacekeeping operations and to carry out forceful interventions in states with conflicts that create humanitarian catastrophes and normative collapse. The report highlighted the role of democracy in enhancing an 'environment where peace and development can flourish', and strongly implied that an annulment of democratic governance — by military coups, say — should be discouraged within the framework of regional initiatives. The Secretary General of the UN, an organization known for a rigidly statist approach to world affairs, was arguing that 'human security' should take precedence over the familiar refuge of autocratic regimes, 'sovereignty'.

Annan's comments were almost certainly influenced by events in West Africa, his home region, coming as they did shortly after Nigerian-led West African troops intervened in Sierra Leone following a highly destructive coup, unseated the military junta and reinstated the democratically elected government that had been overthrown. It would appear from this that West Africa was, for once, shaping global policy, not just being a recipient of it.

Yet the West African peacekeeping initiative was always enmeshed in controversy. With the region being among the most volatile in the world, it was a great source of hope when its leaders met, in August 1990, and decided to set up an intervention force under the auspices of the Economic Community of West African States (ECOWAS), known as ECOMOG. It was a way to respond to a destructive civil war in Liberia

---

[16] Published by African Affairs (Oxford University Press 2003) 102 (406): 147-154

which had, at the time, spawned no less than five armed factions, 60,000 combatants, and led to the deaths of tens of thousands of people in a country with a population of 2 million. Nigeria, the regional giant, contributed the largest contingent of the troops and bore by far the greatest burden of the financial cost. Sierra Leone's President Joseph Momoh appeared to have spoken for all the leaders when he characterized the interventionist force in these terms: 'We view such an initiative as both timely and appropriate and we hope that all the warring factions in Liberia will see reason and agree . . . it is our duty to re-affirm to the world and all those involved in the Liberian conflict that the ECOWAS initiative is a genuine effort aimed at bringing peace and happiness to war-torn Liberia.'

These fine sentiments notwithstanding, controversy was guaranteed right from the start. Unlike most previous peacekeeping missions, ECOMOG intervened in the Liberian crisis before any ceasefire agreement, and indeed against the expressed wishes of the country's most important warring faction, Charles Taylor's National Patriotic Front of Liberia (NPFL). For this reason, Taylor promised to attack the West African troops if they ventured into Liberia, a threat he carried out on the very first day the troops landed in Monrovia, at a base provided them by another, less powerful factional army. Regional rivalries and differences, promoted mainly by France, a long-standing hegemonic rival of Nigeria in West Africa, also complicated the mission. Of the Francophone West African states, only Guinea contributed troops to ECOMOG initially. Outside perception of the force was also blinkered by the fact that almost all the leaders contributing troops (with the exception of tiny Gambia's President Dauda Jawara) were military men who had seized power in coups or in controversial circumstances.

This controversial beginning ignited a debate among African scholars about the role and mandate of the interventionist force. Was it a bold attempt at peacekeeping, offering strong lessons in regional conflict management in a world in which the international community had progressively disengaged from Africa, in the opinion of Maragret Vogt? Or was it, as Max Ahmadu Sesay characterized it, an ill-conceived and regionally divisive intervention exercise by autocratic leaders, with disastrous consequences for regional cohesion and sustainable democracy? This debate reflected, in part, the mixed reviews which ECOMOG operations were earning.

Many West African military forces lacked the basic capabilities, including leadership, for conducting sustained campaigns beyond their own borders. Only Nigeria had an air force and navy of any significance. In Liberia, the quality of ECOMOG's military leadership was patchy. While some commanders, like the Nigerian General Dongonyaro, were astute and decisive, maintaining sustained pressure on the rampaging NPFL fighters, others like the force's first commander, General Arnold Quainoo (a Ghanaian), were distinctly unsuccessful. It was under Quainoo's leadership that one of the factional leaders, Prince Yormie Johnson (of the Independent National Patriotic Front of Liberia, INPFL, a breakaway faction of the original NPFL, and the one that welcomed ECOMOG into Liberia most enthusiastically), captured the beleaguered Liberian President, Samuel K. Doe, and executed him along with 70 of his bodyguards right at ECOMOG's headquarters. Moreover, barely three months after the force landed, the head of the Sierra Leonean contingent, Lieutenant-Colonel Modu Hanciles, had to be withdrawn for cowardice and neglect of duty. Looting was so common among the troops — with stolen cars and household furniture and other goods being routinely shipped to Nigeria and elsewhere — that Liberians corrupted the acronym, ECOMOG, to stand for 'Every Car or Moving Object Gone'. The force was also hampered by what Herb Howe has called 'an incoherent logistical tail'. Its air power, for example, was so limited that by 1995 the only serviceable helicopter was used by the force commander as his personal taxi. In the event, however, the sustained presence of the force in Monrovia, which effectively foreclosed the seizure of state power by any of the rebel groups, finally forced them to agree to a comprehensive ceasefire and disarmament process in 1996, which was followed by general and presidential elections that Charles Taylor and his NPFL won overwhelmingly, in 1997. The Liberian campaign cost Nigeria a reported US$3 billion, and over 500 soldiers killed.

Shortly after this questionable success in Liberia, neighbouring Sierra Leone, which had been battling, since March 1991, with Liberian-backed rebels of the Revolutionary United Front (RUF), erupted into renewed violence after the rebels and rogue government troops collaborated to terminate the elected government (elected in 1996) of President Tejan Kabbah, as well as a tenuous ceasefire and disarmament process. At the time ECOMOG, as a regional force, was not involved in Sierra Leone, but under separate bilateral treaties, Guinean and Nigerian troops maintained a limited presence, in support of the Freetown government, in the country. Kabbah had signed a Status of Forces Agreement (SOFA) with Nigeria, which provided for the deployment of Nigerian troops in defence of the government, and to help retrain the disintegrated Sierra Leone army. It was a small force, and it was easily overwhelmed, in May 1997, by a few dozen armed soldiers who spearheaded the profoundly destructive Armed Forces Ruling Council (AFRC) coup.

The Nigerian leader, General Sani Abacha, a close personal friend of Kabbah, saw the coup as a personal humiliation, and vowed to overturn it. For the majority of Sierra Leoneans, the coup ushered in a reign of terror in which hundreds were killed, and property, both private and public, was destroyed. It triggered a staggering refugee flight of over 400,000 in the first two months after the coup. But the Nigerians' initial attempts were marked by the same lack of clear-sighted strategic thinking which dogged ECOMOG's Liberian operations. On 31 May 1997, with only 3,000 lightly armed soldiers, the Nigerians made a clumsy assault on the more than 15,000 strong AFRC junta troops (including the heavily battle-tested RUF rebels). The operation was easily botched, and 300 Nigerian soldiers were captured and detained. The Nigerians responded by attacking junta positions with gunboat shells, many of them missing and hitting civilian targets. World outrage at these events — few people who spoke about these events failed to mention the incongruous fact that Nigeria was itself ruled by an obdurate and brutal general — forced the Nigerian government to move more systematically, and it enlisted ECOWAS once again to give the campaign broader regional support. This was, in principle, fairly easy to arrange since almost all the ECOWAS states, as well as the OAU and the UN, condemned the coup and called for the reinstatement of the civilian authority.

A four-nation committee comprising the foreign ministers of Nigeria, Ghana, Ivory Coast and Guinea met in July 1997 and agreed to pursue 'any method that would restore the legitimate government of Sierra Leone'. But the agreement did not extend to a specific and concrete method. The problem was not merely a matter of awkward detail. Two of the committee members, Ghana and Ivory Coast, said that they favoured peaceful means, which included the use of sanctions, while Nigeria and Guinea favoured immediate military action. ECOWAS agreed to impose a 'general and total embargo on all supplies of petroleum products, arms and military equipment' to Sierra Leone, plus travel bans on members of the AFRC junta, and called on all member states to 'abstain from transacting any business with' Sierra Leone under junta rule. Both the OAU and the UN quickly endorsed these sanctions, making the campaign against the AFRC a global one. Nigeria was authorized to enforce the sanctions, something it tried to do by completely blockading the country and occasionally carrying out bombing raids on junta targets. This proved to be inadequate to oust the junta, however, and the Nigerians, who had taken over the international airport at Lungi, continued to systematically build up their forces in Sierra Leone to reach 10,000 in January 1998. It was after this that they, along with some Guinean troops and the pro-Kabbah Civil Defence Force, struck at the junta in Freetown, successfully ousting them from the city and then reinstating Kabbah. Hundreds of thousands of Sierra Leonean refugees returned soon afterwards.

This success, the most dramatic display of Nigerian arms abroad, and certainly an interesting example of regional military intervention, made ECOMOG so attractive as a force for restoring democratic governance that when, in June 1998, Guinea-Bissau's army commander General Ansumane Mane triggered a bloody battle in the capital to seize power from President João Bernardo Vieira, Vieira appealed to the West African body to intervene on his side. Senegal and Guinea sent in troops. This led to a stalemate, but the intervening force was otherwise unsuccessful in ousting Mane. ECOWAS stepped up negotiations to end the conflict, and in July 1998 a Committee of Seven was established — consisting of Burkina Faso, Ivory Coast, Gambia, Ghana, Guinea, Nigeria, and Senegal — to map out a solution to the Bissau troubles. ECOWAS decided to broaden its mandate beyond Sierra Leone to include Bissau, and more troops, from Benin, Gambia, Niger and Togo, were dispatched to the tiny country. Mane continued to hold on until 23

November 2000, when he was killed in fighting with pro-government troops.

Adekeye Adebayo's *Building Peace in West Africa* attempts to provide a comprehensive account and analysis of this novel attempt to end destructive internal conflicts and build peace in this unstable region. Adebayo's book, part of the International Peace Academy's (IPA) occasional papers series, argues that, although prone to instability, West Africa "has gone further than any other African sub region in efforts to establish a security mechanism to manage its own conflicts," and notes optimistically that the region's leaders "are currently attempting to institutionalise a security mechanism to manage future sub regional conflicts." This force, which will maintain the name ECOMOG, will consist of troops from all ECOWAS states, and its main task 'will involve observation and monitoring, peacekeeping, humanitarian intervention, enforcement of sanctions and embargoes, preventive deployment, peace-building operations, disarmament and demobilization, and policing activities, including anti-smuggling and anti-criminal activities'. This is obviously a very tall order for a force from states with such limited capabilities and such fractious politics, but Adebayo, a Nigerian scholar with the IPA, is focused on the glorious picture. He is undaunted by some of the problems such a force will encounter, which he outlines with great insight: for example, "parochial, partisan interests" may interfere with a decision to deploy ECOMOG, since a two-thirds majority in support is necessary to sanction deployment; the force will be useless if a country like Nigeria experiences a catastrophic humanitarian situation that merits external intervention; and " if a military coup were to succeed in a francophone state with popular domestic support and tacit French backing, a Nigerian-led ECOMOG intervention would be fraught wit" ' unacceptable political and military risks.

Adebayo's analysis of the historic hegemonic rivalry between Nigeria and France in the region is superb, although this analysis would have been stronger if he had discussed the recent cooperation in the region between France and Britain — including the Franco-British summits — and how this might affect the regional balance of power. The wider implication for ECOMOG of Britain's muscular and universally praised involvement in Sierra Leone is also largely untouched. The fact is that the British intervention, with only 1,000 troops, and following the near-total collapse of the Nigerian forces in Sierra Leone after the January 1999 rebel invasion of Freetown, was so effective that it exposed the bumbling nature of the regional efforts. One must also look elsewhere for a convincing explanation of the origins of the crisis of violent predation, especially in Liberia and Sierra Leone; without an understanding of this, insight into the traumatic peace-building efforts in the region will be limited.

John L. Hirsch's well-written *Sierra Leone: Diamonds and the struggle for democracy*, also part of the IPA occasional papers series, is a brief but helpful account of the origins of the Sierra Leone crisis and the diplomatic efforts to resolve it, especially since the catastrophic coup of 1997. Hirsch was then US ambassador to Sierra Leone, and was involved in some of the diplomatic manoeuvrings that followed the coup, although American involvement was minimal. The book identifies diamonds as "a major source of conflict" but otherwise does not analyze the specific role they have played in the Sierra Leone crisis, which is to have underwritten the RUF's weapons purchases as well as having been the principal motivation of its leaders and foreign backers. Instead, Hirsch focuses on the progressive disintegration of the Sierra Leonean state since independence, and especially during the corrupt reign of Siaka Stevens (1968–85) and his lacklustre successor, Joseph Momoh, whose "seven-year tenure is remembered as a period of the country's economic collapse and disastrous involvement in the evolving Liberian civil war." It is this involvement, Hirsch suggests, that led to Sierra Leone's own war. This account is, of course, skeletal, and it is now generally agreed that the Sierra Leone war is part of a continuous narrative of escalating regional warfare in which resource predation — rather than politics — is the main factor, with Liberia's President Taylor at the centre of this "warlord politics." Hirsch is more thorough in his account of the role of ECOMOG and other outside players in Sierra Leone after the coup, and some of his anecdotes — involving leading players in the crisis — are invaluable. This book should be read as a companion to Adebayo's, as it fills in some major gaps — relating to background events and the less obvious interests of some players in the West African crises — that are absent in the Adebayo book.

In *Democracy by Force* Abass Chernor Bundu, a former Executive Secretary of ECOWAS and subsequently Foreign Minister of Sierra Leone, fulminates against the 1998 Nigerian ousting of the AFRC junta in Sierra Leone, and condemns the intervention as "a complete aberration" which "must never be allowed to contaminate Ecowas' worthy achievements." According to Bundu, Nigeria acted 'unilaterally and precipitately', and ECOMOG got involved in Sierra Leone only after the Lomé Accord of July 1999. A lawyer by training, Bundu uses highly legalistic and sometimes contradictory arguments to make his case. He argues, for example, that humanitarian crisis merits external intervention; but then ties himself in knots desperately trying not to apply this principle to Sierra Leone. He argues that regardless of the clearly praise-worthy outcome of the Nigerian intervention in Sierra Leone – which ousted a sanguinary and utterly lawless and incoherent band from power – it nonetheless was bad for international law. Bundu, incidentally, was a very sour loser to President Kabbah in the 1996 elections in Sierra Leone, and went into voluntary exile shortly after he was accused by the Kabbah government of corruptly selling Sierra Leonean diplomatic passports when he was Foreign Minister of the National Provisional Ruling Council (NPRC) junta.[17] Inelegant statements such as "Kabbah's 'democratically-elected' government joined cause with a dictator to etch in blood its so-called 'sovereign right' to kill its own people in the name of restoring democracy" should therefore not strike the reader as particularly remarkable. If one approaches this book as an honest memoir of a diplomat with unique insights into the momentous developments in the region, one will be disappointed. It is, in many ways, a philippic, the demagogic rantings of a politician who clearly has an eye to a come-back; and Bundu helpfully provides his email address so that "enquiries for speaking engagements" can be addressed to him.

Is ECOMOG something to sustain and build upon, as all of these authors agree? This is undoubtedly a proposition few would argue with, but the force's uneven record gives cause for great caution.

In Liberia, although ECOMOG prevented Taylor from seizing power by force, the fact that it helped eliminate all other armed factions prior to

---

[17] The same government subsequently exonerated Dr. Bundu of these charges, and he became something of an adviser to President Kabbah.

the 1997 elections virtually guaranteed that Taylor would become the undisputed master of the country. And the Liberian President has not ceased since then to be a warlord, his regime of violent predation compounded by an upsurge in fighting as opposition groups coalesced into an armed rebel group struggling to oust him. In Sierra Leone, ECOMOG's failure was more dramatic. After it ousted the AFRC junta, the rebel forces simply moved to hideouts outside the capital, regrouped and out-manoeuvred the Nigerian-led force — which did not have counter-insurgency training, and was badly paid and lacking in morale — in January 1999, in the process destroying a large part of Freetown. ECOMOG's record in Bissau is hardly anything to speak of.

The bottom line is that peacekeeping anywhere, and especially in situations of unconventional (or total) warfare where rules of engagement are at best uncertain, is a serious military activity, demanding the deployment of overwhelming and highly competent force. It also demands basic state building, since most states sucked into such conflicts collapse. West Africa, with its poorly trained and equipped armies, its fractious politics, and its poverty, can only undertake such an ambitious and expensive project, it would appear, with enormous foreign assistance.

3.
Desmond Luke: A Profile in Courage[18]

Desmond Edgar Fashole Luke, former politician and Chief Justice, lives quietly in a modest home on Spur-Loop, Freetown. He doesn't give interviews, and his views are not sought after these days. He staunchly shies away from politics, and seems to follow events mainly in the local papers or on the radio and TV. When I visited him at his home on a Sunday afternoon, the TV in his spacious sitting room was showing a high-pitched African American televangelist, TD Jakes. Luke said Jakes was one of his favourites. He mentioned another favourite of his, another American and a big television personality with the word 'Reverend' prefixed to his name. I was stumped. Luke cares about Christian television evangelism?

Yes, he said, in his mellifluous Oxbridge accent. "Religion has always interested me since I was a student at Oxford back in the 1950s," Luke said. "It didn't come late, not a kind of retirement discovery."

When I went to see him, Luke was getting ready to travel to the UK; he was packing his suitcase in the living room. That explained why he took sometime to come to the door when I rang the bell. He still has, at 77, the same assured and somewhat aloof English public school manner, unsurprised and immensely knowing. His head has now all gone grey; but his looks are still rather dashing, a Sidney Portier lookalike. He was wearing loose flannel pants and a grey pyjama shirt. "Yes, yes, yes. We should have some time to talk," he said, as he led me to the sofa in the sitting room.

The sitting room had an anonymous, almost perfunctory, feel to it. There were no pictures, no shelves with books, no mementos from Luke's long

---

[18] *Patriotic Vanguard*, 13 January 2011.

public career and extraordinarily interesting life. There were stacks of newspapers on the table, and a bible on the coffee table by the sofa.

This, of course, is not the house that Luke, aristocrat, a collector of memorabilia (even from his days as a celebrated sportsman – cricket, hockey, tennis, high jump, everything – at Kings College, Taunton, an English public school), has always lived. That house is further down the Loop, and was thoroughly vandalised, looted and destroyed by soldiers of the Armed Forces Ruling Council (AFRC), in 1997. Luke used to have the largest law library in Sierra Leone, at another house on Lamina Sankoh Street (which also hosted an excellent restaurant run by Luke's long-term partner, Monica), in downtown Freetown. That house, too, was vandalised and torched (the same day as the Nigerian High Commission building) by the AFRC, the library looted, the books burnt or sold in the black market. Few of the country's political elite endured this kind of wrath from the depraved junta. But then none of them were as outspoken against the junta, while still in the country. Luke was a particular target.

On the face of it, this is something of a surprise. In 1996, under the banner of his National Unity Movement (NUM), Luke had contested the presidential elections that brought Ahmad Tejan Kabbah to power. He lost; and his party, for some years the most vibrant because the most outspoken against the National Provisional Ruling council (NPRC) junta, became something of an awkward political presence, without representation in parliament. Luke's presence on the political scene was so assured, however, that when the first peace agreement – the Abidjan Accord – was signed in November 1996, he was made Chairman of the newly-created Commission for the Consolidation of Peace. Then, a few months later, the AFRC coup happened. Luke, though no great friend of Kabbah at the time, was immediately one of the most prominent voices condemning the coup and calling for the reinstatement of Kabbah.

"I felt that this was the most destructive of coups," Luke told me. "We'd gone through a most traumatic transition from one junta rule, and then we had this peace accord. A rather very promising start after all those awful years. The coup was simply unacceptable, and the international community reacted with particular revulsion. Not a single government recognised the junta." Luke was very instrumental in mobilising international opinion against the AFRC, by condemning the junta in many interviews with the international media, in particular the BBC.

Early Celebrity

Luke, of course, is an unusual kind of politician in Sierra Leone: immensely courageous, self-less, principled, with an easy aristocratic disdain for material acquisitiveness. To talk to him, to be close to him, is to have a sense that money doesn't really matter much; that such things are really needed only for the "work of the world" (the quote is from Joseph Conrad, whose inner nobility seems distinctly reflected in Luke).

Born in October 1935 on Rawdon Street in Freetown, Luke's upbringing was privileged. The Luke family was high-achieving, High-Society: education in the best schools and universities in England was taken for granted by the Luke clan, as was the eventual rise to the top of the colonial service in West Africa. A branch of the Luke clan was perhaps the wealthiest family in Fernando Po (now oil-rich Equatorial Guinea), and another was (though black) part of the wealthy elite in Spain. The Luke clan owned massive plantations in Fernando Po (a few years before Luke was born, the League of Nations had censored Sierra Leonean-born Liberian President King for helping to ship forced labour to the plantations at Fernando Po, though the plantation owners were themselves not the focus of the investigation. As it happened, Graham Greene was cajoled into taking a trip to Liberia by the Anti-Slavery Society to investigate the forced labour scandals; he passed through Freetown on the way there in 1935, the year that Desmond Luke was born: that creates a certain context).

The Second World War delayed Luke's travel to England for school: he attended the Prince of Wales Secondary School in Freetown for two years, before proceeding to Kings College in Taunton, Somerset, in pleasant south-west England, in 1949. The school, in that English way with these things, was respectable: two of the younger sons of Haile Selassie, exiled to England after Mussolini invaded his country, went there. Luke was a celebrity at the school: a leading sportsman who got mentioned in national papers like the London Times and Daily Telegraph for setting records in several sporting events. The 1954 (the year that Luke left for Oxford) edition of the school's magazine, The Aluredian, dedicates over a page to Luke's sporting prowess, and carries two pictures of him, one among the hockey team, and the other among the cricket team. The Headmaster's report mentions Luke by name; and the magazine reports Luke reading his last term paper, "The Conditions for the Expansion of Islam." The Aluredian quaintly notes that the paper was "concerned about the position in Negro Africa," and stated that the paper "set a standard for the future that will be hard to maintain." Luke, in other words, was not just a remarkable sportsman: he was also a very good scholar. The magazine wished Luke the very best "as he leaves for Oxford..."

Someone had recently recovered this magazine and given it to Luke: it was now the only memorabilia from those times that Luke possesses; the AFRC had destroyed all the others. "You see," Luke avoided that issue altogether, "my interest in the great world religions has always been there, right from the beginning. I was also interested in Hindu spiritualism."

At Keble College, Oxford, Luke studied Politics, Philosophy and Economics, the famous PPE. He graduated in 1957 but decided to stay for another year to study West African medieval history under the radical leftwing historian Thomas Hodgkin. African independence was approaching: indeed Ghana would gain independence from Britain that year. And Hodgkin (and some other radical British intellectuals; Basil

Davidson was another), who later wrote *Nationalism in Colonial Africa*, was helping prepare for this by looking more sympathetically at the African past, arguing – pace Trevor-Roper – that Africa does have a history beyond the European contact. In 1959, Luke moved to London; two years later, he went to Cambridge to take a law degree.

"I was at Cambridge in 1961 when Sierra Leone gained independence," he said. "I remember celebrating our independence with friends at a pub in the University. It was an immensely joyous moment. We were very optimistic; none of us, in our worst nightmare, would have seen all these coming, coups, rebels, economic meltdown. Our failing as a nation is truly extraordinary."

A Contrarian

Luke returned to Sierra Leone immediately after completing his studies at Cambridge, in 1962. In Freetown, he opened his own chambers, and practised law until 1969, when he was appointed Ambassador to West Germany (accredited to all EU countries) by Siaka Stevens. From there, in 1973, he was appointed Foreign Minister. Two years later, he dramatically resigned. The reason for this now seems as remote and bewildering as it was deeply felt by the brash and earnest Oxbridge sophisticate at the time. It concerned the North/South Korea dispute. At the time, Sierra Leone maintained relations with both countries, but they didn't have embassies in Freetown. The South Korean Embassy in Monrovia, Liberia, covered Sierra Leone; North Korea wanted to establish a mission, but it wanted Sierra Leone to sever relations with the South. The South had recently sent a new Ambassador, who was due to present his credentials to President Stevens in Freetown. On hearing about this, North Korea immediately sent its Finance Minister to Sierra Leone to prevail on the government not to receive the new South Korean ambassador.

That's the kind of diplomatic chutzpah no one can associate with the demented and bankrupt and starveling North Korea of these days. The Finance Minister came with a cheque (or perhaps several cheques), and he, going by his country's template, immediately contacted the Central Committee of the ruling All Peoples Congress (APC). He had read well. Sorie Ibrahim Koroma, the scheming and fanatical Vice President, was on hand. The North Korean promised to build a Town Hall for the government as well as provide assistance to the Central Committee. All this was done behind the back of the Foreign Minister, who was completely ignored. In blissful ignorance, Luke scheduled a meeting with the South Korean ambassador to present his credentials to Stevens. The poor South Korean arrived, and a meeting was duly scheduled. The North Korean deferred his exit from the country and waited. On the morning that Stevens was to receive the South Korean, he was in his office with Luke when SI Koroma arrived. He immediately informed Stevens that the Central Committee had decided that the South Korean was not to be accredited. Stevens was chair of the Central Committee, and he feigned to be ignorant. Luke protested, but Stevens told him he would have to find out first. Meanwhile the poor South Korean had been ushered into the waiting room at State House. Two hours later, he was still waiting. Exasperated, Luke told Stevens he would have to inform the ambassador that the meeting would be rescheduled, which he did.

"I was furious," Luke said. "Nothing happened in the government or the APC without Stevens' approval. He was simply messing around with everyone, and this was unacceptable. The next day, I brought him a draft of my resignation letter, stating that if he can't trust me, his Foreign Minister, on a matter as basic as receiving foreign ambassadors, then there was no point in me serving his government." Stevens was bemused: he simply didn't see how anyone could resign over such a petty matter. To his surprise, Luke submitted the letter the next day and packed out of the Foreign Office.

In 1977, Luke contested his Wilberforce seat as an Independent; SI Koroma mobilised all the APC against him, but the APC candidate lost so badly he forfeited his deposit. Wily Stevens, now planning to introduce a one-party state, saw dangers in having Luke on the back benches. He quickly appointed him Health Minister. Luke accepted. "You see, I would say to Zainab Bangura: you're not the first to be removed from the Foreign Ministry and sent to Health. Cyril Rogers-Wright was the first. It is about service to nation, not hierarchy in government." Luke was, by all accounts, a hugely successful and popular Health Minister. But a year later, shortly after Stevens introduced a one-party state, Luke left the government. He remained in Parliament until 1983, but he was hardly in the country at the time. "Parliament was nothing. I was travelling all the time. The APC tried to get me out with the provision that an MP should not be out of the country for 30 days at a time. But every time they realised I was back on the 28th day," Luke said, smiling.

After 1983, Luke became a single opposition voice in the country. He later set up the National Unity Movement (NUM) to advocate constitutional reforms, and was part of the 1991 constitutional review commission. Then the National Provisional Ruling council (NPRC) coup happened. Luke was a very prominent critic of the regime, and was on a number of occasions prevented from travelling out of the country by the NPRC.

I had got to know Luke at about this time. He had liked what I was writing in the Concord Times, and he invited me for lunch at his restaurant on Lamina Sankoh Street. Every other day after that, I would meet Luke at the restaurant and we would have lunch and drinks. It might be said, though this will be unfair, that this was as much an attraction for the young journalist as the inspiring conversations with the veteran politician and activist. It might have been mutually beneficial. Any time the Concord Times had problems with a good front-page story, the editors would simply urge me to visit my friend Luke, and in no time we would have a great story, with Luke volunteering detailed and cogent criticisms of the junta. He was the only prominent figure in the country to do that at the time.

Luke contested, and lost, the 1996 elections under the banner of NUM. Then the following year, rogues soldiers staged a bloody coup overthrowing newly-elected Kabbah and ushering in what they were pleased to call the Armed Forces Ruling council (AFRC) junta.

"I worked with the Nigerian, British and other foreign diplomats to convince the junta to hand back power to the elected government," Luke said. "My views on the junta were, of course, very well known. They were a despicable lot. But the foreign diplomats convinced me to go, alone, and have a final negotiation with the AFRC. It was a very charged moment. I met with Johnny Paul Koroma and his gang for several hours at night. We made offers to them to leave – cash, study abroad, amnesty etc. The talks went well. As I was leaving, Paul Koroma came to me, furtively, and told me that since he was head of the junta, his own cash payment should be bigger than the rest. It was like that. Disgusting."

Luke got a tentative understanding from the junta that they would handover power to Kabbah. Shortly after, however, the junta announced that no agreement had been reached, and its thugs attacked Luke's home. Luke fled, by fishing boat, to Guinea, joining Kabbah and his exiled government.

Chief Justice

Nigerian troops and the Civil defence Force (CDF) unseated the junta in February 1998, and Kabbah was restored to power. Before they left Guinea for Sierra Leone, Kabbah approached Luke to be his next Chief Justice. He was going to sack Justice Beccles-Davies, for the offence of swearing-in Johnny Paul Koroma. "I wasn't convinced this was a good reason to sack the Chief Justice," Luke said. "It was both unfair and rather frivolous, and I told Kabbah that. I'm almost convinced that had Kabbah been in Beccles-Davies' position, he would have done the same thing."

Kabbah and his then Attorney-General Solomon Berewa, however, insisted. Luke had become close friends with Kabbah in Guinea, and so he told them he would seek help with the Commonwealth to provide an experienced Chief Justice. Kabbah and Berewa, of course, weren't interested; they had plans to try dozens of people for treason and "collaboration", and doubtless they felt that because of the personal suffering that Luke had had at the hands of the junta, he was likely to support the trial. Luke insisted that a foreign judge may be more appropriate at that point. He had personal reasons as well. Luke's father had acted as Chief Justice, and the experience wasn't a very pleasant one. Then his cousin, Livesey-Luke, who would later become Chief Justice of Botswana, had to leave Sierra Leone after falling out with the manipulative Siaka Stevens.

Luke flew to London and met with Commonwealth Secretary General Emeka Anyaoku. By the time he got there, however, Kabbah had already phoned Anyaoku and told him to convince Luke to accept the job. The meeting, in other words, ended even before it began. Undaunted, Luke flew to Botswana to ask his cousin, Livesey, for help. He was there when someone telephoned to congratulate him on his appointment – now announced on the radio – as Chief Justice of Sierra Leone. Kabbah had calculated well: Luke's sense of honour and service to the nation meant that he would have to accept, and he did, returning to Freetown shortly after.

"Within weeks of my taking the job, I had to haul Berewa before Kabbah for interference with my job," Luke said. "Berewa was sending magistrates and judges summarily on leave, telling others to do this or that. This was not his job. He was Chief Prosecutor for the government. I told Kabbah that a permanent solution to this kind of thing was to

119

separate the position of Attorney General from that of Minister of Justice. Stevens had created this problem back in 1978, with the one-party thing. Kabbah agreed in principle."

But there was a looming problem. Luke was approaching 65, the retirement age for judges, when he was appointed. He discussed the matter with Kabbah, and Kabbah promised to revise that upwards: meaning that the retirement age would be pushed to 70, a far more reasonable thing. By that time, however, the vindictive Berewa had gained great ascendancy in the government: in 2002 he became Vice President, and that year, Luke was retired.

Private Life

Luke now mostly passes his time at his home, travelling from time to time. When in Freetown in August 2010, I dropped by to see him. He had been to a "fellowship" – born a Methodist, Luke had become a Pentecostal. I was intrigued. All the same we spent hours together over red wine. He spoke at the time – more in sadness than in bitterness – of the wasted opportunities of Kabbah's government. In December a few months later when I dropped by to see him, his views about Kabbah had somewhat mellowed. There was, in his voice, a sense of disappointment over what had become of the dream of independence, the pathos of the continuing delinquency of his country. "We haven't fulfilled the aspirations of independence," he said. "We haven't succeeded. Can we?" He would, in this mood, adapt Oscar Wilde to say, as the country approaches its 50 years of nationhood: That the waste of the past 50 years has been a mistake. But to waste the next 50 would be sheer carelessness.

4.

Uncommon diplomat: Peter Penfold and Sierra Leone[19]

Peter Penfold was UK's High Commissioner to Sierra Leone from 1997 to 2000 when his services were terminated after disagreement with Tony Blair's New Labour government over Sierra Leone – over the so-called 'Arms to Africa' scandal of 1998. Blair's government told him to keep quiet after his recall and premature retirement after 40 years of service, but he refused. Penfold became the most prominent critic of the Special Court for Sierra Leone (SCSL), a contrivance chiefly of Blair's Foreign Secretary, Robin Cook, whose pretensions to an 'ethical foreign policy' had been exposed by events in Sierra Leone. Penfold has now published a much-anticipated book about his experiences in Sierra Leone and at the hands of Blair's New Labour. The book had tremendous difficulty finding a publisher in the UK, but has now been issued by Pen and Sword, the imprint of the British army. Penfold's old friend and collaborator in Sierra Leone, General Sir David Richards, wrote the Foreward to the book, hailing Penfold as "a brave and determined British diplomat of the Old School," and the book as a 'compelling story of one man's resolute determination to do the right thing.'

I first met Peter Penfold in the summer of 2003 in London. He had been recalled a couple of years back as the UK's High Commissioner to Sierra Leone following a most tumultuous and extraordinarily effective service there, and had been seconded to the Department of International Development (DFID) on the recommendation of Clare Short, who herself would not long after leave Tony Blair's now-discredited government. I had been invited to participate in a study, largely funded by the UK government, on making UN peace operations more effective. (The study was designed to follow-up on the findings of the famous

---

[19] (A review of 'Atrocities, Diamonds and Diplomacy: The Inside Story of the Conflict in Sierra Leone' by Peter Penfold. Published by Pen and Sword, UK 2012), *Pambazuka*, *2012-11-15, Issue 606*

Brahimi Report on UN peace operations in 2000). Penfold was a senior member of our team – representing DFID. Knowing of his reputation, I was awed by his presence on the team. His views carried great weight, but he was always somewhat diffident about what a foreign intervention force can achieve. Context, he would stress, matters. He was insistent on one point: external intervention (ECOWAS, UK and UN) in Sierra Leone was successful largely because it was driven by the principle – accepted by the vast majority of Sierra Leoneans – of support for the democratically elected government of Ahmad Tejan Kabbah against anti-government forces about with little or no support anywhere in the country, and about whom there was nothing ennobling. Penfold formed this view of the Revolutionary United Front (RUF), the then largely amorphous and nihilistic group spearheading a brutal bush war, a few weeks after he arrived in Sierra Leone as Britain's top diplomat there in early 1997. Everything that happened to the country since then merely confirmed his early impressions.

We travelled as a team to Sierra Leone for the research. Once we got to the arrival hall at the airport and Penfold was spotted, the normally vacant or avaricious airport workers sprang into action, and took us all into the VIP lounge. In Freetown, there was hardly any need for prior appointments: Penfold's name opened every office. When we went to see President Kabbah, there was a television crew waiting to record the event, and it was the lead news item that evening. Penfold, though now shunned by his own Foreign Office, was a hero in Sierra Leone: he had been crowned honorary Paramount Chief in the country, the only British official to be so honoured after Prince Phillip. This very important and much anticipated book tells us why he is still revered in Sierra Leone, and much more.

Diplomats from powerful countries who find themselves in degraded or corrupt countries can do one of two things. They can comfortably immerse themselves into the local environment, make friends with the political and business elite, and sit out patiently until they are moved to more salubrious environments or are comfortably retired. That is the careerist option. The other option is to try and do something to influence positive change in the country they find themselves posted, to use the leverage of a representative of the important power which helps subsidise the local government can wield to get things moving in the right direction. This is the more difficult option, for it carries a grave risk. A foreign diplomat falling out with the local government, however insanitary that government is, often finds that his own bureaucracy, full of nibbling careerists who are instinctively against risk-taking, are unsympathetic, and wants to immediately rid of that awkward diplomat. As it happens, the British Foreign Office, with its sense of antique propriety and residual imperial viciousness, is the most practiced and ruthless at this kind of thing.

Penfold's predicament in Sierra Leone was worse. He arrived in Freetown in March 1997 to take over as UK's chief diplomat in the country. He drove from Senegal through Guinea into Sierra Leone, adding drama to an already high-octane situation. Sierra Leone had in the months prior conducted national elections, and the new president – an articulate and presentable former UN civil servant, Kabbah – had signed a peace agreement with the RUF in neighbouring Abidjan, Ivory Coast. Those were glimmers of hope in an otherwise awfully bleak situation: the RUF war, which started in March 1992, had already killed more than 15,000 and devastated the countryside, forcing the displacement of half the population of the country.

Amidst this carnage, the international community, including Britain, the country's former colonial master, pretended that things were under control. Donor funding had been secured for the elections (Britain contributed $3 million), but now what? In the UN Security Council, the US vetoed the setting up of a small military observer force following the signing of the Abidjan Accord on grounds that the RUF had not approved it. Earlier, an important British humanitarian assessment report (April 1995) had fretted about labeling Sierra a 'complex emergency' since this would 'unleash a whole set of responses, including the appointment of a UNSRSG [Special Representative of the Secretary General], a Humanitarian Coordinator, and new arrangements for UN working in Sierra Leone.' This deliberate failure to act when it could have made a decisive difference must be implicated in the subsequent carnage in the country – which finally led to the deployment of one of the largest UN peacekeeping troops ever (UNAMSIL), at a cost of $2.5 billion in five years.

In the event, both the elections and the Abidjan Accord would become only seriously effective in terms of the country's international relations in their breach: as reaction to the sanguinary Armed Forces Ruling Council (AFRC) coup of May 1997. No coup has been more ill-timed.

Penfold had previously served in the British mission in Nigeria during that country's civil war in the late 1960s, in Ethiopia in the 1970s during the neurotic Derg revolution, and in Uganda in the 1980s during two coups. In Sierra Leone, he quickly became a passionate advocate for the democratically-elected government, helping to fundamentally change the UK's policy towards the country. His efforts gained immense traction when Blair became Prime Minister on 2 May 1997, a few months after Penfold took post, and only three weeks before the fateful AFRC coup. Blair's father had been a lecturer at Sierra Leone's Fourah Bay College, and though Blair made this discovery much later, he characteristically embraced it with missionary zeal. That changed attitudes within the British establishment towards Sierra Leone: the sentiments of a popular new Prime Minister perforce quickly became state policy

Blair's earnest moral tone – he and his foreign secretary Robin Cook spoke about an "ethical foreign policy" – seemed congruent with the field reports Penfold was sending back, in which Penfold depicted the war in Sierra Leone as a conflict in which there was a clear division between good and bad – on one side the legitimate, democratically-elected government and on the other a bunch of thugs without a reasonable political agenda. The AFRC coup of May 2007 made this view compelling.

Penfold's account of the coup and its consequences are the most stirring parts of his immensely riveting book – and the best I have read anywhere. His valiant attempts – aided by other diplomats and notably the courageous Desmond Luke – to cajole the mutinous soldiers failed, but it is worth studying closely for the astonishing possibility it offered. Promised money, cars and a comfortable exile, Johnny Paul Koroma and his gang agreed to cede power back to Kabbah, but this was scuttled by the RUF, which had been invited by Koroma to join his "peoples' army." Penfold then organised one of the most complex evacuations of foreign nationals from a war zone ever – an effort that involved several planes and warships from Britain, France and the US, among others. In the final episode in the evacuation drama, the USS Kearsarge landed dozens of heavily armed marines and positioned combat helicopters all around Lumley beach in Freetown, overlooking the main military barracks where the AFRC officers and their RUF allies had based themselves. The junta had one combat helicopter, and the Americans made a point that though they were not authorised to strike at the junta, the helicopter was a danger to foreign nationals and would be destroyed if it took off the ground. Interventionists prayed for that to happen, and at one point the junta's only pilot was seen walking towards the helicopter. Suddenly he turned back, failing to perform a terminal service for the rest of humanity: had he moved closer, the marines would have blasted him apart along with the helicopter, and in the ensuing firefight, the rest of the AFRC thugs would doubtless have been obliterated. (That helicopter, by the way, was later used by the junta to destroy villages in places like Moyamba and Bonthe, killing hundreds, on the excuse that they were habouring Kamajors.)

For his leadership role during the evacuation, Penfold received letters of commendation from both Blair and Cook. He was now based in Guinea along with the exiled Kabbah government. There is little doubt that without his support Kabbah, a reluctant flag bearer if ever there was one, would not have sustained the resistance against the AFRC. And it was in providing this support that Penfold, in the latter judgment of his senior colleagues in London, may have faltered. It involved what came to be famously known as "Arms to Africa" scandal: an agreement between the exiled government and a British mercenary outfit, Sandline International, to supply arms to pro-government forces resisting the AFRC in Sierra Leone. Penfold was accused of facilitating the deal, though he had fully briefed the Foreign Office in London about the negotiations going on between Kabbah and Sandline's Tim Spicer. The problem was that at that time there was a UN Security Council-mandated arms embargo on Sierra Leone, and the resolution had been sponsored by Britain. The scandal – or so the British press called it – was first publicised by Lord Avebury, an unctuous Liberal peer whose motives were extraneous to Sierra Leone's interests. It turned out that the arms themselves never actually got to the pro-Kabbah forces: they were impounded by Nigerian troops, who must be credited – along with the pro-government Kamajor militia fighters – for unseating the AFRC and restoring democracy to Sierra Leone. But the ill-fated arms had been shipped out to Sierra Leone, and the fidgety and dull civil servants in London could not be persuaded that a law had not been broken. It didn't matter that the spirit of the resolution clearly did not intend the ban to apply to the exiled government – who Blair called the "good guys." The episode, described here in painful detail, wrecked Penfold's career.

It led to his early retirement, and even there he was not left alone by the British government. When he was in 2002 offered the post of Africa Program Director by the International Crisis Group (ICG), for which he was eminently qualified, the offer was quickly withdrawn "on the advice of senior figures in the Foreign Office."

Penfold is rarely judgmental about the politicians and diplomats he deals with in this book, though he is sharply critical of American machinations in the run-up to the shambolic Lomé Accord. The story of how Jesse Jackson, Bill Clinton's Africa adviser, manipulated and coerced Kabbah into an outrageous peace agreement is now well known, but Penfold adds useful details. Jackson took Kabbah in his plane from Ghana and he refused to allow James Jonah and Julius Spencer – two of Kabbah's closest aides, and both known anti-RUF hardliners – to travel alongside. In Lomé, American lawyers drafted both the ceasefire agreement and the final accord. Foday Saybanah Sankoh, the RUF leader, indulged himself in an "orgy of food, drink and sex" in a Lomé hotel, and mounted a bill of over $400,000, to be paid by the UN. Britain sent an inexperienced and disinterested diplomat with no knowledge of Sierra Leone to Lomé, leaving Penfold uninvited in Freetown. The result, Penfold writes bitterly, was that the US and Britain 'acted disgracefully in forcing through the Accord.' (The Accord in effect made Foday Sankoh Vice President and gave him control of the country's mineral resources, including its coveted diamonds. For good measure, the flippant Jesse Jackson compared Sankoh to Nelson Mandela at the time.)

What does Penfold really think of Kabbah, the man at the centre of all this drama? Clearly, Penfold had far greater respect for Hinga Norman – an activist minister after Penfold's heart – and enormously admires Desmond Luke, James Jonah and the great activist at the time, Zainab

Bangura. Kabbah was merely a symbol of the great struggle for democracy, though a rather flawed one. Penfold's judgments of Kabbah are made by accretion, and two impressions stand out. Kabbah was too quick to flee Sierra Leone after the coup announcement in 1997, and in exile in Guinea, Kabbah did not once visit either the Sierra Leone government office – converted from a disused restaurant – or even the Sierra Leone embassy (where hundreds of his exiled countrymen met every day) a few yards from his house. When, in the aftermath of the devastating January 1999 attacks Penfold visited Kabbah, he found a thoroughly devastated and lonely man who had not even taken the time to visit the national stadium, where tens of thousands of his derelict people had sought shelter. (Penfold had earlier been there, distributing medicine, food and other necessities). To be fair to Kabbah, at this point he been struck – in addition to the calamities of the rebel onslaughts – with a great personal tragedy: his wife of many years had only recently died, and he was already a very broken man (he never actually recovered from that tragedy, as anyone close to him knows).

Penfold's harsh judgment of the Special Court for Sierra Leone (SCSL), which was set up in 2002 to try those "most responsible" for the atrocities of the war and which recently convicted former Liberian President Charles Taylor (among others), deserves to be quoted at length. He writes: 'Supporters of the court, citing the example of Charles Taylor…say that it demonstrates that no one can get away with such barbarous acts with impunity…However, Sam Norman's indictment and subsequent death is a stain on the Special Court's legacy. Who else will come forward to fight the cause of peace and democracy in the future if they face the threat of being treated as a war criminal? Resolving conflicts diplomatically elsewhere has become more difficult as a result of the Special Court's antics. When resolving conflicts it is usually necessary to persuade both sides of the conflict to cease fighting and killing, lay down their weapons and negotiate a peaceful agreement. Often this will require not only understanding, patience and skillful diplomacy but also some form of concessions such as pardons and/or amnesties. The Special Court demonstrated that such provisions and assurances negotiated on the ground in good faith become meaningless once the juggernaut of international justice comes on the scene. What incentive, therefore, will there be for some of those involved to stop fighting. [where does the quote end?]

It is a sobering thought – and from a man who witnessed firsthand the atrocities of the Sierra Leone – documented here in great detail – as well as the efforts to end it through negotiation.

Of some curiosity is the title of the book *Atrocities, Diamonds and Diplomacy*, since Penfold never subscribed to the ham fisted view – peddled by the likes of David Crane, the Special Court's first prosecutor – that the Sierra Leone war was all about diamonds. Diamonds were important in funding the war and ensuring the sustained interest in support the RUF by the likes of Charles Taylor, but the war was not caused by diamonds, he writes.

This superbly well-written, well-documented and passionate book should be read by everyone interested in Africa, as well as in the grave issues of war and peace.

5.
At Home with Tejan Kabbah[20]

Ahmed Tejan Kabbah has been living at his Juba mansion, in the far west-end of the Sierra Leonean capital Freetown, since his retirement in2007. The mansion, at the end of a short "special" road called Kabbahya Drive, is in the modern style, but it is completely devoid of flash or shoddiness. From outside, it is not at all imposing among the dozens of similar expensive buildings in the area; and its understated part-ochre exterior suggests a deliberate drabness.

Inside the huge compound, however, the view is breathtaking: the elevated Italianate balcony of the four-bedroom house (a protruding elevator in the sitting-room adds a piquant touch to an otherwise curiously domestic ambience) overlooks a well-designed and sedate-looking swimming pool (the water very blue and inviting, and seeming to await use) and, above it, Freetown slopes majestically, stunningly beautiful. There is an inexpensive abstract painting in a corner of the sitting-room, and another canvas in the sombre style of an early Picasso. The most remarkable pieces of art are a beautifully framed Ashanti bronze cast with an insctiption from Ghana's former president, John Kuffour, and a finely framed anonymous Arabic inscription, a gift from the Libyan leader Muammar Gaddafi. Kabbah is clearly not a collector.

There is a glass-encased bookshelf, but with not many titles: noticeable are Bill Clinton's *My Life* (not surprising since Kabbah is writing his own memoirs), a book about empire by the historian and apologist of British imperialism Niall Ferguson, about half a dozen volumes of UNESCO's History of Africa series (Kabbah, a former UN man, is particularly proud of these), and several other (mainly obscure) titles. The place suggests tranquility, rest--and rest is important to Kabbah who, at 77, can claim to have achieved all his life's ambitions and more, including attaining the very pinnacle of the public service he dedicated his entire life to.

---

[20] *New African*, July 1, 2009

After two terms as president of Sierra Leone, Kabbah gracefully handed over power in November 2007 to the leader of the opposition All Peoples' Congress (APC), Ernest Bai Koroma, rather than to his vice president and preferred candidate, Solomon Berewa, who lost the elections to Koroma. In retirement, Kabbah exudes the serenity of a man whose work has been done. "I have suddenly developed this phobia for flying," he said, apropos of nothing. "I spend almost all my time here now." Almost: Kabbah had monitored elections in Kenya as an African Union statesman, and was in Zimbabwe on a similar mission.

Kabbah speaks slowly, deliberately. He hardly gestures, and only his clean shaven, preternaturally smooth face shows emotion--intense interest and a little humour mainly, with occasional flashes of irritation. The irritation came early in our meeting. A local daily had carried a front page story that morning alleging that a Lebanese businessman, Mohamed Wanza, had contributed a hundred million leones to Kabbah's 2002 presidential campaign. The story, one might say about six years late, apparently had a powerful extraneous purpose: it seemed to have been published as part of the new government's effort to award millions of dollars to Wanza for services he markedly failed to provide for the country over a decade ago.

Kabbah brushed aside the newspaper report without contesting its veracity. "Wanza was very close to the NPRC [the National Provisional Ruling Council junta, which ruled Sierra Leone from 1992-1996]," Kabbah began. "He monopolised all business dealings with the regime, and at one point entered into some agreement to purchase a gunboat for the Sierra Leone Navy. As well as that, he was given millions of dollars to equip Connaught Hospital. None of this was done, of course."

Under the NPRC, this little detail -non-deliverance--would not have been any problem: a contract had been signed, the military boys had had their percentages, and the Lebanese would be paid in full. To his shock, when Wanza submitted the final invoice--totalling $10m--to the new President Kabbah (who Wanza had reasons to think was an ally), he was told to wait, pending further clarification.

"First, I asked my officials to tell me where the gunboat was, and I was told that the boat was somewhere in Liverpool [England], where it would be inspected," Kabbah explained. "Then I realised that my minister of health, Tejan Jalloh, had submitted a long list of equipment items needing to be purchased by Connaught. As it happens, Wanza had not delivered any equipment to the hospital."

Soon enough, an expert consultant hired by Kabbah found that the gunboat was junk. Kabbah duly had Wanza informed that he would not be paid a single cent by the government until several awkward questions relating to the procurement were answered. Normally this would perhaps have provoked a court action or prolonged negotiations, but Wanza had far more potent weapons. A few months later, in May 1997, rogue soldiers overthrew Kabbah's government in a bloody coup, and Wanza once again became the key contractor--supplying weapons, army uniform and petroleum products--for the new Armed Forces Ruling Council (AFRC). The pathos of it is not lost on Kabbah, a politician who can sometimes exude a charming unself-consciousness.

"We never said that Wanza--who since we took office was moving between Nigeria and The Gambia--played a role in that coup," Kabbah said. "But we were determined on the reinstatement of my government in 1998 that the person who funded the killing of our people should face certain consequences."

Wanza was stripped of his naturalised Sierra Leonean citizenship, and was told he would not be paid any money. He now lives in Nigeria, where during the 2007 elections in Sierra Leone he allegedly made serious financial contributions to the APC, which succeeded in defeating Kabbah's vice president, Solomon Berewa, in the polls. Shortly after the new president Bai Koroma took office, Wanza's Sierra Leonean citizenship was restored. In short order, the Lebanese orchestrated a court action against the Sierra Leone government in the Ecowas Court for Human Rights over the non-payment of his contract millions. Parody outdid tragic parody as the new minister of information, I. B. Kargbo, announced that the Wanza case posed such embarrassment to the government that it had to be settled out of court. Translation: Wanza was to be paid millions of dollars for allegedly delivering no service to Sierra Leone other than arms and other support to the military junta.

The vibrations of the Wanza issue rang loudly, a presage, perhaps, of what the country could expect in the future? Said Kabbah: "I'm very much concerned and worried that people are getting agitated. First, you had all this sacking of people perceived to be SLPP [Sierra Leone People's Party] supporters in the civil service and government agencies. These are professionals, people who had dedicated years to serving the nation. And you get them replaced by largely unqualified people who don't know how proper systems operate. And I see this growing bad feeling among groups and regions."

Kabbah, not at all a taciturn man, can be as laconic as that. "Bad" is a word he likes, as in "bad heart" (malevolence). Politics still agitates him, but most of his interest in our conversation was the self, the "I" in the lunch company. Part of it was generous, embracing, nostalgic; the other part was narcissistic, self-congratulatory.

Retirement denotes home, so these days Kabbah likes to begin conversations with visitors with an anecdote involving how he acquired the land where his mansion stands. He bought the four acres of land, at the cost of 300 pounds (sterling), in the 1960s from the late Chief Yumkella. Kabbah was then a UN employee based in New York. Sierra Leone's confusing land law--only marginally now improved--required the land to be registered with the government within 10 days. Kabbah had flown back to New York after the purchase without registering the land.

"I was in New York when I got a phone call from friends telling me that Chief Yumkella wanted to sell the same land again because I had not registered it," Kabbah explains. "This entire place was bush at the time. There were no houses here, so I didn't understand the rush. But I had to fly back immediately and hire Joko-Smart [a prominent lawyer and academic] to stop Yumkella. I had the place registered. But I actually finished building this house in 1992, just before my retirement from the UN."

This recollection did not lead to comments from Kabbah on the country's murky land market, and 1 did not press the point. The interest was the famous guests who have stayed at the house since: Libya's Gaddafi, for example, who stayed there for three days in 2007, just before Kabbah's retirement from politics.

The Libyan leader, who likes to affect the hardy lifestyle of his Bedawin people, built a tent in Kabbah's compound, where he stayed. An additional block of security fence and other devices were added by the Libyan.

Kabbah once told me that Gaddafi had readily admitted to him that he had supported the RUF (Revolutionary United Front) rebels who waged a brutal war in Sierra Leone for more than a decade beginning in 1991 because, Gaddafi's view (according to Kabbah), the APC party then in power was "fascistic."

This time our conversation veered into an unexpected--and improbable but not at all implausible--revelation that Kabbah had played a crucial role in getting Gaddafi and Britain's former prime minister, Tony Blair, to thaw their once-frosty relationship. It was during Blair's visit to Sierra Leone sometime before Kabbah's retirement. Gaddafi had visited earlier.

In the car, Blair suddenly turned to Kabbah and asked whether he could get him to have direct contacts with Gaddafi. The two leaders--Blair and Gaddafi--were not on speaking terms. Kabbah quickly made a call to Al Gathafi ... and shortly after, Blair made a well-publicised visit to Libya.

It just so happened that a day before Blair's visit, Gaddafi telephoned Kabbah, almost begging him, in a long conversation, to be put in touch with Blair. Would Kabbah have been so self-congratulatory if he had known, as was evident, that British intelligence had long bugged his phone? I cannot say.

I first met Kabbah in 1995, a year before he became president. He was then the chairman of the National Advisory Council to the NPRC government. This role would later--after the 1997 coup that overthrew Kabbah's government -be rendered sinister, but in fact members of the

Advisory Council, mainly civilians, worked behind-the-scenes to pressure the NPRC to begin peace talks with the RUF rebels and reintroduce multiparty democracy.

It was a delicate balancing act: lacking constitutional power, Kabbah and his colleagues (Solomon Berewa being the second most influential in the Council) relied on their superior knowledge and experience to goad the young military rulers towards more conciliatory politics, and if they found resistance, would brief selected journalists to give particular slants or emphasis in their stories. It was their way of putting pressure on the junta to encourage them to leave office.

I was introduced to Kabbah by the late Garvas Betts, a cigar-smoking, Oxford-educated lawyer of easy charm and aristocratic bearing. Kabbah had hired his firm, Betts and Berewa (housed in a curiously drab building in a far-from-posh area of Freetown). Berewa was a junior partner.

When the ban on politics was finally lifted by the NPRC junta, Kabbah contested the leadership of the SLPP. He appeared unprepared for the nastiness that followed. His rival, Charles Margai, a veteran bare-knuckle operator, quickly distributed a 30-year-old Commission of Inquiry report which had said a number of very unflattering things about Kabbah.

That afternoon, I got a call from Garvas Betts, who suggested that Kabbah would like to give his side of the story to a trusted journalist. Would I go to see him? I quickly made my way to Kabbah's private office in downtown Freetown, and found an enraged Kabbah seated with his friend, Abdul Karim Koroma.

Koroma rescued the faltering moment, suggesting to Kabbah that he and I have an extraneous conversation over tea before the interview. It was smart advice: after that Kabbah was composed and articulate, and the interview went on very well.

Kabbah, of course, won the elections, and to the surprise of many he brought the prickly Charles Margai into his government later. Kabbah can be as generous as that. In fact by some counts, nearly half of his cabinet in the last year of his presidency were people who probably did not vote for him.

This makes Kabbah's malevolent treatment of a very staunch ally, the late Sam Hinga Norman, stand out in sharp relief. Chief Norman led the resistance against the AFRC junta which had overthrown Kabbah in 1997, and remained loyal to him until the very day that he was obscenely arrested by the Special Court for Sierra Leone--with Kabbah's approval--and detained along with the notorious killers of the RUF.

Norman died in the custody of the Court, an appalling end for such an august figure. It was a very low point in Kabbah's political career, a fact which should have become clearer to him at the end of his term: his party lost the 2007 elections mainly because of this fact.

A myth has percolated since the defeat of the SLPP in 2007 that Kabbah did not support his presumed successor, Solomon Berewa. Kabbah himself brought up the matter, in our conversation: "I have kept quiet about these rumours," he said. "But the idea that I did not vote for my own party, that I did not support someone I nominated to succeed me, is simply outrageous."

But was it true, I asked, that he was not on speaking terms with Berewa? Kabbah ignored the question, and instead ripped into his former allies--the British--for undermining the SLPP government and contributing immensely to its electoral loss in 2007.

He mentioned the withholding, by the British Department for International Development (DfID), of budgetary support to his government, and other unfulfilled promises made by the British, including one about providing two helicopters for the Sierra Leone military. "The opposition, of course, claimed during the elections that the helicopters had been delivered by the British, and that we had sold them to fund our campaign," Kabbah said, laconically.

He also mentioned the insulting fact--a major breach of protocol--that on the inauguration day of President Ernest Koroma, the IMATT (International Military Assistance and Training Team) commander, a

British brigadier and part of the presidential security detail, saluted Koroma even before he had been sworn in as president, a not-so-subtle signal to Kabbah not to be wobbly at that point.

The politician in Kabbah could not relate this final humiliation to the fact that in his last term as president, he had all but abdicated major national responsibilities to his foreign donors, and that he would have been handing over power to a member of his party if he had not abandoned Chief Norman to be destroyed by foreign prosecutors.

And now Kabbah speaks to visitors, lately more and more urgently, about his anxieties over the rising political tensions in the country as a result of confrontations between the APC and the SLPP. Like many people, he blames Koroma's government for failing to rein in violent APC supporters.

"I see my role as helping promote peace and stability," Kabbah said. But here he does not sound very convincing: he seemed resigned...

6.
On Tejan Kabbah's 'Coming from the Brink'[21]

In the concluding chapter of Jean-Francois Bayart's penetrating 1993 study of African politics, 'The State of Africa: The Politics of the Belly', there is a picture of Guinea's Ahmed Sekou Toure, triumphantly crossing a rope footbridge – the final symbolic steps towards Guinea's defiant independence from France in 1959. And Bayart sardonically comments: "We know what was waiting for Guinea, on the other side. Nevertheless, how can one be indifferent to the joyous forces which leap out of this snapshot, to the certainty that the film has indeed captured history in the making?"

The picture did indeed capture a luminous historical moment of pure joy, but much of what followed in Guinea after this – a long period of terror and sadness, the neutering of civil society, that inexorable force that had propelled Toure to that grand moment of history – was never foreseen at the time. I was brought to mind of this extraordinarily striking vignette while reading Ahmad Tejan Kabbah's memoir in Freetown, Sierra Leone, during the country's 50th anniversary of independence from Britain in April. Kabbah, who retired as President of Sierra Leone after two turbulent terms, now lives quietly in his villa in the far-west end of Freetown, and I had lunch with him on 27 April, the day of the anniversary (Sierra Leone gained independence on 27 April 1961.) Kabbah turned 79 this year [2011] and, somewhat to my small surprise, is a little short of memory. One has, therefore, to turn to his memoirs (written during the preceding three years since he retired, and published early this year) to get a sense from him of how he reflects on the country's 50 years of statehood. The effort is immensely rewarding and frustrating by turns.

---

[21] Published in Patriotic Vanguard 25 May 2011 and in New African June 2011

Kabbah showed me the manuscript of *Coming from the Brink* in early 2010. I introduced it to my London publishers Hurst, who were instantly interested. In the event, however, Hurst sent the manuscript to be read by one of their reviewers. Kabbah felt that the publisher was delaying, and he abruptly pulled out of the arrangement. The book, beautifully jacketed, has now been issued by EPP books Services, a Ghanaian firm (Kabbah had told me that he would much rather prefer an African publisher to issue his memoir).

Kabbah's career trajectory spans Sierra Leone's entire post-independence period. After graduating from the University of Wales in 1959 (with a bachelor's degree in economics), Kabbah returned to Sierra Leone and was appointed to a post as an administrative officer in the colonial civil service. As he writes, he was "among the first crop of qualified Sierra Leoneans to replace the British administrators." At that time, "the level of social, political and economic development in Sierra Leone compared favourably with that of other West African countries," Kabbah writes. Sierra Leone gained independence in 1961, opening up opportunities for Kabbah, whose rise thereafter was meteoric. He became District Commissioner a year later. In 1965, at age thirty-three, Kabbah was made Permanent Secretary in the Ministry of Trade and Industry. His emergence as an important player in the new nation's political elite was signalled that year when his marriage to Patricia Lucy Tucker became a news item in the Sierra Leone Daily Mail, the country's main newspaper.

But the glories of independence, so liberating at the time, had its perils. While at the Ministry of Trade and Industry as Deputy Permanent Secretary in 1964, Kabbah played a role in the Sierra Leone Produce Marketing Board's (SLPMB) purchase of a palm kernel oil mill and refinery. Sierra Leone's first Prime Minister, Milton Margai, died at about this time, and was replaced by his unscrupulous half-brother, Albert Margai. Kabbah's advice, as Acting Permanent Secretary, that the SLPMB should consider several vendors and compare the cost was ignored. The oil mill and refinery were purchased, at an exorbitant cost, from a favored company.

In the event, when the SLPP government lost power in a military coup in 1967, the new junta set up a commission of inquiry to investigate the Margai regime. On the matter relating to the purchase of the oil mill and refinery, the Beoku-Betts Commission found that though he was "very intelligent" and had "qualms of conscience" about the entire deal, Kabbah was "instrumental in making the conspiracy possible."

Kabbah is understandably tetchy while narrating this part, omitting even the quotes from the Commission above. He writes, plausibly, that there was a case of mistaken identity in Commissioner Beoku Bett's rebuke of him. That the ambience was one of vindictiveness and political skullduggery could be seen in the fact that Prime Minister Siaka Stevens, who the junta handed power to, seized Kabbah's property—a house and land in the west end of Freetown—though the Beoku-Bett's Commission had not recommended that action.

In 1974, Kabbah began petitioning the government to return his property; this was only done when then-Attorney General, Abdulai O. Conteh, reviewed the Commission's findings and Kabbah's petitions, and concluded that "a combination of errors, flawed actions, etc have unfortunately militated against Mr. Kabbah" and that Kabbah's "constitutional and fundamental protective rights" had been violated. Kabbah's property was restored on 20 May 1988 by the government, which effectively repudiated the Commission's findings against Kabbah.

By that time, Kabbah was an international civil servant. He joined the United Nations (UN) while in England; his first appointment was as Deputy Chief of the West Africa Division of the United Nations Development Programme (UNDP) in New York. Kabbah thereafter took up a series of posts with the UN, returning to Sierra Leone only in 1992 after his retirement. By that time Sierra Leone was experiencing what Kabbah calls "state failure": a civil war had started, and a coup by young soldiers had overthrown the one-party dictatorship of President (formerly Major General) Joseph Momoh. The junta appointed Kabbah to a senior advisory position, and in 1996, on the return of the country to civilian rule, Kabbah was elected President of Sierra Leone, the first Muslim Head of State of Sierra Leone. He immediately began negotiating peace with the Revolutionary United Front (RUF) rebels but in 1997 Kabbah was forced into exile after a bloody military coup. Nigerian troops and Kamajors restored Kabbah to power in 1998. The war officially ended in 2002. Kabbah was re-elected to a second term that expired in 2007. He comfortably retired.

Coming from the Brink is refreshingly brief on Kabbah's ancestry and early career, concentrating on his political life as President. He was born at Pendembu, Kailahun District, in eastern Sierra Leone, on 16 February 1932. His father, Abu Bakr Sidique Kabbah, was an ethnic Mandingo businessman who had migrated to the predominantly Mende and Kissi town from Kambia District, in northern Sierra Leone. His mother was from a prominent Mende ruling family, the Coomber family of the Mandu chiefdom, Kailahun District. The family later relocated to Freetown, allowing Kabbah, a member of a devout Muslim family, to attend the Catholic St. Edward's Secondary School in Freetown. Reflecting his country's fabled religious tolerance, Kabbah later married Patricia Tucker, a Catholic who was of the Sherbro/Mende ethnic group.

One would think that this is impressive enough, but the politician in Kabbah seemed unable to avoid wrapping his origin in myth. He writes that he had a 'mysterious' birth (he is self-conscious enough to have that mysterious in quote). He was told, much later by his beloved first wife, that Kabbah "entered the world with a clasped left hand containing what was thought to be a piece of paper with an Arabic inscription," augury of great things to come for him.

As presidential autobiographies go, this one is not too bad. Liberia's President Ellen Johnson-Sirleaf wrote in her 2009 memoir that on her birth a visiting old man had looked at her and pronounced "This child shall be great. This child shall lead." She modestly used this happy premonition as title for the memoir.

What is good in Kabbah's memoir is often very good. In one breathtaking moment, the former president narrates how he was violently unseated in January 1999 by a band of brutal rebels and his own (rogue) soldiers.

He was woken up at 3am by a Nigerian military commander (from the West African intervention force, Ecomog, then based in Freetown), and was taken to Government Wharf (the grimy oceanfront celebrated in Graham Greene's *Heart of the Matter*) to board a boat that would take him to a Nigerian warship anchored a few miles away. It was a chilling and immensely symbolic moment. The Sierra Leonean state had atrophied; even the boat would not start. It took 30 minutes of trying before its creaking engine finally roared, and it left just before the rampaging rebels overran the place.

They fired at the fleeing boat, which nearly capsized, and once it got to the ship, a rope was lowered and President Kabbah was pulled up into the ship - and taken to Guinea. That extraordinarily telling scene - a fleeing president being rescued like a drowning man by a foreign ship - was not captured on camera at the time, which perhaps partly accounts for the high drama of the revelation.

For, as it happened, during that attack the rebels who nearly killed Kabbah succeeded in killing about 5,000 people in Freetown, abducting thousands of children, and torching large parts of the city.

We learn, very importantly, of the existence of the so-called Special Task Force, a secret Liberian militia set up by the Sierra Leonean armed forces under the National Provisional Ruling Council (NPRC) junta whose existence, Kabbah writes, was unknown even to him until the very day of the Armed Forces Ruling Council (AFRC) coup against him in May 1997, by which time he had already been President for over a year. This group participated in the coup against Kabbah. He is right to bash the roguish Sierra Leone army for its "reckless disregard for the security of the country" for not bothering, in Kabbah's felicitous view, "to trace the real origin and the real motive of members of [the Task Force]." But Kabbah should also have reflected that as Commander-in-Chief, he bore some responsibility for an evident lack of vigilance towards such a flawed army at that point.

Kabbah provides some insights into the prolonged negotiations leading to the end of war, in particular into the ghastly and treacherous character of RUF leader Foday Sankoh. But he disappoints by a failure to provide a first-hand account into the complex political impulses, alliances and deals that drew in presidents and prime ministers from several countries to get intimately involved in Sierra Leone, which was of no great strategic interest to some of them. What does Kabbah really think of the role of Nigeria's General Abacha? Or of Britain's Tony Blair, for that matter? On matters of the personality and role of important foreign players, Kabbah maintains polite reticence bordering on blandness.

Kabbah even attempts to minimise Gaddafi's destructive role in the war, doubtless because the Libyan leader, a fellow Muslim, later became a close friend. Gaddafi trained and funded the original insurgents, through Liberia's Charles Taylor, that invaded Sierra Leone in 1991. But he is first mentioned on page 111, where Kabbah confronts him with evidence the Sierra Leone authorities had wrung out of Yair Klein, a notorious Israeli thug and arms trader. That evidence, which I have seen, clearly implicated Gaddafi in the carnage in Sierra Leone. Kabbah writes that when he showed Gaddafi the evidence the scrofulous Libyan leader was "very shaken" and told him that he had provided support to some Sierra Leoneans who had "appealed to him to assist them get rid of what they considered a fascist government" (the absurd reference is to Momoh's gloriously incompetent and ramshackle regime). And: "Gaddafi swore that his support to the RUF had stopped when I assumed the presidency," Kabbah writes.

Kabbah, of course, knows that Gaddafi was lying. On page 52, Kabbah quotes from a letter Foday Sankoh wrote on 4 December 1996 (months after Kabbah came to power) to his "international contacts" thanking them for assistance in procuring "fighting materials" [sic] What Kabbah markedly leaves out is that Sankoh wrote the letter to Mohamed Talibi, of the Libyan Peoples Bureau in Ghana (I have seen the letter and several others implicating the Libyan leader, and I quoted some in my book, *A Dirty war in West Africa: The RUF and the Destruction of Sierra Leon*', 2005).

The same frustrating evasiveness can be seen in Kabbah's treatment of the Special Court for Sierra Leone (which he helped bring into existence) and particularly of the indictment of his own minister, the late Chief Hinga Norman. He writes that he was "stunned and upset" by the arrest of Norman (page 329), and that some of the court's activities were among the most "agonising of my Presidency." But he is defensive about his role in bringing about the court and in this memoir he resorts to legalese, rather than introspection or a proper analysis of the court's impact, to account for his dealings with the court. This is most clear in his obtuse reason for testifying on behalf of Issa Sesay (a brutal thug who, however, made a "significant contribution" to ending the war) and not on behalf of Norman, a true hero who risked his own life to save Kabbah's presidency and the nation (something that no one can accuse Kabbah of doing).

The last part of Kabbah's memoir makes an impressive list of important institutions that he set up in his final term of office, including a Truth and Reconciliation Commission (TRC), a new National Revenue Authority (NRA), an Anti-Corruption Commission (ACC), and a new

National Social Security and Insurance Trust (NASSIT). He also revamped the security sector, and enacted major new laws protecting children and promoting gender equality. There are reports of the systematic downgrading of some of these institutions by Kabbah's graft-addled successor government, and it would have been most helpful for the ex-president to have reflected on how they have fared.

Curiously, Kabbah is at pains to take credit for the so-called Attitudinal Change business which current President Ernest Koroma made the sort of ideological – for want of a better term – cornerstone of his government. That anybody can associate with such an idea is beyond me, and I said this even before the leaders of the bureaucracy Koroma set up were convicted for theft (something that was inevitable).

The entire sordid episode only add up to the impression of the degradation of that idea of nationhood and independence that the country's founding leaders exemplified, and which Kabbah himself tried so hard, in his final years as President, to reclaim – it is a very tragic 50-year journey indeed. One cannot escape the conclusion, going through Kabbah's memoir, that though not at all a great man, Kabbah is (aside from Milton Margai, the country's first Prime Minister) without doubt the most successful, as well as the most personable, leader Sierra Leone has had in its decades of independence.

A few days before Sierra Leone celebrated its golden jubilee, a friend, who is close to Kabbah, told me about an episode involving Kabbah that was steeped in pathos. He met the ex-President at a petrol station in Freetown giving 20,000 leones to his driver to fill the car's tank. But that amount could only buy a gallon: Kabbah had not done his own petrol purchase in years. He was still steeped in good days gone.

7.
Michael Schulenburg and Sierra Leone[22]

On 6 February 2012, UN Secretary-General Ban Ki-moon - recently given a second term in office - abruptly withdrew his executive representative from Sierra Leone following a request by the government of President Ernest Bai Koroma. Michael von der Schulenburg, a respected German diplomat, had been in the post since 2008, first as acting executive representative, and then, since January 2009, as head of the UN mission in Sierra Leone called UNIPSIL.

The announcement did not come as much of a surprise to anyone who has been following the vicious attacks on his person by sections of the media; but surprisingly it was a shock.

Schulenburg had worked hard to create a level playing field, getting the opposition and the government to dialogue and reduce tensions ahead of elections slated for November 2012.

That, caused offence to President Ernest Bai Koroma, who is desperate for re-election.

A terse statement from the UN Secretary General thanked Schulenburg for his "open and fruitful work with all sections of the Sierra Leonean society including with political parties and stakeholders [and] his effective cooperation with the Peace building Commission."

It was a well-deserved compliment for a man whose commitment to Sierra Leone went way beyond the call of duty, and that's simply a fact.

Just before the end of 2011, Sierra Leone announced that it was sending 850 peacekeeping troops this year [2012] to Somalia, joining troops from

---

[22] *New African* April 1, 2012

Uganda and Burundi. That event was barely noticed internationally. That showed how far Sierra Leone has come.

When in 2009 the country announced that it was sending its first batch of peacekeepers – 160 soldiers to Darfur, Sudan since its war ended, the Economist reported the event with the predictably unflattering caption:"From Butchers to Peacekeepers." The magazine wrote that; "what used to be one of Africa's worst armies turns a new leaf."

Schulenburg liked to proudly point to this stunning turn-around for a country once dismissed as beyond salvage.

I first met him in September, 2008, shortly after he was posted to the country. The UN was then occupying the heavily-fortified and once-luxurious Mammy Yoko hotel in the far west of Freetown.

Schulenburg never concealed his disdain for such extravagance. The war had been over since 2002, and Sierra Leone had successfully conducted its second presidential elections. Violent crime was low.

The key anxieties in the country, when he got there, was the growing threat of organised crime syndicate using Sierra Leone as a base for transiting cocaine to Europe, and the rising tide of intra-party political violence, since the election of President Ernest Bai Koroma and his All Peoples Congress (APC) party to power.

Within a few months, Schulenburg completed a plan that transformed the UN mission to a much smaller office with less than 3% of the budget of the large peacekeeping mission (17,500 troops) that the country previously hosted. He moved his much reduced staff, and rented an accessible and modest former hotel close to downtown Freetown.

And more energetic and resourceful than his careerist predecessor Victor Angelo, he sought to put in practice the inchoate notion of 'peace building' only recently enunciated by the UN, which quickly set up the

Peace building Commission (PBC) and placed Sierra Leone and Burundi as its first clients.

Under this new arrangement, all the UN programs in the country were integrated under Schulenburg's leadership, whose political mandate was underlined by Security Council resolution 1886.

This mandate was severely tested in March 2009 amidst a rash of violent confrontations between the ruling APC and the opposition Sierra Leone Peoples Party (SLPP), in which supporters of the APC, led by a former rebel combatant (turned presidential guard) with the un-improvable name Leather Boot, besieged the headquarters of the SLPP and nearly destroyed it.

There were 22 people trapped in the building, some of them women (and some of whom were allegedly raped). The ill-equipped and probably conniving police stood by doing nothing.

Schulenburg drove into the crowd and such was the prestige of the UN which had lost soldiers and spent over $2.5 billion to bring peace to the country, he was able to persuade the drunken, murderous crowd to disperse.

Shortly after, Schulenburg brought the two parties together and had them sign a Joint Communiqué, which committed them 'to work jointly in preventing all forms of political incitement, provocation and intimidation that could lead to a recurrence of the disturbances' that the country had witnessed since the 2007 elections.

The pathos, that political leaders in the country had to be cajoled by a foreign body to make this basic commitment, was that while a once-depraved army was now behaving responsibly, the top political leadership was anything but.

I got close to Schulenburg after this event. When I moved to Sierra Leone after nearly two years in Liberia, Schulenburg asked me to travel around the country and write a report that could form the basis of a conflict mitigation strategy ahead of the 2012 elections.

In my many meetings with him, I found him to be the most intellectually curious and engaging senior UN official I have ever met. He was interested in every detail, and constantly challenged my conclusions.

I felt at the time that he viewed Koroma who he told me he liked and trusted, and with whom he was in almost daily contact much too favourably. He had to, of course, have the confidence of the president and his government; but he was also determined to learn more about the country from many different sources.

I told him at the time that Koroma was a politician and that since he was running for re-election, his motives and actions are likely to be as base as any politician desperate for power.

In fact, in my research, I came to a conclusion that actually stunned me at the time: almost all the political violence since 2007 was initiated by people or groups linked to the ruling APC.

I also found that the parties had very tenuous infrastructure outside of Freetown and the major cities, and so the initiative for any organised political activity or fission had to have come from the top leadership, mainly in Freetown.

It seemed simply not feasible, certainly not the practice for local groups – even unruly youth groups, to initiate any serious violent political confrontation without the blessings or signals of top political leaders.

The young people who actually carry out the violence, in Freetown and elsewhere in the country, merely respond to such signals, however vaguely expressed by the party leadership.

Almost all of the violent political clashes that have happened in the provincial towns and cities, since the elections of 2007, were preceded by visits from Freetown or Bo by high-profile party leaders or activists.

I suggested that a conflict prevention strategy must therefore focus on the top echelons of the main political parties, and especially on the more vociferous and 'visible' sectors.

By 2010, the SLPP was complaining loudly that Schulenburg was an ally of Koroma, and its robustly ham-fisted chairman, John Benjamin, was barely on speaking terms with Schulenburg.

I met Benjamin several times during my research, and he told me that I was wasting my time since the facts are well known to the UN, which had in any case connived to inflict Koroma on the country by rigging the elections of 2007. The UN people, he said, have an interest in covering up for Koroma.

When the UN Secretary General – Ban Ki-Moon visited the country that year, I spent nearly an hour on the phone with Benjamin trying to convince him that Schulenburg meant well, and that he should therefore put on a positive face when meeting Ban, even if he had to complain about things he didn't like.

He took my advice, and after the Ban visit his relationship with Schulenburg improved.

Ever resourceful, Schulenburg was influential in mobilising international support for President Koroma's Agenda for Change, then merely a set of rather high-sounding political sentiments, by fashioning a UN Joint Vision from Sierra Leone, whose blueprint gave meaning and direction to Koroma's Agenda.

Schulenburg focused on good governance and the rule of law; youth employment; and combating drug trafficking, with gender and regional perspectives as cross-cutting issues.

The problem was money to make any difference. The UN Security Council and the General Assembly, which jointly created the PBC as a subsidiary body, still appear unable to make the necessary commitment to have it work.

In fact, the Security Council appears singularly dilatory in its attitude to the PBC: the permanent five members, at any rate, often treat it as an inconvenience, the kind of nation-building approach that unnecessarily expands the role of the UN in an uncertain and needful world.

Funding for the PBC is voluntary, and for the whole of 2011 PBC contribution towards the Joint Vision was: Australia ($1,000,000), Canada ($500,000), Italy ($685,000) and the United States ($200,000), falling far short of promises made at the beginning of the year.

Since 2006, Sierra Leone has received less than $45 million from the PBC funds. Schulenburg's frustration over this state of affairs was deeply felt: it impacted on the prestige and leverage that the UN has in the country.

As a respected German diplomat, however, Schulenburg was able to attract enormous bilateral assistance for Sierra Leone, as well as used UN funds to help refurbish the SLPP HQ after the APC attack, and assist civil society groups doing valuable advocacy work in the country.

He was especially close to such groups, including the media, seeing them as key guarantors of the country's democratic future.

In March 2011, Schulenburg submitted a memo to the UN in New York setting out an uncharacteristic plan: abolish his office after what he hoped to be the success of the 2012 elections and transfer responsibilities to the lesser office of a resident UN coordinator.

"Within only nine years," he argued, "Sierra Leone has evolved from a country that was engulfed in anarchy to a country with an evolving democratic culture; from a country with institutions that had all but collapsed to a country with functioning central as well as regional governance structures; from a country where some of the worst human rights abuses were committed to a country in which its people now live largely at peace with each other and from a country that was only recently the beneficiary of one of the largest UN peacekeeping operations to a country that is now sending its own armed and police forces to UN peacekeeping operations in other countries." Problems remained, he wrote.

The greatest challenge facing the country, he wrote, may well be the recent massive investments into iron ore and off shore oil and gas deposits.

"Presently, the country does not have sufficiently strong governance structures, adequate regulatory frameworks, the technical know-how, the trained human resources, the physical infrastructure or even the economic basis that would be needed to cope successfully with and take full advantage of such large investments in extractive industries," he wrote.

"A particular challenge in dealing with emerging extractive industries will be; managing public expectations, maintaining an open dialogue on the likely impact of such activities on the lives of ordinary Sierra Leoneans and creating an environment of inclusiveness that open opportunities not only for the élites but also for the unemployed youth, for fresh university graduates as well as for the rural and urban poor.

"A particular risk is that unrealistic expectations could lead to imprudent public investment decisions and a failing budgetary discipline that in turn would create only new dependences.

"The Government's ability to manage these potentially huge natural resources for the benefit of all Sierra Leoneans will probably more than any other challenge determine the future stability, peace and prosperity of this country."

He made some of his concerns public, drawing the ire of Koroma's government, which was busy signing non-transparent and lopsided deals with several mining companies.

The memo also emphasized the coming November 2012 elections as the "critical political test for Sierra Leone's stability, the maturity of its political system and the capacities of its national institutions."

In the event, it was those elections, still several months away, which determined Schulenburg's future in the country, in a rather unexpected ways. The issues are difficult to disentangle from the mix of interests and sentiments, some counter-intuitive, others plainly baffling, but one thing seems to stand out:

It appears that Schulenburg had in 2010 advised President Koroma, after considering the potential implications for overall security and good governance, to drop the idea of holding an inquest into the extra-judicial killings of 29 people by the National Provisional Ruling Council (NPRC) in 1992.

The issue, as it happens, was extensively looked into by Sierra Leone's Truth and Reconciliation Commission (TRC), which recommended drawing a line under the matter. At the time, Koroma had no problems giving up the idea of an inquest.

There occurred something of a zeitgeist change within the ruling party: from a complacent belief that a second term for Koroma was a matter of course to a sense of mortal political struggle ahead.

Koroma stopped taking Schulenburg's calls, and the APC as a party, made it clear that it would not be cooperating with the UN as long as Schulenburg remained in the country. Pro-APC newspapers launched a campaign against Schulenburg, falsely accusing him of a number of untoward things.

The leader of a brand new political party linked to the APC was taken to New York by Koroma, where he delivered a rambling and ungrammatical letter accusing Schulenburg of undue meddling in the country's affairs.

The dignity and prestige of the UN were under attack: Schulenburg had to go.

Political violence, meanwhile, has continued: a by-election for a local council seat in Freetown in January, which was won by the SLPP, was accompanied by violence, and Koroma's government promptly arrested and detained the winner.

Sadly, these developments portend pace the bright optics of a once demented army on peacekeeping missions something truly sinister: that the politicians may well be bracing for bloody battles in November.

Part IV

War and Memory

1.
Truth and Justice on Trial in Liberia[23]

On 8 January 2008, almost without notice elsewhere, public hearings of Liberia's Truth and Reconciliation Commission (TRC) began at the Centennial Pavilion, a large mock-Roman structure flanked by the country's national museum and an imposing Baptist Church in downtown Monrovia. The TRC had been established by an Act of the Legislature in 2005, and had prior to the public hearings collected 16000 statements from victims as well as alleged perpetrators of the country's nearly fifteen years of brutal civil war, 1989-2003. The timing of the hearings appeared propitious, for it coincided with the opening of the trial, for crimes against humanity and related offences, of Liberia's former President Charles Ghankay Taylor, several thousand miles away at the Special Court for Sierra Leone in The Hague. In contrast to the TRC hearings, the opening of the trial attracted significant international media coverage. It appeared that at long last accountability – and 'closure' – was being sought for the terrors and depredations of Liberia's recent past.

The only problem is that the trial focuses not on crimes Taylor committed in Liberia – where before becoming president he was head of the National Patriotic Front of Liberia (NPFL) rebels - but on Taylor's alleged role in the war in neighbouring Sierra Leone. Meanwhile in Liberia itself, the TRC process has been wobbly and controversial, and its many critics say that it will neither create a "clear picture of the past" nor "facilitate genuine healing and reconciliation" (its core mandate). What the TRC process has done beyond dispute, however, is neatly complement, at least to Liberians following the two processes, the prosecution's case against Taylor: the picture that has emerged of the former Liberian leader from the public hearings is roughly what the Special Court prosecutors have sketched – that of a monster and warlord beyond politics, who not only caused untold suffering for his own

---

[23] This article, with full citations, appeared in *African Affairs* (Oxford University Press) (2008) 107 (428): 455-465. June 2008

people, but also, with criminal deliberation, sent his fighters to support the Revolutionary United Front (RUF) and loot Sierra Leone. This picture is likely to endure whatever the outcome of the Hague trial.

Truth and Justice

The TRC was launched on 20 February 2006 (nine Commissioners had already been appointed to staff it on 22 October 2005), as provided for by Liberia's Comprehensive Peace Accord, 2003 (CPA). Article XIII of the CPA stated that a "Truth and Reconciliation Commission shall be established to provide a forum that will address issues of impunity, as well as an opportunity for both the victims and perpetrators of human rights violations to share their experiences, in order to get a clear picture of the past to facilitate genuine healing and reconciliation." The Commission was to "deal with the root causes of the crises in Liberia, including human rights violations," and it was ultimately to "recommend measures to be taken for the rehabilitation of victims." The Commission is mandated to investigate "gross human rights violations and violations of international humanitarian law," as well as other serious abuses, including massacres, rape, murder and extra-judicial killings. It is also to investigate "economic crimes, such as the exploitation of natural or public resources to perpetuate armed conflict." The Commission was to end its work in September 2009, but it could request the National Legislature to extend its tenure for an additional period of three months; this request cannot be repeated more than four times, however.

The Commission was to inquire from as far back as January 1979 – the final year of Americo-Liberian rule, and ten years before the war began – to 14 October 2003, the day of the inauguration of the National Transitional Government of Liberia. This timing was a compromise reflecting a fundamental division in Liberian society, a problem that has continued to cast a shadow on the entire process. The tiny but still-powerful Americo-Liberian elite tend to view the crisis of state collapse and violence as beginning with the coup of 1980, which overthrew William Tolbert (whose father was actually US-born). On the other hand, the vast majority of Liberians, the so-called 'natives', tend to think that the coup resulted from the inherent deformity of the Americo-Liberian state, and see the entire period of Americo-Liberian rule as disenfranchising, a period of distress which laid the foundation for the war that began in 1989. In fact, Article IV of the TRC Act states that the Commission could look at 'any other period preceding 1979.' With little insight into the politics behind it, Amnesty International welcomed this broad timeframe since 'narrow limits in the period of time under a truth commission's investigation can hamper the effectiveness of its work.'

Liberian law makes mandatory that officials of statutory national bodies must be Liberian citizens, and all nine Commissioners are Liberian (unlike Sierra Leone's TRC, which had Commissioners from Canada, South Africa and The Gambia). The result is that none of the Commissioners have had previous experience with truth commissions or related institutions. The Chair, Jerome Verdier, is a young activist lawyer with little political and – even less – moral clout, both necessary for leadership of an institution of huge potential national and international importance. Funding was an immediate problem, causing significant delays. Once this was partially overcome, the Commission began work in earnest. Predictably, it has been further beset by institutional and other problems that have seriously undermined respect for the entire process.

The Past as Memory

The Commission initially determined it would collect statements from 34,000 Liberians, or approximately one per cent of the country's population. In view of the serious capacity constraint of the Commission, this was a purely theatrical gesture, and was quickly abandoned. In the event, by end of 2007, the Commission had collected 16,000 statements, and was anticipating a further 2,000 to be collected from the important Liberian Diaspora in the US (an innovation: the Liberian TRC is the first to take statements from citizens living abroad). Then in early January, public hearings, intended to take place in all of Liberia's 15 counties, and to feature 600 witnesses who would testify openly or in camera, began.

I arrived in Liberia shortly after the hearings began. Already, by mid January, the political impact was palpable. Two dramatic testimonies were made in the first week. At the opening of the hearings, attended by the President and cabinet ministers, the first witness, David Saweh, identified a prominent musician and close aide to the President, Marcus

157

Davies, otherwise known as Sundaygar Dearboy, as a former NPFL fighter who caused the gang-rape and killing of his sister. Saweh claimed that his father was also killed in the attack by Dearboy. It was an extraordinary moment. Dearboy is a national star, something of a role model, and he has an office at the Executive Mansion, the presidential palace. It was a huge embarrassment for Johnson-Sirleaf, who appeared visibly flustered, and left the Centennial Pavilion unceremoniously. Thereafter, she took a markedly unfriendly attitude towards the Commission, which did not help its own cause by exhibiting sordid infighting, including an actual fist-fight between two (female) Commissioners. Johnson-Sirleaf promptly described the TRC as a "charade," and vowed never to appear before it. Instead, she said, she will reserve her testimony for her memoirs, which is her key retirement plan. [Her eminently valuable book, *This Child will be Great* (Harper Perrenial) appeared in 2009, long before her retirement. But it is somewhat economical with the truth with respect to her involvement with Charles Taylor during the early stages of the civil war.]

The presidential criticism looked suspiciously like a cop-out, and it was widely condemned by the vocal Liberian press. Johnson-Sirleaf was Finance Minister in the Tolbert administration that was overthrown in 1980, and was one of the most prominent supporters of Taylor in the early stages of the war. This support continued even after thousands had been slaughtered in ethnic pogroms and Taylor was besieging Monrovia. As for Dearboy, he at first denied the charges, and then admitted that he was recruited by Taylor as a child soldier. He has, however, denied committing atrocities, and has launched a noisy campaign against the TRC, refusing to appear before it. The musician was influential in the Johnson-Sirleaf election campaign, helping to rally thousands of young people to her side.

The other sensational testimony was that of Joshua Blahyi, a former fighter for the Krahn-dominated ULIMO-J faction and later leader of the Butt Naked Brigade, a band of naked child fighters who believed that nudity protected them from bullets, and who allegedly participated in ritual cannibalism. This faction fought in the very destructive battles of Monrovia in April 1996, in which Blahyi was said to have played a leading role. Shortly after this, Blahyi became a born-again Christian, and established a popular church in Monrovia. In his testimony, Blahyi claimed that he was responsible for the deaths of 20,000 people during the war, and he made clear that his confession was a form of contrition, calling on other factional leaders to come forward and confess to the TRC.

In fact, the testimony looked suspiciously histrionic, and Blahyi – preening and evidently proud of himself – behaved less like a contrite sinner than a hero seeking a national platform. I met him a week after his testimony. As we walked to a nearby restaurant, he was embraced by passers-by, and the 37-year old saluted everyone who recognised him in triumph. I was stumped. Blahyi has already self-published a book, *Trading Priesthood for Priesthood: A Testimonial Account of a Liberian Brutal War General and Traditional Priest that dramatically met Christ and is now a Christian Ambassador*, in which he writes that he and his thirty-six naked but armed children who constituted the Butt Naked Brigade would pluck out the hearts of 'little girls' and eat them before going to battle (the book is banned in Liberia). I asked him about his 20,000 victims. Why 20,000 and not, say, 19,999? Blahyi said that he did not want to understate his atrocities; that the 20,000 included those he killed when he was a Krahn "tribal priest" (he said he became a priest in 1982 at aged 11), and that ritual killings were an integral, weekly necessity. He said that none of his fighters was hurt or killed throughout their many battles, and that he was himself armed only with a machete. He seemed energised while explaining this part – it looked like a boast. "In some encounters," he said, "I would kill seventeen people at a time. And there would be sometimes three or four such encounters a day. On some days, I would kill up to fifty." He was trying to explain the 20,000 figure. "But you don't appear convinced?" he asked. I wasn't, but all the same I admired as much as was repelled by his determination to convince me that he is indeed a mass murderer.

I was to see this same attitude on display when I attended the hearings at the Centennial Pavilion that week. None of the alleged perpetrators who appeared asked for amnesty before they gave their testimonies, and all of them behaved as though what they did – gang-raping women, disemboweling people, participating in mass killings, or leading gangs of fighters (on the orders of Taylor, many said) to invade neighbouring countries where they exported their brand of cruelty – unusual but not particularly despicable. Often even the Commissioners, looking un-shocked, would smile or laugh, the early solemnity of the proceedings abandoned. Worse, onlookers, including some Commissioners, would giggle when victims narrated unusual forms of atrocities, including particularly creative forms of rape. In fact, the Commissioners often tend to subject victims to more probing examination, as in actual trials, than they do alleged perpetrators (whom the lawyerly Chairman routinely refers to as 'accused.') A witness protection scheme put in place by the Commission, costing $500,000, has tended to benefit alleged perpetrators more than it has victims; in March four alleged perpetrators were said to be 'protected' yet only one victim was benefiting from the scheme. Reflecting on this, Paul James-Allen, of the International Center for Transitional Justice (ICTJ), who has worked with the TRC since it was established, regretted the shrill tone of the Commissioners when questioning victims, and noted that 'the perpetrators have almost been treated on the same level as victims.'

These regrettable but telling episodes can be read as something of a variation on the phenomenon observed by Frantz Fanon during the Algerian War of Independence in the 1950s: the congruent abasement of victim and victimisers, of oppressors and the society they oppress. It is as though, after over a decade of near-universal experience of distress and pain, the sense of a moral universe had been obliterated in the country; and as though, because of a long history of injustice and casual violence, notions of justice are no longer contemplated or easily grasped; and as though ideas of truth and memory are simply meaningless. Cruelty, of course, had long ceased to have any meaning; it had been a part of life for so long.

The hearings, however, have been partially redeemed by a number of clarifying disclosures which have firmly put Charles Taylor at the centre of most of the murderous violations. Perhaps the most important so far has been the testimonies on the Harbel or Camp Carter massacres of 6 June 1993. On that day, 600 mostly displaced women and children at the camp, which was on the Firestone Plantation – an area which both the NPFL and the Liberian army, the Armed Forces of Liberia (AFL), claimed to control at the same time – were massacred by armed fighters.

It was a shocking display of terror, made more dramatic by the fact that negotiations to end the war, sponsored the Economic Community of West African States (ECOWAS) and the United Nations (UN), were in progress at the time. The NPFL promptly accused the AFL of the killings, which the AFL denied, blaming the NPFL. The UN set up a Commission of Inquiry headed by a markedly incurious former Kenyan Attorney General, Amos Wako. In September 1993, Wako submitted his findings, blaming the AFL for the killings. Few were convinced. The historian Stephen Ellis, who was then an investigator for Amnesty International, later wrote that the "most plausible explanation... is that [the massacre] was carried out by elements in the NPFL, as a means of gaining world attention and increasing the pressure for a ceasefire, which was now in the NPFL [increasingly under attack] interests."

Appearing before the TRC on 15 January, M. Allen Nicholas a.k.a. 'Mission Ant', a former child soldier of the NPFL, said that he was one of dozens of NPFL fighters under the command of General 'Jack the Rebel' and Christopher Varmoh ('Mosquito'), who carried out the killings. Nicholas, now a born-again Christian, alleged that NPFL fighters were ordered by Charles Taylor to carry out the killings in a way that would cast suspicion on the AFL, thus helping legitimize his campaign during the aforementioned negotiations to end the war.

Two days later, on 18 January, at the Special Court in The Hague, General Zigzag Marzah, a former NPFL commander who is now a key prosecution witness, with no apparent knowledge of the disclosure at the TRC in Monrovia, made the same claim about the massacre in this exchange with the Prosecutor:

> Pros: You told us about a Death Squad. Are you familiar with Camp Carter?

> > Wit: Carter Camp in Harbel (sp?). Carter Camp massacre was done by Taylor through [Benjamin] Yeaten. Yeaten said they were civilians at Camp Carter working with the AFL at Camp Shefflin. He said none of those people should live. Ben came to my house - I was sick. Mosquito - Christopher Varmoh, a small boy, carried out the execution with Joe Tuah (and

others). All the people there were executed. The people killed were more than 600 at Carter Camp. The same thing happened at Depot (sp?) Road.

Pros: Do you know if that massacre at Camp Carter was blamed on anyone else?

Wit: Yes. After that massacre, he [Taylor] left the blame on the AFL, then Prince Johnson.

Pros: Do you know how the blame was put on the AFL?

Wit: For NPFL not to be blamed for that instruction, the blame was cast on AFL. Because you cannot go and say it was NPFL that massacred, or the civilians would turn against us.

Pros: Do you know how they made it look like it was the AFL?

Wit: I don't know. I only heard over the radio that the NPFL massacred, I heard Taylor say it was the AFL.

Marzah also explained in detail how, on the orders of Taylor, he led fighters to support the RUF in Sierra Leone, a testimony buttressed by another prosecution witness, Varmuyan Sheriff, formerly head of Taylor's security (1997-2000). At about the same time, a former NPFL Brigadier-General testified to the TRC that on becoming a marine in the rebel group in 1992, he was sent by Taylor, along with hundreds of NPFL fighters, to support the RUF. This was after a coup had brought to power in Sierra Leone young officers who were now fighting the war more vigorously than the overthrown Joseph Momoh's decrepit government. The NPFL fighter also stated, casually, that Taylor later sent other soldiers to fight in Ivory Coast and Democratic Republic of Congo (then Zaire). Amidst the piling-up of such disclosures, Moses Blah, Taylor's former Vice-President, warned the TRC, in an interview with a local newspaper, to "beware of false statements from so-called Generals," but he himself did not volunteer to testify.

A difficulty faced by the TRC is that although many alleged perpetrators have voluntarily testified without even asking for immunity first, many of these, with the exception of Blahyi, were fairly minor and largely unknown figures during the war. The major players, like Prince Johnson (the rebel leader who killed Doe), who is now a Senior Senator, have so far refused to testify. Johnson has claimed that he has made peace with the family of Doe (even though he continues to insist, against the evidence of widely circulated video footage, that he did not kill Doe), and that he would only testify if makers of the 1980 coup testify as well. Only Alhaji Kromah, the former leader of ULIMO, and now a professor at the University of Liberia, has clearly stated that since his rebel faction did not have a policy of targeting civilians, he was willing to appear before the Commission at any time. He made this statement in mid-January, but has still not appeared before the Commission. Winston Tubman, the grandson of William Tubman (the longest serving President of Liberia) and a former United Nations Secretary General's Special Envoy to Somalia, has dismissed the hearings as a "joke" and a forum for promoting "ethnic interests." Tubman is Americo-Liberian, and his anxiety is widely shared by others within that small but old and highly influential community.

At first glance, the anxiety is curious. Of the nine Commissioners, at least two – Pearl Brown Bull and Ambassador Gerald Coleman – are Americo-Liberians (who constitute only five per cent of the population), and the current government has Americo-Liberians occupying important cabinet positions. But those in the TRC have felt harassed; in March, the TRC chair announced the sacking of Bull for alleged conflict of interest. The decision was ill-advised and probably illegal, and the Supreme Court quickly annulled it. Earlier, Bull, believed to be very close to the Johnson-Sirleaf government (increasingly seen as too weighted towards Americo-Liberian interests) was involved in a fistfight with another female Commissioner, Massa Washington. Post-war Liberia, it seems, is still involved in a serious identity struggle.

The more corrosive issue for the TRC, however, is the very public criticism of the Commission by the President and key players in the war. The Commission can legally compel Liberians to appear before it, but the use of such a blunt instrument can defeat the purpose of the entire exercise, which is to record voluntary and truthful statements. In view of this, the Chairman in March issued a series of statements underlining the amnesty and immunity provisions of the TRC Act. The amnesty provision states that the Commission can recommend prosecution, but it can also recommend amnesty for those who make "full disclosure of their wrongs and … [express] remorse for their acts and/or omissions, whether as an accomplice or a perpetrator, provided that amnesty or exoneration shall not apply to violations of international humanitarian law and crimes against humanity in conformity with international laws and standards."

In the March statement, the TRC chair amended this provision somewhat, stating that the TRC "will determine what constitutes international human rights law violations," and that it will take into consideration "the strong desire for national unity and reconciliation." This gives it a measure of flexibility clearly not anticipated by the TRC Act. And Article VIII, Section 30 of the TRC Act provides that "The TRC shall grant immunity to all persons or groups of persons, organizations or institutions from prosecution or tort actions on account of statements made or evidence given before the TRC…" It remains to be seen whether these would be enough enticement to leaders of the various militia groups to come forward and testify voluntarily.

Until this is done, the work of the TRC will look incomplete, and its findings will be hotly disputed, and probably lack credibility. Truth itself, in other words, is being held hostage to the whims of those who started the problem that led to the setting up of the Commission in the first place.

Conclusion

In its brutality and anarchic colourfulness, its factional fluidity, and in the gruesome perversion of religious rituals, the Liberian war was quite unique. The hearings have been dominated by accounts of ritual cannibalism, the drinking of the blood of human beings, the gouging of human hearts for consumption in the hope that this would make the consumers' bodies impervious to bullets. There is no point dismissing these accounts as deluded or merely sensational, since they form the dominant narrative of the war, and they are widely believed. Liberians are generally religious; over 90 per cent are said to be Christian, many of them Baptist Christians. But Christianity in the country has always been fused by the vast majority of its adherents with other traditional religious practices; outside of Monrovia few people are literate in the Western sense. Some of such practices are both bizarre and clearly harmful.

Since her election, Johnson-Sirleaf has made reform of key governance institutions, including the justice sector, and economic recovery the top priority for her administration. The President promised to govern 'differently, decisively breaking from the past.' But the capacity constraints are overwhelming. Liberian law states that magistrates and judges must hold law degrees, and that they must be Liberian citizens. In practice, however, because of the dearth of educated and trained Liberians, 90 per cent of judicial officials barely finished high school; only three per cent attended university. This has severe consequences for individual human rights - and the capacity of the degraded justice system to cope with the needs of the country. At present, only nineteen of the 790 people in prisons in Monrovia have been convicted; the rest are on remand, which can be indefinite.

One measure of progress in governance in Liberia is the degree of openness with which the government conducts its business, as well as the robust anti-corruption posture of the President. Anti-corruption measures have included the prosecution of the former Transitional President Gyude Bryant on corruption charges and the sacking of key government officials for the same reason. In March 2008, a Deputy Minister and an assistant minister were sacked for allegedly granting bogus mining licenses, and a top official very close to the President was forced to resign early in the year when his picture – showing him in a lewd act with two young women – surfaced in local newspapers.

There is an ongoing process of decentralisation, which includes efforts to extend the writ of the state or strengthen its capacity in long-neglected areas outside of Monrovia. The UN has created County Support Teams (CSTs) in each of the 15 counties, with the aim of strengthening the capacity of local administration and extending modern justice systems across the country from its concentrated area of Monrovia. Implementation has, however, been stymied by poor infrastructure and the constricting powers of traditional chiefs: Liberia has about 250 Senior Chiefs along with over 500 Clan Chiefs.

Institutional reform, then, can only go so far – in other words, not far enough. It means that the problems that caused the war and ensured its gruesome character will not, at least in the short run, be tackled by governance reform so favoured by outsiders and some of the enlightened members of the governing elite, like Amos Sawyer, now the head of the Governance Commission. So what other options are there?

Many other Liberians see their predicament in a religious sense. In his account of the Liberian war, James Youboty, a journalist, writes that the war 'could be partly blamed on the segregational way in which the ex-slaves from America founded the country and kept the majority of the native population benighted for more than a hundred years. All these disparities in the society set the stage for Satan to take advantage in brutally turning brothers against brothers.' Even Charles Taylor, Youboty writes, is not unlike most Liberians – among the 'most generous people on the face of the earth.' 'But Satan, the devil, came from hell and corrupted the minds of the peace-loving Liberian people to start killing one another for no good reason.'

Given the overtly religious perspective of most Liberians on their country's problems, it might be that true reconciliation and closure should most appropriately be sought, at least in part, from religion. Stephen Ellis made this point in an article for the journal *African Affairs* 1995, long before the end of the war. He wrote:

> Healing [in the circumstances of the religious nature of the Liberian war] lies in the spiritual field at least as much as in the political one, and at the local level rather than the national one. The spirit world is the only domain in which constructive action is still detectable, and in this a leading role may fall to the churches. Unlike Poro society or other traditional cults, they are universal in orientation, having the potential to incorporate all Liberians. In their own symbolic language, the Holy Spirit is pacific and universal in nature and can enter anybody. The Christian God can forgive any crime, no matter how terrible. In the case of the international and other former

missionary churches, they also have the connections and even the material resources to help in the process. Their greatest disability is the unwillingness to come to grips with the anarchic spiritual world of Liberia which may well necessitate assuming more of the symbolic language of Liberian spirituality than is the case at present.

Most liberals recoil at any assertion of religion in the political and even social life of states, but it is important to remember that the church in Liberia, unlike that in Rwanda, played a positive role during the war – it condemned the atrocities, and was one of the spearheads of the attempts to forge a negotiated solution. It seems clearly central to Liberian life. Two of the TRC Commissioners are clergymen, and it is curious that one of them was not made chair of the Commission. Certainly both of them are older (an important issue in Liberia) and of a higher national standing than Verdier, the chair, and either one of them could have given greater traction to the Commission. If Liberia's truth and reconciliation process is that to have success, the church ought surely to play a more important role.

2.
On Child Soldiers[24]

The most difficult ones to deal with, the earnest UN official told me, are the "teenage ruffians." I was talking to him in Monrovia, capital of Liberia, in 2004.

A large UN force, 15,000 strong, was desperately trying to disarm the mostly deranged combatants who ravaged the place for over a decade. Many people had thought that the disarmament would be fairly easy because a large number of the Liberian militias have gone through such a process before, some of them twice.

There had been the incomplete process, supervised by ECOMOG (the West African intervention force) just before the shambolic 1997 elections. Some of the Liberian fighters had actually been disarmed as fighters in Sierra Leone during that country's (earlier) UN-supervised disarmament process.

But the first attempted demobilisation turned chaotic after the militias, desperate for the small cash incentive to hand in their weapons before Christmas, stormed Monrovia. At least eight people were killed in the ensuing violence. In the event, the UN paid 12,000 soldiers but received only 8,000 weapons.

The UN official calmly told me about a two-hour long meeting he had had with 48 "Generals." "Most of them were children, of course," he added. "And the trouble is that these bush Generals are absolutely jealous of their ranks! It makes the word 'feral' meaningless."

The official suggested that I go with him to Gbarnga to see for myself. With some reluctance I agreed. Gbarnga was once the headquarters of Charles Taylor's National Patriotic Front of Liberia (NPFL), which

---

[24] (Review of *Allah is Not Obliged*, by Ahmadou Kourama and Ishmael Beah's *A Long Way Gone: Memoirs of a Boy Soldier*), Pambazuka Issue 304, 16 May 2007)

started Liberia's war. It had become an immense ruin. The pathos of its decrepitude was that it had now edged itself, once again, towards the centre of Liberia's woes: the militias encamped there had become frighteningly restive and violent.

By the time we got there, a long line of them had formed at the cantonment site to hand in old AK 47 rifles and collect their money. Things seemed to be going well when suddenly a scrawny teenage fighter with a bandana around his head jumped ahead of the queue, raised his old rifle and started shouting abuses at the UN officers. "Mother fuckers, Give us our money now or we'll go to Sierra Leone, to Guinea, to Ivory Coast, and start fighting all over again." I sneaked quietly away.

I was reminded of this chilling incident recently when I started reading Ahmadou Kourama's haunting novel *Allah is not Obliged*. Its obscenely loquacious central character, Birihima, an ex-child fighter who has seen service in the wars in Liberia and Sierra Leone, happily describes himself as "rude as a goat's beard," and given to swearing "like a bastard."

He continues: "I don't give two fucks about village custom any more, 'cos I've been in Liberia and killed lots of guys with an AK-47 (we called it a 'kalash') and got fucked-up on kanif [cannabis] and lots of hard drugs." He is now, he says, stalked by "the ghosts of many innocent people" he killed. This is not "an edifying spectacle."

The novel was first published in France in 2000. Its Ivorian author died three years later. It was a huge success in France, but its English edition, published by William Heinemann last year got a few respectable mentions and then was quickly forgotten.

The novel's liberal and somewhat foolish use of the word "nigger" was probably too off-putting; and it doubtless it makes the story – a powerful psychological exploration of the terrible phenomenon of child soldiery – less exalted for a reader of the English translation than it actually is.

The narrator says at the outset in the novel that "the full, final and completely complete title of my bullshit story is Allah is not obliged to be fair about all things he does on earth." It is an insight of sort, capturing the kind of cynicism that has, until recently, surrounded the phenomenon of child soldiery.

The use of children in armed combat is probably as old as warfare itself – the word 'infantry' is obviously a derivative from 'infant'. It has never been limited to irregular armies. Even Clauswitz, the great theoretician of conventional warfare, joined the Prussian army at age 13. There were hundreds of thousands of children in all the major armies that fought the two world wars.

After much foot-dragging, in 1989 193 countries signed the UN Convention on the Rights of the Child, which sets 15 years as the minimum age for recruitment into armed forces.

Incidentally the US (and Somalia, no doubt because it didn't have a government) signed, but refused to ratify the convention. The convention was largely ignored even by those who signed it. There was no legal instrument to enforce it.

In the 1980s Renamo, a uniquely brutal (and mercenary) rebel group in Mozambique, which anticipated Sierra Leone's Revolutionary United Front (RUF) in the use of amputations as a war tactic, had made widespread recruitment of children into its militia (also anticipating the RUF) a core part of its insurgency.

Other African rebel groups, also markedly mercenary, followed this pattern. The spectacle of drug-addled children armed with AK 47 rifles and gamely inflicting terror against defenceless civilians became a ubiquitous part of African warfare: a metaphor for the continent's underdevelopment and mindless brutality.

After an intense campaign – led by Graca Machel, the Mozambican wife of Nelson Mandela, with the active support of then Canadian foreign minister Lloyd Axworthy – against this appalling new reality, the UN Security Council in 2000 passed the Optional Protocol on the Involvement of Children in Armed Conflict, which made no distinction between formal militaries and non-state militias, and which defined the recruitment of children under 18 (instead of 15) years of age as a war crime.

Since then, UN-sponsored war crimes trials, like the one in Sierra Leone, have included recruitment of children into armed groups as a crime against humanity.

As I write, however, it is estimated that 300,000 children are serving in various armies or militia groups around the world. During Sierra Leone's war, the RUF would have its child recruits branded with red-hot bayonets: the figures R-U-F were literally carved on their body, making defection – because RUF fighters caught by government troops and sometimes by civilians were often summarily executed – almost impossible. These children – hysterical, flagellant, and immensely lethal – would then roam the countryside, destroying every living thing they encounter.

Shortly before the Optional Protocol was issued, I attended a conference about child soldiers, organised by Axworthy in the Canadian city of Winnipeg in 2000. In one of the sessions, I attempted to make a distinction between children kidnapped and inducted into militias (like the RUF did) and those who, orphaned and left homeless by the terror campaigns of insurgents voluntarily join armies or pro-government forces, finding for themselves a home and some kind of security.

The Liberian activist andpolitician Conmany Wesseh, who was actively engaged with the problem in West Africa, took me aside and remarked: 'This issue does not admit of such a fine distinction. Recruitment of children into any armed group is bad, full stop. You provide a loophole for all kinds of opportunists by fudging: what moral and professional difference is there between some armies and all these rebel groups?' His point was unanswerable, and I kept quiet about the issue henceforth.

Ishmael Beah's phenomenally successful, but flawed account, *A Long Way Gone: Memoirs of a Boy Soldier* (Farrar Straus Giroux, 2007) makes this same point in another way, though his pained but fluent account does not exactly resolve the central dilemma.

Beah served as a child soldier in the Sierra Leone army during the country's decade-long war. His book, which recounts his traumatic experiences during the period, has been on the top of the New York Times bestseller list for several weeks now, and it is being offered by Starbucks in its thousands of coffee shops in North America. It has been a sensation.

While reading my copy on the plane during the short flight from Chicago to New York City recently, a handsome teenage girl leaned over my seat. Giggling, she asked me whether I found it interesting. 'I heard him [Beah] speak yesterday and I bought a copy there and then', she said. 'I am so excited about it!'

It was the most unalloyed compliment that can be made of a recently-released book, pure in its curiosity and innocence. It almost made me – someone who has also written about the war of which Beah's memoir is concerned – green with envy. So let me report that I found Beah's astonishing story both unsettling and hugely satisfying: the author, who is now 27, emerges as a highly intelligent young man with remarkable literary flair. But his account has obvious flaws.

Beah was just ten when the war in Sierra Leone started. He was attending school in a village in southern Sierra Leone, which became one of the key theatres of the bloody conflict. At that age, he had already read Shakespeare. He could quote passages from Julius Caesar from memory. He had also become interested in American hip hop.

The book is a sustained study in such contrasts: high culture versus low, a Shakespeare-loving teenager committing barbarous atrocities, frightened civilians versus red-eyed murderers, a friendly people versus brutal politics, demented cruelty versus pure kindness, poverty-stricken Sierra Leone versus affluent New York.

It is soon clear that the book is aimed, first and last, at an American readership. No problem with that: for Beah tells us early on that he intends to address the curiosity of his former schoolmates who had always suspected that he was not telling them all about his past.

This past, therefore, comes to include his memory of some "nice summer days" in Sierra Leone – the torrential rains in the country, which should surely form one of the most vivid of experiences for a barefoot straggler in the bush there, is barely mentioned (and when mentioned only perfunctorily).

Hip Hop is evoked throughout – and why not? It can be readily associated with gun violence and drugs in America, important aspects, he tells us, of Beah's experience as a boy soldier. One should not quibble too much here, even when Beah calls Yele 'a big village with more than ten houses' – it is actually a small town with over a hundred houses.

The area that Beah lived in, somewhere in Moyamba District in southern Sierra Leone, was largely unaffected by the war in its early stages. But then rebels – aided by rogue government troops – attacked the Sierra Leone Rutile Mines, where Beah's father worked, in 1994.

They killed some of the people, apparently including Beah's parents, and kidnapped some European ex-patriate workers and Sierra Leonean senior staff.

Beah was then living in a village not far away, and soon his village was also attacked. He fled with a few friends. Then he began a traumatic trek through the bush to virtually nowhere.

Beah devotes a lot of space to this depressing bush trek – the night spent in the forest living bare, grim encounters with the rebels in some places, the death and destruction they encountered along the way, the occasional kindness he and his friends got along the way, the more general fear that people they met had for child stragglers who could well have been rebels, the debilitating hunger and near-collapse into insanity – about three times more space, in fact, than for his actual experience as a child fighter.

The intention is plain. Without this background, without knowledge of the hopelessness of Beah's situation, one would be far less prepared for this:

"My face, my hands, my shirt and gun were covered with blood. I raised my gun and pulled the trigger, and I killed a man. Suddenly, as if someone was shooting them inside my brain, all the massacres I had seen since the day I was touched by war began flashing in my head. Every time I stopped shooting to change magazines and saw my two young lifeless friends, I angrily pointed my gun into the swamp and killed more people. I shot everything that moved, until we were ordered to retreat because we needed another strategy."

Beah is describing his first real battle with the rebels after his recruitment into a contingent of Sierra Leone Army by an officer who, like Beah, would quote Shakespeare for fun. The recruitment, unlike those into the rebel Revolutionary United Front (RUF), was not coerced. But it was not voluntary either.

It was also ad hoc: the new recruits were not registered as government soldiers, and were not paid. They accounted only to the officer, acting on his own whim, who had recruited them.

After the months trekking in the bush, the starving young boys having completely run down to seeds, Beah and his friends really had no choice when, after spending some days in the village where the army had occupied in some comfort, they along with everyone else in the village were asked to help defend the village from the rebels who had started mounting attacks against it. Two of Beah's very young friends were killed at the first encounter with the rebels. A line had been crossed. Beah becomes a killing machine. He tells us:

"I grabbed [a] man's head and slit his throat in one fluid motion. His Adam's apple made way for the sharp knife, and I turned the bayonet on its zigzag edge as I brought it out."

All this may be true, but what one remembers about one's past is always a choice – a choice partly conditioned by what one feels one's audience expects. It is hard not to feel, on reading this account, that Beah is keen on playing to all those voyeurs after adolescent terror and mindless African violence who perhaps are his targeted readers, in the United States.

This may be a curious judgment, but one thinks that Beah is perhaps guilty of a chilling excess of candour – or dreadful fantasising. Killing people becomes a way of life, an obligation: in war you have to kill to remain alive. The lieutenant who recruited Beah tells him, according to Beah's account: "Visualise the enemy, the rebels who killed your parents, your family, and those who are responsible for everything that has happened to you."

He would add: "[the rebels] have lost everything that makes them human. They do not deserve to live. That is why we must kill every single one of them…It is the highest service you can perform for your country."

Beah takes the message to heart – so much so in fact that he is made an officer, having command over his own troop of child fighters. W.H Auden's famous poem, "September 1, 1939," about that "low dishonest decade" of "darkened lands of the earth" comes easily to mind:

"I and the public know/What all schoolchildren learn/

Those to whom evil is done/

Do evil in return."

It was terribly traumatic for Beah, all the same. For months after his rescue from this murderous life by the UN and an NGO dedicated to rehabilitating ex-child soldiers, he suffered from nightmares and frequent bouts of migraine (the side effects of the heavy drugs they fed on daily).

The rehabilitation turns out to be far more difficult than his induction into the army, and there were moments of extreme violence – fights broke out between child soldiers who had served with the Sierra Leone and those who had fought with the RUF, leading to loss of lives.

On arriving at the camp, Beah encounters another ex-child soldier who looked to him like a RUF rebel. Beah, who had hidden a grenade in his pocket, took it, and the boy pulled out a bayonet. Beah asked who the boy was. "We are from Kono district," the boy replied. "Ah, the diamond district!", Alhaji, Beah's friend, responds.

Finally the boy says: "I fought for the army. The rebels burned my village and killed my parents, and you look like one of them." A deadly fight was averted. It is a telling moment, but quickly Beah relates another encounter which seems to make another, more profound point. He and his other friend, Mambu, accost another ex-child soldier who looks different in appearance. "What kind of army person wears civilian clothes?" Mambu asks of the boy. The boy responds: "We fought for the RUF; the army is the enemy. We fought for freedom, and the army killed my family and destroyed my village." A nasty fight breaks out immediately, and several people are killed. This account, which looks so staged, has been disputed: no other person has reported the incident, and it is very likely that Beah – who is given to fictionalising or fantatising – made it up.

It does not really matter, in other words, on what side one fought during the war: all sides had reasonable claims to have been wronged: all the armed groups in the country committed atrocities, and all should be held to account on the same level. There is no difference, this incident seems to suggest, in the methodology of recruitment and induction into the various fighting forces. The problem is that this is not true, and it is clear from Beah's account overall that this point is absurd: it looks like a sop to the campaigners against child soldiery.

It is a noble campaign, but as I said at the Winnipeg conference, there was a marked difference in how the RUF recruited its child fighters and how the army and the Civil Defence Force (CDF) did. The end result may have been pretty much the same, but I doubt whether any official – UN or NGO – could have ventured into a RUF camp (as they did to many army and CDF camps, including Beah's) to take away child soldiers for rehabilitation camps. The RUF fighters in the rehabilitation camps were, before the war ended, very few, and they certainly were not handed over by their commanders.

Beah's book does not provide a history of the war or the background to the conflict. Its singular value is that it gives an insight into the thinking of the child soldiers, and it shows – in the subsequent career of Beah – that rehabilitation is eminently possible.

Beah left Sierra Leone after a bloody in 1997 coup. He had earlier acted as a spokesman at a UN conference in New York on child soldiery. He returned to New York and was adopted by an American woman he had met during his first visit. There he attends college, earns a degree, and has now provided us this valuable memoir. For this reason alone, the book deserves the recognition it has been accorded.

3.
Sierra Leone: Remembering a Difficult Disarmament Process[25]

The Revolutionary United Front (RUF) fighter was probably no more than sixteen, but he was already well-practiced in the front's affecting sententiousness. "What we want," he said, his voice sounding like some old recording, "is peace that does not leave us in pieces."

I was talking to him in the diamond-rich district of Kono, eastern Sierra Leone, in 2001. The disarmament process, thrown into chaos after the RUF abducted 500 peacekeepers in May 2000, had picked up again, and a large contingent of heavily-armed Pakistani troops were camped a couple of miles to the other side of the ravaged district. Many of the RUF fighters, some still with weapons, were digging for diamonds. Fatorma – for that was the RUF fighter's name – said that his gun, an old AK 47, was all that he had in the world. It was a life and death matter for him. Without it he feared he would be killed. "This is what makes me a man," he said. "Why should they ask me to give it up? It will be end of our Revolution."

Fatorma was right. The RUF, which was almost entirely without political support, surviving only because it was armed, would cease to exist once its weapons were taken away. The UN, which was funding the process, did not seem very aware of this. They had also put in place an elaborate political programme which would allow the rebels to participate in elections that were to be held the following year, 2002. The psychology of the armed in an atmosphere of lawlessness has been commented on by many, but to face someone like Fatorma – very young, rootless, without any other skills, in an environment degraded by warfare in which he was a prime participant – is to add a new, totally frightening, meaning to the phenomenon. With their weapons – small, cheap, easy-to-hide guns – they have a feeling of real power and a stake in what goes on

---

[25] *Pambazuka, 2006-09-28, Issue 271.*

around them; and they can be highly destructive, especially when drugged (as is often the case). Without them they feel alienated and hopeless, but far less dangerous to overall society. It is the reason why the UN has made disarming of militias and their encampment and reintegration into the wider society a cardinal part of any process of transition from war to peace in every war-affected country that the organisation has been involved with.

"A successful DDR/RRR process," concludes the National Programme for Disarmament, Demobilisation and Reinsertion, a 2004 document produced jointly by the Ivorian government and the UN mission in the country, ONUCI, "makes the difference between peace and a return to war." Put so starkly, the question whether DDR (Disarmament, Demobilisation and Reintegration) is a requirement for peace looks like a no-brainer. Can there be any question about the need for disarming combatants and having them completely demobilized and reintegrated, as civilians or into the professional military, in any transition from civil war to peace programme? In fact, DDR programmes have been such a core aspect of peace missions in the recent past that peace operations have become almost unthinkable without them.

It has not always been like that, however. The problem of dealing with unwanted combatants, or ex-combatants, is as old as warfare itself. The current policy of DDR is a distinctively UN strategy; its humanitarian provenance cannot be doubted. This, as we have noted, has not always been the case. As Marx noted, when Julius Caesar, the great Roman general, wanted to demobilise some unwanted Gallic rebels who had, at various times, caused him serious problems, he had the right hand of hundreds of them cut off. This was not recreational cruelty in the manner of some of the neurotic indulgences of Sierra Leone's Revolutionary United Front (RUF); it was deadly rational business. The soldiers, if not put out of business, could have posed a grave danger to Caesar's emerging dominion, and Caesar had no time for a protracted programme of a more humane nature – these were cruel and turbulent times. Napoleon, the French revolutionary leader and a child of the Enlightenment, would have found Caesar's tactic too barbaric. So, as soon as he was sure of his own imperial ambitions, he had thousands of his own soldiers, suspected of Republicanism, shipped to Haiti, there to be killed by the revolutionary forces of Toussaint L'Overture and the plague.

The UN-monitored programmes of disarming and demobilising West African civil war combatants have involved essentially the same logic: most combatants in such wars were hastily recruited, sometimes forcefully, and although they always get coarsened by warfare, normal life for many of them can really only be found outside of the armed forces. Conventional militaries in any case cannot absorb many of the ex-combatants, who, increasingly, are children anyway.

Sierra Leone's war began in March 1991 when a former army corporal and photographer, Foday Saybanah Sankoh, invaded the country from Liberia with a small band of Sierra Leonean dissidents and mercenaries from Liberia and Burkina Faso. In a very short time, the war engulfed the country with a destructive force. The war led to a complete normative collapse. It directly triggered three military coups - one in 1992, the National Provisional Ruling Council (NPRC) coup led by Captain Valentine Strasser; another in 1996, a palace coup that led to Strasser's replacement by his deputy, Brigadier Maada Bio [who had promoted himself from captain within a few years]; and the most destructive, in 1997, a bloody putsch that temporarily terminated the democratically elected government of Tejan Kabbah. By the end of 1996, upwards of 15,000 people had been killed and almost two-thirds of the country's population of 4.5 million displaced.

The economy collapsed, with a negative annual growth rate of minus 6.24 per cent between 1991 and 1995. By March 1996, an estimated 75 per cent of school-aged children were out of school, and 70 per cent of the country's educational facilities, already troubled by the time war started, were destroyed. Only 16 per cent of the country's health facilities were functioning by March 1996, and almost all of these were in the as yet untouched capital (untouched by war, that is). By the end of 1999, the casualty figure had risen, by most estimates, to upwards of 70,000, and Freetown had itself been partly destroyed in a devastating attack by the rebels and rogue government soldiers in January 1999. Thousands of civilians, including young babies, had their hands crudely amputated by the rebels in a campaign of insane terror.

Understanding why disarmament is so important in such a situation requires a mere examination of how difficult the whole process was. In May 2000, months into the process, the UN announced that it had disarmed 24,042 militia combatants, but that these combatants had turned in only 10,840 weapons. That same month, a RUF commander invaded one of the disarmament camps on grounds that the UN had disarmed some RUF combatants without first clearing it with him. He had some UN soldiers and military observers tied up, beaten and detained. That RUF commander, who was later convicted by the UN-Sierra Leone Special Court of crimes against humanity, is now jailed in Rwanda. It was a week after this incident that the RUF captured the 500 UN troops (of the Zambian contingent), precipitating one of the biggest crises in the UN's peacekeeping history.

At the end of Sierra Leone's disarmament process, over 70,000 combatants were disarmed and demobilised. They were mainly Revolutionary United Front guerrillas and their main nemesis, members of the Civil Defence Force (CDF). An interesting report on the aftermaths of the DDR process, entitled "What the Fighters Say: A Survey of Ex-Combatants in Sierra Leone June-August 2003" makes a number of important comments on the motivations of the combatants in the two groups. The survey took place over a year after the disarmament process, and since it relies on the expressed views of the ex-combatants to draw its conclusions, so these comments should be regarded with healthy skepticism. The report argues that "Overall, the data support the view that the fighters in the conflict were largely underprivileged individuals who had been failed by the Sierra Leonean state." It states:

"Over one-quarter of fighters came from households in which the father had passed away before the war; fully one third had lost at least one parent by the time the war started; and almost 10% had lost both parents at the start of the fighting..."

Moreover, nearly 60% had been displaced from their homes before they joined a faction. These figures are much higher for the CDF – where more than three-quarters of the combatants had been forced from their homes [by RUF attacks] before they decided to join. Particularly for the

CDF, the uprooting of their lives caused by the war was an important part of their story of participation.

The report argues that:

"Across factions, both political and material motivations mattered for the recruitment of fighters. RUF combatants claimed that they fought to express dissatisfaction, to root out corruption, and to bring down the existing regime. CDF fighters argued that they aimed to defend their communities from the violence brought by the war. Political motivations notwithstanding, there were strong material incentives as well. RUF combatants were promised jobs, money, and women; during the war, they received women, drugs, and sometimes more valuable goods. [My emphasis] The CDF helped to meet the basic needs of the members and provided increased security for their families."

The issue of political motivation with respect to the RUF – that business of fighting to "root out corruption" – is seriously undermined by the fact that, as the report notes, "87% of RUF combatants reported being abducted [and forcefully inducted] into the faction and only 9% suggest they joined because they supported the group's political goals." On the other hand, the CDF, which was aggressively pro-government, had "62% of [its] combatants [reporting that they joined] because they supported the group's political goals," with only 2% suggesting they were "forcibly recruited." The rest said they participated because they were "scared of what would happen if they did not join or to take revenge on the RUF." There are other interesting sets of statistics. With respect to corruption and governance, "more than half" of the ex-combatants "believe things are about the same or worse than before the war." But "while members of different factions have found distinct ways of reintegrating, they tend to share a largely positive assessment of the progress made by the government in addressing fundamental economic and political challenges in the country," with fully "83% of the respondents" [the survey interviewed 1000 ex-combatants] believing that "access to education is better now than it was before the war," and 65% believing that "access to medical care has substantially improved."

How can one make sense of the apparent cognitive dissonance in these views? It probably reflects a profound issue at the heart of the war: most of the combatants, particularly those in the RUF, can hardly be expected to have a good idea of conditions before the war, because they were mainly children when they were recruited to fight. Now a good number of them are grown-up and are now facing the usual challenges of eking out a legitimate living in an impoverished country with few opportunities. What to do?

Francis Kai-Kai, who managed Sierra Leone's DDR programme, recently told me that his National Committee on the DDR got the ex-combatants quickly through the Disarmament and Demobilisation phase – which included some technical training and a little cash support – and then had them integrated within the general ambience of poverty. "We didn't want them to feel privileged for a long time," he said, "that would pose problems in the future." The Sierra Leone government went on to work on a Poverty Alleviation Scheme, with World Bank support, and with Kai-Kai as one of the key players. The success of this scheme would lead to a more general improvement in the living standards in the country, from which the ex-combatants will presumably benefit.

DDR processes are expensive, time-consuming, and often irritating. It challenges one's sensibilities, for example, to come to terms with the idea that fighters who have been guilty of gross atrocities will be compensated and helped to resettle and reintegrate into society, while millions of their victims, whose lives have been battered by the combatants, will remain derelict. Patient work, however, can pay off. One of the more creative steps taken by the UN and the Sierra Leone government was the Community Arms collection initiative. Officials decided to go beyond the combatants and ex-combatants, and target various communities in Sierra Leone in an effort to induce ordinary people to give up deadly weapons. The initiative was so successful that since the war ended there have been fewer incidents of violent crime in Sierra Leone than even before the war started – which is to say, crime is very low in the country.

At the end of the disarmament process in Sierra Leone, the UN Secretary General Kofi Annan issued a statement welcoming the development. The statement noted that it was time for "the extension of State authority throughout the country, the restoration of ex-combatants, the restoration of the Government's control over natural resources, and the resettlement of returning refugees and internally displaced persons, as well as forging national reconciliation, remain crucial tasks for the peace process which also requires generous support from the international community." The very difficult and less dramatic task of governance and economic development, in other words, would now start. That task, like the reintegration process, is still ongoing; Sierra Leone's future stability will depend on it. The jury is out on the whole process.]

4.
Memory and Politics: Liberia's TRC report[26]

James Joyce was right that history is a nightmare, James Baldwin wrote, reflecting in a somnolent Swiss village on the racial tensions in his country: "But it is a nightmare from which there is no awakening. People are trapped in history and history is trapped in them." The words were written about 40 years ago, in a specific context. But they seem to have a particular resonance for post-war Liberia.

Over five years after its brutal insurgencies ended with the signing of the Comprehensive Peace Accord (CPA) in 2003 and the deployment of thousands of UN troops (at a cost of over $600 million per year), Liberia is enmeshed in another conflict altogether, a contest over its past and soul. The outline of the story is jarringly seductive, and there were tantalising hints of it at the 15–20 June 2009 National Conference of Reconciliation organised by the country's Truth and Reconciliation Commission (TRC). It was held at the Unity Conference Center in Virginia, just outside Monrovia; the centre was built for the jinxed Organisation of African Unity (OAU) – the precursor of the more robust Africa Union (AU) – in Liberia in 1979 by President William Tolbert, who would be murdered in his bedroom by his own soldiers less than a year later.

Part of the once-famous Hotel Africa, the hall's main structure – a massive high-rise building – is now a monstrous ruin, making the conference centre, still intact and even elegant, something of a minor wonder. On the walls of the annex, which the casual visitor is likely to miss, there is a very telling mural of a group of confident black people dressed in Western-style clothing getting off a boat to be greeted by apparently dissolute and benighted Africans in their "native" attire. This is not an accurate historical representation, of course, but this is exactly the point. And that point is also captured in the flowering communiqué issued at the end of the conference, the delegates of which, "representing

---

[26] Pambazuka, 2009-07-23, Issue 443

citizens of Liberia from all 15 counties and from all walks of life, background, race, clan [sic] and tribe [sic]," were still able to recall, with no hint of irony, "the spirit of all our great ancestors, who through love of unity, freedom, justice and liberty founded this great nation." This is the standard, vainglorious narrative of Liberia's history, and here we are told that it is shared by "perpetrators and victims of crimes of all forms and degrees against our fellow brothers and sisters" during the country's recent wars.

Surely the presence of perpetrators and victims imply contest – and so an unruly voice among the drafters asserts itself – calling for "a historical review commission [to] be established to review Liberia's history and produce a version of it that reflects the lives of the people met here by the settlers in 1822." It continues to Point 24 of the communiqué, declaring that "the motto in the seal of Liberia should be changed from its current form, 'The love of liberty brought us here,' to instead read 'The love of liberty unites us here." In this same revisionist mood, the communiqué also called for "a national culture center [to] be established to promote Liberia's diverse culture[s]," as well as for "a national consultation process [to] be set-up to determine a single indigenous dialect to be spoken throughout the country and taught in Liberian schools."

You now get the basic idea. In its modern form, Liberia was established by the American Colonization Society (ACS) in 1827 as a colony for American freed slaves. The condition of freed blacks in the United States at the time was both pressing and complex for America's (racist) white masters like Thomas Jefferson, for they amounted to hundreds of thousands, if not millions. Jefferson and his revolutionary colleagues clearly did not envisage that their ideas of independence and liberty, which had led them to revolt against British colonial rule, should extend to their own black population. These leaders thought that the chief solution would be to repatriate the blacks to Africa, where they would live in liberty with themselves. This point has been much stressed by various writers – from the English novelist and travel writer Graham Greene to the Liberian (indigenous) nationalist and academic George Boley, who later emerged as a factional leader during Liberia's recent civil wars, but it surely had been settled over a century ago by that erudite

Lansana Gberie

pan-Africanist Edward Blyden. Noting the influential African voices in America who were yearning at the time for a return to Africa, Blyden wrote that while some of the American whites clearly wanted to expel the freed slaves, the Liberian project "was in harmony with the instincts and desires of the Africans in America."

The only problem was that by a cruel sub-Freudian dynamic, the "instincts and desires" of these Africans would come to reflect exactly the pathos and contradictions of the American revolutionaries. In Liberia they replicated the system of servitude they had known in the antebellum South, only this time with themselves as masters and the majority indigenous Africans as virtual slaves. This is hardly surprising: the classical writers of ancient Greece and Rome, the world's first organised slave societies, had thousands of years ago postulated something about the "slave mentality," the idea that a slave remains a slave even when freed, because the mind remains shackled and conditioned by an experience which makes freedom meaningful only if it exists side-by-side with servitude. This is Liberia's foundational deformity, if you will, and it is why post-war Liberia today is burdened by a very special anxiety, the fear that it is relapsing into that condition against which the struggles of the late 1970s, the nihilistic coup of 1980, and the subsequent collapse into bloody anarchy was triggered.

That anxiety is most clearly expressed in the TRC report released early in July 2009, the month that Liberia celebrated its 163th year as a republic, making it the oldest in Africa. The TRC had been established by the Act of the Legislature in 2005, and in the course of its ponderous work collected more than 20,000 statements from victims as well as alleged perpetrators during the country's nearly 15 years of brutal civil war over the period 1989–2003. The commission was mandated to inquire into Liberia's tragic past from as far back as January 1979 – the final year of Americo-Liberian rule, and 10 years before the war began – to 14 October 2003, the day of the inauguration of the transitional government which replaced Charles Taylor's rule. This time-span was a compromise reflecting a fundamental Liberian problem, the fact that the tiny-but-still-powerful Americo-Liberian elite tend to view the crisis of state collapse and violence as beginning with the coup of 1980, which overthrew William Tolbert, the last of Americo-Liberian oligarchs. On the other hand, the majority indigenous Liberians tend to think that the coup resulted from the disastrous nature of the Americo-Liberian True Whig rule, contending that the entire period from 1847 to 1980 was disenfranchising, laying the foundation for the war that began in 1989. In fact, Article IV of the TRC Act stated that the commission could look at "any other period preceding 1979" in order to create an "accurate historical record" of the past which would form the basis of reconciliation.

Thoughtful Liberians have long deplored the paucity or absence of such a historical record. In Wilton Sankawulo's vastly underrated novel *Sundown at Dawn: A Liberian Odyssey* (2005), a very wise character (doubtless the author's alter-ego) vents his frustration about this fact, noting that Liberia will move forward in peace and stability 'Only if we know our history – history that highlights our strengths and other resources. But the true history of Liberia is yet to be written. All we have is a jumble of journals, reports, and memos which tell us when Liberia was founded, who have been its presidents – what parties have been in power – what nations aided us…we're thriving on chaos and mistrust because we don't know our true history.' The 370 pages of the TRC's Consolidated and Final Report attempts to fulfil such a task, but it is not hard to imagine that Sankawulo, Liberia's foremost literary figure who died early in2009, would have found it almost entirely disappointing.

Here I must state, by way of full disclosure, that from January 2008 to June 2009 (shortly before the report was submitted) I was head of International Center for Transitional Justice's (ICTJ) Liberia programme, and that the TRC was one of the core institutions we worked with rather closely. It was, however, a very difficult relationship, to put it no stronger, though it continued till the end of my tenure without open rancour.

Predictably, the report has a long list of "causes" for Liberia's slide into civil war, including the "over-centralisation and the oppressive dominance of the Americo-Liberian oligarchy" (who at no point have constituted more than five per cent of the population) over the indigenous Liberians, a weak judiciary, tribalism, disputes over land acquisition, distribution and accessibility, and a "lack of clarity and understanding of Liberia's history including its history of conflicts."

Few would have any problem with this, though one can certainly quibble. A large part of the report is taken up by interesting but somewhat extraneous discussions around concept, methodology and the personalities of those involved with the commission, and various other mundane details. The historical section, deemed the most important, is brief to the point of terseness, and it is rather problematic. It opens, bewilderingly, with a notorious quote from Hugh Trevor-Roper, a former Regius Professor of History at Oxford, dismissing the idea of African history ('it does not exist')! Perhaps the report writers should have pressed further with Trevor-Roper, who for much of his career had to fend off accusations of racism and anti-Semitism, for he elaborated his foolish thesis by arguing that before the European arrival in Africa, there was only "the gyrations of barbarous tribes in picturesque but irrelevant corners of the world." Would such a dubious authority aid the TRC's efforts in trying to include the contributions of indigenous Liberians to the development of the modern state of Liberia? Is the TRC saying that pre-settler Liberia is irrelevant?

There is truth in the following observation (appearing in the historical section): "Central to understanding the socio-political conflict and its degeneration into armed conflict in the evolving history of Liberia is the choice made by the early leadership of Liberia from colony, to commonwealth and statehood. It was a choice of purpose or political direction for the new enterprise. One option was a Euro-American orientation with the idea of a civilizing and christianizing mission at its core. The other option was to attempt to build an African nationality that blended Western and African values, as Edward Wilmot Blyden and others have advocated. The choice of the former is at the root of Liberia's yet unresolved historical problem of political identity and legitimacy. The choice, in time, alienated, marginalised, degraded not only the majority of the inhabitants of the Liberia area, but implicitly the very westernised black leaders who bought into and adopted the views derived from American colonialist sentiments."

Again, one can quibble. Blyden has recently emerged as the great intellectual and political hero of Liberia, the most important inclusive personality among the settler types (in Boima Fahnbulleh's remarkable historical novel *Behind God's Back,* published in 2005, the same point is made even more forcefully, with Blyden appearing in the novel as "Dr. Caldwell"). This is largely a myth, of course, and its appearance in the TRC report is telling. Blyden, as a highly cultured man, was certainly disdainful of the vulgarities of settler politics, and he had little time, himself a proud "unadulterated Negro," for the Mulattos who dominated early Liberian politics: his quaint racial theory had them as degenerate and effeminate, an inferior breed. But far from being a consistent spokesman on behalf of indigenous Liberians, Blyden advocated the bringing in of more blacks from America and the Caribbean. Reflecting the views of some of his European friends, he looked upon indigenous Africans as degraded and benighted – the issue of social equality with them did not arise in his mind.

Blyden himself was forced to flee Liberia by his political enemies, and he settled in Sierra Leone, where he died. Liberia remained in its state of inertia; at the end of the 19th century the settlers numbered only 25,000. When in 1874 the Liberian government decided that other groups adjacent to Monrovia would be allowed representation in the national legislature as "referees and advisers," their advice was restricted to matters involving their own ethnic groups, and they were denied the vote. It is entirely moot given their background and demographic disadvantage whether the settlers could have afforded a more inclusive state; for political purposes, history does not make room for such nuances. Liberia, in fact, was probably too weak and indigent to have expanded its writ much; by the end of the 19th century, its entire budget, about £25,000 (sterling), was less than half what its neighbour Sierra Leone was spending on education.

Liberia's fortune changed radically when in 1926 President Charles Dunbar Burgess King (who was born in Sierra Leone of settler descent) signed an agreement with the American Firestone Company to invest US$20 million in rubber plantation; the company also gave a loan of US$5 million to the government, and then took the management of the country's customs to ensure the loan was paid back. Firestone fuelled both a measure of economic growth and an extreme form of patrimonial corruption, with receipts from its taxes and royalties being controlled directly by the presidency. This ensured that the Liberian government had enough resources to ignore the overall socio-economic development of the country, as well make the presidency a potent and overwhelming force. The relationship between the Monrovia government and the indigenous population was so skewed that a League of Nations investigation in 1931 actually recommended that Liberia be deprived of its independence and colonised. In the mid-1950s, William Tubman, the embodiment of this new patrimonialism, had made the presidency utterly personalised; maintaining his personal yacht – bought at crippling cost by the indigent state – cost more than the allocation for education for Liberia's 2 million people. He was succeeded, after 27 years in power, by Tolbert, who was overthrown by the nihilistic Samuel Doe, a former master-sergeant. Under his bloodthirsty reign, Liberia dissolved into anarchy.

However fair one wants to be about Liberia's settler elite, it is clear that they, out of ignorance, avarice or existential necessity, refused to adhere to Edmund Burke's vision of a state as a partnership with its citizens in all arts and sciences, in all virtues and vices, in all endeavours great and small. And they refused to see that disenfranchisement, the relegation of a large body of people to a position that Baldwin called that of "disesteemed," leads to rage. That rage, as Baldwin saw clearly, may be "personally fruitless, but it is also absolutely inevitable; this rage, so generally discounted, so little understood … is one of the things that make history." Liberian history for the past quarter-century – from the Doe coup to the Taylor-inspired insurgencies – has been driven exactly by this rage of the disesteemed.

While the TRC report captures some of these undercurrents, the analysis often seem breezy and pat, as though what is being presented is self-evident; the writers do not even bother to make attributions like footnotes.

Attention is likely to focus on the recommendations around lustration and prosecution, but the manner in which these are made is rather irresponsible and foolish. The report notes that 'Prosecution in a court of competent jurisdiction and other forms of public sanctions are [sic] desirable and appropriate mechanisms to promote the ends of justice, peace and security, foster genuine national reconciliation and combat impunity.' And it asserts – without careful, deliberative evidence-based demonstration – that a number of groups, entities and individuals were "involved in a joint criminal enterprise or conspiracy, which planned, instigated, ordered, commanded, aided or abetted in the planning, preparation or execution" of crimes against humanity during the Liberian wars. The phrase "joint criminal enterprise" is the reductive, depoliticising and intellectually slovenly formulation of David Crane, former prosecutor of the Special Court for Sierra Leone. Its use in the TRC report that pretends to weigh the political, economical and social factors that led to the civil war in Liberia is unfortunate, and utterly inapt.

The following, deemed the "Significant Violator Groups" in the category of culpability, are well-known and deserve little comment: Charles Taylor's National Patriotic Front of Liberia (NPFL), which is found to have been responsible for most of the violations, 41 per cent; Liberians United for Reconciliation and Democracy (LURD); George Boley's Liberian Peace Council (LPC); Militia [sic]; Movement for Democracy in Liberia (MODEL); United Liberation Movement (ULIMO); Armed Forces of Liberia (AFL); Unknown [sic]; United Liberation Movement-K (ULIMO K); Independent National Patriotic Front of Liberia (INPFL); United Liberation Movement-J (ULIMO J); and Anti-Terrorist Unity (ATU). In all, 106 people, including leaders of all the warring factions, are recommended for prosecution by an extraordinary court for "gross human rights violations and war crimes." But 36 persons, except for Joe Wylie, are rather unknown characters and are exempted by the TRC from prosecution "though found to be responsible [for violations] because they cooperated with the TRC process, admitted to the crimes committed and spoke truthfully before the Commission and expressed remorse for their prior actions during the war."

Doubtless the most unexpected, and certainly the most outrageous, recommendation is the one dealing with lustration. The TRC recommended that 52 persons, who were "political leaders and financiers of different warring factions," should be barred from holding public office for 30 years. This category includes – sigh! – the current President

Ellen Johnson Sirleaf. It also includes the academic Byron Tarr, whose very useful analysis of the early stages of the war has been much cited by other academics. The list seems to come from nowhere; there is little in the entire report to suggest that most of the personalities were culpable in anything. In fact, few of the names on the list are mentioned in the actual report, making the recommendation seem rather glib and asinine. President Johnson Sirleaf appears a few times in the report, and her name is thrown about rather carelessly; we are told somewhere that "Amongst Doe's staunchest and most active political opponents in the Diaspora were Dr Amos Sawyer and Ellen Johnson Sirleaf, both victims of Doe's brutality," and that Sirleaf "led the pro-Taylor elements while Dr Amos Sawyer led the opposition to any form of engagement or support to Charles Taylor." Again, we read that as Taylor became "increasingly unpopular, he lost the popular support of the Liberian people and his traditional political allies and financiers in Liberia, including Ellen Johnson Sirleaf."

This is about all. Sirleaf was not in a leadership position at the time, and she has provided a convincing account of her dealings with Taylor, both to the TRC and in her memoirs, *This Child will be Great* (2009). Her first meeting was when "sometime in 1989" Taylor was presented to a group she belonged to in the US, the Association for Constitutional Democracy in Liberia (ACDL); the second was in a Paris hotel just before the war started in Liberia, at which Sirleaf suggests buying breakfast for Taylor and Tom Woewiyu, who had unexpectedly visited. Taylor said, "The money you spend for breakfast you could give to us." She gave them the money, adding with a touch of pathos, "It was clear to me that whatever their plans, they were not going well at the moment if they needed the price of breakfast to keep on." And finally Sirleaf ventured into Taylor territory during the war to present him with US$10,000 her group had raised, to feed his troops and civilians trapped on his side of the frontlines. Sirleaf writes that she was appalled by Taylor's viciousness and his lack of a reforming vision for Liberia. She cut her ties with Taylor after that.

This account may well be abbreviated, incomplete, but the TRC does not present an alternative narrative; it simply makes assertions, perhaps convinced that by simply doing so they would be taken at face value.

This really in a way defeats the purpose for which more than US$8 million was expended on the TRC – Sirleaf's government, as well as many other donors, was supportive throughout – over a period of two years. In fact this very dull, padded and somewhat shabby report is rescued from utter irrelevance by its being so outrageous and irresponsible in the recommendations section. Can any sensible person who has seen the immense accomplishment of the Sirleaf government since it came to power in 2006 suggest with a straight face that she is unfit for public office?

More useful and interesting is the statistical data, analysed for the TRC by the US-based charity Benetech. We learn that forced displacement accounted for the most violations, 36 per cent (or 58,849 cases), to be followed by killing at 17.1 per cent (or 28,042 direct war-related killings). This should cause some reflections on some of the casualty figures usually bandied about for the war. The TRC accepts these figures, but curiously rejects another set of statistics produced for them by Benetech, which had determined that about 60 per cent of Liberians would rather 'forgive and forget' the crimes of the past; in other words, the overwhelming majority of Liberians rejected prosecution for the offences committed during the war. I have myself recommended some kind of prosecution for the egregious crimes committed with impunity in Liberia during the war, but I found this statement by the TRC totally confusing: 'The catalogue of violations enumerated [in the report] evidences the distinct nature of violations of human rights that characterized the conflict in Liberia. Rightly so, the TRC has determined that gross violations of international human rights and humanitarian laws, egregious domestic violations and other forms of violations were very much pervasive in Liberia's several wars and armed conflict during the TRC mandated period of review.' The TRC 'determines'; so what was the point of the public hearings, the very elaborate effort to collect statements and views from across the board all over Liberia? Are these to be dismissed so glibly? This cavalier approach seriously undermines the relevance of the report itself.

5.
Sierra Leone's Truth and Reconciliation Commission[27]

Sierra Leone's South African-style Truth and Reconciliation Commission (TRC) finally submitted its long-awaited report to the government in late2004. The main report is 1,500-pages long, and there is a CD-ROM version (Vol. 4), along with transcripts of testimonies. The transcripts are more than 3,500 pages. Put together, the report is 5,000 pages long.

The report is well-organised and reader-friendly. There is an Executive Summary (of about 40 pages), which very well captures the substance of the massive report; and the main report is broken down into several sections dealing with various aspects of the decade-long war that ravaged Sierra Leone from 1991 to 2001: the historical antecedents of the war and other preceding events; the causes of the war, with a particular focus on issues of governance; the conflict itself, including military and political events; its nature, with a focus on such demented atrocities as amputations and sexual slavery; the role of external actors, and circumstances that fuelled the war, such as mineral resources; the impact of warfare on various groups, particularly on women, children, and youths; the relationship between the TRC and the Special Court for Sierra Leone; and the efforts made to help Sierra Leone reconcile with its past, including the proposed reparations programme and the National Vision for Sierra Leone, a still-inchoate project which was the direct offspring of the TRC. A set of well-detailed and cogent recommendations (including, with exquisite fitness, a call for the abolition of the death penalty) constitute a whole chapter: this section should be treated with particular urgency by the government and people of Sierra Leone.

---

[27] Znet, 14 October 2004

The Commissioners had initially planned to submit the report in October 2003. When this proved impossible—the Commission was handicapped throughout by its poor finances and by the rather serious shortfall in quality personnel—an extension was granted it in September 2003. The TRC was then to submit its report to the President in March 2004, a deadline it again failed to meet. What has been submitted, however, is rather worthy of the long wait, and a read through its thousands of pages will repay many times over. No doubt there will be questions about the report's methodology, interpretation of events, and its often idiosyncratic political and military analysis, but there is no question that the report is one of the most important documents on Sierra Leone's recent history.

Congratulations are due to the Commissioners, the diligent staff of the Commission, including its senior staff (notably Ozonia Ojielo, a brilliant human rights lawyer and former civil society activist in Nigeria, who almost single-handedly ensured that the process remained on track even after the Commission ran out of funding), the researchers, and the donor community.

MANDATE

The TRC was set up as a result of the Lome Accord of July 1999 (the highly controversial but definitive agreement that ended Sierra Leone's war), whose Article XXVI states thus: "A Truth and Reconciliation Commission shall be established to address impunity, break the cycle of violence, provide a forum for both parties and perpetrators of human rights violations, to tell their story, get a clear picture of the past in order to facilitate genuine healing and reconciliation'" On 10 February 2000, the Sierra Leone Parliament passed an Act legally setting up the Commission. The Act made provisions to compel persons to appear before the Commission where Commissioners were convinced that this would be necessary to get important statements from them. The Act described the purpose of the TRC as an instrument designed to create "an impartial body of historical record' of the war and to 'help restore the human dignity of victims and promote reconciliation." The TRC was required to conduct a year-long nationwide process of collecting testimonies and research, and to foster "inter-change(s) between victims and perpetrators." At the end of the year, the Commission was to present a report to the Sierra Leone government, which would then share the findings with the UN Security Council. A budget for the exercise was initially set at $10 million, but this was reduced to $6.5 million after potential donors complained that the earlier figure was too high. The cash-strapped Sierra Leone government was to contribute only a small fraction of this. In the event, it was not until 5 July 2002 that the TRC was finally inaugurated in Freetown.

The Commissioners and staff were from various backgrounds and of various nationalities, and they saw themselves clearly as being above the undue influence of any party to the just-ended conflict. This was an undeniable strength, but in the report they also curiously affected to be above the moral sensitivities that come naturally in such a situation. They write that it was not part of their mandate to "assess the justice of the conflict itself." This is also the position taken by the Special Court for Sierra Leone, another instrument of transitional justice in Sierra Leone— and it is one of the few things on which these two instruments agree. It is a hugely problematic position, of course. It is not that a fiercely evenhanded approach to assessing the war's protagonists and responsibility for the destruction and atrocities is inherently bad or misguided; it is just that a report like this should seriously attempt to provide a proper context in which groups emerged or acted the way they did. And this should involve, clearly, assessing the justice or rationale for which the various groups resorted to arms and did what they did.

Sifting through thousands of testimonies, mainly from victims but also from some perpetrators, the TRC sought to establish what it called "social truth," by which it meant the establishment of a kind of "consensus" about the nature of the conflict. This obviously involved making judgments about the 'personal or narrative truths' that were collected from individual testimonies, although the report is rather coy about this. It emphatically submits its findings as mainly a matter of statistical truism, which is reasonable and fair, as far as it goes. We read: "The Commission finds the RUF, the AFRC and the SLA (the Sierra Leone Army, when it operated with the AFRC) to be the primary organisations that committed violations against children. Of the violations known to the Commission with a victim with known age and alleged to have been committed by the RUF, 15.4% (3090 out of 20125 violations) was against a child. The corresponding statistic for the AFRC, (including the SLA when it operated with the AFRC), was 10.7% (603/5610). The leaderships of these organisations are held responsible for permitting the commission of gross human rights violations against children. There are no mitigating factors to justify such inhuman and cruel conduct." The report states that overall the RUF committed 60.5 % of the atrocities; the AFRC 9.8 %; the SLA 6.8 %; the Civil Defence Force (mainly Kamajors) 6 %; and ECOMOG, the Nigerian-led West African intervention force, 1 %.

As stated earlier, this statistical apportioning of blame for the violations appears reasonable and fair, as far as it goes. But since the report evokes the concept of "just war," one would expect certain judgments, of a broader more cosmic nature, to be made about responsibility for the war itself, and therefore for the atrocities that resulted from it. The war was started by the RUF, and it is arguably true that only the RUF ensured its continuation and even its character. The RUF was a predatory and self-interested, even criminal, organisation, and the report's statement that some people may argue that "those who initiated the attempts to overthrow the Momoh regime were justified in taking up arms" (an obvious reference to the RUF), betrays a certain lack of insight into how the RUF was organised and inflicted on Sierra Leone.

The TRC in fact does make strong judgments, and not only in the matter of naming prominent names and assigning responsibility (the RUF leadership is held responsible for RUF's actions; the government of Sierra Leone, including the President, is held accountable for the depredations of the CDF etc). It also makes pronouncements on what it considers caused the war, although the broadness of culpability it assigns makes such pronouncements of rather little value. It dismisses the "commonly held view, both within and outside Sierra Leone, that the Sierra Leone conflict was a war fought over diamonds' as 'only partly true." The report stresses that issues of bad governance, endemic corruption and poverty, disenchanted youth, a dictatorship that closed legitimate avenues of political expression, the dubious policies of the former colonial administration, uneven development in the country, capital punishment, a sclerotic elite, autocratic chiefs, a demented gerontocracy, patrimonial politics—all of these "laid the grounds for the war which would have taken place even without the existence of diamonds in the country." The report concludes that the "exploitation of diamonds was not the cause of the conflict in Sierra Leone, rather it was an element that fuelled the conflict," and that "diamonds were used by most of the armed factions to finance and support their war efforts."

Isn't there a non sequitur here? Did anyone ever doubt that other armed factions benefited from diamonds or used them in their war efforts? The government of Sierra Leone certainly used profits from the diamond trade to fund its war effort, as well as run the government; and the Civil Defence Force (CDF), which fought to protect civilians, also mined diamonds and used the profits to fund its activities. To make this recognition, however, is different from attempting to blur the distinction between the various groups by arguing that the RUF was just another armed faction. The war was the RUF's war, and diamonds for the RUF were more than simply an available resource to fund its war effort: they were also a principal motivation for its crucial external supporters, particularly Charles Taylor and various arms dealers, as well as most of its core fighters.

These are only preliminary comments, and the criticism here certainly do not detract from the overall value of what is, in my view, a profoundly important and well-researched document, one that should be read and evaluated with great care by all Sierra Leoneans and those interested in Sierra Leone. Below, I reproduce some important findings made by the

Commission; I highlight them because they are rather fresh, in some ways surprising, but ultimately rather reasonable and intriguing:

WHAT THE REPORT SAYS, IN ITS OWN WORDS: Most of the violations reported to the Commission were committed against adult males (59.6%, 6816 violations out of 11429). Of the victims reported to the Commission for whom age and sex are known, 66.5% (7603 out of 11429 victims) are male while 33.5% (3826 out of 11429 victims) are female. Female victims reported to the Commission comprised 31.9% of adult victims (3186 out of 10002 victims) but made up 44.9% (640 out of 1427) of the child victims....

The Commission finds the RUF, the AFRC and the SLA (when it operated with the AFRC) to be the primary organizations that committed violations against children. Of the violations known to the Commission with a victim with known age and alleged to have been committed by the RUF, 15.4% (3090 out of 20125 violations) was against a child. The corresponding statistic for the AFRC, (including the SLA when it operated with the AFRC), was 10.7% (603/5610). The leaderships of these organisations are held responsible for permitting the commission of gross human rights violations against children. There are no mitigating factors to justify such inhuman and cruel conduct...

The Commission has identified an astonishing 'factional fluidity'☐ among the different militias and armed groups that prosecuted the war. Both overtly and covertly, gradually and suddenly, fighters switched sides or established new 'units'. These 'chameleonic tendencies' spanned across all factions without exception...

The factional fluidity that defined this conflict was drawn into its sharpest focus in the latter stages of the conflict. Many of the early members of the RUF on its Southern Front in the Pujehun District reappeared as Kamajors under the banner of the CDF after 1997. Theirs was not so much a switching of sides as the identification of a new vehicle on which to purvey their notions of empowerment as civil militiamen...

The Commission finds that the RUF was responsible for more violations than any other faction during the period 1991 to 2000: 60.5% (24353 out of 40242) of all violations were attributed to the RUF. Furthermore, the RUF committed more violations than any other group during every individual year between 1991 and 2000...□

The AFRC was responsible for the second largest number of violations during the period 1991 to 2000. Some 9.8% (3950 out of 40242 violations) of all allegations made in statements to the Commission were attributed to the AFRC...□

The Sierra Leone Army (SLA) was responsible for the third largest number of violations during the same period. Some 6.8% (2724 out of 40242) of the allegations made in the statements were levelled at the SLA. 6% (2419 out of 40242) of violations alleged by the statement-makers are attributed to the CDF, and 1.5% (of violations alleged by the statement-makers are attributed jointly to the SLA and AFRC during the second quarter of 1997...

Other groups such as ECOMOG, the Special Security Division (SSD) of the Sierra Leone Police and the Guinean Armed Forces (GAF) account for less than 1% each of the recorded violations. 5.0% of the recorded violations are considered to have unknown perpetrators....

Knowledge of CDF Atrocities: The Commission finds that the Government was aware of human rights violations and abuses carried out by the CDF, through the role of its Deputy Defence Minister, Chief Samuel Hinga Norman, who served as CDF National Co-ordinator and members of the War Council at Base Zero. The Government was further kept informed through its Security Committee briefings and through reports received from ECOMOG, but failed to take steps to stop them. The Commission, accordingly, holds the Government responsible for the violations and abuses of human rights committed by the CDF...

Of the various groups that comprised the CDF, the Kamajors received the most scrutiny by the Commission as they were responsible for largest number of violations committed by the CDF after 1996. A defining characteristic of the CDF is the initiation ceremony, described by many witnesses before the Commission as entailing gross abuses and violations of human rights...

The War Council in Exile established by President Kabbah struggled to assert its mandate. Indeed, the War Council's efficacy depended largely on the extent to which its directions converged with Hinga Norman's own views…

Nonetheless, the Commission finds that the War Council and the President were fully and timeously apprised of events that were taking place on the ground in Sierra Leone during their period in exile. They did not act to stop the violations being carried out by CDF elements nor did they speak out against them. As such, they are held responsible for the acts of their agents on the ground… The failure of the pro-Government forces to halt the AFRC advance on Freetown in January 1999 represents a blunder on the part of the Government of Sierra Leone and ECOMOG. Both parties had multiple prior warnings of the impending disaster. Their joint neglect and poor analysis of the situation culminated in the wanton destruction of Freetown by bands of thugs and hooligans…

Citizenship should be acquired by birth, descent or naturalisation. Race and gender must not be a consideration in the acquisition of citizenship. The Sierra Leone Citizenship Act should be amended accordingly. This is an imperative recommendation…

Prosecution of corruption cases should be free of any scope for political interference. The Commission recommends that the Anti- Corruption Commission (ACC) should be permitted to pursue its own prosecutions in the name of the Republic of Sierra Leone. The Commission recommends that the ACC Act 2000 should be amended to include a provision deeming prosecutions undertaken by the ACC to be in the name of the Republic…

The Commission calls on the Sierra Leone Association of Journalists and the Media Commission to be more proactive in monitoring standards of journalism practiced in Sierra Leone and to establish mechanisms for effective self-regulation. These organisations can do much to advance a culture of human rights in Sierra Leone…

Part V

War on Trial

1.
Special Court begins Trials[28]

On 3 June 2004, the UN-created Special Court for Sierra Leone began prosecution of those it alleged bear "the greatest responsibility" for war crimes, violations of humanitarian law and related offenses during Sierra Leone's decade-long dirty war. It was a "solemn occasion," said the court's American prosecutor, David Crane, whose many shortcomings surely does not include modesty or under-statement. Crane summoned all of mankind to "once again [assemble] before an international tribunal to begin the sober and steady climb upwards toward the towering summit of justice." Waxing poetic—rather in the manner of high-pitched tele-evangelists of the American south—Crane declared: "The path will be strewn with the bones of the dead, the moans of the mutilated, the cries of agony of the tortured, echoing down into the valley of death below. Horrors beyond the imagination will slide into this hallowed hall as this trek upward comes to a most certain and just conclusion."

The prosecutor must surely be thinking of the depredations of Foday Sankoh, the nihilistic and self-adoring ex-corporal whose petty army, known as the Revolutionary United Front (RUF), terrorized Sierra Leone from 1991 to 2000 by crudely mutilating civilians and burning down towns? No. Sankoh died peacefully in2003. Charles Taylor, the buccaneering Liberian thug-president who helped set up the RUF after unleashing a catastrophic war on his own country? Not a chance. Taylor is hundreds of miles away from the court, in comfortable exile in the Nigerian port city of Calabar. In fact, what inspired Crane's pithy eloquence was Sam Hinga Norman, a former Sierra Leone government minister and the putative leader of the Civil Defence Force (CDF), a group of civilians who organized to liberate villages overran by the RUF,

---

[28] Znet, 6 July 2004

keep the bloodthirsty rebel force in check, and restore a democratically-elected government which had been overthrown by the rebels and rogue government soldiers. Bathos is too limited a word to describe this grandly demented exercise in how not to pursue international justice: even Joseph Conrad, with that cold eye for heroic absurdity and hypocrisy, would not have invented this.

The notion of international humanitarian law is still inchoate, evolving. But one is sure that two rules of justice will, at least in the minds of decent people, remain valid. The first is that a justice system should be fairly sure that the guilty is held to account; and the second is that a justice system should be absolutely certain that the innocent is not punished. We know that this has not always been the case. When the baronet's sister in one of Dicken's novelexclaims, on hearing of the murder of the baronet, "Far better hang wrong fellow than no fellow!" we are reminded that a certain vengefulness and zealous desire to punish others have always underpinned the modern justice system. Indeed we are reminded, as George Bernard Shaw cynically commented, that the wrong fellow is in some circumstances the right fellow to hang.

THE CHARGES

Crane's charge sheet against Norman and the two other CDF leaders—Moinina Fofana and Kondewa— is a long one. The first part is largely forensic: it describes, in colourful detail, the conditions and ideas that supposedly guided the activities of the CDF. The purpose of the CDF, we learn, was "to use any means necessary to defeat the RUF and AFRC forces and to gain and exercise control over Sierra Leone territory." The CDF sought to do this by the "complete elimination of the RUF/AFRC, its supporters, sympathizers, and anyone who did not actively resist the RUF/AFRC occupation of Sierra Leone." Specific acts of war crimes are all limited to about the end of 1997 to about April 1998—when the fighting against the rebels forces was at its most intense—and they are alleged to have included "practices of elimination" of the RUF/AFRC in Tongo Field, Kenema, Bo and Koribondo. These included "human sacrifices and cannibalism." There is also the conscription of children below the age of 15; "multiple attacks on Tongo Field and the surrounding area and towns, during which the Kamajors unlawfully killed or inflicted serious bodily harm and serious physical suffering on an unknown number of civilians and captured enemy combatants;" the killing of "collaborators", including "an unknown number of police officers" in Kenema by the Kamajors on 15 February 1998; and the so-called Black December operation, in which the Kamajors allegedly killed "an unknown number of civilians" in 1997.

Crane noted, "Despite the obvious political dimension to this conflict, these individuals are indicted for those crimes, the most grievous of acts" adding that each of the accused "acted individually and in concert with subordinates to carry out this plan, purpose or design." We are solemnly informed, in case we still do not get it, that "The light of this new day-today-and the many tomorrows ahead are a beginning of the end to the life of that beast of impunity, which howls in frustration and shrinks from the bright and shining spectre of the law. The jackals whimper in their cages certain of their impending demise. The law has returned to Sierra Leone and it stands with all Sierra Leoneans against those who seek their destruction."

Even the great scribes of the Old Testament would not better this. But how valid is the implication that the CDF leaders should even be remotely considered as "most responsible" for the recently-ended war and its almost unique atrocities? And how do we react to this odd American awakening to the necessity to address impunity and rights violations around the world?

LIKE THE RUF, LIKE THE CDF?

Sierra Leone's war started in March 1991 when a self-adoring former army corporal and photographer, Foday Saybanah Sankoh, led a petty army—of mainly Liberian rebels and a few Sierra Leonean insurgents—from territories controlled by then Liberian warlord Charles Taylor into southern and eastern Sierra Leone. Sankoh had trained in Libya with Taylor, and he fought alongside the Liberian from the start of Liberia's civil war in 1989 until intervention by West African troops, known as ECOMOG, led to a bloody stalemate in late 1990. It was then that Taylor opened another front, so to speak, in Sierra Leone by launching the Sankoh-led Revolutionary United Front rebels. The new conflict, like the one in Liberia, was characterised by vandalism and terror, and soon enough it became evident that pillage—of mainly the country's forest resources and diamond mines—was a far greater motivation than politics. Sierra Leone's feeble and corrupt army almost imploded, and a large number of its members collaborated with the RUF. Hundreds of thousands of the country's rural population were displaced by the fighting. It was out of this dreary displacement that the civil defence force, the Kamajors, mobilising from makeshift camps, and drawing upon the traditional coherence and resources of a putative hunters' guild, organized to fight back the rebels and reclaim their lost villages and towns. They soon became the only bulwark against the complete over-running of the country by the RUF—and the main saviors of Sierra Leone's new experiment in democracy.

No one can dispute that the Kamajors, an inchoate group lacking logistical support, committed excesses in its fight against the RUF and to protect the general civil population. But then the demented nature of the RUF's total warfare ensured that in order to effectively challenge them one could hardly have avoided using brutal tactics. The mealy-mouthed argument—so vigorously enunciated, with ringing and seductive familiarity, by the Special Court's prosecutors—that those combating the depredations of the rebels should not have themselves been drawn into similar excesses flows from a well known pathology: the complacent "humanitarianism" of people from more secure societies, people who in the end do little more than celebrate their own security. When the military theorist Martin van Creveld wrote that prolonged 'low-intensity' conflicts, like that which occurred in Sierra Leone, always ensures that combatants on both sides would look and act in the same way, he was stating an objective fact, not explaining away state or civil brutality.

208

What is striking about the war crimes trials going on in Sierra Leone at the moment is that, defying comprehension and every form of decent sensibility, the star accused is not a member of the RUF or one of its foreign backers but Hinga Norman, the man who provided inspiration and leadership for the civil defence forces. It simply beggars belief. One commentator on the issue, Abdul Bangura, has even gone so far as to accuse Crane of racism for this suspect failure of discernment as well as for making a number of stock statements. This is an extraordinary charge; it is far from the truth. Crane is no racist. What Crane represents is an irresistible old tragicomedy, the parable of simple and very good-natured people who substitute doctrine for knowledge, and who in the process cause great damage in good conscience. In the past they could have appeared as missionaries in colonial outposts, but they are really best represented in fiction. Conrad, in one of his famous stories—set in the bloodstained Belgian Congo—has his narrator speak of "the outraged law" coming from beyond the seas to a helpless people who had been labeled "criminals," the law appearing to them as "an insoluble mystery from the sea." This may be too cynical in this context: horrible crimes were committed in Sierra Leone, and the effort to account for them is a noble one. Mr. Pyle in Graham Greene's novel appears more appropriate: the "quiet American," a decent and very simple man, seeking to apply some crackpot theories he had learnt from a book, causes great pain with his simple mind assured that it is all for a good cause.

I do not suggest this because Crane is American, a former Pentagon lawyer. But there is something to be said about the fact that the country which is so aggressive in resisting the efforts to institutionalise an international justice mechanism is the chief backer of the limited and "hybrid" experiment that is the Sierra Leone Special Court. But then again this suggests an interesting line of speculation but is otherwise irrelevant to the point of this article, which is that in aggressively prosecuting the CDF leaders the court may not only be doing a grave injustice, it may also be doing a grave damage to Sierra Leone's future ability to defend itself if such predatory groups as the RUF were to emerge again. Who will emerge to lead the effort given the appalling example that has been made of Norman?

As for the charges, well the trial has begun and it would be in very bad taste to examine them here. But one can't help observing how suggestive the inclusion of "cannibalism" is. The narrator in the Conrad story referred to seems obsessed with the notion of Africans as cannibals. This was a strong motif in colonial self-justification. The British seemed to have been particularly determined to have it suppressed in Africa. But the testimony of a former British colonial Acting Attorney General in Sierra Leone long, long ago is worth keeping in mind. He had heard many stories of cannibal rituals in the country, he said, and had even heard vivid descriptions of cannibal acts by supposed eye-witnesses. But "No District Commissioner has ever been able to get hold" of the instruments, knives and other paraphernalia that were supposed to be integral to the rituals. In other words, he found no evidence.

But then, unfortunately, the myth stuck. Such may be the sad legacy of the Special Court for Sierra Leone, Crane's eloquence notwithstanding: "The ghosts of thousands of the murdered dead stand among us. They cry out for a fair and transparent trial-to let the world know what took place here, here in Sierra Leone. The tears of the maimed, the mutilated, and the violated will dampen these walls. These victims, their families, their towns, their districts-their country ask all of us here for a just accounting for the agony of those ten long years in the valley of death." 'Just accounting': that is not going to happen until the Nigerian President Obasanjo hands over Charles Taylor to the court, something he— another daunting mystery—seemed determined not to do.

2.

Charles Taylor: the bitterness of war, the sourness of justice[29]

I have been asked by many people about my views on the conviction, on 26 April, of Charles Taylor, Liberia's former president, for aiding and abetting Sierra Leone's Revolutionary United Front (RUF). He is the first head of state - after Admiral Doenitz, who very briefly led Germany after Hitler committed suicide, and was convicted by the Nuremburg court after WWII - to be convicted by an international court for war crimes and crimes against humanity. The RUF that Taylor supported waged a nasty bush war against successive Sierra Leonean governments from 1991 to its defeat by a combination of forces, mainly foreign, in 2001. Throughout that war, Taylor mentored the RUF and provided it with weapons and fighters; in turn, the RUF gave him diamonds looted from Sierra Leone's mines. This is the sum of the judgment against Taylor, and it narrowly reflects the argument that I have been making for over a decade now.

Sierra Leone's war started in March 1991 when Foday Saybanah Sankoh, a self-aggrandising former army corporal, led a ragtag army from territory controlled by Taylor, then an insurgent leader in Liberia, into southern and eastern Sierra Leone. Like Taylor, Sankoh had trained in Libya and, according to the trial judgment, met Taylor there. The judges, however, rejected the prosecution's overdrawn argument that Taylor and Sankoh "made common cause" in Libya to wage wars in West Africa. The judgment accepted the prosecution's submission that Taylor facilitated the training of RUF recruits in Liberia and helped launch the RUF's war, noting that Taylor's National Patriotic Front of Liberia (NPFL) forces "actively participated" in the RUF's initial invasion in March 1991. (*Witness to Truth*, Sierra Leone's Truth and Reconciliation report of 2004, estimated that as many as 1,600 NPFL fighters were involved in the early phase of the Sierra Leonean war, or about 80 per cent of the RUF forces. This grew to 2,000 within a few months of the invasion.)

---

[29] Pamzazuka, *2012-05-02, Issue 583*

However, striking a balance between the prosecution's claim that Taylor "effectively controlled" and led the RUF at this point, and Taylor's claim that only former NPFL members joined Sankoh and that he had nothing to do with the RUF after the Sierra Leone invasion, the judgment delicately noted that the prosecution did not prove beyond reasonable doubt that Sankoh took orders from Taylor - or that Taylor participated in the planning of the invasion.

This point was always a difficult legal one, not least because the trial was not about the crime of aggression (which had not even been defined by the time Taylor faced the court). The indictment period did not even cover the origins of the war - the temporal jurisdiction of the court is from November 1996 to the official end of the war in 2002. Compounding this problem was the fact that the most credible person that would have definitively testified to this would have been Sankoh, but he died long before Taylor faced the court. In fact, it is a testimony to the tenacity and industry of the prosecution that it was able to sufficiently prove even the crime of aiding and abetting, since Taylor had effectively eliminated key witnesses to that crime. He allegedly had Sam Bockarie, his key link to Sankoh and the RUF during the period of the indictment, murdered in Liberia shortly after Bockarie was indicted. Johnny Paul Koroma, a notorious Sierra Leonean coup maker who also dealt intimately with Taylor, simply disappeared: he was also allegedly murdered either in Liberia or Ivory Coast on Taylor's orders after his indictment. These events must count as the most comprehensive and effective evidence-tampering in an international war crimes trial ever.

I have always thought that the prosecution's invocation of the notion of "joint criminal enterprise" (JCE) was ill-advised, and successive judgments by the court rubbished the concept. This concept was first used by the International Criminal Tribunal for former Yugoslavia (1991-1999). It considers each member of an organised group individually responsible for crimes committed by that group within the "common plan or purpose." The Appeals Chamber of the ICTY decided on 21 May 2003 that "insofar as a participant shares the purpose of the joint criminal enterprise (as he or she must do) as opposed to merely knowing about it, he or she cannot be regarded as a mere aider and abettor to the crime which is contemplated."

The concept was roundly rejected by the court in the trial of the leaders of the admirable Civil Defence Forces (CDF), since "the evidence led by the Prosecution in this case to show a joint criminal enterprise [is] insufficient to prove its existence against those named persons beyond reasonable doubt." Conviction around the concept was entered only in the case of the leaders of the RUF, and even here the judgment involving the pathetic and roguish Augustine Gbao was problematic, looking very much like guilt by association. Though the prosecution did not establish Gbao's direct involvement in crimes during the war, the judges concluded that because he was the RUF's "ideological trainer," Gbao "significantly contributed to the [Joint Criminal Enterprise], as the leadership of the RUF relied on the RUF ideology to ensure and to enforce the discipline and obedience of its forces to the RUF hierarchy and its orders, this being a factor which contributed to the furtherance of the Joint Criminal Enterprise." Justice Shireen Fisher dissented, noting that Gbao's conviction "abandons the keystone of JCE liability as it exists in customary international law." Gbao was nevertheless given a global sentence of 20 years and flown to jail in Rwanda. Many observers feared that the same approach would be used to convict Taylor.

The prosecution had argued that Taylor had made a "common cause" with Sankoh to invade Sierra Leone and loot is diamond reserves, and that the RUF's terror campaign was a direct result of this blood pact. Taylor's Defence made no effort to deny Taylor's support for the RUF, but it stated that "diamonds only financed the procurement of arms and ammunition" for the RUF between 1998 and 2001. The Defence denied that diamonds were the reasons why Taylor supported the RUF, stating in the Final Brief what no one has challenged: that the RUF diamond mining began "post the invasion" which happened in March 1991. It stated: "There is no evidence of any discussions relating to diamonds pre the Sierra Leonean invasion to suggest that the invasion might have been motivated by a desire to pillage Sierra Leone's diamonds." The point was that the Defence's key argument was not that Taylor did not support the RUF, but that he did not do so either as part of JCE or with "an underlying intention to cause terror." The Defence contends that there was a "purely political motive" for Taylor's support of the RUF war, which may be immoral but certainly not illegal in international law (since the law of aggression was not at issue).

The judgment on 26 April broadly agrees with this, dismissing the notion of JCE as it involved Taylor's role. But while the judgment agreed with Taylor that he and Sankoh had "a common interest in fighting common enemies" - the Liberian anti-Taylor insurgent group ULIMO and the Sierra Leonean government supporting ULIMO - this is actually tangential to the case, since the period (1991-1992) falls outside the temporal jurisdiction of the court.

Of profound importance to many people in Sierra Leone and elsewhere is the finding involving Taylor's role in the events surrounding the Johnny Paul Koroma coup in 1997, and in particular the resurgence of rebel forces leading to the devastating attacks on Freetown in January 1999. Close to 6,000 people were killed, including hundreds of Nigerian peace-enforcement troops, and the hands of dozens of people were crudely amputated by the rebel forces during those attacks. The judges established Taylor's direct role in instigating the attacks on diamond areas of Kono as well as the subsequent attack on Freetown. Here the judgment uses the word 'instructed' to describe Taylor's orders to Johnny Paul Koroma and Sam Bockarie. With his eyes ever on diamonds, Taylor "emphasised" to Bockarie that taking over Kono was more important than attacking Freetown at that point. He also told Bockarie to make the attack "fearful." As a result, the demented Bockarie, who called himself Maskita, announced "Operation No Living Thing," with predictable results. More crucially, the judgment establishes that Taylor arranged "a large shipment of arms and ammunition from Burkina Faso" to the rebels in Makeni; these arms were instrumental in the attacks on Kono and later Freetown. It is important to note that the UN Panel of Experts on Liberia had established in 2000 that the arms were supplied by Victor Bout, recently convicted on unrelated charges in the US, and that they were presumably paid for by diamonds from the RUF in Sierra Leone.

It is of interest that a number of names appearing in the judgment as playing a facilitating role in this sordid and murderous business were neither indicted by the court nor even invited as witnesses: Gaddafi,

Ibrahim Bah, and, of course, Blaise Campaore (who as president of Burkina Faso surely knew and supported it all).

Also of interest has been the unenthusiastic - sometimes even hostile - reaction of a good number of Liberians to the conviction of their former president. This is partly because Taylor was not charged with his many crimes in Liberia but for his role in supporting a foreign war. But there are quite a few Liberians who actually do not think that Taylor should have been held accountable for his crimes at all, local or international. This reflects a deep-rooted culture of impunity in the country. I lived in Liberia for nearly two years during its truth and reconciliation process, and attended dozens of testimonies there. Many of these, by former commanders in Taylor's NPFL, proudly narrated how they participated in attacks inside Sierra Leone, and how they were fully supported by Taylor to do so. None of them to my knowledge expressed remorse about what they did - but then none of them, with the quirky exception of General Butt Naked, apologised to Liberians for the atrocities they committed in Liberia itself.

Was it all necessary, this expensive and long trial? I think that the proceedings were unnecessarily prolonged by overpaid judges and lawyers, and I think that the court erred very badly in indicting and convicting the leaders of the CDF. The Taylor trial alone reportedly cost $250 million, nearly six times more than the total revenue officially generated by Liberia in 2003 ($44.2 million), the year that Taylor was forced to relinquish power. Still, I think that the conviction of Taylor - as nasty a gangster as ever become president in Africa - is a signal event, something we should all celebrate in our region.

As I write this, I remember the day that Taylor was helicoptered into the Special Court compound in Freetown. I stood among the small crowd of people there that evening. A woman in the crowd turned to me after Taylor was sent to his cell and said, apropos of a statement made by Taylor in 1990, "Well, he told us that we in Sierra Leone will taste the bitterness of war. We did. But now he will taste the sourness of justice." The sourness of justice: that indeed is a lovely phrase there.

3.

The Special Court for Sierra Leone – A Final Word[30]

On 26 September 2013, the Special Court for Sierra Leone made its last significant decision when its Appeals Chamber upheld the 50-year sentence of former Liberian President Charles Taylor. Presided over by Samoan Judge Richard Lussick, it had in April 2012 found Mr. Taylor guilty of five counts of crimes against humanity, five counts of war crimes and one count of other serious violations of international humanitarian law perpetrated by Sierra Leone's Revolutionary United Front (RUF) rebels. Taylor was convicted for his role in murder, rape, other inhumane acts, acts of terrorism, pillage, outrages upon personal dignity, and recruiting children under 15 as soldiers. The 2493-page judgement, including annexes of maps, sources, and a long table of authorities, found that Mr. Taylor was the main backer of the RUF, and was aware of its atrocities at the time. He was guilty, in other words, of aiding and abetting the RUF.

Taylor was transferred to a prison in the UK on 15 October 2013 to serve the remainder of his sentence – the result of an agreement signed between the court and the UK government on 10 July 2007. By the rules of the UK judicial system, Taylor has 43 years left to serve and will only be eligible for early release after serving two-thirds of his sentence, at which point he will be 91. He is 65.

This was a verdict with important international implications. Taylor was the first head of state, after Germany's Admiral Doenitz (who was convicted by the Nuremburg court after WWII) to be convicted by an international court for war crimes and crimes against humanity. But though now hailed as one of the landmark achievements of the Special Court, this was hardly anticipated by some of the court's creators. The same is true of the court's other important achievements, including the

---

[30] Published by *African Renewal* 24 March 2014; and *Global Times* (Freetown)

first-ever convictions for attacks against UN peacekeepers; convictions for forced marriage as a crime against humanity; and for the recruitment of children for combat. They are testimonies to the resourcefulness and determination of the court's prosecutors and judges, but also to the rather protean nature of its mandate. Some of the court's creators fretted about its apparent overreaching, and none was pleased that it lasted three times longer than planned and cost many more times. For these reasons, and there are others, it is an experiment which is highly unlikely to be tried again.

UN Secretary-General Ban Ki-Moon on 30 December 2013 hailed the court's contribution towards establishing peace and stability in Sierra Leone, as well as its "impressive legacy" in helping the global quest for "an age of accountability." Ban has a point. But in Sierra Leone, the court is seen as a result, not the cause, of the country's peace and stability; and its record on accountability, despite the singular charm of Taylor's conviction, may strike many critics as overblown.

Money and Control

The Special Court for Sierra Leone was established by an agreement signed between the UN and the government of Sierra Leone on 16 January 2002, the month that Sierra Leone's civil war was officially declared ended. Meant to last for only three years with an initial budget pegged at $75 million, the court formally closed in December 2013 after spending about $300 million dollars.

The Court's customs-made compound in Freetown is a massive fortification of high barbed-wired walls with its own prison house and, while it was in operation, with rifled Mongolian soldiers standing at guard. The premises cost $3.5 million, minus the land. Opening it in 2004 Sierra Leone's then President, Tejan Kabbah, was enthusiastic. Sierra Leone, he said, had become the first country to establish "an independent mixed court to bring to justice persons responsible for serious violations of international humanitarian law and national criminal law."

Kabbah, a lawyer, had clearly given serious thought to the issue. In his letter (of 12 June 2000) to the UN Secretary-General calling for the setting up of the Court, he had conceptualised the court as "a symbol of the rule of international law, especially at a time when some State and non-State actors are increasingly displaying, shamelessly, contempt for the principles of international law, including international humanitarian law and human rights law." It is of interest, therefore, to note that Mr. Kabbah would, in his memoirs (*Coming from the Brink*, published in 2011), profess to be "stunned and upset" by some of the court's activities. Mr. Kabbah's buyer's regret can, of course, be dismissed as an example of a parable of wishes granted: like King Midas, he merely got it in excess.

The point is that once a prosecutor – an energetic, not to say theatrical, American Defence Department lawyer, David Crane – was appointed, Mr. Kabbah realised that all pretence that he was even marginally in control of the court was effectively repudiated. We now know that Mr. Kabbah's useful letter to UN was only that: useful as a convenient cover for the driving forces behind the court. David Scheffer tells us in *All the Missing Souls* (Princeton University Press 2012) that the US and the UK were those driving forces. He was the first US ambassador for war crimes throughout Clinton's second term, and it was he, in fact, who decided on the character of the court. It was to be *sui generis*, meaning that it was to be very different from all other tribunals. It was to be wholly specific and limited to the Sierra Leonean context. It wasn't to have any overarching ambition. The Special Court was to "correct the perceived excesses of the *ad hoc* tribunals and shrink the enforcement of international criminal justice to a manageable and sustainable size." This was a dig at the UN tribunal for Rwanda, which was being widely criticised for being antiseptic and dilatory, and which has now spent over a billion dollars and hardly made any important conviction.

Particular effort was made to present the Special Court only as UN-backed, and not as an instrument of the UN, to distinguish it from the International Criminal Court (to which many powerful figures in the US remain anathema) and the tribunals for Yugoslavia and Rwanda. It wasn't given the status of Article VII, which would have made its funding and compliance with its rulings mandatory as a UN Security Council instrument. The UN Secretary-General wanted all the funds for the court to be set aside before starting, but this was rebuffed by the US and UK, the better to keep control over the court's operations and decisions. It was to be funded by voluntary contributions of member states, which meant that those with the most geopolitical interests in the subregion, US and UK, would be the key funders. The court was to be governed by a management committee which comprised (prominently) these countries as well as Nigeria, which also had an important interest, as the key peace-enforcer in Sierra Leone, in the decisions of the court. The statute of the court ruled out prosecution of peacekeeping troops – something which, given the evidence of apparent gratuitous killings of civilians by Nigerian peace-enforcement soldiers in the widely-circulated documentary, *Cry Freetown*, was a little suspect. Grumbling about all this to the present writer in 2003, Robin Vincent (UK), the court's first Registrar, referred to "our pathetic lack of international clout."

The Special Court was to be a hybrid, a joint enterprise of the government of Sierra Leone and the UN. In truth, however, this was limited to a provision in the court's statute for the Sierra Leone government to appoint the deputy prosecutor and two of its six judges. Article 8 (2) of that statute stated that the Special Court "shall have primacy over the national courts" [of Sierra Leone] and that "[a]t any stage of the procedure, the Special Court may formally request a national court to defer to its competence in accordance with the present Statute…" This clause was evoked later, when some of the defendants before the court raised objections that it violates the Sierra Leonean constitution, which gives primacy to the country's Supreme Court. The judges of the Special Court argued that "it is immaterial to the validity of the Special Court Agreement and to Sierra Leone's obligation under the Agreement whether the conclusion of the Agreement by the Government of Sierra Leone was not in fact in conformity with the Constitution."

Critics soon began to note that a judge at the court, paid $240,000 tax free per annum plus huge allowances, was earning several times more than the President of Sierra Leone. The office of the prosecutor's annual budget of more than $4 million was more than the budget of the Sierra Leone Supreme Court. The Court's permanent staff of 422, many of them foreign nationals, meant, in fact, that about 70 per cent of its entire budget was used up as salaries and bonuses for these employees. Reflecting on this awkward imbalance, Stephen Rapp, a former chief prosecutor of the court, said in an interview with *Time* magazine (September 2009) shortly after he left to take a job in the Obama administration that this was a concern. We were, he said, "conducting justice in a comfortable courtroom with long trials and well-paid attorneys. Prisoners had single cells, and they had committed the worst crimes. A mile away in the local prison there were simply no resources. Cases can't go forward, witnesses are lost, and people stay in detention for many years at a stretch. [If I was] to do it over, I would try to develop a court within the national system. That would be my preference. Maybe not a court that costs $30 million a year like the Special Court, but an appropriate court."

The procedurally languorous and expensive Special Court, in other words, was inappropriate in the circumstances: this was a most damning of criticism.

"Most Responsible"

In conceptualising what he was told should be a modest enterprise, Ralph Zacklin, the UN's lawyer who negotiated the court with the Sierra Leone government, contrived the notion of "most responsible" for war crimes to be the focus of court's prosecutorial efforts. In a report to the Security Council in October 2000, he defined those "most responsible" as "obviously including the political or military leadership," as well as "others in command authority down the chain of command… judging by the severity of the crime or its massive scale."

Though the Sierra Leonean war started in 1991, the Court decided that prosecution would be made only for crimes committed after the signing of the first (failed) peace agreement, the Abidjan Accord of November 1996. On 7 March 2003, David Crane announced the first set of indictments, which included members of Revolutionary United Front (RUF), which started the war, and the Sierra Leone Army and the admirable Civil Defence Force (CDF), which resisted the RUF. In all, the court would indict 14 persons, of which two – the RUF leader Foday Sankoh and his former commander Sam Bockarie died before their trial began – and a third, Hinga Norman, the putative leader of the CDF and cabinet minister in President Kabbah's government, died during his trial. Taylor, who had gone into voluntary exile in 2003, was handed over to the Court in 2006, and was tried in The Hague under a special arrangement.

Clearly the indictment of persons from all armed groups which participated in the war in Sierra Leone was meant to create an impression of even-handedness but it puzzled many in Sierra Leone. In the popular imagination, the CDF was a heroic civil militia which battled to protect civilians and reinstate the legitimate government of Mr. Kabbah after it was overthrown in 1997.

The proceedings of the court, as well as its judgments, benchmarked a problematic new legal contrivance: "Joint Criminal Enterprise" or JCE. This concept, first used by the International Criminal Tribunal for former Yugoslavia (1991-1999), considers each member of an organised group individually responsible for crimes committed by that group within the "common plan or purpose." It is an ingenious way of de-legitimising leaders of violent groups in poor countries, and, as many critics have noted, it can easily translate into guilt by association.

It is little wonder that the court entered convictions in all the cases it tried – an extraordinary achievement indeed!

Legacy

At the formal closing ceremony of the court, UN Under-Secretary-General for Legal Affairs and UN Legal Counsel Miguel de Serpa Soares hailed this achievement as "a landmark, not only for the Special Court, but also for international criminal justice in general."

An important argument for the Special Court's legacy in Sierra Leone and West Africa is that it demonstrated that the law is no respecter of persons, and that no one, however powerful, is immune from it. However, many people implicated in the Mr. Taylor's crimes in Sierra Leone escaped justice. Burkina Faso's President Blaise Campaore's role in supporting Mr. Taylor and the RUF is documented in the trial judgment on Mr. Taylor, but he was never indicted or even called as a witness. Ditto the late Libyan leader Gaddafi. Surely, the court was a geopolitical mechanism, and although the fetish of the law as blind and equal is all very well, the court excused President Kabbah from testifying – even though his testimony would have been of immense material and symbolic importance in the trial of the CDF (which he helped organise up).

As important as Mr. Taylor's conviction and sentencing are, it is unclear what impact his case would have on powerful politicians in the region. The point is that Mr. Taylor was tried for supporting a foreign war, not for the terrible crimes he committed in his own country. Liberia's civil war, fought about the same time as Sierra Leone's, was far more destructive than the latter; it certainly killed far more people (about 200,000 to Sierra Leone's 75,000). But no one has faced justice for the immense atrocities committed in Liberia, which have been documented by the country's Truth and Reconciliation Commission in a report in 2009. Perhaps more pertinent, several UN reports have documented Rwanda's role in supporting destructive and predatory "rebel" activities in eastern Democratic Republic of Congo – exactly the kind of thing for which Mr. Taylor is now serving a long jail sentence. President Paul Kagame sits pretty in Kigali.

The struggle to combat impunity in Africa, in other words, is still an uphill one, despite the great strides made by the Special Court for Sierra Leone. Perhaps the Residual Court which has now replaced it in Sierra Leone can make a useful contribution in this direction by conducting a major continent-wide study of what may be needed to entrench the values of the rule of law in Africa.

Part VI

War on Screen

1.
'Man Den Nor Glady'O': A film[31]

Dramatic atrocities, extreme human suffering and the cruelties and psychosis of dirt poverty and slum life make for memorable documentaries, and the Sierra Leone civil war (1991-2002) combined all of these in excess. Man Den Nor Glady'O, a 57-minute documentary produced by the charmingly named Rice N Peas, an alternative London-based production company, is the latest to relentlessly focus on these vulgar aspects of the country's recent and current condition. The film maker – who is both narrator and director - is one Ishmail Blagrove, a Caribbean British (or Black British) journalist who previously worked for the BBC.

Blagrove brings a passionate and affectionate tone to the subject, and he is most convincing when he is portraying the dereliction and disenchantment of young people in their depressed environments. The young people that Blagrove meets – some in their slums, some secondary school students scrounging in someone else's veranda to study because the house happens to be the only one in the area providing electricity (Blagrove was staying there, so he had a generator on all night), some in the diamond mines in Tongo, eastern Sierra Leone – are articulate, oddly high-spirited, and are a striking reminder, if this were necessary, of the terrible disillusionment which continues to make Sierra Leone a highly fragile state. Blagrove is at his best here: he allows them to speak, some even debating in a refreshingly informed way the democratic choices that the country faces. The film's title, Man Den Nor Glady'O (a Krio word meaning The People Are Not Happy) is fully realized here. This part of the film should be used as an instruction manual for the politicians and hustlers who have contributed to making the country such a blighted place.

---

[31] Znet, August 21, 2006

Blagrove, however, has a bigger ambition. Here is what he says about the making of the film in a promotional interview published on the website of his production company (www.ricenpeas.com): "Man Den Nor Glady'O "is documentary about how the United Nations and other international supporting bodies dealt with the consequences of war in Sierra Leone but failed to deal with the causes. So although the guns are presently silent, the issues of poverty, corruption and bad governance are still endemic and may yet again be the igniting factors of a future conflict," he said. Blagrove had wanted to do a story like this when he shot Blood Diamonds for the BBC in 2001, but the BBC "placed restrictions" on him because the corporation wanted a story about diamonds. The BBC wanted to do a simple, focused story. Blagrove, on the hand, wanted to do a story about "why the war started." His intention here is to "make the story I wished to make originally and in the process correct some of the fallacies that have permeated the public's perceptions about Sierra Leone: namely that this was a war fought for control of diamonds." In his view, the war "began as a campaign to eradicate the corrupt and inept practices that had forced this mineral rich nation to the bottom of the international development chart. It later mutated into an anarchic free-for-all, governed by complex variables of factional and tribal loyalties."

On the evidence of Man Den Nor Glady'O, the BBC was right, and Blagrove, in spite of his necromantic appeal, seriously confuses and conflates – not to say simplifies – the issues he takes on.

The film focuses almost entirely (as a cause of the war) on corruption – a very important and vexed issue, but also a catch-all trope that therefore explains nothing. Indeed the key evidence that Blagrove gives for his quite seductive assertion that the war "began as a campaign to eradicate" corruption is an interview with Fatou Sankoh, one of the wives of the late Revolutionary United Front (RUF) leader Foday Saybanah Sankoh! Mrs. Sankoh is Senegalese, and she first came to Sierra Leone after the 1999 Lome Accord that, at least formally, ended the war. Why her view, or indeed the view of any of those associated with the rebel group, can be taken at face value is not made clear. The fact is that the RUF started its war in 1991, and only published "Footpaths to Democracy" – which must be considered, in the absence of any other document, its manifesto – in 1995, well after thousands of people had already been killed. It was written by two outsiders (Ghanaians), and in its denunciation of corruption and poor governance (not to mention the indulging in environmental romance) is certainly an elaborate ex post facto rationalisation.

There is no hint of the role of outsiders – the likes of Charles Taylor, the arms dealers and diamond smugglers – in the conflict. This, of course, is a core part of Blagrove's aim: to show that the war was a purely internal matter: a war fought by Sierra Leoneans who were disenchanted with a corrupt state. I think that there is merit in showing that bad governance contributed in making the war possible, and to focus on its manifestations. But corruption is only one of the manifestations of bad governance, and in the view of this reviewer not the most important. The focus on corruption is too pat, too easy, and it certainly is more caricature than serious analysis. In any case, the film fails to show how corruption works or what form it takes: all it relies on is interviews with a few young people (whose views should be obvious), a few politicians (actually only Vice President Solomon Berewa and opposition politician Charles Margai), and the activist Zainab Bangura. The BBC's 1990 Trade Slaves, which shows how local politicians connive with foreign mining companies to rip off Sierra Leone, is far more illuminating in this respect.

I have already hinted at Blagrove's skewed methodology. His idea of illumination – showing that corruption is really the core problem in Sierra Leone – is to relentlessly focus on deprived communities in Sierra Leone (his favourite is Kroo Bay, the worst slum in Sierra Leone, which however contains probably less than 10,000 people: Abidjan's slum, not to mention the far more horrible slum in Nairobi, has more than one million), and to interview its inhabitants about the state of the country, which he then contrasts with the more optimistic views of Berewa. Berewa's views are then contrasted with Margai's or Bangura's, as though all of these should be given equal weight. On the question of corruption, Berewa notes, deliberately and somewhat animatedly (as though relishing the self-parody) that the government's commitment to rooting out corruption can be seen in the setting up of the Anti-Corruption Commission (ACC); to which Zainab Bangura responds, a few minutes later, that the ACC was in fact set up as a result of pressure from external donors, and that in any case it is ineffective. Margai, for his part, repeats his formulaic talk about poor leadership and his desire to provide a better one: in the background are his supporters chanting about the braces-wearing lawyer as "Our Mandela."

When a student states that his house had electricity "last night," and is told by his comrades that that's because he lives in Aberdeen "where the politicians live," Blagrove does not show us Aberdeen (or the more prosperous Hill Station or Juba); in fact he does not show any prosperous area of Sierra Leone. This clearly robs his viewers of context. Anyone watching this film would be forgiven to conclude that Sierra Leone is one sprawling slum. How can anyone make sense of the corruption the film so hysterically talks about?

At the end of the film – shown at Tricycle in Kilburn, London, on 11 August – Blagrove exhorts viewers to contribute to a fund he has set up to support a few people who appear in the film, the students and slum dwellers shown. Then we know what the film is for: a sop to our finer instincts, a call for charity. So the problem of bad governance, after all, can be solved by pumping a bit of money into the slums of Sierra Leone.

The idea of charity in its present form developed in Victorian Britain as a result of the well-held fear of the poor by aristocratic Britain. But can it really be a substitute for fundamental programmes of social reforms? The Marxist playwright Bertolt Brecht exhibited some cruelty when he sneered at the idea of "a bed for the night" (his rejection of charity), and the (now) neo-conservative French philosopher Bernard Henri Levy may have gone too far when he dismissed charity as a form of "neurosis" and an abdication of politics. But one feels that these positions are more to the point when one places them side by side with Blagrove's.

Man Den Nor Glady'O makes an important commentary of a somewhat unintentional nature: it leaves one perplexed why a government, any government, seem so incapable, or unwilling, to provide reliable electricity and running water for, at the very least, its capital city. This speaks more of incompetence and neglect than corruption. But of course it is corruption of a different, more visceral, nature.

2.
Blood Diamond: A Film[32]

For fleeting moments almost every decade now, the rich world tends to embrace Africa – a continent badly wracked by poverty, wars and related crises – as its pet project. Africa as the object of the fantasies of the West is an old pathology, and it is not limited to the entertainment industry – though Hollywood has represented its most crude and egregious form in recent decades. Stalked by the disaster of Iraq, British Prime Minister Tony Blair (who, to be fair, cannot by any means be accused of prior indifference to Africa) embraced the old continent with renewed vigour, in 2005 producing "Our Common Interest," a sprawling, well-meaning document which sets out detailed plans for wiping out African poverty and related crises. Less than two years later, the document is all but forgotten.

Africa, however, has not been, at least by Hollywood. By the end of 2006, Africa became "suddenly hot" to the entertainment industry, to use the appropriately frivolous words of the New York Times. Before the end of the year, the continent somehow managed to attract the interest of big name stars – and therefore big media – beginning with Bono, then Clay Aiken, Jessica Simpson, Angelina Jolie and Brad Pitt, George Clooney and a few others. Even Madonna, not usually associated with high-mindedness, was "suddenly casting an ice-blue eye toward Africa" (this is from the New York Times), that year famously adopting a child from Malawi. Ed Zwick and Leonardo di Caprio and Jennifer Connelly took the pathology a step higher (or lower), coming from nowhere and seeming to adopt a whole country, Sierra Leone. Their "Blood Diamond," a film that purports to recreate the horrors that befell Sierra Leone mainly in 1990s, came out just before Christmas. The producers of this film, which makes the word narcissism inadequate, claim that the intention is to save Sierra Leone (and countries like it) from the predatory degradation of diamond hunters and their wretched native allies who pressgang children into their militia and commit unspeakable atrocities.

---

[32] Znet, 13 February 2007

There was a time, a few years back, when films like "Blood Diamond" would have been most welcome, not least by the long-suffering people of Sierra Leone. The diamond-fueled war in the country began in 1991, but scarcely got a mention in most of the world's media until 1999, after fighters of the demented Revolutionary United Front (RUF), a criminal, nihilistic group, attacked and nearly destroyed Freetown, the country's capital. Their campaign was distinguished by gratuitous attacks on civilians, including the crude mutilations of women and children. A large UN force, 17,500 strong, backed by some British troops, was then sent in, and two years later succeeded in disarming most of the militias. In 2002, with the successful conduct of nation-wide democratic elections, the war was declared over. Most estimates put the number of those killed at 70,000; well over two-thirds of the country's infrastructure, already seriously troubled by the time the war started, was destroyed during the conflict.

It is nearly five years since the war ended, and the country is planning to conduct its second democratic elections, in July. Sierra Leone's economy has registered marked improvement: growth for the past two years has been at 7 per cent. Sierra Leone's critical diamond industry, while still problematic, is much improved. In 2006, after rigorous application of the international control system, the Kimberley Process Certification Scheme (KPCS), Sierra Leone officially exported over $140 million worth of diamonds, about the same as in the previous year, and doubling that for 2004. In 1999, at the height of the war, official export was slightly more than $1 million; needless to say, most of the country's diamonds were then stolen and smuggled by the RUF and its allies, through Liberia and into the international diamond market. In return, the RUF was showered with weapons, with which they killed and maimed defenceless women and children.

That diamonds, universal symbol of love, can actually be implicated in hate and destruction and frenzied violence is a highly compelling story. And "Blood Diamond," featuring Leonardo di Caprio as a charismatic and gruff South African diamond smuggler and mercenary against the backdrop of larger intrigues and all-consuming violence, is, by any measure, a compelling thriller. But since Zwick makes very large claims for the film – as a "socially-conscious" effort, as something more profoundly cerebral than the usual Hollywood offerings of tear-filled love or mad lust violence – 'Blood Diamond' has to be evaluated as such.

I feel even more convinced saying this because "Blood Diamond" has been immediately preceded or followed by a number of other lesser known efforts, some of them offering starkly different, sub-revisionist versions of what Sierra Leone went through during its war. There was Ismail Blagrove's "Man Den Nor Glady'O," produced by a London-based company, which rather obliquely disputes the popular claim that the war was all about diamonds; and there has been the stupid film, "Empire in Africa," produced by a Frenchman named Philippe Diaz, which actually shows the RUF thugs as misunderstood and romantic heroes who were thwarted by murderous UN troops and corrupt local officials (Diaz's key informant, who appears throughout this film as interviewee, is the drunken and insipid RUF commando Mike Lamin, for whom the word wretched might have been invented.) Just before the year ended, History Channel produced "Blood Diamonds," an excellent documentary which should be viewed by anyone interested in the subject. Soon to be shown will be "Bling," produced by the New York-based Article 19 Films. "Bling," on which I marginally cooperated, tells the Sierra Leone diamond story by using American rap artists, juxtaposing their vulgar use of diamond products ("bling") and the destruction and terror that diamonds have caused in Africa. A Canadian company, Kensington Studio, will also be showing "Diamond Road;" since I know the producers and have somewhat followed what they are doing, I can say that "Diamond Road" will probably be more exalted and comprehensive that the previous films.

"Blood Diamond" (notice that it is singular) centres around a single pink diamond which had been found and hidden in the bush by Solomon Vandy (Djimon Hounsou) while mining under the RUF's grim watch. Vandy had recently been violently enlisted into the RUF's army of miners after his capture in a brutal attack on his village which left many dead and his family (including his much loved son) captured and taken away. Danny Archer (Di Caprio) learns about this diamond while in a crowded cell (after his capture by Sierra Leone government troops as he tries to smuggle diamonds through the skin of a goat) which also features both Vandy and the rebel commando who saw him hide the diamond (they were both immediately after captured by government troops).

Archer works for bigger interests (De Beers, the giant diamond conglomerate, is hinted at but never mentioned by name), but his interest is purely himself. Intrigues and bloodshed follow more intrigues and bloodshed (one of the film's merits is its quite realistic portrayal of attacks by RUF fighters). Archer and Vandy agree to make a trip together to the rebel-infested area where the diamond is hidden; incredibly they are successful (even though a band of South African mercenaries, hired by the government, are trying to kill them to take the diamond for themselves). But Archer is critically wounded; he couldn't make the trip out with Vandy and his son (who had been found already a RUF fighter). Before all this, Archer had enlisted a beautiful Western journalist he had met at a sleazy bar (which looks quite like the famous Paddy's Bar in Freetown), Mandy (Jennifer Connelly). Mandy had been in the country for sometime, but she is almost completely uninterested in the country's people, its politics or history. She is obsessively interested only in the diamond story, believing that she would end the war by simply showing to the Western world – prime consumers of diamonds – that the diamonds they value as symbols of love were in fact causing death and destruction in Africa. Once Westerners realise this, they would stop buying diamond products (valued at nearly $70 billion a year), and rebels like the RUF which fund their armies with proceeds from diamonds would be starved of funds and collapse. She is clearly not being treated with irony. Although she looks very much the part of a starry-eyed fool, the simplicity is not hers; it is the film's core defect.

Now there is absolutely no doubt that diamonds helped fund, and therefore fuelled and prolonged, the war in Sierra Leone (as they did that in Angola). This aspect of Sierra Leone's tragic recent past has been exhaustively studied, following "The Heart of the Matter: Sierra Leone, Diamonds and Human Security", co-authored (with Ian Smillie and Ralph Hazleton) by this writer in 2000. The study exposed the unregulated nature of the international diamond trade at the time, documenting evident smuggling of Sierra Leone's diamonds by the RUF through Liberia (under Charles Taylor, now an indicted war criminal), which then exported the gems as its own. As reaction to this study (as well as a UN report which it precipitated) showed, Mandy's approach, on the face of it, is utterly reasonable: the outside world may not able to do anything about the degraded politics of Sierra Leone that helped breed the nihilism so much in evidence in the film, but it can do something about diamonds – and ultimately this (along with thousands of UN troops) would be crucial. The problem is that the diamond story is allowed to run completely berserk, making almost everyone in the film look silly. An old man, surviving a rebel attack, is heard saying "It's just the diamonds. I hope they don't find oil here as well!" Excuse me, but this looks very much like some desperate NGO campaign stunt: it is completely incredible and absurd in the context.

The most obvious objection to the film, voiced by De Beers (which strangely – given its unwholesome history – now seems to be saying all the right things) and the government of Sierra Leone, is that Sierra Leone's war ended a long time ago, and recreating it now and blaming diamonds for it all as though it is still ongoing is misleading and a disservice to the long-suffering country as it tries to project a new image of stability to attract external investors and tourists. This is a very important objection, although De Beers' self-interest was soon made clear – partly by it setting aside millions of dollars to fight the negative publicity around diamonds that it envisaged the film would generate. A less clear-cut objection is that even at the height of the wars in places like Sierra Leone and Angola, blood diamonds accounted for just a fraction of the billions of dollars worth of diamonds traded internationally, and to tar the entire diamond business as bloodstained is potentially to undermine economies, like Botswana's, which completely rely on the diamond trade but whose diamonds are undoubtedly conflict-free. This objection was rejected by many when it was first voiced out at the height of the NGO campaign against blood diamonds, in the 1990s and early 2000s. I think that in fact it is also a legitimate position. It is easy to argue, from a distance, that the good economies of Botswana and the hundreds of thousands of jobs elsewhere cannot quite compensate for the lives lost in Sierra Leone or Angola. But this position is glib, and does little to address the issue. An effort in this direction was the Kimberley Process Certification Scheme (KPCS), which was initiated by the South African government, some NGOs and De Beers, and which aimed to make sure that only diamonds traded by legitimate governments would enter the international system. The agreement was signed in 2002, and was adopted by the UN Security Council. It is far from being perfect – diamonds continued to be smuggled, as anyone should expect, and have continued to move from conflict areas in places like Ivory Coast – but as such agreements go, the KPCS is reasonably effective, and there is continuing efforts to improve its monitoring activities.

"Blood Diamond" acknowledges both that the war in Sierra Leone has ended and that the KPCS is in place, but only at the end of the film – after the manic violence, the destruction, the pious effusions about the evils of the diamond trade – and in writing which many viewers would probably not stay around to read.

Such inanity surely should excuse a bit of bitching from a reviewer. The film is about Sierra Leone but it is obviously not set in the West African country. If one didn't know that already, the zebras and elephants (none of which could be found in present day Sierra Leone) should be the giveaway; as should the very bad, almost incomprehensible Mende (Vandy is Mende) spoken throughout the film. In fact the landscape tells you this is Mozambique, in Southern Africa – close enough to Sierra Leone in recent experience but very far indeed geographically. The seductive little scene where Mandy and Vandy and Archer, surviving many attacks by the rebels, run into an apparently disciplined and determined Kamajors (the pro-government militia) goes well enough until you remember, if you knew already, that the Kamajors would not have allowed a woman to so flirtingly hobnob with them, as Mandy (as usual) does. (It is against their ritual to touch a woman when they are in action – which explains why incidence of rape was completely absent among the Kamajors, as various commentators have observed). I am not also sure why it is Archer, a foreigner, who leads Vandy (who, as a denizen of the place, should be expected to know his way about a lot better) through the bush to Kono, except that the leading, macho role had to be exclusively reserved for Di Caprio.

These are trifling observations perhaps; but high-mindedness, as that which "Blood Diamond" represents, always invites uncomfortable scrutiny. The film's denouement takes its morality pitch to another level of (celluloid) clumsiness and fantasy. As Archer writhes in pain critically wounded, he gives the 'pink' diamond to Vandy, arranges for a helicopter to pick up Vandy and his son, and phones his friend Mandy (who had since gone to London) to arrange a flight to Europe for Vandy (plus sales arrangement for the diamond). Di Caprio's earnest, passionate, selfless "Titanic moment" is evoked: a remarkable twist for a hardcore mercenary and smuggler. Mandy gets her full story when Vandy arrives in London and meets the representatives of the great diamond cartel (Mandy is seen frantically snapping pictures. Later we see Vandy, in nice suit (and 2 million pounds rich), appearing to address a conference on the evils of the diamond trade...

The film ends.

I have to admit, as I stated earlier, that this is a powerful thriller. The acting, particularly Di Caprio's, is stunningly good. As a credible recreation of Sierra Leone's tragic story, well that is another matter altogether...

Part VII

Elections and the Political Future in Sierra Leone, Ivory Coaast and Nigeria

1.
Sierra Leone's 2007 Elections[33]

The peaceful transfer of power from ruling party to opposition after democratic elections in West Africa still merits headlines. When this happens in a country with a history of political violence, coups and a brutal civil war (only recently ended), the effect is chastening. There is, of course, an added bonus if it comes after the theatrical incompetence and corruption that marred elections in the region's largest and most important state, Nigeria, a country that seems simply incapable of doing anything – even simple theft – right. This is the recent story of Sierra Leone, a country which until 2002 was wracked by a devastating war (which led to the death of an estimated 70,000 people), the near-total collapse of the state, and three coups, one of them extremely bloody.

Elections, first conducted on 11 August to choose a successor to Ahmed Tejan Kabbah and a 118-member Parliament, dominated by Kabbah's Sierra Leone Peoples Party (SLPP) for the past ten years, proceeded to a run-off on 8 September. The opposition All Peoples Congress (APC) party, the SLPP's old nemesis, won 59 parliamentary seats in the first round to the SLPP's 43. A brand new party, the Peoples Movement for Democratic Change (PMDC), which is in effect a breakaway from the SLPP, won 10 seats. In the presidential polls in August, the APC's Ernest Bai Koroma got 815,523 or 44% of the votes cast, compared to the SLPP's Solomon Ekuma Berewa, Kabbah's Vice President (and until the polling the frontrunner), who won 704,012 or 38% of the votes. The PMDC's Charles Margai came third with 255,499 or 14% of the votes. Several minor parties also contested, barely gaining votes at all in the tightly contested three-way run. The polls were entirely violence-free and without controversy.

---

[33] Znet, 15 October 2007

Because none of the presidential candidates gained the required 55 per cent of the votes, the presidential polls had to proceed to a run-off, on 8 September. Shortly after the September date was set, apparently carefully-choreographed series of violent clashes were reported in parts of the country between supporters of Koroma and those Berewa. Both campaigns suffered attacks of one form or the other. Koroma's convoy was reportedly assaulted in the east of the country (an SLPP stronghold) and the SLPP's offices burnt to the ground in the incident. There then followed frantic assaults on the SLPP's offices in Freetown by supporters of the APC. Alarming incidents; but in fact no one was hurt throughout (let alone killed), and controversy remained over who exactly set fire on the SLPP's offices in Segbwema.

The run-off votes were held on schedule, and the atmosphere was largely peaceful and free. The final results were announced after over a week of controversy-wracked vote counting, on 17 September. The results showed that Koroma won 950,407 (54.62%) to Berewa's 789,651 (45.38%), representing a difference of 160,756 votes – a clear win for Koroma, since, unlike the first round, the run-off is won by a simple majority. The problem was that results from 477 polling stations were invalidated by the head of the National Electoral Commission (NEC), Christiana Thorpe. Thorpe, a former Catholic sister and (subsequently) education minister under the corrupt National Provisional Ruling Council (NPRC) junta, had improbably emerged as a single-minded, courageous and incorruptible electoral boss, but her decision to invalidate the votes – which led to the apparent disenfranchisement of an estimated 250,000 – left many observers baffled. She explained that voter turnout in these polling stations exceeded 100%, and that those who perpetuated this fraud should take the blame for the disenfranchisement. Thorpe added that the invalidation did not, in any case, affect the outcome of the ballots in any significant sense, a point which would have carried more weight if – as the SLPP demanded – recounting in the presence of agents of both parties had been done, and the excess votes eliminated. In fact, the SLPP contended that 426 of the invalidated stations were in their strongholds, and a recount would have tilted the elections in favour of its candidate. In the event, two of the five electoral commissioners refused to endorse the final results, and walked out of the press conference where Thorpe announced the results.

A few hours later, the SLPP candidate, citing a desire to maintain the peace, accepted the results, and Koroma was sworn in as President. What happened next bewildered most observers. Hundreds of young people, in apparent celebration of the APC victory, stormed the National Secretariat of the SLPP, and thoroughly vandalised it. Glass windows were destroyed and equipment completely looted. The party's newspaper and radio station were all destroyed. The homes of several leading members of the party were also attacked. Some arrests have since been made, but ultimate culpability for the attacks has yet to be determined.

The elections were the third in the West African state since its war ended. The first, held in March 2002, re-elected Kabbah and the SLPP in a landslide. The second, nation-wide local government elections held in 2004, led to important gains by the APC, including a win of the strategic municipality of Freetown, the capital.

Nor were they the first to see the APC defeating an incumbent SLPP government. This happened in 1967, when Sierra Leone's first post-colonial government, the SLPP, was defeated by the APC under Siaka Stevens. The outcome of those elections was also disputed, with consequences far graver than the tepid protest of the SLPP after the recent APC win. The SLPP was then led by Albert Margai (father of the leader of the PMDC), who had appeared to have lost grounds to Stevens. Shortly after Stevens' APC was declared winner, the army, under Margai protégé Brigadier David Lansana, stepped in at the crucial moment to prevent Stevens' swearing-in as Prime Minister, and suspended the constitution.

About those vertiginous days, a perceptive writer for the left-leaning British magazine *New Statesman* wrote at the time words which still have strong resonance: "The inability of outsiders to take West Africa seriously does injustice not only to the complexities of political societies like that of Sierra Leone, but also to the seriousness with which the people take their own politics. For, far from it being the case that the Sierra Leonians [sic] cared so little about their democratic party system that it just collapsed, they cared enough about it for as many as (probably) 26 of them to be killed trying to make it work. Nor was it the case that an African election…was unable to produce a change of government through the ballot box – that was exactly what it did do, and the real trouble began as a result of the successful exercise of democratic change."

Junior officers later restored the electoral mandate, and the APC was brought to power. Afterward, it was downward spiral for the country – a trajectory that included the banning of opposition parties, the introduction of a one-party state, widespread corruption, the collapse of state institutions and a brutal insurgency. No doubt both Kabbah and Berewa had all of this in mind when they decided to conform to the apparent will of the electorate: if the electorate wanted the SLPP, a party whose record they were all too keenly aware of, to remain in power, they would have voted overwhelmingly for it, as they did in 2002.

The new APC government, with well-known and credible figures like the veteran journalist Ibrahim Ben Kargbo (as minister of information) and the political activist Zainab Bangura, certainly inspires some confidence. It has taken a platform of zero tolerance for corruption, a necessary campaign that must, however, be accompanied by real and visible changes in the ordinary life of Sierra Leoneans, which is currently characterised by high unemployment, drudgery and the lack of a reliable electricity grid and running water in the capital and other cities.

2.
Liberia's 2005 Elections[34]

In the end, bizarrely, they made it all look like an anticlimax. Liberia's recent elections, the milestone of the country's difficult transition from brutal low-intensity warfare to peace, had been choreographed in advance to fit a well known narrative. The famous football star George Weah, a high school drop-out from a deprived background, was running against urbane Harvard-trained economist and longtime politician Ellen Johnson-Sirleaf. The Western media has a traditional fascination for this kind of study in contrast, and it is a foregone conclusion who they would favour: Weah's rags-to-riches story, a classic American narrative, won the contest from the start. The elections themselves, however, would prove to be different. And when Johnson-Sirleaf won the run-off polls by a handsome margin (60 per cent of the votes), the media quickly magnified Weah's sour, frantic claims that the polls had been rigged. So the first election of a female President in Sub Saharan Africa – a signal event – became somewhat peevishly qualified.

I first met Johnson-Sirleaf, while an exile in Ivory Coast (she had fled former President Charles Taylor's despotic rule) in 2001, and met her again a few weeks before the elections. Articulate and energetic, Johnson-Sirleaf is probably Liberia's most accomplished national figure; and in a region full of sadly effete and colourless leaders, she is bound to stand out, her sex and battered country aside. When we met in Ivory Coast, she was busy coordinating a grassroots women's group involved in rural development in Liberia. (This group would prove extremely important in mobilising the tens of thousands of women voters who ensured Johnson-Sirleaf's victory). She struck me as someone who intensely knew her country, was always thinking about its problems, and therefore knew what was needed to start addressing them: all qualities that would make for a successful leader.

<hr>

[34] Znet, 5 December 2005

It is probably too early to say, but it seems Liberians made the right choice this time around. In 1997, when Taylor ran after conducting a brutal insurrection, the slogan that catapulted him to power was: 'He killed my ma. He killed my pa. But I will vote for him!' Weah's supporters made a variation on this grim rallying point, to good effect, in the first rounds of the polls in October: 'Did he kill your ma? No. Did he kill your pa? No. Then vote for George Weah!' Weah was the anti-Taylor, the one who could credibly claim not to have been a player in Liberia's tragic recent past. The first round had a number of ex-militia leaders also running. But when the contest was brought down to Weah and Johnson-Sirleaf, who herself could claim not to have killed no ones pa or ma, Weah supporters invented another, less inspired line: 'He know book, he nor no book, but I'll vote for him!'. Liberians, it turned out, knew better than to elect someone who would celebrate the lack of educational accomplishment.

Having spent two weeks in Liberia shortly before the elections, what struck me afterwards wasn't the cry of foul play by Weah and his supporters; this was almost predictable. What struck me was that the elections were held at all, to say nothing about the high turn-out and the orderly behavior of voters during the polls. One key anxiety before the elections, quite apart from the logistical nightmare of conducting elections in a country a large part of which is largely inaccessible, was over how such an obviously traumatised and militarised people would behave during such a high-octane moment. About half of the registered voters had never voted before, and this was surely Liberia's first ever transparent elections. Compounding this was the fact that some of the militia leaders who helped ravage the country emerged among the 22 candidates vying to become president. The fact that at the end of the elections the two leading candidates would be people with empathically civilian backgrounds shows how far Liberia has come.

This tiny West African state, like its neighbour Sierra Leone, was a beacon of hope and inspiration to many people of African heritage for much of the 19th and part of the 20th centuries. Writing about the two in 1887, Edward Blyden, the great Pan Africanist, was highly optimistic about the salutary effects the two countries would have on the continent of Africa. "There is no part of West Africa where the openings and opportunities for introducing civilisation and Christianity into this continent are greater than these contiguous states present," he wrote. "The attractions which they offer to the efforts of the philanthropist and African Colonisationist (in the American sense of that phrase) are not without just grounds it is not difficult to predict the effects [of these two countries] upon the general interests of civilisation, upon the welfare of the Negro race, and upon the great cause of humanity." ☐

The "great cause of humanity." The irony is that, at the turn of the 20th century, the two countries would come to represent a great blight on humanity instead. Predatory warfare ravaged the two, and it became all-too-clear that the fortunes of the countries are indeed inextricably linked. This is why Liberia's elections have been perhaps the most closely watched such event in the region; its ramifications go well beyond its borders.

I spoke to Dr. Amos Sawyer, a former President of Liberia and perhaps the country's best known intellectual, on the phone shortly after the elections. He was ecstatic. A "great opportunity," he said, has been opened up by the elections. The elections have "opened up space for civil society, and would bring clarity☐ to a lot of issues." In Dr. Sawyer's view, the elections would help bring traction to the peace and reconciliation process that the entire region is engaged in at present, and help to focus attention to serious issues economic development.

One would only hope, given the region's extremely unhappy recent history, that Dr. Sawyer is right. West Africa, at long last, needs a break.

3.
The Crisis in Ivory Coast: First Impressions[35]

In the early 1980s, the British writer V.S. Naipaul visited Ivory Coast. The country was then one of the most stable and prosperous in Africa. As everyone knows, Naipaul is a deeply cynical and unabashed Afropessimist. But in the piece that he subsequently wrote about Ivory Coast, enchantingly entitled "The Crocodiles of Yamoussoukro," Naipaul was genuinely admiring. Yamoussoukro, the political capital, Naipaul called "one of the wonders of black Africa." "Out of apparently little," Naipaul observed, "wealth had been created. And this wealth has been shared and used; something extraordinary had been accomplished." Never one to give unqualified praise to achievements in the so-called Third World, however, the Trinidadian-born writer wearily reflected that the success of Ivory Coast "induces a kind of anxiety. Will it last?" As he reflected further, the great city of Abidjan now "seemed sinister: proof of a ruler's power, a creation of magic, for all the solidity of the concrete and the steel: dangerous and perishable."

That, as we have seen, was still in the 1980s. Ivory Coast, surrounded by countries that were sucked into what Naipaul colourfully described as either "chaos or nullity," was a thriving place. A relatively small country, it was sub-Saharan Africa's fourth largest economy, with a GDP per capita that was more than double the continent's second largest economy, oil-rich Nigeria. Its largest city, Abidjan, which began as a small colonial port town built on the side of a bleak lagoon, had become a commercial centre of great sophistication. Today, it is the only country in West Africa with an industrial base that contributes more to its GDP than the agricultural and extractive sectors. The little red guide-book for the Basilica, which features the country's first President, a very dapper Felix Houphet-Boigny, sitting besides Pope John Paul, carries a message which, when it was first issued, would be overlooked by the casual visitor but which now carries particular resonance: "This House of God

---

[35] Znet, 24 June 2004

witnesses to the desire to transmit a particular message: a message of Peace and Love. 'O, Our Lady of Peace, keep the human family always in peace!'"

Almost as though to fulfill the grim prophesies of Africa's doomsayers, the country today appears to be unravelling. And it all started in September 2002, when a group of about 750 retrenched soldiers—they had been hastily recruited by a former military leader—attempted to take over the government in a violent coup. As a result, Ivory Coast, once so tranquil and prosperous, is now enmeshed in a civil war, and the country has been effectively split into two, with the northern (and largely Muslim) half controlled by a near-mysterious rebel group, the southern (and largely Christian) half by a frequently churlish and pedestrian government.

A Failed Coup

Most rebel insurgencies in West Africa start as incursions from neighbouring countries by armed groups, beginning with attacks from the border areas and gradually progressing towards the capital city, often far removed from the initial scenes of fighting. This was the trajectory of the Liberian and Sierra Leonean conflicts. In the Ivorian case, however, the violence flared up, suddenly and unexpectedly, in Abidjan, and very quickly, with little apparent movement of forces, spread to the northern cities of Korhogo and Boauke. The attacks appeared to have been well-coordinated, and were bloody. In the first few days of fighting, 400 people were killed, many of them in Abidjan, including the country's Interior Minister, Emile Doudou, and a former President, General Robert Guei (the country's first successful coup-maker) and his entire family.

Ivory Coast's army was an ill-equipped and ill-prepared force. It was created in 1960 with little prospect that it could one day get involved in armed combat. It had never even participated in any peacekeeping mission that involved combat, and 80 per cent of its budget was, until the current crisis, used to pay the soldiers' salaries. Facing a threat that could well destroy it, however, the army (known as FANCI), quickly mobilised, and in a few days of fighting repelled the rebels from Abidjan. The rebels, though, had already taken over the northern cities of Bouake and Korhogo. A less than spirited attempt by FANCI to retake the cities was repulsed. A crack force of French troops, long stationed in the country as a result of a defence pact, staged a dramatic rescue of foreign nationals, including hundreds of American students, from Boauke in the first weeks of fighting, and a reinforced French contingent established camps just outside Bouake and along a zone roughly dividing the country into two parts—a formal acknowledgement, if this were needed, that the rebels now controlled the northern half of the country. The government of President Laurent Gbagbo, elected just over a year before in a popular but controversial vote, reinforced its control of the southern half.

The stalemate was disrupted, in November 2003, by the emergence of two new "rebel" groups in western Ivory Coast. The two groups, the Mouvement Populaire du Grand Quest (MPIGO) and the Mouvement pour la Justice et la Paix (MJP), said they were fighting to avenge the death of General Guei, and determined to do so by removing from power Gbagbo, whom they accused of the killing. It emerged, however, that the rebels were really former Revolutionary United Front (RUF) soldiers from Sierra Leone and units from Liberia's army loyal to then President Charles Taylor, and that pillage, not politics, was driving their "insurgency." Unlike the group holding the north of the country (the Mouvement Patriotique de la Cote d'Ivoire (MPCI), which established itself as a rather well-behaved force in key cities, the new groups in the west of the country soon became notorious for vandalism and terror, and they soon after clashed with French troops, leading to serious casualties. Tens of thousands of Ivorians fled the country.

But who were the far more important northern rebels? Were they simply mutinous soldiers hungry for power? Or were they champions of a marginalised sector of the country, the mainly Muslim—and Dyula-speaking—half of the country (the north), as they claimed? Or were they, as Gbagbo's government claimed, foreign mercenaries carrying out a plot by Ivory Coast's neighbours, particularly Burkina Faso, to destabilise the country? These questions persisted months after the failed coup and the beginning of the insurgency. Western reporters who ventured into the rebels' stronghold generally found them genial and charming, behaving well to the civilian population but otherwise not engaged in any form of governance. A reporter from a major American newspaper found the rebels "lazing about," and possessing "more satellite phones than battle scars." The reporter noted that five months after the rebels' occupation of Bouake, the banks there were not functioning, businesses were boarded up, schools closed and half the town's population had fled. As the months progressed, the World Food Programme announced that 50 per cent of residents in Boauke had no savings, and that the rest had lost 80 per cent of their purchasing power. Starvation loomed, precipitating still further mass exodus from the city.

At War with Itself

I visited Ivory Coast for three weeks in December 2002, a few months after the failed coup. Just before I flew to the country, the BBC World Service news program showed dramatic footage of thousands of apparently frenzied young men storming a recruitment centre in Abidjan in answer to a government call for new recruits to help fight off what officials called "terrorists" who had occupied large swathes of the country. I thought I had seen something like this before—in Sierra Leone, in 1991, at the start of what would turn out to be an extremely destructive conflict, with hundreds of young men, many of them drifters and thieves, turning up to be recruited into the country's feeble army, only to become "rebels" and "sobels" and the principal despoilers of the country. I had been properly appalled by events in Ivory Coast, but now I knew things were taking a sharply more sinister turn: the country was setting itself up to unravel. Ivory Coast had been a bad player in West Africa's linked crises; now it appeared the country's well-fed elites had learnt nothing from what had happened in Liberia, Sierra Leone and Guinea.

It was a mark of the confusion surrounding the conflict that the circumstances of its beginning, so recent, sounded almost like legend even when recounted by hard-headed diplomats. Over lunch a day after I arrived in Abidjan, a Western diplomat tried hard to explain how it all started. Less than two weeks before the failed coup plot in September, there had been a dramatic heist at the headquarters of the Central Bank for the West African CFA Francs, in Abidjan, by armed men using a car with the State House number D-10. The car had been stolen, and in spite of the sophisticated security system at the Bank, which is located in downtown Abidjan, the robbers made away with CFA 2.5 billion. The chief of security at the bank, a fellow named Siapopo, fled, and was later arrested in Burkina Faso carrying a Ghanaian passport. What was the point of this story? "There are strong indications that the robbers were the rebels who later led the coup attempt," he said. "It was almost certainly a way of funding their assault on the state. It was classic guerrilla tactic." Little was known about the rebel leadership. All that was clear about it was that it comprised of mainly ex-soldiers and that a prominent figure in the group was a former radical student leader named Guillaume Soro. Soro soon emerged as spokesman for the group, and in one interview he reacted impatiently to questions about his group's real identity. "Who are we? We are young Ivorians, and we are ready to fight and die." He then described his group as a mix of exiled soldiers and former students furious at the Ivorian government's mistreatment of northern Ivorians. "If you are from the north," he said, "you are subhuman, according to the government. We want a united Ivory Coast. We want a country that lives in harmony and includes everyone. We want a Pan African nation where the Ivory Coast is a melting pot."

Self-serving no doubt, but the rhetoric clearly taps into long-simmering grievances among the relatively impoverished, and largely politically marginalised, inhabitants of Ivory Coast's northern regions. Since independence in 1960, the country has been ruled by people from the southern part of the country, who as a result constitute an elite class dominating the country's government, civil service, the academia and the business sector. This charmed circle, from mainly the Baoule and Bete ethnic groups—the first two Presidents of the country, Houphet Boigny and Konan Bedie, were Baoule, and Gbagbo is Bete—has in the past even contorted the country's constitution to maintain the lopsided status quo. The most striking case was the adoption of a new electoral code by the National Assembly, at the instance of Bedie, which stipulated that Presidential candidates must be born in Ivory Coast to parents who were themselves born in the country. Gbagbo, then an outspoken opposition figure, angrily described the electoral code as "liberticide, racist, xenophobic and dangerous."

The intention, of course, was to exclude from participation in the polls Bedie's chief rival, Alasane Ouattara, of Dyula ethnicity from the north, and a former Prime Minister of the country. Ouattara's mother is said to have come from Burkina Faso, and he was subsequently barred from contesting the 1995 Presidential polls, which Bedie won. But the code, which sedulously created a distinction between "pure" and "mixed" Ivorians, had much more far-reaching implications. Now it is Gbagbo, a self-styled socialist, who has been exploiting *Ivoirité*, using coded language. When he returned to the country after the failed coup, he said in a televised speech: "In this country, once and for all, we need to know who is who and who wants what. We need to put on one side those who are for democracy and the Republic, and on the other those who are against democracy and the Republic." He called for a sweep of the shanty towns, where many foreign workers reside, displacing them and arresting a large number of them (at the site of one shanty town, by the middle-class suburb of Cocody, only a small bar, belonging to a gendarme, was left standing when I visited there in December 2002). This demagogic approach alienated many potential supporters, including some West African regional leaders. For Ivory Coast has been, truly, a West African melting pot.

Boigny's Vision Betrayed

When Ivory Coast gained independence in 1960, it had a population of 3 million; in 2002 the population stood at 17 million. The remarkable increase resulted as much from natural growth as from labour immigration. Under the patrician President Felix Houphouet-Boigny, who led the country to independence in 1960 and ruled it until his death in 1993, the Ivorian government made it a policy to encourage huge immigration into the country of other Africans from the more depressed—and sometimes chaotic—states adjacent to Ivory Coast. The new immigrants were smoothly integrated into Ivorian society, with some of them holding important governmental positions, and the majority employed in the country's booming agricultural sector. By the 1980s, world market prices for cocoa and coffee (the country's key export commodities) slumped drastically, and the huge presence of nationals from other African states began to be seen as a burden. In 1990, Houphouet-Boigny named Ouattara, a senior official of the IMF, Prime Minister partly to handle the economic crisis. Ouattara introduced residency permits for foreign nationals in the country. They cost $50 per annum for nationals from ECOWAS states and $500 for non-ECOWAS nationals. Houphouet-Boigny died in 1993, and Bedié, then head of the National Assembly, won a power struggle with Ouattara to become President. It was then that the toxicity of ethnic politics was smuggled into the debate about non-native Ivorians. In 2002, there were an estimated 3 million Burkinabes, 2 million Malians, 500,000 to 1 million Ghanaians and over 250,000 Guineans in Ivory Coast plus tens of thousands of Liberian refugees in Ivory Coast. In his power-struggle with Ouattara, Bedie's rhetoric persistently hammered on the concept of Ivoirité or "pure Ivorian-ness." It was his way of ensuring that he remained at the helm, one of the most invidious uses of ethnicity. And it irked the millions of non-native residents of Cote d'Ivoire, and, more significantly, Ivorians in the north who generally supported Quattara.

In December 1999, non-commissioned officers, led by Staff-Sergeant Ibrahim ("IB") Coulibaly, ousted the incompetent Bedie in a bloodless coup, and invited former army chief Robert Guei—who had been sacked by Bedie for refusing to use the army to crush civilians protesting the flawed electoral process of 1995—to become the new Head of State. Guei was himself forced to organise elections in October 2000 in which he contested for the Presidency. Making use of the Bedie electoral code, he banned Ouattara from contesting. Longtime oppositionist Gbagbo stood, however, and he appeared to have emerged victorious by a wide margin. Guei's attempts to rig the results were scuttled by massive demonstrations in Abidjan, and he fled the country in a helicopter. Gbagbo became President. Less than two years later, the foiled coup and insurgency occurred, with the rebel leaders citing the controversial elections which excluded Ouattara as one of the reasons for their rebellion.

The question of national identity in Ivory Coast, in other words, is instrumentally used by all parties, but it has become a key issue in the conflict, one that has threatened to unravel all the best efforts at bringing peace to the country. The country's famous musician, Alpha Blondy, called *ivoirité* "black Nazism," noting that the "only people benefiting from the madness are the people in politics."

France Intervenes

France, Ivory Coast's former colonial master, remains the most important Western presence in the West African nation. Before the September 2002 crisis, there were 20,000 French nationals—some of them simultaneously holding Ivorian citizenship—in Ivory Coast, and a further 20,000 Ivorians who held French citizenship. A 600-strong contingent of French troops was based in Abidjan. These troops, however, did not participate in crushing the coup attempt of September 2002, and France became involved in the crisis only after its spread to engulf much of the country threatened a serious humanitarian catastrophe. Many Ivorians suspect that this was because the French wanted to punish Gbagbo, whose mouthing of African nationalist and socialist rhetoric did not endear him to the French. Worse, Gbagbo had begun to actively court the Americans and Chinese—no contradiction here—and on one occasion offered a lucrative contract to the Chinese for which a French company had applied. But France's hands may also have been held by a more searing pathology.

France, whose investment in Africa is 5 percent of its external trade, and whose sense of "national grandeur and power: —to quote Rachel Utley's seductive phrase —has been a projection overseas of its potential to exercise unmistakable influence and power, has since the 1960s militarily intervened in at least nine African countries. France intervened in Mauritania, Senegal, the Congo, Gabon, Cameroon and Chad in the 1960s; in Chad again, as well as in Djibouti, Western Sahara, the Central African Republic and Zaire in the 1970s; and in Chad twice more in the 1980s; in Togo in 1986; and finally—and most controversially—in Rwanda in the 1990s. These interventions earned France the title 'the gendarme of Africa.' In fact, in early 2001, French President Jacques Chirac was a prominent proponent of intervention in Guinea, during a time when Liberian-supported guerrillas were ravaging the southeastern parts of the country; and France still maintains significant military bases in Senegal and Djibouti. Unlike other former colonial powers, especially Britain, France continued to regard much of its ex-colonies in West Africa as its traditional sphere of influence and maintained a policy of *rayonnement* towards them. France's military aid to Africa was 800 million French francs in 1984, and in 1990, France had 6,600 troops stationed in Africa. This military presence by a major European power was a source of great disquiet among other, non-French-speaking African states, especially the West African regional power Nigeria, which viewed the intrusive French presence in West Africa as a kind of Trojan Horse strategy and the recipient African nations as neo-colonial client states.

France could no doubt afford to ignore the African nationalist rhetoric of neo-colonial intervention. But it could not brush aside the deeply embarrassing episode of its Rwandan adventure, which amounted, in the eyes of many around the world, to collusion in the genocidal campaigns of the Hutu leadership of the country in 1994. After that episode, France decided to be more cautious about militarily intervening in an African crisis. When the Ivory Coast crisis broke out, France's initial impulse was to use its forces to protect its interests and foreign nationals in the country. French troops staged a dramatic rescue of Western nationals from Bouake during the first two weeks of the crisis. After that, the

French called on the warring parties to observe a ceasefire and to resolve the crisis be peaceful negotiations. Meanwhile, 200,000 Ivorians fled rebel-controlled Bouake on foot and by bus in the first four weeks of the crisis.

In January 2003, the French, concerned about the escalating crisis, proposed peace talks between the government of President Gbagbo and the rebels, to be held in France. Earlier, in November 2002, less than two months after the crisis started, French Foreign Minister Dominique de Villepin visited Ivory Coast and held talks with the government. His visit coincided with a government offensive, said to have included foreign mercenaries, on Vavoua, which alarmed the French. De Villepin visited the country again, in January 2003, and obtained a promise from President Gbagbo to expel mercenaries from the country and halt air attacks against supposed rebel strongholds. The French foreign minister was quick to disavow support for either side in the conflict. "France," he said, "has no other camp except the one for peace." Through ECOWAS and French mediation efforts, a ceasefire agreement between the government and the western rebel groups was signed on 13 January, and the participation of the rebel groups in proposed talks in France was assured.

Talks began on 15 January in Linas-Marcoussis, just outside Paris, and ended on 24 January with an Agreement that was signed by all the parties. The Agreement called for the establishment of a Government of National Reconciliation with wide executive powers, and was to be composed of ministers from the main political parties and the rebel groups on a roughly equal basis, but the current government of President Gbagbo was to be given primacy in the arrangement. Gbagbo was to remain president, but a Prime Minister with wide-ranging powers was to be appointed in agreement with the other groups.

The Linas-Marcoussis Agreement was anchored on three main principles: the need to maintain the territorial integrity of Ivory Coast; the creation of a Government of National Reconciliation, with a new

Prime Minister; and the need to conduct transparent and free elections in which people would not be excluded by means of fraudulent electoral requirements.

Other concerns included the need to re-organise the army, the granting of amnesty—only slightly qualified—to the army mutineers and other militia forces which constituted the insurgent forces; and, most far-reaching, the need to address the issue of identity or nationality with new legislation that integrates and protects the millions of immigrants residing in the country. The Agreement states that "foreign nationalsâ€¦ have made a major contribution to national wealth and have helped confer on Ivory Coast its special position and responsibility within the sub-region," noting that "the petty annoyances perpetrated by the administration and the police and security forces, which often disregard the law and human rights and which often affect foreigners, can be caused by using willful misapplication of identification laws." The new government, therefore, "will immediately eliminate the residence permit requirements for nationals of ECOWAS countries and will carry out the immigration inspection needed by using means of identification not subject fraudulent misuse." The Agreement also called for changes to land ownership laws to grant the immigrants access to land.

Appropriate measures were also to be taken to ensure the freedom of the media, but the Agreement condemned "the incitement to hatred and xenophobia propagated by certain media." Measures were also to be put in place to facilitate the liberation of prisoners of war. In quick order, the French government dispatched Force Licorne to Ivory Coast, on 6 February 2003, partly to facilitate the implementation of the Linas-Marcoussis Agreement and to protect French interests across the country. Force Licorne, which beefed up the French military presence to 4000 troops, quickly deployed across the country and was able to check the spread of the violence. Troops from West African states, acting under the Economic Community of West African States, ECOWAS, also deployed to bolster the French effort. On 27 February 2004, the UN Security Council passed a resolution authorizing a full peacekeeping operation for Ivory Coast, and mandating nearly 7,000 UN troops to monitor and help implement the peace agreement. Both the ECOWAS and French forces have been, as a result, subsumed under the UN mandate, although the French still maintain an independent command structure, and officially pledged only to playing a supporting role to the UN. West Africans troops, on the other hand, have been 'rehatted' by the UN and brought under UN command—the commander of the ECOWAS forces, Senegalese General Ibrahima Fall, is now the commander of the UN force. Very little, however, has changed on the ground since this new development: the country remains divided, and the rebel forces have refused to disarm, saying that they won't do so ahead of the elections slated for October 2005. It is, really, back to Square One.

Some observers now say that the Linas-Marcoussis Agreement is dead in the water, destroyed by the insincerity and waffling of the signatories. Popular sentiment in Abidjan, where the government is now effectively based, is against making any concessions to the anti-government rebels, and the government has often acted in a heavy-handed manner to crack down on perceived opponents. In March 2004, demonstrators calling for concrete progress in the peace process were shot at in the city. The UN said that 120 people were killed in several days of clashes with the security forces, and that the clampdown had been "carefully planned and executed" and was ordered from "the highest state authorities." Earlier, shortly after the failed coup in 2002, several mass graves were discovered just outside of Abidjan, and it was reported that the government had set up "Death Squads" to hunt down opponents.

A Big Question

The big question now in the region is: Will Ivory Coast survive this crisis and emerge out of it a unified nation? No one now thinks that the country would, any time soon, return to the grand tranquility which so famously set it apart from the rest of unstable West Africa for many decades. That it would come to this—come to, that is, a question of basic survival for a country that offered so much hope just a few years before; and that still functions, in parts held by the government, far better than, say, Nigeria—to come this point is to utterly unsettle ones idea of nationhood in Africa. Just what does this mean for the much-vaunted notion of African Renaissance? The government of President Gbagbo appears in no mood to appreciate the gravity of the situation: just this week it stirred up an unnecessary frenzy over a sensible decision by the United Nations peacekeeping mission in the country, UNOCI, to set up an FM radio station which would be used to 'sensitise' all parties and the general public about the mandate and limits of the UN operation. Gbagbo's government announced that it would ban the station, claiming that the mission had set up a 'pirate' radio station which would aid the 'enemy'.

At a seminar in Accra, Ghana, recently, West African diplomats and military officers went almost over the top in praising France for its intervention in Ivory Coast—intervention that has supposedly averted a major humanitarian catastrophe. That signaled a new, more positive image for French military presence in Africa. It also means that African leaders must work harder to take full charge of their continent.

4.
Some thoughts on Ivory Coast[36]

On a visit to Ivory Coast in December 2002 – shortly after a bloody coup attempt had plunged the country into civil war – an old friend took me to meet her former college mate in Abidjan, Picasse Damana (simply Picasse). Picasse had been, as a student, linked to virulent student leader Blé Goudé, who (like Picasse) came from President Laurent Gbagbo's cocoa-growing region. It was during the nineties: Gbagbo was then a university professor of history, and a pretend socialist who had been a part of the fringe opposition against Houphouët-Boigny's benign long-term rule. Gbagbo was an inspiration for the likes of Blé Goudé who, like his mentor, was sent to prison many times. The student movement Goudé (nicknamed "Machete" because of his proneness to violence) founded split into two factions, he leading the most important, and Guillaume Soro, a student from the north, leading the other (which eventually lost the power struggle).

When I got to Abidjan that December, the fire-spitting Blé Goudé was now the leader of the aggressively pro-Gbagbo Young Patriot movement; Picasse was, once again, a strong ally of his mentor Gbagbo. Soro had become the political leader of an inchoate rebel group, the Patriotic Movement of Ivory Coast or New Forces, which had emerged out of the failed September 2002 coup attempt, and was fighting Gbagbo's government.

I met Picasse at a restaurant in Cocody, a neat suburb in Abidjan. He was accompanied by half a dozen young men, some of them wearing bandanas. He spoke furiously about the "foreigners" trying to rip apart Ivory Coast, and of the need to "purge" the country of its "internal enemies."

---

[36] Patriotic Vanguard, 25 January 2011.

At the end of the short meeting, I felt drained and gripped by a deep melancholy: Picasse seemed to me at that point to be the new face of the nihilism overpowering the once-prosperous country. I was somewhat shocked, but not at all surprised, to see on TV in December last year this same Picasse, now an Elections Commissioner, grabbing the paper carrying the recent Ivorian presidential elections results from the Chief Electoral Commissioner and tearing it to pieces. So Gbagbo had made this murderous thug an Electoral commissioner?

One does not need to recall this incident to understand that Gbagbo's shrill objection to the recent elections result on grounds that they were rigged by the opposition is hopelessly weak and cynical. But it is a reminder, if this were necessary, of the very high stakes that his continuing squatting in the presidential palace have for the people of that country and for the region. This must be taken into account as we weigh the potential consequences of an ECOWAS-led intervention in Ivory Coast to oust Gbagbo and install the democratically-elected President Alassane Ouattara. I am, needless to say, all for that intervention, and for the following reasons:

• Ivory Coast has been, in effect, in a state of war or heightened emergency since September 2002, and only the large presence of foreign forces – the UN and France's Licorne – has prevented a bloodbath. Remove those forces today, as the desperate and power-drunk Gbagbo has recently been shouting, and you will have a full-scale civil war in the country. Despite his shrill insistence, everyone who knows knows that that Gbagbo's inept army, FANCI, has no way of defeating the rebel forces, and that the war will escalate to involve Liberia, Mali, Burkina Faso and potentially Sierra Leone. That prospect alone justifies a UN intervention.

• Gbagbo's forces are already engaged in mass atrocities – targeting supporters of Ouattara in a campaign of mass murder. In plain terms this means that people are being targeted for killings on account of their ethnicity (most of those targeted are people of Ouattara's Dyula ethnicity). We know that Gbagbo and his so-called Young Patriots have been doing this for a while now. In March 2004, demonstrators calling for a political resolution of the crisis in the country were shot at in Abidjan. The UN said that 120 people were killed in several days of clashes with the security forces, and that the clampdown had been "carefully planned and executed" and was ordered from "the highest state authorities." Earlier, shortly after the failed coup in 2002, several mass graves were discovered just outside of Abidjan, and it was reported that the government had set up "Death Squads" to hunt down opponents. We know from credible reports that this Squad, controlled by Gbagbo, has been very active since he lost the elections. By most accounts, about 5000 to 6000 people have been killed and more than a million displaced since the troubles began in 2002.

• Gbagbo won the previous elections in Ivory Coast, in 2000, entirely by default. Through the use of the corrosive and idiotic policy of *ivoirité*, Ouattara was disqualified on the dubious ground that he was not of complete Ivorian parentage (his father was from Upper Volta, now Burkina Faso). Gbagbo took office amid riots, during which his supporters killed hundreds of Ouattara's primarily Muslim followers. Using his Young Patriots thugs, Gbagbo has fanned xenophobia in the country since 2002: the consequences of that in such a polyglot country if left unchecked is not hard to imagine.

• Elections were to have been conducted in Ivory Coast over five years ago, in October 2005. But in early September 2005, when I last visited the country, the UN peacekeeping mission in the country, UNOCI, announced that the country was unprepared for the elections since Gbagbo and the insurgents had obstructed all attempts to conduct proper voter registration. In other words, Gbagbo's (flawed) mandate expired over five years ago, and he has been squatting in the presidential palace since then. It is time for him to go.

• The other compelling reason why Gbagbo should be forced out underscores the complexity of the Ivorian situation – but also the urgent need for its just resolution. When Ivory Coast gained independence in 1960, it had a population of 3 million; in 2002 when the troubles started the population stood at 17 million. The remarkable increase resulted as much from natural growth as from labour immigration. Under the patrician President Felix Houphouet-Boigny, who led the country to independence in 1960 and ruled it until his death in 1993, the Ivorian government made it a policy to encourage huge immigration into the country of other Africans. The new immigrants were smoothly integrated into Ivorian society, with some of them holding important governmental positions, and the majority employed in the country's booming agricultural sector. In 2002, there were an estimated 3 million Burkinabes, 2 million Malians, 500,000 to one million Ghanaians and over 250,000 Guineans in the country plus tens of thousands of Liberian refugees. When the troubles started, Gbagbo's xenophobic rhetoric inspired his Death Squads and Young Patriots to start attacks against these people, but he held them back in check after Nigeria's President Obasanjo threatened to militarily intervene. So we know that this is not just about Gbagbo and his Bete ethnic group (about which he wrote a foolish book praising their singular virtues). We also know that Gbagbo knows when to back down.

• Ivory Coast was a very bad player in the wars that engulfed Liberia and Sierra Leone: the country provided support to the rebels that ravaged both countries. In fact, Gbagbo's Defence Minister at the time of the coup attempt in 2002, Moise Kouassi, was named by the 2000 UN report on Sierra Leone and Liberia as the official who was signing end-user certificates for arms illegally transferred to the Charles Taylor government and then to the Revolutionary United Front or RUF (this fact should give pause to those who now claim that the rebel forces expressing support for Ouattara were the ones who brought the Liberian and Sierra Leonean rebels into the Ivorian conflict.) As it happens, Gbagbo has recently been trying to recruit these same forces to back up his very fragile position. The risk of such irresponsibility dragging the region into renew widespread violence is very high, and cannot be tolerated.

In the UK Guardian recently, Paul Collier suggested that a coup by the Ivorian military removing the obdurate Gbagbo will be the ideal solution, earning rebukes from several quarters. But his position is not at all original. Reflecting on the overthrow of his former friend Kwame Nkrumah in the exalted pages of the *New York Review of Books* (June 1966), Conor Cruise O'Brien, whose principled stance as a senior UN official in the Congo so impressed Nkrumah that the Ghanaian President had the Irish intellectual appointed Chancellor of the University of Ghana, wrote that a situation—such as that which prevailed in Ghana under Nkrumah— "where the government cannot be changed except by force, the armed forces have no choice but to be in politics. If they obey orders and suppress rebellion, they are playing the highly political role of blocking the one route to political change. They cannot 'stay neutral' in such a situation for they have to decide whether or not to obey the orders of the Supreme Commander and Head of State. Whether they obey or disobey, their act will be of political significance. Even without a rebellion, their very presence, in a condition of putative loyalty to the regime, is a major political factor, inhibiting the flow of political change through the only channel by which such change can come. The armed forces are therefore faced with the choice of guaranteeing the perpetuity of the regime or of overthrowing it. It is not the second option only that is political."

The chief objection to this position is, however, too strong to be ignored. It is that once you start getting the military to settle political issues through coups, then you instill into the army a sense of political indispensability: coups become the only solution to every political problem, and coups will become, once again, a ubiquitous part of the political landscape in Africa. This year alone 17 African states are holding elections, 16 of them including presidential. It is of utmost urgency, if the admirable stance of the African Union (AU) and ECOWAS on good governance is ever to gain traction that a major country like Ivory Coast shouldn't be allowed to so brazenly vitiate such a core principle of good governance: respecting democratic outcomes. Gbagbo needs to be unseated, if necessary by force of ECOWAS' arms...

261

5.
Politics in Nigeria: 'A Paradise for Maggots'[37]

> Nigerian politics revolve around the distribution of the oil money, whether officially (in the form of debates over oil revenue allocation) or unofficially (as military and civilian politicians seek favour with those in a position to reward them with opportunities to 'chop' - **Human Rights Watch**, *The Price of Oil: Corporate Responsibility and Human Rights Violations in Nigeria's Oil Producing Communities*, **1999**.

Paradise for Maggots is the title of a book published on the work of the anti-corruption campaigner and presidential candidate in 2011, Nuhu Ribadu; the book was published in 2010. It is, needless to say, about corruption in Nigeria, and this corruption is centred on oil.

Oil, whose commercial exploitation by the British company, Shell, started in Nigeria in the 1950s, has shaped the country's character and politics more than any other factor – more than even its extraordinary ethnic diversity (there are over 250 language groups in the country), and more than its religious diversity (more than half the population confesses to be Muslim, 35 per cent Christian, and the rest thought to be practicing various African indigenous religions.) Nigeria produces the much-valued 'sweet crude', and it supplies the US with 25% of its oil needs. Nigeria is by far the largest exporter of oil in Africa. The country may have earned more than $400 billion from its oil and gas to date. Oil accounts for 95 per cent of Nigeria's exports, and therefore hard cash earnings. With rising oil prices, Nigeria actually now earns $30 billion-40 billion a year from its oil.

This overwhelming dominance of a single, extractive commodity has undoubtedly been a curse. The country that produces so much oil can only satisfy ten per cent of the (mains) electricity needs of its main commercial city, Lagos. Oil is responsible for the corruption of Nigeria's politics, and

---

[37] This is excerpted from a long report on Nigeria's 2011 elections written for the Institute for Security Studies; I spent three weeks in Nigeria researching the report in March and April 2011.

has distorted its development efforts in many insidious ways. Because revenue from oil is enough to run the government, keep the ruling elite immensely wealthy, and with enough left to maintain a vast patrimonial network – what passes for governance in the country – effective, Nigeria's rulers have over the years neglected the agricultural and even manufacturing sectors. The textile industry, for example, which used to be a major employer, is now in a state of collapse; and from being able to feed itself and even export food (in the 1960s and early 1970s), Nigeria has become a net importer of rice and other foodstuffs; it spent $1 billion in 2010 on the importation of rice alone. Moreover, because wealth, in the form of oil revenues, is totally controlled by government, competition for access to state offices has become deadly – as the country's former President Obasanjo crudely put it, a "do or die affair."

In February 2011, the country's opposition parties accused the government of failing to account for over US$27 billion in state accounts. The money was more than in the Excess Crude Account (ECA) set up in 2004 by Obasanjo to keep savings from excess earnings from crude oil in case oil price rises above that set in the national budget. Perhaps in response to this scandal, the government in March 2011 announced plans to abolish the ECA because, Olusegun Aganga, the Minister of Finance explained, the account "is not transparent and clear to the Nigerian people, therefore there is a general perception that there is some level of mismanagement." "Some level of mismanagement": the delicious understatement is the farthest the earnest minister could go to acknowledge official corruption. This was, of course, elections seasons, and corruption allegations like this tend to be carelessly made, but Jonathan's PDP government made no convincing explanation regarding the use of the funds.

The allegations certainly resonated with the public, and for good reasons. Successive Nigerian leaders are believed to have embezzled billions of dollars. In 2003, the Auditor General's report of Federal ministries and companies revealed the embezzlement of 23 billion nairas through financial fraud. The previous year, the Obasanjo government, in order to avoid a long drawn-out litigation, reached an agreement with the family of the deceased former President, General Abacha, and various European banks to return $1 billion stolen by Abacha to the country with an agreement that 10 per cent of this will be returned to the Abacha family; in the event the government got $700 million of this. Much earlier, in 1987, the country's General Accountant estimated that corruption in the civil service was costing the state between $1.2 billion and $1.5 billion a year. Even the pension's scheme is not spared. In March 2011, a N13 billion scam involving the country's Pension's Office was reported in the local newspapers. Another report suggested that state governors may have embezzled N1.3 trillion (several billions of dollars) in funds released by the federal government in development funds in 2010 alone.

In 2010, the respected (former) Governor of the Central Bank accused members of the National Assembly of allocating for themselves nearly 25 per cent of country's annual budget of about US$29.6 billion. This was perhaps an exaggeration for effect, but each Assembly member carried home about $1.5 million a year, among the highest paid law makers in the world. In the budget announced in March 2011, in fact, the law-makers added close to $1 billion to their share of what they like to call "national largess." This is obviously scandalous for a country where 92 per cent of the citizens are, by every international measure, absolutely poor, earning less than $2 a day, according to the World Bank. Unscrupulous foreign oil companies are inevitably complicit in this widespread and corrosive graft. An audit report prepared by the Extractive Industries Transparency Initiative (EITI) noted many discrepancies in reported royalty payments by companies to the government and what was actually deposited into the consolidated revenue – several hundreds of millions dollars were unaccounted. In 2006, the un-reconciled difference in royalty payments was $437 million. The un-reconciled difference with respect to crude oil exportation from 2006 to 2008 was 3.1 million barrels of oil, with an estimated cost of $240 million. The report noted that foreign companies had fleeced the country of hundreds of million dollars during the period.

In such a situation, moreover, anti-corruption efforts are quite easily stymied. Nigeria was ranked in 2010 as 130th of 180 countries on Transparency International's corruption perception index. This was perhaps partly because serious corruption cases against many senior politicians and state officials indicted for corruption by the Economic and Financial Crimes Commission were inexplicably quashed. In March 2011, for example, Bode George, the former Chairman of Nigeria's Ports

Authority and Vice Chair of the PDP, who was convicted (along with five others) in October 2010 for embezzling $500 million, was released from prison. His release was heralded by a big party sporting many PDP big wigs, including senior ministers, leading to a national outcry. The previous year, Attahiru Bafarawa, former Governor of Sokoto convicted for stealing tens of millions of dollars, was released on bail soon after his arrest. The trials for corruption of the following were also quashed last year: Adenike Grange, the former Health Minister; her ex-Minister of State, Gabriel Aduku; the ex-Governor of Delta State James Ibori; Ezebonwu Nyeson, the Chief of Staff of Rivers State; Kenny Martin, the ex-Chair of Police Equipment Foundation; and Hammand Bello Ahmed, the former Comptroller-General of Customs.

Such a deformed system inevitably encourages political violence, as the Afari-Gyan Report noted: the "widespread extreme poverty amid massive wealth concentrated in the hands of a few creates the context where political elites enjoy enormous advantages over the impoverished public, and where voters and other stakeholders are vulnerable to financial inducements and intimidation."

ELECTORAL VIOLENCE

In March 2011, 63 political parties signed a Code of Conduct undertaking, among others, not to hijack ballot boxes, use thugs or weapons, or use inflammatory language in their campaigns, take provocative actions, or make images or manifestations that incite violence. It was also agreed that INEC would monitor all political rallies.

These frantic commitments speak volumes, needless to say. Hundreds of people have been killed during elections in Nigeria since 1999. Elections in Nigeria since 1999, a British 'hotspot' report has colourfully noted, are "fought down the barrel of the gun", generating 'a general atmosphere of intimidation and threats, assassinations, arson, bombings, random shootings and pitched battles between opposing bands of thugs using sundry weapons.' The report lists nearly 100 political assassinations in the country since 1999. In March 2011, Amnesty International issued a short report entitled *Loss of life, insecurity and impunity in the run up to Nigeria's elections*. The report noted that hundreds of people had already been killed in "politically-motivated, communal and sectarian violence across Nigeria ahead of presidential and parliamentary polls."

These assassinations, moreover, remain unsolved. One of the most brazen and significant of these cases involved the murder of Bola Ige, the country's former justice minister under Obasanjo. Ige was killed on 23 December 2001 after, critics of the government allege, he signaled to Obasanjo that he will be quitting the PDP to focus on building his own party, the Alliance for Democracy (AD). Ige was former governor of Oyo State (1979-1983). Leaked US embassy cables last year quoted the former US Ambassador to Nigeria, Howard Jeter, reporting Nigeria's then Assistant Inspector-General of Police, Abimbola Ojomo, as saying that "undertrained and ill-equipped" police bungled the investigation in Ige's killing. Jeter noted: "Absent a credible confession or outside assistance, the Nigerian police investigation will fail to identify the assassin or his paymaster because of the lack of preserved evidence and the weak investigative skills of the police." The Police Chief dismissed claims that the murder was related to Ige's firm actions against drug barons: "Possible drug or organized crime-related motives for the murder have been investigated and rejected, claimed the AIG." The real motive, the cable suggested, was political, and the culprits were probably associated with the ruling PDP. The case remains unresolved.

On 3 March, "unidentified people" drove by a huge campaign rally of the ruling Peoples' Democratic Party (PDP) in Suleja in Niger State and lobbed bombs at it, killing 13 people and wounding scores more. This catch-all police phrase, unidentified people meant only that this is a political crime that will never be solved. Just before the end of last year, three similar bomb attacks happened across the country leaving dozens dead and far many more mutilated: in the capital Abuja (just as the country celebrated its fiftieth independence anniversary); in the perennially bloodstained Jos (riven by communal low-intensity warfare), in which 80 people were killed; and in Bayelsa, the grimy oil-rich state from which the presidential career of Goodluck Jonathan was launched while acting as Governor in 2000.

There have also been assassinations of senior political figures on the campaign trail. A candidate for Governor of Bornu State, Modu Fannami

Gubio, was gunned down in January this year along with six of his supporters allegedly by young men on top of motor cycles with AK 47 rifles. The Deputy Chairman of Gubio's party (All Nigeria Peoples Party, ANPP) had already been gunned down by unknown assassins a few weeks before. Blame for the killings was placed on the Boko Haram, an inchoate Islamist sect sometimes known as the Nigerian Taliban – though some analysts contend that the notorious sect is being blamed for atrocities that other more sophisticated political actors perpetrate.

Such assassinations and casual political killings have clearly now become commonplace in Nigeria – it is called "Point and Kill." The assassins usually drive in cars with tinted windows – the shootings are often drive-by. As a result, the government in March this year banned all cars with tinted windows, though enforcement is highly problematic and ramshackle. By the end of March, no arrest of would-be assassins was reported.

In January this year, the government announced the establishment of a new Army Division (called 82), 17,000-strong, solely to be deployed across the country to tackle elections-related violence. That Division alone is larger than any other army in the region, and is far larger than the UN forces deployed in Liberia to help put together the ravaged country. The government also announced in March that all of the country's 370,000-strong police force will be deployed on elections day across the country to prevent or curb violence.

6.
Nigeria's 2011 Elections: One Man's Burden[38]

Stepping outside Abuja`s Nnamdi Azikwe Airport in early March, I was suddenly aware of a convoy of SUVs and other sleek vehicles leaving the parking lot. It looked presidential, but the small crowd of people around the parking lot was waving reverentially at the convoy, and the security wasn't particularly tight. On inquiry, my taxi driver, beaming, told me: "That is our savior, Commissioner Jega. He is the only one that can fix things here, and he is conducting our elections." He was referring to Attahiru Jega, formerly Vice Chancellor of Bayero University, and appointed in August 2010 as head of the country`s wobbly Independent National Electoral Commission, INEC.

I muttered something about the danger of putting so much hope in one man in such a large and complex country. The driver`s friendly smile vanished; and he looked at me scornfully, as at a cynical foreigner and a fool, and never regained his good humour throughout our long trip to my hotel. It was a good introduction to the country as it prepared for what is billed as "make or break" elections this April [2011].

The elections are certainly the most open since Nigeria gained independence in 1960, and the fourth nation-wide polls since. Breaking a cycle of coups and praetorian dictatorships, it returned to civil rule in 1999. Of the 17 or more elections being held in Africa this year, the elections in Nigeria are certainly one of the most important, and their successful conduct will have ramifications all over the continent.

Nigeria's last nation-wide polls, in 2007, were so contested that they generated an astonishing 1,250 petitions, and 6,180 electoral litigations at the courts. Incredibly, some of these litigations are still pending. While the resort to the courts by aggrieved parties is a welcome sign that Nigerians generally respect the judiciary for its independence – a potential insurance against resorting to organised violence – the long

---

[38] *ISS Today*, 6 April 2011. Jega also conducted the universally praised elections in 2015.

delays in passing judgments undercuts this reassurance. As it happened, over 300 people were killed during the 2007 elections.

Shortly after those elections, Umaru Yar'ADua, who won the disputed presidential polls, set up the Electoral Reform Committee (ERC) chaired by the respected Justice Muhammadu Uwais to make recommendations about the conduct of future elections. Not entirely satisfied with the work of the ERC, the government in 2009 took the highly unusual step of requesting the British and American governments to arrange an independent electoral assessment team to make recommendations for credible elections in 2011.

The team produced a comprehensive report in January 2010, which made ten concrete recommendations. The key recommendations included the following: the Independent National Electoral Commission (INEC) should be reconstituted; funding from INEC should be independent of the Presidency and should come directly from the consolidated revenue and voted by the National Legislature; INEC should be transparent and should share vital information with all stakeholders, including all political parties, the media and civil society; elections results should be transparently verified; the judiciary should commit to timely adjudication of electoral disputes and allegations of vote rigging "with possible timeframes specified;" and the state-owned media should provide "equitable, impartial, balanced coverage." □

The government, to its credit, moved quickly to implement a good number of the recommendations. INEC was reconstituted with the respected Jega as chair, though several of the discredited Commissioners who conducted the 2007 polls were not removed. Funding from INEC was delinked from the Presidency, and shortly after Jega requested, and got, over $570 million for the conduct of the polls. INEC then embarked on voter registration, which was completed early this year at the cost of about $230 million. It registered close to 74 million voters, said to be 92% of the voting population, and a significant increase over the about 60 million of 2007.

Jega late last year [2010] announced that votes for the National Legislature were to take place on 2 April, those for the Presidency 9

April, and those for Governors on 16 April. A day before the first votes, however, Jega announced that ballot papers and result sheets were not in place for some polling places, and a new schedule for the elections was announced. National Legislative elections would be held on 4 April, presidential elections on 19 April, while gubernatorial and local elections will be held on April 26. On Monday 4 April, however, the elections were again postponed. Some ballot materials had arrived too late at polling stations and Jega said "we cannot proceed with these elections if we want them to be free, fair and credible if there are no result sheets." This time the blame was placed on the earthquake in Japan, which somehow had diverted the plane bringing the voting materials to Nigeria. This means that the entire calendar will have to be revamped.

This was testing the patience of Nigerians to the limit, and the public would have none of Jega's soothing assurances. The Lagos daily, *The Punch*, not at all a rowdy tabloid, came out with a frontpage editorial denouncing the "sheer incompetence" of INEC which "has turned a moment of celebration to a flash of queasy foreboding for an enthusiastic nation."

Others will not celebrate however timely the polls would have been. Electoral violence, including bomb attacks and assassinations, has already killed dozens.

Meanwhile, there are 21 presidential candidates, but only four have campaigned across the country and, therefore, have any serious chance. Leading is President Goodluck Jonathan, flagbearer for the Peoples' Democratic Party (PDP), which advertises itself as "the largest party in Africa." It is certainly the richest and most powerful in Nigeria.

Jonathan's key challengers, however, are no push-overs. Leading them is former military Head of State, General Muhammadu Buhari, of the Congress for Progressive Change (CPC). Buhari overthrew the civilian regime of Shehu Shagari in 1983, and ruled with an iron fist until he was unseated, less than three years later, by General Ibrahim Banbagida.

The other is Nuhu Ribadu, who gained national and international prominence as chair of the Economic and Financial Crimes Commission.

Ribadu is Presidential candidate of the Action Congress of Nigeria (ACN). During the course of his work as head of the country's anti-corruption commission, Ribadu embarrassed the government by exposing key Governors, State and National Government officials for corrupt practices, and he had to flee the country after receiving death threats.

The fourth leading candidate is Mallam Ibrahim Shekarau, the Governor of Kano State. Shekarau's appeal, however, is limited largely to the Muslim-dominated northern half of Nigeria, making him a rather long-shot candidate.

All the key challengers of Jonathan, in other words, are from the North. This is likely to play to Jonathan's favour. From the minority Ijaw (albeit the fourth largest ethnic group) in Nigeria, Jonathan appeals to other minority groups, as well as having the support of heavyweights from all the major groups in the country.

A likely scenario – and one which the three opposition candidates clearly hope for – is that none of the candidates will win outright, and there will be a run-off between the two leading candidates. The Constitution stipulates that a candidate wins outright only if he/she secures at least 25% of the votes in at least two-thirds [or 24] of the states of the Federation, and moreover must gain the highest number of votes cast nation-wide.

Jonathan alone can conceivably achieve this feat, though the intensity of the contest puts even that in doubt. Nigeria, in other words, may be having a long and uncertain electoral season. But of course it is a more reassuringly familiar season than the so-called Arab spring.

7.
Nigeria's Elections: Goodluck Triumphs, Again[39]

When he emerged on the Nigerian national scene as vice-presidential candidate for the People's Democratic Party (PDP) in 2007, Goodluck Ebele Jonathan, a bland zoologist in an ill-fitting fedora, was a kind of curiosity. From an impoverished fishing village in the oil-rich but badly neglected Bayelsa State, Jonathan was dismissed by many in the country as a nonentity who would not, on his own, survive the rough and tumble of Nigeria's politics. He was acting governor of Bayelsa at the time. He had been deputy to Governor Deprieye Alameyesiegha, a ghastly figure who combined gluttony with gangsterism and made his backwoods state famous: pocketing millions of dollars from his state's federal allocations, he traveled to Europe in grand style, but was arrested in London and detained for money laundering. Under house arrest, Alameyesiegha had his contacts forge a passport bearing the picture of a woman – and, dressed to match, complete with a woman's wig, he escaped detection at Heathrow airport and fled to Nigeria. He was impeached by his state, and Goodluck – always lucky – replaced him. It was how he was picked as Umaru Yar' ADua's running mate.

They won in the most messily rigged elections in Nigeria's history. Two years later, President Yar' Adua was diagnosed with a terminal kidney problem, and was flown to Saudi Arabia for treatment. In February 2010, the National Assembly, acting extra-constitutionally, declared Jonathan "Acting President" by resolution, and, a few months later, Yar'Dua died. Jonathan quickly became the substantive President. Because he lacked a political base and does not belong to the three major ethnic groups in the country – he is from the minority Ijaw – Jonathan was, of course, expected merely to serve out Yar' Adua's term, and then give way to a Northern candidate. Instead, he repudiated the supposed elite consensus called "zoning," and ran as his own man, as the flagbearer of the PDP, after winning a hotly-contested primary poll.

---

[39] www.the-african.org, June/July 2011. Goodluck would be soundly defeated by Buhari in elections in 2015.

Goodluck's most important moment came on 18 April, two days after presidential votes that had been delayed twice, with this terse announcement from Attahiru Jega, Nigeria's unusually well-respected chair of the Independent National Electoral Commission (INEC): "I, Attahiru Muhammadu Jega, hereby certify that…Goodluck Ebele Jonathan of the People's Democratic Party, PDP, having satisfied the requirements of the law and scored the highest number of votes is hereby declared the winner and returned elected."

There had been initial doubts about whether the result would be announced at all, since Jonathan's key opponent, former military leader General Muhammadu Buhari (of the Congress for Democratic Change, CDC), was already crying foul as the returns from were coming in, and riots had broken out in the northern half of the country. But Jega made clear that Jonathan had fulfilled the requirements by not only winning the highest number of votes, but also the more tasking requirement of winning 25 per cent of the votes in two-thirds of the 36 states.

He failed, however, to carry a single state of the 16 main northern states, which Buhari comfortably carried. Buhari for his part failed to carry or even poll significantly in any of the southern states. Youths chanting 'Only Buhari!' rampaged through northern cities, killing supporters of Jonathan and burning down houses. In all, as many as 1000 people may have been killed, a number far higher than that for those killed during and after the elections of 2007. The army had to be deployed – a 17,000-strong division had been set up for just that eventuality.

Buhari claimed that the returns in Jonathan's southern strongholds had been rigged, and he called for a forensic examination of the ballots. Though Jonathan commanded majority support in the country, there are certainly grounds for Buhari's objection. While overall voter turn-out was low, hovering around 45-55%, voter turn-out in the south were in some places way higher. That could perhaps be explained by the fact that enthusiasm for Jonathan in these areas was very high, though Jonathan's People's Democratic Party (PDP) is far from being popular there. The official results of the balloting are certainly somewhat suspect – they indicated perhaps some sophisticated tampering by the PDP, which has a notorious record of rigging elections. The results from Akwa Ibom state in the south of the country, for example, gave Jonathan 95 per cent. The mainly Igbo Anambra state, not at all a major stronghold of either Jonathan or the PDP, gave the incumbent 99 per cent. Jonathan modestly accepted only 99.63 per cent in his home state of Bayelsa.

The National Chairman of Buhari's Congress for Progressive Change (CPC) party delivered a formal petition to INEC rejecting results from the 22 states, demanding that the "ballot papers and result sheets…from these zones and states" be subjected to further "scrutiny in the interest of peace, prosperity, free, fair and credible elections."

There could be a long legal tussle, though Buhari had earlier rejected claims that he was seeking legal recourse. To his credit, though he initially dithered with respect to condemning the spreading violence, he finally disowned the perpetrators. Buhari has been defeated now three times by the PDP in his presidential bid.

The presidential results were very disappointing for the anti-corruption crusader Nuhu Ribadu. He got only 2,079,159 to Jonathan's 22,495,187 and Buhari's 12,214,853. Initial indications suggested that key governors and notables of his party had made deals with the PDP to support Jonathan in return for future favours. In any case, Ribadu, a new-comer to Nigeria's tough electoral field, never really had a chance even in areas where his party held governorships (mainly the south-west), since as a northerner he was deemed far less palatable than Jonathan, from the minority Ijaw in the south. He also had little chance against the veteran campaigner Buhari.

The post-elections violence in northern Nigeria should not be viewed as merely a reaction to the suspicion that the votes had been rigged in favour of the incumbent, Jonathan, though it was clearly part of the reason for it. Northerners – civilian and military – have ruled Nigeria for 38 of its 51 years of existence as an independent state. This putative dominance is the cause of the great anxiety which Nigerians cryptically call the "National Question," or, using another formulation, the "Federal Character" of the nation: the idea that no region or cluster of states or related ethnic groups would dominate national politics in the country. It is the reason why Nigeria has progressively tended to be fissiparous, breaking up old political units or states into smaller new ones that are, because non-viable in themselves, wholly dependent on the largess of the Federal government, making secession all but impossible. At independence, Nigeria had three regions and 301 local governments; since 1996, the last time new states were created, Nigeria has 36 states and 774 local governments. The conspiracy theory around the violence emanating from Jonathan and others supporting him – that the violence was orchestrated by disgruntled political figures and was not at all spontaneous – should be understood partly in this context.

This brings in the issue of zoning – the elite consensus forged by the PDP to make sure no part of the Nigerian Federation would be politically dominant. This is highly significant politically. Zoning was far from being perfect, but the fact that it may be principally responsible for the political stability Nigeria has enjoyed since 1999 – the longest period of civil rule since its independence in 1960 – should be a cause of deep reflection. Clearly disgruntlement runs deep in the north as a result of Jonathan's repudiation of the 'zoning' agreement, which in effect has denied the north a chance to provide a two-term president for the country. The fact that Jonathan is Christian, and from an impoverished backwater – albeit oil-rich – state, make matters worse in the eyes of many northern Nigerians. The violence was perpetrated by young, impoverished people, many of whom probably did not vote. Nigeria is a country where politicians hire assassins to kill opponents, such are the stakes. Inspiring mobs to create mayhem to make a political point or gain political mileage is not at all inconceivable in Nigeria.

Nigeria surely needs such a consensus if it is to remain together, or is to have a stable democratic future. An important step forward would be for Jonathan to organise something like a national conference to debate the issue and forge an elite consensus to replace zoning.

An important development during and after the elections was the support thrown behind Jonathan by the violent militants of the Niger Delta state. Yar'Adua had negotiated a peace agreement with the militants in which they were offered amnesty in exchange for laying down their arms. Violence, however, continued in the region, some of it no doubt perpetrated by the militants, but some perhaps by extraneous political elements wishing to undermine Jonathan, who hails from the region. The Amnesty Office set up by Yar'Adua in Abuja, the federal capital, went up in flames on 3 March 2011. No one claimed responsibility for this. After the Jonathan win precipitated violence in the north, the Niger Delta militants vowed to fight to death to protect Jonathan's tenure.

If militants' support for Jonathan holds, and they finally accept the jurisdiction of the federal government over that key oil-producing state, then Jonathan's presidency could have made a highly positive contribution to keeping Nigeria together and stabilizing its oil production. That, however, is only the very beginning of the effort to establish good governance, peace and stability in Nigeria.

Nigeria is Africa's largest democracy, its most populated country, and the most strategic in West Africa. It is the continent's largest oil producer, and its most enthusiastic peace-enforcer. Nigerians have high hopes that the country, disfigured by decades of corruption and mismanagement, will finally turn the corner by entrenching practices of good governance. This will demand major reforms in all public sectors in the country, which can only be guaranteed by strong and visionary leadership. Entrenched corruption around the oil industry should be a key focus. From the oil-rich Bayelsa State himself, Jonathan must be keenly aware of the ravages caused by rapacious elite exploitation of this key industry, including distorting the country's development, creating an exploitative and unproductive ruling class, causing massive environmental degradation, as well as the impoverishment and oppression of citizens of the oil producing regions.

With an apparently strong mandate of his own, and with his promise to serve out only one term, Jonathan ought surely to immediately start working on these issues, even if that means, once again, going to battle with his PDP.

8

A Postcript

Revisiting Sierra Leone's 'Rebel' War: Evidence from the TRC and Special Court

On 14 JULY 2009, in an open session at Trial Chamber II of the Special Court for Sierra Leone (SCSL) sitting in The Hague, Charles Taylor, the former Liberian president, was finally giving testimony on a crucial and much-debated point about the origins of Sierra Leone's 'rebel' war. He was being questioned by his lead counsel, Courtenay Griffiths:

Griffiths: Now moving on, Mr. Taylor, did you knowingly assist Foday Sankoh and the RUF [Revolutionary United Front] to invade Sierra Leone?

Taylor: I, Charles Ghankay Taylor, never ever at any time knowingly assist Foday Sankoh in the invasion of Sierra Leone.

Griffiths: Did you plan such an invasion with him?

Taylor: I never ever planned any invasion of that friendly country with Foday Sankoh.

Griffiths: Did you have prior knowledge that such an invasion would take place?

Taylor: Now, I may have to probably just seek some clarification. I was aware from Libya that a Sierra Leonean group, the Sierra Leonean Pan-African Revolutionary Movement, harboured the intent to carry on such operations in Sierra Leone at the time in Libya, and so that's why I said I need some clarification. But as to the Foday Sankoh operation, no.

Griffiths: Did you ever provide the RUF with military assistance?

Taylor: I did not provide the RUF with any military assistance to invade Sierra Leone.[40]

---

[40] Trial transcripts from the SCSL's website http://www.sc-sl.org accessed on 1 November 2011: Taylor added, however, that months after the initial incursions by the RUF into Sierra Leone, "between the periods of August 1991 throughout May of 1992," his National Patriotic Front of Liberia (NPFL) had forged some kind of

This vehement denial notwithstanding, the prosecutors on 17 January 2011 submitted their voluminous final brief to the judges, arguing with great cogency and detail that Taylor "created, armed and supported" the RUF which, in the view of the prosecutors, was little more than "an extension" of Taylor's NPFL. This claim, which is unlikely to be definitively decided by the SCSL because the origin of the RUF is not covered in the indictment period of the trial proceedings, has been at the heart of the difficulty in reaching consensus about the character of the RUF and, even more important, about the nature and purpose of the so-called rebel war in Sierra Leone.

More than many other small wars in Africa, and more than even the Liberian civil war from which it allegedly derived, the Sierra Leone 'rebel' war (1991-2002) has over the years attracted significant scholarly attention, and debates about the origin and nature of the war still rage among academics, policy analysts, and, before the SCSL, jurists. This article will revisit the beginning of the debate, both in order to see how consistent the points of contention have been for the past 15 years or so, as well as to evaluate the new evidence that have been brought up to illuminate the issues principally by the report of the Sierra Leone's Truth and Reconciliation Commission (TRC) in 2004 and the data produced by SCSL over the years.

A recent article in the journal *African Affairs* on the war by four academics ask, "Was the civil war in Sierra Leone (1991–2002) fought for diamonds, or was it a peasant insurgency motivated by agrarian grievances?" The evidence on both sides, it noted, "is less than conclusive."[41] It is a curious way of framing the issue, since the

---

'cooperation' with the RUF after an anti-Taylor group, ULIMO, entered Liberia from Sierra Leone to battle Taylor. "They had been armed, trained and sent in by the [President Joseph Saidu] Momoh government [of Sierra Leone]. Now, I provided for the protection of the borders of Liberia, as was my duty and responsibility at the time - I provided small amounts of arms and ammunition, more ammunition than arms to that particular group," Taylor said.

[41] Esther Mokuwa, Maarten Voors, Erwin Bulte and Paul Richards, "Peasant Grievances and insurgency in Sierra Leone: Judicial Serfdom as a driver of Conflict in Sierra Leone" (*African Affairs*, May 2011, Vol. 110, Issue 440, 339-366.)

proponents of the view that diamonds helped fuel the war – including this writer – have never suggested that the war was all about diamonds. In this article, I describe key findings relating to the origins and causes of the war by both the TRC and SCSL, showing how they illuminate, contradict or support what is already known about the war from published sources. I engage with theoretical debates about the war only in so far as they relate to these findings.

Understanding the Origins and Character of the War

In his magnificent novel, *War and Peace*, Tolstoy mordantly reflects on the arbitrary nature of historical stocktaking. "The first thing history does is to take an arbitrary series of continuous events and examine them separately whereas no event can *ever* have a beginning, because an individual event flows without any break in continuity from another," he writes. "The second thing...is to treat the actions of a single person...as the sum total of everybody else's individual will."[42]

Tolstoy makes a very important point. Unfortunately, in considering historical events, especially modern wars which are subject to juridical reviews, one perforce must make judgments about the approximate origins, the trigger causes, and individual driving forces. This is particularly true of the Sierra Leone 'rebel' war, which has been so subject to conflicting interpretations and reinterpretations, and about which there has been an expensive and prolonged international criminal proceeding.

On a number of issues regarding the war, however, scholars, analysts, policy makers and jurists agree. The first is that Sierra Leone's war started in March 1991 when Foday Saybanah Sankoh led his fighters from territories controlled by then insurgent leader, Charles Taylor, in Liberia into southern and eastern Sierra Leone. Like Taylor, Sankoh had trained in Libya, though there is some disagreement about whether the two met there and forged a relationship.[43] There is no dispute, however, that Sankoh spent considerable time with Taylor's National Patriotic Front of Liberia (NPFL) forces in Liberia in the initial stages of Liberia's

---

[42] Leo Tolstoy, *War & Peace* (London: Penguin Books, 2005 edition), 912.
[43] See the SCSL trial transcripts cited above.

civil war (from 1989 to 1991) and that he recruited and trained most of his initial RUF fighting force under Taylor's patronage in territory controlled by the NPFL in Liberia. This is of particular interest, in part because the SCSL prosecutors have charged that Taylor and Sankoh made "common cause" to launch a war in Sierra Leone from their time in Libya as well as in Taylor's territory in Liberia at about this time. The prosecutors charge that this was in furtherance of a "joint criminal enterprise" (JCE) to loot Sierra Leone's mineral resources, mainly diamonds.

The trial transcripts show that all the so-called Vanguards – the fighters who constituted the original invading RUF force from Liberia – were trained at Camp Naama in Taylor's occupied territory in Liberia by Isaac Mongor, a Liberian NPFL who had been a guard at Monrovia's Executive Mansion (the presidential palace). These included future leaders of the RUF: Issa Sesay, Sam Bockarie, and Morris Kallon. Sankoh was clearly now leader of the RUF; Rashid Mansaray was battle front commander (and No.2 in the RUF hierarchy), and Mohamed Tarawalie was battlefield commander (No.3). All three had trained in Libya, and were known as Special Forces. The prosecution's argument that Taylor "created and effectively controlled the RUF" is based on these facts, as well as on the evidence that the majority of the original RUF fighters who entered Sierra Leone in 1991 were Liberians who were members of Taylor's NPFL.

Trial transcripts show several witnesses testifying that many of the Sierra Leoneans who were recruited into the RUF at that point were already prisoners held by Taylor's forces, and almost certainly would have been executed had they not joined Sankoh's RUF. On this, even Taylor's defence conceded, noting in its final brief that "recruitment into the RUF was accomplished in part by deceit and blackmail; and many were...reluctant volunteers preferring the relative safety of joining the RUF to the prospect of indefinite detention in a NPFL camp. The Sierra Leoneans recruited by Sankoh were predominantly expatriate Sierra Leoneans from Liberia and Ivory Coast." But it noted, in defence of their client's claim that he never entered into a pact with the Sankoh before the launch of the RUF war, that only "former members of the NPFL and some ordinary citizens of Liberia chose to throw in their lot with the RUF." Even Issa Sesay testified that he was forced to join the RUF on threat of death. A key prosecution witness testified that the RUF's plan to attack Sierra Leone was drawn at Voinjama between Taylor and Sankoh. *Witness to Truth*, the TRC's final report, estimated that as many as 1,600 NPFL fighters were involved in the early phase of the Sierra Leonean war,[44] or about 80% of the RUF forces. This grew to 2000 within a few months of the invasion. The report called the original RUF recruits in Liberia "detainee-turned-vanguards," noting that:

> Sankoh personally accompanied members of NPFL 'hit squads' who visited some of the detention facilities, apparently for the sole purpose of enlisting the men and women he wanted to make into his first revolutionary commandos... Sankoh's favoured means of recruitment depended on convincing people that their lives lay squarely in his hands and that if they refused to join him, they would be responsible for their own fate – effectively, he blackmailed them into becoming members of the RUF. Many of those enlisted by this means were acutely aware of what Sankoh was doing, but were equally powerless to prevent it in view of the all-pervading dangers at that time of being a Sierra Leonean in Liberia...[45]

Once they invaded Sierra Leone, trial transcripts show that the RUF targeted children for recruitment, and that this continued as a policy. The judgment in the case of the three RUF indictees – Issa Sesay, Moriss Kallon and Augustine Gbao, delivered on 2 March 2009 – determined that "thousands of children" were forcibly recruited by the RUF. It noted:

> The military training of children by the RUF dates from its inception as an armed movement. Between 1991 and 1992, children between the ages of eight and 15 were trained at Camp Naama in Liberia3081 and Matru Jong and Pendembu in Sierra Leone. Prior to1996, the RUF also trained children in military techniques at their Headquarters at Camp Zogoda... In the

[44] *Witness to Truth: Report of Sierra Leone's Truth and Reconciliation Commission*, vol. 3A, para. 126.
[45] Ibid.

Chamber's view, this evidence demonstrates a consistent pattern of conduct by the RUF of recruiting and training children for military purposes that began as early as 1991 and continued throughout the Indictment period. Children were of great importance to the RUF organisation. As the RUF had no formal means of recruitment, it relied heavily on abducted children to increase the number of fighters within the RUF. Young boys were of particular value to the RUF due to their loyalty to the movement and their ability to effectively conduct espionage activities, as their small size and agility made them particularly suitable for hazardous assignments. The younger children were particularly aggressive when armed and were known to kill human beings as if they were nothing more than "chickens."

Some witnesses testified that the RUF was not well-armed at the time it invaded Sierra Leone, and the prosecutors produced a letter in court from Sankoh begging Taylor to send him more armaments and weapons. Taylor's defence seized on this to suggest, in its final brief, that this would mean that the RUF was not a wing of the NPFL since it otherwise would have been significantly well-armed by Taylor before it was launched in Sierra Leone. But it admitted to Taylor being aware of the RUF training in territory under his control, emphasing, however, that there was "ideological training" of the RUF. This training was meant to induce in the fighters a need to "give good treatment to the civilians because they needed their support; people's property was to be taken care of and maintained, fighters were to have access to food." It continued: "Ideology training involved offering someone a chance to surrender; no raping; and allowing civilians to leave for safer locations."

No doubt the "ideological" training was not entirely successful, as many witnesses testified to a regime of terror and rapine imposed on areas that the RUF immediately controlled after its initial incursions. Blame for this were largely placed by several witnesses on the Liberian elements in the RUF. This concurs with the findings of the TRC, which noted that in fact Sankoh was effectively held hostage by the NPFL elements (or so-called 'Special Forces') both because of their huge number as well as by the fact that having brought them to Sierra Leone, Sankoh "had to accept that in the eyes of the population these people were the RUF."

In addition, the Commission insightfully notes of the Liberian training in general:

> The Commission recognises that the period spent in training by the vanguards of the RUF was to provide a benchmark for the formation of other militias and armed groups that participated in the Sierra Leone conflict: in character, this group of people stands to be considered as a highly unconventional fighting force; its members were taken on board in troubled circumstances, many of them under false pretences, duress, or threats to their lives; and they were only loosely bound together by superficial bonds, more out of a sense of common adversity than any true notion of unity. It is therefore hardly surprising that the relationships of these vanguards among themselves would fluctuate between friendly camaraderie and mutual suspicion.

When the RUF gained a foothold in Sierra Leone, particularly in Kailahun and Pujehun districts, long a stronghold of opposition to the All Peoples Congress (APC) one-party dictatorship in Sierra Leone, several witnesses testified that there were many "willing recruits" joining the RUF. Paul Richards was the first scholar to draw attention to these types, as he was the first to write about the brutalities of the Liberian and Burkinabe elements in the RUF at the early stages of the war, in a pioneering article that appeared in 1995. Among the willing recruits, he wrote, there were "signs of voluntary adhesion" to the RUF.[46] The TRC report has a particular section on such recruits in its Volume 3, and it treats the matter with appropriate circumspection and sensitivity. Referring to "a variety of individuals in both the East and South of the country, with particular emphasis on young men from rural areas" who "joined the RUF of their own volition, stayed with the movement until the end of the conflict and, in many cases, have gone on to become members of the Revolutionary United Front Party (RUFP), which they feel still embodies their ideas for change," the report noted that "some complicated sociological dynamics [are] to be considered when looking at the concept of 'volunteering' one's own or a family member's services to the RUF." The 'willing recruits' were mostly, the TRC concluded, of the

---

[46] *Paul Richards*, 'Rebellion in *Liberia and Sierra Leone: a crisis of youth?*' in Oliver Furley, ed., Conflict in Africa (London: I. B. Tauris, 1995), 134-170.

'stereotype' which would "fit a young man who had come from a lower-class background of abject poverty and whose parents had not enjoyed any favour or good fortune under the APC, despite often having worked hard in the agricultural sector." Such a young man "had nonetheless been able to acquire enough education to perceive some of the blatant injustices to which he was being subjected; but at the point the RUF found him, he had lost all social bearing and was therefore open to the option of taking up arms."

The SCSL, partly to demonstrate the ultimate culpability of Augustine Gbao – who is described as the "ideology trainer" of the RUF – goes to great lengths to describe the RUF's ideological training as an integral part of the movement, one which determined the character of the war and ensured the coherence of the RUF throughout the war. In its judgment on the RUF indictees, the SCSL has this to say:

"A crucial aspect of the political ideology of the RUF was the acceptability of taking up arms to further the goals of its revolution. The ideology consisted in "the use of weapons to seek total redemption"; "to organise themselves and for a sort of People's Army"; "to procure arms for a broad-based struggle so that the rotten and selfish government is toppled". The RUF claimed to be fighting to overthrow a corrupt military Government in order to realise the right of every Sierra Leonean to true democracy and fair governance. Nonetheless, when democratic elections were held in 1996 the RUF boycotted the ballot box and continued active. A critical pillar of the ideology was thus the notion that the people of Sierra Leone were tasked with helping the revolution succeed. It was common practice for the RUF, upon capturing a village, to conscript its civilians, including children, into the ranks of the fighting forces. Accordingly, despite the ideological focus on the revolution as the embodiment of the will of the people, there was often no alternative to accepting the RUF ideology: civilians who did not support the movement were perceived as enemies and therefore legitimate targets. It is notable in this respect that many of the senior members of the RUF were originally forced recruits, including Sesay, Kallon and Gbao."

A key evidence popularly tying Taylor to the RUF from the very start of the war in Sierra Leone was Taylor's statement on the BBC on 1

November 1990, threatening to attack and destroy Sierra Leone's international airport, arguing that by allowing its territory to be used as an operational base of the West African intervention force, ECOMOG, Sierra Leone had made itself a legitimate target. The SCSL prosecutors presented this as one of evidence of Taylor's involvement in the war in Sierra Leone, but the defence dismissed it as mere bluster on the part of Taylor, not a policy statement. Evidence is incontrovertible that in the late 1980s, and long before this threat, Taylor traveled to Freetown and bribed the compulsively venal Joseph Momoh government of Sierra Leone to allow him to use Sierra Leone as a base to launch his war in Liberia. Momoh's government at first agreed but later reneged on the agreement, arrested and detained Taylor for several days.[47] Was this the root of Taylor's animus to Momoh, and the reason why he supported the RUF's incursions? On this, the TRC report states:

> "The Commission has confirmed that Taylor was indeed detained at Freetown Central Prison for a limited period in 1989, but must caution against the story being afforded any undue credence or significance as a motivation for his later involvement in the Sierra Leone conflict. Taylor had developed multiple other reasons for attacking Sierra Leone by March 1991 and his period of imprisonment ranked very low among them. Acknowledging that the detention itself was not the main cause of Taylor's rancour, some commentators have made claims that Foday Sankoh was incarcerated in the Prison alongside Taylor and that their friendship grew out of this common plight. Testimonies before the Commission do not support this version of events. Several firsthand testimonies place Sankoh in Libya and the Ivory Coast during the period in question. Taylor and Sankoh had met in Libya in 1988 and had become part of the deal between Sierra Leonean and Liberian revolutionaries to mutually support each

---

[47] The trial transcripts are clear about this – even Taylor has not denied it. In his testimony to the Liberian Truth and Reconciliation Commission (TRC) in 2009, Prince Johnson, who was Taylor's chief commander at the initial stages of the Liberian war, said that Taylor gave President Momoh $50,000 as inducement for his facilitating role, but that Momoh later arrested and detained Taylor. Johnson suggested that there was some kind of understanding from that point that Momoh would be punished once the NPFL became successful. I attended the hearings in Monrovia and took notes.

other in their respective plans. Thus when Taylor was released from custody in Sierra Leone and returned to the Ivory Coast to pursue his incursion on a single front, he would meet Sankoh on Ivorian territory and the two of them would continue their joint plans from there."

The TRC gives more weight, with respect to reasons for Taylor's support of the RUF's invasion, to the fact that Momoh had permitted ECOMOG, the "Ceasefire Monitoring Group" of the Economic Community of West African States (ECOWAS), the use of Sierra Leone's Lungi International Airport, "to be used as a launch pad for air raids that were essentially levelled 'against' Taylor." The fact that Momoh sent at least two sets of troops in support of ECOMOG only added to Taylor's ire, in the TRC's view.

Both the TRC and the SCSL prosecutors, in other words, are agreed that Taylor played a critical role in the launch of the RUF war in Sierra Leone – though the SCSL's approach has been less nuanced because narrowly focused on proving "joint criminality" and "common cause" between Sankoh and Taylor than the TRC's.

Diamonds and War-Atrocities

On the controversial issue of the role of diamonds in the war, especially as motivation for Taylor's involvement, the SCSL prosecutors submitted several key documentary and witness evidence to assert that "as early as 1992" the RUF captured the diamond district of Kono "and took captured diamonds to Charles Taylor." They stated as well that in 1995, the RUF again took Kono and Tongo Fields, another diamond area, and extensively mined diamonds there. The prosecutors noted: "However, it was during the AFRC/RUF Junta period that Taylor began to taste the real benefits of Sierra Leone's abundant diamond resources." Their final brief noted that in order for Taylor to arrange shipment of arms to the AFRC and RUF forces – now united as the Peoples' Army – Taylor's emissary Ibrahim Bah "informed Junta leaders that it would be necessary to pay cash for the flight and provide diamonds to Taylor." Diamonds mined in Tongo Field, then under the control of the RUF's Sam Bockarie, "were taken to Taylor by Daniel Tamba." The brief noted that when the AFRC was expelled from Freetown, "Taylor ordered the rebels to concentrate on retaking Kono," which they did, and committed widespread atrocities, including mass execution and amputations in the process of establishing their control over the diamond-rich district. Taylor "arranged shipment of multiple truck-loads of ammunition" into Sierra Leone, which "enabled the late 1998/early 1999 offensive in which the rebels were able to take control of all diamond areas," the brief charges. It noted Issa Sesay's testimony to the effect that after Sam Bockarie left the rebels for Liberia following the 1999 attack on Freetown, "Liberian security closed the border to all with the single exception that Taylor's emissary, Ibrahim Bah, was allowed to cross the border into Sierra Leone with trucks filled with [diamond] mining equipment." The brief noted that twenty-five witnesses "provided information about the AFRC/RUF's diamond business with Taylor or his designees."

In response, Taylor's Defence did not deny these statements, stating that "diamonds only financed the procurement of arms and ammunition" for the RUF between 1998 and 2001. But the Defence denied that diamonds were the reasons why Taylor supported the RUF, stating in the *Final Brief* what no one has challenged: that the RUF diamond mining began "post the invasion" which happened in March 1991. It stated: "There is no evidence of any discussions relating to diamonds pre the Sierra Leonean invasion to suggest that the invasion might have been motivated by a desire to pillage Sierra Leone's diamonds."[48] It should be noted that the Defence's key point is not that Taylor *did not* support the RUF, but that he did not do so either as part of JCE or with "an underlying intention to cause terror." The Defence contends that there was a "purely political motive" for Taylor's support of the RUF war, which may be immoral but certainly not illegal in international law.

The TRC attached a very interesting appendix to its report on the ghastly issue of amputations during the war, which became perhaps the defining mark of the Sierra Leone war.[49] Though the report mentions a number of

---

[48] Charles Taylor's Defence's *Final Brief*, 273.
[49] 'Appendix 5: Amputations in the Sierra Leone Conflict,' (*Witness to Truth*) put together by friend Artemis Christodulou, a PhD student from Yale University, who was an intern at the TRC in 2003: I shared some of my notes, which formed a section of my

intermittent cases of amputations in the region based on mainly colonial and missionary records, it wisely refrains from historicising the phenomenon. The report noted that "intentional amputations" had been carried out by Taylor's forces in Liberia before they were reported in Sierra Leone. The report cites the testimony of Francis Momoh Musah, of the RUF's Internal Defence Unit for Kailahun District, as claiming that the notorious Liberian Special Forces "introduced this specific kind of brutality into the Sierra Leonean civil war of the 1990s." Analysing the telling case of a Sierra Leone government soldier, Tamba Ngauja, who was amputated on 21 November 1992 by Liberian elements in the RUF in Kono, the report notes:

> If the details of this story are credible and if they are representative of the actions of other RUF rebels at least, then we may conclude that the Liberians did, in fact, influence the Sierra Leoneans to commit amputations (the history of amputations in Liberia in lends further credence to this view) and that the Sierra Leoneans, as represented by this commander, willingly accepted the suggestion and made it into their own. We may also conclude, on the basis of this testimony, that, at least at this point in the war (November 1992), the RUF did not have a planned strategy to amputate, but that amputation resulted instead from improvisation on the field.

The report noted that amputations came to be widely practiced by both the RUF and rogue government soldiers, particularly after the ousting of the AFRC from power in Freetown in 1998. The report noted that the AFRC "demonstrated a 'specialisation' in the practice of amputations in the period from 1998 to 1999." From the point of the advent of the AFRC, "similarity of the structure [of amputations] points to a systematic strategy on the part of the perpetrators" and that amputations "were reportedly regularly performed by young boys, often in their teens, though on occasion children were also used." The report quotes a famous amputee, Jusu Jaka, the Chairman of the association for amputees in Freetown, as testifying that "there was one queue for amputation of one hand and another for the amputation of both" during

book (*A Dirty War in West Africa*), with her. In 2004, she was involved in a horrible road accident in Sierra Leone, and remained in coma for many years.

the attack on Freetown in January 1999. It also quotes claims by amputees and the UN that there were 'special units' devoted to cutting off of hands, especially during the horrendous attack on Freetown in 1999. Much of this agrees with my analysis, in which I characterized the amputations as 'violence-as-spectacle'.

The SCSL, on the hand, did not treat amputations in any special way, noting that they were "a hallmark of the retreating" AFRC and RUF forces from Freetown. It noted in the verdict against the three RUF and AFRC leaders charged by the court that "many civilians were subjected to this crime at locations including Calaba Town, Upgun and Kissy." It states: "According to witness George Johnson, AFRC Commander Five-Five issued an order to commit 200 civilian amputations and to send the amputees to the Government," and that several "witnesses testified that rebels asked civilians whether they wanted 'short sleeves' or 'long sleeves' and their arms were amputated either at the elbow or at the wrist accordingly. Rebels were also known to amputate four fingers, leaving only the thumb, which they referred to as 'one love' and which they encouraged the victims to show to Tejan Kabbah." Based on this evidence, the SCSL concluded that "the scale of violence was such that there can be no doubt that the infliction of violence on civilians was a primary objective of the attacking forces."

It is chilling to read the different types of the abuses committed by the AFRC soldiers as they retreated from Freetown even in the dry legal prose of the SCSL: "Expert Witness TF1-081 testified that of 1,168 patients examined between March and December 1999, 99% had been abducted following the 6 January 1999 invasion, the "vast majority" of whom originated from Freetown. Out of these patients, 274 (23.4%) had been beaten for refusing to engage in sexual relations or carry heavy looted goods; 648 (58.5%) of the abductees had been subjected to rape, some by more than two and up to 30 men; 281 (24.1%) complained of vaginal discharge and 327 (27.9%) had pelvic inflammatory disease, both of which are transmitted through sexual intercourse; and 200 (17.1%) were pregnant, over 80% of whom were girls between the ages of 14 and 18."

Lansana Gberie

The Sobel Factor

One of the most confusing – and disturbing – aspects of the war was the emergence of what came to be known as 'Sobel phenomenon' – government soldiers transforming themselves into 'rebels' to partake of the foraging activities of the RUF: soldiers by day and rebels by night. The TRC report discusses this phenomenon in Vol. 2 of its report as part of the 'chameleonic character' of the war. The report notes that a "small but significant number of Army officers and private soldiers engaged in connivance with the RUF to plunder resources out of ambushes and raids on civilian convoys and settlements during the phase of guerrilla warfare." These soldiers engaged in this unwholesome activity "entirely unscrupulous reasons": they "pursued their own self-enrichment and betrayed the state they were enlisted to serve." The report identifies Captain Tom Nyuma, a leading member of National Provisional Ruling Council (NPRC) and praised at the time as a 'war hero', as "foremost among the officers who put his personal interests ahead of his constitutional duties." The report notes: "On many occasions, the SLA acted against the Sierra Leonean people – the very people it was meant to defend. Soldiers perpetrated extensive human rights violations against the civilian population. A large number of soldiers collaborated with the RUF and later the AFRC. At times, troops masqueraded as rebel fighters while attacking convoys and villages in order to loot and steal."[50]

David Keen was the first scholar to graphically describe this phenomenon, though he was to change his mind later about the nature of the war and the character of the insurgents who constituted the RUF.[51] In a paper presented at a seminar in 1995, Keen reported on the phenomenon thus:

> [Government forces would] withdraw from a town, leaving arms and ammunition for the rebels behind them. The rebels pick up the arms and extract the loot, mostly in the form of cash, from the townspeople and then they themselves retreat. At this point,

---

[50] *Witness to Truth*, Vol. 2 Chapter Two Findings, 51

[51] See his 2005 book *Conflict and Collusion in Sierra Leone* (London: James Currey/Palgrave Macmillan, 2005) for a rather different analysis of the RUF war.

290

the government forces reoccupy the town and engage in their own looting, usually of property (which the rebels find hard to dispose of) as well as engaging in illicit.[52]

It is unclear from the testimonies from the TRC and the SCSL whether such a fully-rationalised relationship was ever forged between the RUF and government soldiers before the coup of 1997, but dozens of testimonies at both the TRC and the SCSL make clear that individual commanders and personnel in the two apparently warring rivals collaborated on countless occasions for the sole purpose of looting and rapine. More important, the testimonies indicate that after the National Provisional Ruling Council (NPRC) coup of 1992, some army officers from the north of the country, who dominated the army and continued to maintain residual loyalty to the overthrown All Peoples Congress (APC) government which had recruited them into the force, actively sabotaged the NPRC's war efforts by collaborating with the RUF at various levels. I discuss this issue in my book, in which I characterized the phenomenon as "perhaps the most important element of the war" in much of the 1990s.[53] The Sobel phenomenon profoundly shaped the war in many ways: it led to widespread distrust of the army in Sierra Leone; triggered the emergence and near-preponderance of civil defence forces like the Tamaboros, Kapras, Gbenthis, and Kamajors; and certainly influenced the highly destructive AFRC coup of 1997.

On 24 January 2006, there was a very interesting exchange at the SCSL between Chief Hinga Norman, the putative leader of the Kamajors facing trial at the court, and his lead counsel, Dr. Bubuakei Jabbi:

Norman: A comment that was ringing around Sierra Leone [in 1994 when Norman was regent chief of Jaiama Bongor] was Sobels.
Jabbi: What did that mean?
Norman: Soldiers and rebels combined.
Jabbi: Sobel?
Norman: Sobel. Soldier/rebel, rebel/soldier.
Jabbi: What's the spelling?

---

[52] David Keen, "'Sell-Game': The Economics of Conflict in Sierra Leone," paper presented at Queen Elizabeth House, 1995 (in author's possession)
[53] See Gberie, *A Dirty War*, 80-85.

Norman: That was the name given to soldiers that were viewed by civilians who did not understand whether rebels were wearing soldier uniform or soldiers were actually behaving, or rebel activities. So it was a confused situation in this country…

Jabbi: Any other example of such name?

Norman: Everybody used to call them their own names. The Mendes, instead of saying rebels, they say 'lebels' and others gave other names to them. But you and myself would be very difficult -- it would be very difficult for you and myself to say which was really true, whether the soldiers had really transformed their loyalty into becoming rebels or it was the rebel that was trying to cause confusion among the population. And eventually, if that was the situation, they succeeded in putting us against our soldiers. So when chiefs, including myself, decided to arm young men in our chiefdoms to protect our land, homeland, property and life, soldiers viewed this as a disservice to their loyalty, and so Hinga Norman, being a soldier they were looking up to.

Jabbi: Who is that Hinga Norman?

Norman: Myself, and also a chief who had then sided with his colleague chiefs…As Deputy Minister of Defence, all soldiers thinking that I [was] against them. So I was only lucky to survive. That was how it was when, in 1997, I had a lot of intelligence covert in the army and they did their best in giving me information that later proved accurate. Most, if not all, of this information I did not keep to myself. I passed them to my boss.

Jabbi: Meaning?

Norman: The Minister of Defence, the commander-in-chief of the armed forces and the president of Sierra Leone [Ahmad Tejan Kabbah]. I requested measures to be taken to safeguard the armory where guns, explosives and other dangerous weapons are kept and this is where, when I heard that I have been selected as one of those who bear the greatest responsibility for whatever happened in Sierra Leone resulting into massive deaths and destruction of life and property for which I am sitting down here, I feel aggrieved. That I am also held for omission - that is, not doing what I should have done to prevent that, whether it was by punishment or by preventing what happened to Sierra Leone. I do feel aggrieved and that is why I am very grateful that after all my long stay from this Court, finally their Lordships did not walk me out of this Court to say, 'Go back. You said you were not coming here, so we are not accepting you.' I have been given the opportunity to tell this Court, this nation and the world whether it is me or those two people over there…those who are now there in detention that have been picked, that are responsible, they're to be left to Their Honours…[54]

Norman's cautious framing of the issue in the court is understandable – in an interview with this writer shortly after a bloody attack on Telu Bongor, his chiefdom headquarter town where he started recruiting young men into a civil defence militia unit, at the time, nearly led to his death in 1994, he categorical blamed the attack on rogue government soldiers posing as RUF rebels.[55]

Judging the AFRC coup from a narrow technical legal point, the SCSL – in its judgment in the case of the AFRC indictees – found that the coalition formed by the soldiers and RUF rebels after the coup in 1997 was "not based on longstanding common interests."[56] In fact, the transcripts of the testimonies of dozens of people, including ex-soldiers and ex-RUF rebels, persuasively show that mercenary interests shared by elements within the army and the RUF shaped this collaboration at least since 1992, after the NPRC coup.

Early Analyses of the War

The RUF's brutality, its reliance on foreign fighters at the initial stages of the war, and on child soldiers throughout the war, bewildered most analysts from the start. The first attempt to understand the war had to grapple with this unique characteristic. As it happens, the basic outline of this analysis – which depicted the war as part of a wider narrative of youth nihilism, state collapse, and mercenarism in West Africa – has been significantly modified, but not entirely rejected. It began with the publication, in 1994, of Robert Kaplan's highly influential "The Coming Anarchy" article in the *Atlantic Monthly* magazine.[57]

---

[54] SCSL trial transcripts at http://www.sc-sl.org/LinkClick.aspx?fileticket=zlBenCP64OM%3d&tabid=154 (accessed on 6 November 2011)
[55] I discuss this attack in *A Dirty War*, 85-86.
[56] Trial Chamber 2, *Judgment against Alex Tamba Brima, Brima Bazzy Kamara, and Santigie Borbor Kanu*, 20 June 2007, 43.
[57] Robert Kaplan, 'The Coming Anarchy,' *Atlantic Monthly*, February 1994.

Kaplan's article, which posited youth discontentment and dislocation in West Africa as among the most important drivers of conflict in the region, however, addresses the problem only tangentially, as a footnote to much more important factors at play. Uneasily welding together the thesis of Martin van Creveld about post-Cold War wars by non-state actors, Thomas Homer-Dixon's pessimistic environmental prognosis and Samuel Huntington's thesis about the unavoidable 'clash of civilizations', Kaplan described the war in Sierra Leone - and in Liberia at the time, after lightning stops in both countries - as anarchic, criminal (as opposed to political) violence that would lead to a Hobbesian state of nullity and terror. The widespread armed violence in both countries, he wrote, was not war in the sense in which Clausewitz defined wars as a continuation of politics by other means. Instead, what was happening in Sierra Leone was

> ... a microcosm of what is happening in West Africa and much of the underdeveloped world: the withering away of central governments, the rise of tribal or regional domains, the unchecked spread of disease, and the growing pervasiveness of war.[58]

This kind of war is not politically motivated but criminally driven, with dispossessed urban youths – 'loose molecules in an unstable social fluid' - wreaking vengeance on societies that had left them despairing and poor. Kaplan suggested that these armed youths were Africa's modern day *écorcheurs* who were roaming and ravaging the countryside in a manner reminiscent of the ravages of armed mercenaries in Germany during the Thirty Years' War. It was the phrase, West African youth as 'loose molecules in an unstable social fluid', that captured the mercenary essence of the war, and upon which other analysts seized.

It provoked Paul Richards, a British anthropologist with very intimate knowledge of Sierra Leone, to write the first scholarly analysis of the war. In 1995, Richards published "Rebellion in Liberia and Sierra Leone: a crisis of youth," as a chapter in Oliver Furley's volume on *Conflict in*

[58] Ibid.

Africa.[59] It is impossible now, with all the many volumes and thousands of pages of data that has been produced on the war, to accurately capture the refreshing impact of this path-breaking article. It was the first serious study that drew a conceptual and practical connection between the RUF and the NPFL in Liberia, even tracing their roots to anti-state student and youth activism, as well as the support from ideological connections in Gaddafi's Libya – though only tantalisingly. Richards did not appear to have the evidence to flesh out the linkages. The following year, he wrote a book-length account of on the war, *Fighting for the Rainforest: War, Resources and Youth,*[60] in which, stung perhaps by a robust critique of his 1995 article by Ibrahim Abdullah, he somewhat abandons those critically important aspects of the war to instead concentrate on providing a rationalist framework for the RUF's demented brutality. Though he makes the case that student radicalism had been a factor in the rise of the RUF, Richards devotes a large part of the book to debunking Kaplan's ill-thought out thesis on the Sierra Leone war. Youth is central to understanding the crisis in Sierra Leone, Richards wrote, but not in the context that Kaplan placed it. There is nothing like the breakdown of social order, population pressure, family breakdown and environmental degradation that Kaplan claims to have happened in "this well-resourced country." Sierra Leone, Richards wrote in a spirited piece which came not long after Kaplan's article, "is one of Africa's less likely candidates for neo-Malthusian disaster." The problem really, according to Richards, is that there was a rebellion of marginalized youth to take control over the country's forest resources from the capital city-based elites and their exploitative foreign friends. He analysed the RUF now as a "group of embittered pedagogues" fighting to replace the corrupt patrimonial state with a "revolutionary egalitarian one" and appealing "directly to deracinated youths with blighted educational prospects." The RUF also, he wrote, appealed to a "younger generation of rural primary and secondary school teachers, long disgruntled by poor and uncertain pay" and to a "mass of less educated youth in the diamond districts [who had] a more intuitive revolutionary consciousness shaped notably by reggae-style Rasta and exposure to Rambo genre of post-Vietnam movies." Richards noted certain "communitarian principles" practiced by the RUF

---

[59] *Paul Richards,* "Rebellion in *Liberia and Sierra Leone: a crisis of youth?*"
[60] Paul Richards, *Fighting for the Rainforest: War, Resources and Youth in Sierra Leone* (London: Heineman, 1996).

in areas it controlled, including redistribution of "food, drugs, clothes and shoes from 'liberated' government sources," taking at face value the RUF's stated pronouncement: "Every member of the community has rights to basic needs (food, housing, health, and transport)."[61]

Once again, Ibrahim Abdullah descended on Richards in an important article, "Bush Paths to Destruction: The Revolutionary United Front of Sierra Leone," first published on the Sierra Leone email discussion forum Leonenet in November and December 1996 and later as part of a collection of articles on the war.[62] In it, Abdullah provides a convincing account of how some university students in Sierra Leone, expelled by the authorities for involvement in arson attacks on campus, were led by their leader, Alie Kabba, to train in Libya for a revolutionary project in Sierra Leone. These students subsequently recruited mostly urban drifters ("lumpens") and spirited them off to Libya to train. Foday Sankoh, who had been cashiered out of the army for involvement in a failed coup plot and gaoled for many years in the 1970s, also joined the group. He had been a commercial photographer after his release from prison. It was this group that Taylor referred to when he testified to the SCSL on 14 July 2009.[63]

Abdullah offered his own interpretation of the war as a "rebellion" driven by "lumpen youth," and, inevitably, characterised by terror and lacking in ideological motivation. Abdullah defines lumpen youth as socially uprooted and criminally disposed young people among whom had emerged, after decades of a corrupt and ultimately failed one-party system, a lumpen youth culture - a despairing anti-social movement of drug addicts, petty thieves and gamblers, growing up mostly in the slums of Freetown. People from this group formed the core leadership of the

---

[61] Richards, *Fighting for the Rainforest*, 52-54.

[62] Ibrahim Abdullah, 'Bush Paths to Destruction: The Revolutionary United Front of Sierra Leone,' in *Between Democracy and Terror* (Dakar: CODESRIA, 2004).

[63] In fact, according to all other accounts, the project went nowhere at the time, and the group scattered. Sankoh and a few of the revolutionary enthusiasts, however, were later to join Taylor in his insurgency in Liberia, and from there launched the RUF war.

RUF, which is why the group was pathologically disposed to criminal violence and terror. The war, in other words, was a kind of rootless urban youth revolt. The "mutilation, murder and rape of innocent women and children by the RUF are acts that are incompatible with a revolutionary project," Abdullah argues. "The 'revolutionary' acts…were committed again and again precisely because of the social composition (of the RUF)…A lumpen social movement breeds a lumpen revolution."

The transcripts of testimonies from the SCSL trials make clear that the RUF did make an attempt to establish some form of communitarian order in Kailahun once the district had been fully pacified, but that the effort was not at all consistent, as the RUF's regime of terror superseded all such efforts. Some witnesses, mainly for the defence, testified that civilians worked willingly on the "community farms" and mines run by Issa Sesay in Kailahun district, and that the farm workers were well care for. As in certain slave plantations in the antebellum South,[64] some workers on these farms and mines were said to have gone about their work "singing and dancing." The RUF, again true to form, allowed some of the workers on the agricultural fields to keep the proceeds from the farms. A picture of harmonious cooperation between the RUF overlords and the peasant farmers was painted by some witnesses; Issa Sesay was said to have been particularly generous to the workers, giving them salt, pepper, cigarettes and other food items. The SCSL Trial Chamber rightly rejected this glorious picture, noting:

> The Chamber recognizes that there may have been a limited few privileged people who had access to such amenities. The Chamber is of the considered view that the overwhelming evidence presented during the trial contradicts this reality for most civilians in RUF controlled areas of Sierra Leone during the war. The Chamber observes that the majority of these witnesses testified that they were adherents of the RUF ideology. Some of these witnesses testified out of loyalty to the RUF and their superior Commanders, and evidently were trying to assist Sesay and Kallon in this trial, and not necessarily to assist the Chamber in its search for the truth. Accordingly, the Chamber has rejected

[64] See Eugene Genovese's *Roll, Jordan, Roll: the World the Slaves Made* for an insightful discussion of this phenomenon.

the version of events presented by these witnesses because their testimony to this effect, in the circumstances, is not credible.[65]

In fact, the SCSL noted:

> Numerous witnesses testified before the court and gave personal accounts of suffering brutal and violent crimes such as amputations or rapes, or had personally witnessed crimes such as amputations, rapes and killings committed against relatives and friends. The re-telling of such traumatic experiences was difficult for many of the witnesses, some of whom became understandably emotional and distraught during testimony. The Chamber recognizes that, as an obvious consequence of recounting such horrifying events, some witnesses were unable to give the Chamber a full account of what they had endured, either because it was too painful, or because they had mentally repressed the event. Other witnesses, while able to remember the event, had difficulties in recalling all of the details in full.

On the matter of whether the RUF was an urban or rural rebellion, Krijn Peters cites a study by Humphreys & Weinstein in 2004 which "make clear that a majority of ex-combatants in the Sierra Leone civil war (more than 80 per cent) were from a rural background." This, he writes, "is seemingly at variance with the urban "lumpen" thesis of Abdullah (1997) and others, which states that the RUF rebellion was implemented by a group of people with urban underclass backgrounds."

Peters notes:

> The root causes of the conflict in Sierra Leone suggested by rural ex-combatants can be divided into two kinds. One group of reasons consists of issues playing out on the local level: complaints about a general unwillingness of seniors to help their juniors, the injustice meted out by local courts controlled by corrupt elders and chiefs, and the control these elders exercised over productive and reproductive means, such as land and

---

[65] *Trial Chamber verdict in the Case of the RUF Accused*, 181.

labour, and the resources necessary for marriage. The other group of reasons plays out at national or state-level. Here, the focus is on the state's failure to provide accessible education for all, lack of job opportunities and desire for a democratic system to replace an unfair and divisive clientelism.[66]

Peters interviews mainly such rural ex-combatants, and mostly in the eastern part of the country (Kailahun and Kenema districts). One would assume, of course, that ex-combatants who partook of a defeated and discredited "revolution" would provide such ex post facto rationalisations, though the issues raised – petty injustices and even oppression at the rural level – are real indeed. The problem is that these deprived rural youths only took up arms when an essentially outside force came in, and in most cases, as is clear from the foregoing, their recruitment was far from "willing."

Conclusion

In this article, I have engaged only with a few of the major works on the war in Sierra Leone, juxtaposing arguments made by them against the findings and data produced by the two institutions tasked with establishing the historical record of the war, the TRC and the SCSL. These institutions had vastly greater resources and access than any individual author, and both sought to be as dispassionate with the evidence as possible.

I have concentrated on the RUF, as I did in my by book *The Dirty War in West Africa*, in part because the war was started by the RUF, and arguably only the RUF ensured its continuation and character. A number of very important works have appeared on the CDF, in particular the Kamajors; the most authoritative account in this respect is Danny Hoffman's *The*

---

[66] See introduction of Krijn Peters, "Footpaths to Reintegration: Armed Conflict, Youth and Rural crisis in Sierra Leone" (PhD thesis Wageningen Universiteit, 2006); a slightly revised version of the thesis has been published as *War and the Crisis of Youth in Sierra Leone* (Cambridge University Press, 2011.) Like the thesis, the book appears to seek to recast the RUF and its demented war as a "rural crisis expressed in terms of unresolved tensions between landowners and marginalized rural youth" disenfranchised by the legacy of domestic slavery.

war Machine, which more than any other work integrates the Sierra Leone conflict within the wider Mano River wars that started in Liberia and spread into Guinea and Ivory Coast.

Since I am one of the authors reviewed in this paper, my bias is plain; but I have tried as best as possible to do justice to the various scholars who started and sustained the debate on the war in Sierra Leone. To them, Sierra Leone owes a debt of gratitude.

This article is preliminary. A full discussion of the issue should perhaps involve a book-length assessment of the roles of all the various parties to the war, the RUF, the CDF, the Sierra Leone Army, politicians, mercenaries, forces of foreign countries and regional organisations, and civil society, in light of the findings by the TRC and the SCSL.

Part VIII

Other Wars

1.
Africa and the War on Drugs

The publishers claim for *Africa and the War on Drugs* that it is a vital book on a neglected subject. The book is indeed timely and makes important points, but the subject is far from being overlooked, as the authors themselves acknowledge when they complain about the "sensationalizing of the drug situation in Africa." Neil Carrier and Gernot Klantschnig, the co-authors, begin their argument from this point, noting that the simplifying narrative spurned by the American-driven war on drugs has been utterly counterproductive in Africa. This is because the effort has merely led to increased militarization, repression and corruption without tackling the "real problems surrounding the production, trade and use of drugs" on the continent (p.2).

There is much truth in this observation, but the authors' conclusions in this brief, well-written and tightly-argued book – an extended polemic rather than a substantial study – are overdrawn. This is partly because they anchor their arguments on their distaste for the Reagan-inspired war on drugs and its depredations before seriously considering the evidence of its manifestations in Africa. More importantly, they seem somewhat dismissive of African anxieties around the pernicious problem of drug trafficking, and are almost entirely ignorant of the work of African researchers and policy makers who are looking at the problem from within Africa.

The African Union (AU) Plan of Action on Drug Control and Crime Prevention 2007-2012 captures African anxiety in this respect by noting the "increased linkages between drugs and conventional and organized crime in Africa." I attended the 4th session of the AU Conference of Ministers for Drug Control and Crime Prevention, held at its headquarters in Addis Ababa, Ethiopia, on 29 September to 2 October in 2010. Meant to review the implementation of the Action Plan, the meeting stressed increased investment in medical treatment, collaborative law enforcement to prevent trafficking, and preventative measures to curb addiction. South Africa and Kenya appeared to possess more advanced treatment programmes, but all the countries agreed on a multidimensional approach to limit the problem. Some experts at the meeting, mainly from South Africa, expressed the fear that the increased use of intravenous drugs may well undermine the largely successful efforts to limit the spread of HIV Aids, a point which is not often discussed in the debate on drug abuse in Africa.

The authors of Africa and the War on Drugs mention the AU Action Plan in passing among other regional initiatives, but only to underline their key argument in the book: that policies implemented based on such plans "have prioritized the tougher interdiction, prosecution and punishment of drug criminals" (p.129). This sounds glib in the context.

Of the three case studies in the book – Nigeria, Guinea-Bissau and Lesotho – the authors identify only Nigeria as using outright repression to tackle the problem. Guinea-Bissau is said to be complicit in international trafficking, and Lesotho merely neglectful. The authors tediously wrestle with the notion of "weak" (and "criminal") states in Africa, and with respect to Guinea-Bissau – which has seemed to be the complete manifestation of this notion – they argue that though there is "strong evidence" of its military's involvement in drug trafficking, "some of the subsequent claims of the state-crime nexus made in the media can be considered unfounded" (p.113).

I quickly checked the publication date for this book – 11 October 2012. This is way after army officers known for their participation in the international narcotics trade in the country overthrew the internationally-credible civilian administration in between national elections on 22 April 2012. The coup showed that these soldiers *were* the state; and as it happens, recent reports suggest that drug trafficking through the country has increased exponentially. It makes nonsense of the authors' claim that political instability in the country "might be the best guarantee for the decline of Guinea-Bissau's status as a 'narco-state.'" The absurd statement is made in the context of the authors' view that the country's political instability means that narco-traffickers have to constantly look for local collaborators – anyone minimally familiar with Guinea-Bissau knows that its military has remained the unshakable power for decades.

The undoubted merit of this book is in its providing of historical depth to understanding the problem, using mainly the penetrating works of the Harvard (and Ghanaian) scholar Emmanuel Acheampong and the distinguished British Africanist Stephen Ellis, among others. This aspect, however, is almost obscured by the extended discussion that the authors give to perfectly legitimate and largely non-controversial drugs like alcohol, cola nut, cigarettes and khat (the latter a highly valuable export for the Ethiopian government, and a popular and mild narcotic, as I found out while living in Ethiopia in (2010-2011).

I spent sometime in 2011 looking at the narcotics problem in West Africa, traveling to Ghana, Nigeria, Sierra Leone and Liberia, and speaking to dozens of local and international officials and journalists interested in the issue. I was particularly keen on examining the problem of internal drug use, especially among youths, since clearly West Africa, contrary to widespread views, is more than just a transit point for South American drug traffickers. Once traffickers establish a foothold, they tend to start paying local agents in kind rather than in cash, and the drugs are then sold in local communities, leading to the emergence of competing gangs. The UN Office on Drugs and Crime (UNODC), in fact, had in 2010 estimated that cocaine abuse among Ghanaians of 15 years and older at 1.1% of the population was the highest in Africa, and was almost as high as that in the UK (1.7% of the population). Ghana also has a high rate of amphetamine abuse within that demographic group, 0.1%.

For these reasons – and there are more – Ghana should provide the most important case study of the problem. I interviewed Yaw Akrasi-Sarpong, the Executive Secretary of Ghana's Narcotics Control Board, in April 2011. He said that because of its stability, reasonably sophisticated banking system and large property market, Ghana is attractive as a base for big time cocaine traffickers and dealers. Money laundering was a key concerned. "We have the highest convictions for narcotics-related offences in the region," he told me, "but the problem is manifold." Akrasi-Sarpong said that the problem has to be tackled regionally, but law-enforcement mechanisms are extremely weak in neighbouring Francophone countries and this trafficking from those countries into Ghana and elsewhere in the region. A May 2010 report by the Dakar-based GIABA entitled "Corruption–Money Laundering Nexus: An Analysis of Risks and Control Measures in West Africa," not mentioned by the authors of Africa and the War on Drugs, made similar points.

In the past, Ghanaian nationals have been convicted in the US for drug trafficking, including a member of parliament who was arrested in November 2005 in New York and was linked to a trafficking network operating in New York. While I was in Ghana in April 2011, six people were sentenced to long terms in prison for unlawful possession of 22 boxes of cocaine "found hidden in a concealed compartment behind a big-sized mirror." Some high officials of the previous government in Ghana – the Kuffour administration – were widely believed to be complicit in the illicit business.

Developments such as those largely informed the anxieties expressed in the July 2009 UNODC report, "Transnational Trafficking and the Rule of Law in West Africa: A Threat Assessment," which noted that drug trafficking in West Africa has undermined the rule of law, deepened corruption and jeopardised state and human security in the region. This report led to the first UN Security Council debate on this issue, on 8 December 2009, during the rotating presidency of Burkina Faso. The debate led to a presidential statement urging the UN Secretary General to "consider mainstreaming the issue of drug trafficking as a factor in conflict prevention strategies, conflict analysis, integrated-missions' assessment and planning and peace building support." Since then, the sheer scale of the cocaine seized in Liberia, the Gambia and elsewhere in the region underline the seriousness of the problem: the worth of the drugs are several times more than that of the budgets of those countries.

A 100-page judgment in a major trial of cocaine traffickers in Sierra Leone in 2009, by Justice Browne-Marke, showed why these anxieties are not misplaced, and why the problem goes way beyond the implications for health, pace Neil Carrier and Gernot Klantschnig. The trial revealed the range of networks the traffickers had in Sierra Leone, including very senior government officials, top security agents, businessmen, fake NGOs, a fake mining company, safe houses in the interior of the country, and young people, including students, co-opted into the operation. The judgment noted that the country's chief intelligence agency, CISU, as well as the Special Branch of the police in charge of serious criminal cases, "had become penetrated institutions, accepting shop-worn wares as good intelligence."

It may well be, as *Africa and the War on Drugs* argues, that African "discourses on drugs" are shaped by "western ideas on drugs and the supply-sided control" (p.7). But is that not because the "discourses" are rooted in lived reality? This brave little book unintentionally reveals, once again, the danger of substituting one's irritation with some of the awkward policies of western governments with concern for the African predicament. Friends of Africa should always have this trap in mind.

2.
Ebola: Brueghel's Hell[67]

The impulse to regard infectious diseases that cause sudden deaths as forbidding mysteries that befall only the despised 'other' is an ancient one. The Hebrew authors of the Old Testament did not evoke mystery when they happily narrated how, responding to the wish of their necromantic leader Moses, God inflicted ten plagues on the ancient Egyptians who were holding their ancestors captive. But they were less certain about a latter plague which befell their mortal (and far superior) enemies, the Philistines.

The story is narrated in the First Book of Samuel which tells us how, after the Philistines defeated the Israelites in battle and captured their ark of the covenant, "rats appeared in their land, and death and destruction were throughout [their] city". Feeling triumphant at first at the horror that had befallen their enemies, the Israelites were shocked to find that when the Philistine tactfully returned the ark to them, they, too, became afflicted, and many of them died. The deaths were sudden, the victims apparently afflicted with hemorrhoids whose pathogens may have been buboes (from rodents), perhaps the first instance of the bubonic plague. The Israelites, however, knew God, but not science – so that every instance of defeat or disaster was ascribed to their failure to please their God, and their deviation from His often stern and bewilderingly cruel commands.

Modern Europeans, children of the Enlightenment, are bound to think differently. When the first modern outbreak of the bubonic plague occurred in 1894-1901, Europe had had centuries of devastating encounter with such killer viruses, and they quickly found its origin: in Asia, from where it spread from the port of Hong Kong to the rest of the world, its movement facilitated mainly by British merchant ships and the logic of Empire. It killed many people in the port cities of Africa, and this movement – through the lines of anxiety drawn by the

British Empire and the imperatives of European merchant capitalism – may have helped coin the phrase "diseases of civilisation."

There have been many such "diseases of civilisation" in Africa – new diseases or more potent variations on indigenous ones. They include all kinds of venereal diseases (syphilis in particular), tuberculosis (the result of unhealthy industrial work environments mainly), even malaria, and, most notorious, cholera. Today, 95% of all cholera cases happen in Africa, in its ever-sprawling neocolonial slum-cities.

It was only a matter of time for a properly indigenous African killer virus of a highly infectious nature to emerge. At first, HIV Aids seemed like it was an affliction of a biblical nature (remember Sodom and Gomorrah – there go our Hebrew fantasists again) on California's Bay Area. Some researcher, very soon however, traced it to the monkeys in the Congo. It helped, perhaps not that slightly, that the area was the same place that Ebola had first been detected a few years earlier, so please excuse my long preliminary digressions.

This article, I make haste to say, is about the current [2014] Ebola outbreak. This highly infectious and deadly disease – variously called Ebola virus disease (EVD) or Ebola hemorrhagic fever (EHF) – affects human beings as well as primates. It was first identified – by Peter Piot, a Belgian scientist who now heads the London School of Tropical Medicine – deep in the rainforest in Zaire, the nonsense name that Joseph Mobutu gave to the Congo. A variety of it has been found in monkeys from the Philippines (the virus was isolated in the United States in 1989) and there may have been an earlier outbreak in the Sudan, but its Congo origin has long been firmly embedded in the popular imagination. The Congo, after all, is the setting for Conrad's *Heart of Darkness*, a place where "civilisation" (as represented by Mr. Kurtz) succumbed to the imperatives of "primitivism;" and Ebola is, if anything, the quintessential disease of "primitivism," of the "other" in Western imagination.

The remote rural rainforest origin of Ebola appears to be its most consistent truism. The current outbreak began in early February in the southeastern forest region of Nzérékoré in Guinea. But though hidden in the verdant wet forests, this area is strategically placed among a system of inter-connected waterways tied to the large Moa (or Makona) river which connects Guinea to Sierra Leone and Liberia. The ruling elite in Conakry have long regarded people in this remote rainforest community – formerly a veritable source of slaves for the Fulani and Mandigo elite – as fetish worshippers beyond the pale. The virus quickly spread from there, taking one route, to Conakry, and another, to Lofa County in Liberia, by late March. When I was in Monrovia that month, few people I met among the country's effete elite thought the affliction in Lofa was happening to Liberians, despite President Ellen Johnson-Sirleaf's very early radio messages about the virus' ravages.

Ebola struck Sierra Leone in May, well over two months after the Guinea outbreak. Nearly two months into the outbreak, with over 100 people dead in Kailahun and Kenema districts, few among the country's Freetown-based political elite took any notice. This reaction was shocking but not surprising; it mirrored almost exactly the attitude of the ruling elite then to the rebel war when it started in almost the same places in 1991. And it is the result of the debilitating mix of graft, smug 'tribalism' and simple incompetence that is the bane of the country's politics.

When I was in Freetown in June, I heard dark talk among some of those people that the afflicted people in Kailahun had brought the virus on themselves by their quaint culinary habit. I also heard talk about a herbalist from those parts who had crossed the Moa river to attend a funeral of a relative in Guinea and who then brought the disease to Sierra Leone on her return. She died; and because of her fame, her burial attracted the helpful hands of many people who naturally contracted the virus, helping to start a pandemic.

Out of this fairly pedestrian story clueless young Frankie Taggart, a reporter for Agence France-Presse, sought, as is common among so many starry-eyed journalists thrusting themselves like connoisseurs of death-bed anecdotes into hot zones, his own more mysterious version. "Tribal chiefdoms" have been laid waste, he wrote in a report for that agency on 20 August 2014, by an outbreak which need "never have spread from Guinea …except [sic] for a herbalist in the remote eastern border village of Sokoma" in Kailahun. Taggart quotes from a Mohamed Vandi, "the top medical official in the hard-hit district of

Kenema", as saying: "She was claiming to have powers to heal Ebola. Cases from Guinea were crossing into Sierra Leone for treatment."

A lot of blame has been spread all around for the engulfing calamity. President Ernest Bai Koroma, who did not bother to visit Kailahun himself to find out how people there are doing until ten weeks into the outbreak, glumly blames the "international community" for not being as helpful as it presumably should be. He then skewedly distributed funds he had collected to combat the disease, so that Koinadugu, then unaffected, got more money than Kailahun – the epicentre accounting for 40% of cases! Poor overwhelmed Dr. Vandi can only blame a dead herbalist!

The entire Kailahun and Kenema Districts have, meanwhile, been militarily cordoned off from the rest of humanity, in an operation – *The New York Times* has helpfully reminded us – reminiscent of medieval Europe during the Black Death. Cut-off, a version of remoteness, is another Ebola truism.

Its broader application to the region can be dated to 20 July 2014, when Patrick Sawyer, an American citizen who happened to also call Liberia his home, boarded a flight from Monrovia for Lagos, Nigeria, taking Ebola along with his bulky self. Sawyer had been told in Liberia that he had contracted Ebola – probably from his sister, who had died in his care of the disease – and was told not to travel. He should have been forced not to travel, but as an elite figure, such rules had no applicability to him. He flew in the Nigerian airline ASKY from the near-derelict Sprigs Payne Airport, which few other commercial airlines use; and the CCTV camera showed him lying down, obviously very sick, at the airport minutes before boarding the plane. He must have been assisted to board the flight, probably spreading the virus from that point. For that singular act of callousness or desperation, all major airlines are now shunning Liberia, Sierra Leone and Guinea, against the entreaties of the World Health Organisation, which continues to insist that Ebola is not airborne.

And now from a distance these effectively quarantined countries only evoke Pieter Brueghel's famous painting, inspired by the Black Death, of hell (which is its perfect definition): a horror and neurotic zone where you cannot *live*, and cannot *leave*.

3.
Ebola: Fighting Back in Sierra Leone[68]

On 5 November 2014, the World Health Organization (WHO) issued its eleventh situation report on Ebola. It was a mixture of good and bad news. A total of 13,042 Ebola cases had been confirmed, resulting in 4,818 deaths. This is an appalling figure, but far short of the 20,000 fatalities that WHO and Imperial College London had predicted in September. More encouraging still, the outbreaks in Senegal and Nigeria were declared over in October, indicating that with robust measures taken early, West African countries can contain and eliminate the deadly virus.

The report also noted that the weekly incidence appeared to be stable in Guinea, while in Liberia – the worst hit by the Ebola outbreak so far – it seemed to be declining. In Sierra Leone, which seemed to have been managing the crisis better than Liberia, the weekly incidence appeared to have spiked in October, and continues to rise. Much of this, the report said, "was driven by intense transmission in the capital of Freetown, which... remains one of the worst affected cities in this outbreak."

There were bright spots even in this bleak picture: "There is more evidence of a recent decline in the number of cases reported weekly in Kenema and Kailahun," the report noted cautiously. These two districts were the original locus for the outbreak, between them recording close to 700 deaths. Now, they reported only 14 new confirmed cases in a week. In fact, the declining trend had been evident for over four weeks.

So what accounts for this turnaround in Kenema and Kailahun districts, formerly epicenters of Ebola?

There is, of course, the heroic work of aid agencies, in particular Médecins sans Frontières (Doctors without Borders), which set up a

---

[68] This briefing note was prepared for the Ottawa-based Development Diamond Initiative in November 2014.

64-bed emergency clinic in Kailahun in June and which has expended enormous resources in the area.

The government also revamped its facilities in Kenema under the leadership of Dr. Sheik Umar Khan, the country's leading virologist. Dr. Khan himself is credited with saving the lives of more than a hundred Ebola patients. He died in Kailahun at the MSF facility on 29 July of Ebola-related complications. More medical assistance, from the government and international health agencies, poured into the area after this widely publicised death.

The real turning point, however, may have resulted from the containment efforts of local authorities. This includes social mobilization, education, proscriptions around burial procedures, and the imposition of fines for breaking new bylaws focussing on the reporting of sickness and the movement of people in the area.

There has been much debate about the role of traditional rulers in the context of the modern state in Africa, and the activities of chiefs in Ebola-wracked eastern Sierra Leone are likely to give the debate new texture. In the absence of governmental infrastructure in many of the stricken areas, chiefs have played the critical role in the containment effort, and have demonstrated that they can be more relevant to ordinary village people than the modern state.

In July, at the height of the outbreak, Paramount Chiefs and representatives from all 14 Chiefdoms in Kailahun District met to develop a common strategy to contain and eradicate Ebola from their chiefdoms. At the end of the meeting, they issued a communiqué which contained a uniform set of bylaws that were immediately adopted in every chiefdom.

In addition to measures already in place, such as the closure of schools and other venues where people normally congregate, the bylaws impose stiff fines on anyone concealing an illness, refusing an Ebola test or interfering with contact tracers, community mobilisers, Ebola burial teams, or any other healthcare personnel. Any new arrival in a town or village, whether known or not, is treated as a possible carrier, and must be reported and assigned a contact tracer for three weeks. Heavy fines are imposed on anyone found negligent in enforcing the new bylaws, including people in positions of authority. And finally, anyone stigmatising a recovered Ebola patient is also subject to a fine.

Chief Mandu Farley Keili-Coomber wrote in an email on 6 November 2014: "We felt that only chiefs enjoyed the moral and legitimate authority of our people to get them to willingly comply with behaviour-changing regulations, which central government organs, with all their resources had failed to achieve. This was at a time when nobody wanted to send their sick people to hospitals, people were still burying their dead in the traditional ways and, government Ebola intervention units were routinely attacked because of our people's historic mistrust of central government."

Within weeks, the results were palpable. By August, infection rates began dropping dramatically in Kailahun District. Chiefs in the adjacent Kenema District adopted the bylaws in August, and there, too, infection rates began to drop significantly in September.

By October, the quarantine measures that the Government of Sierra Leone had adopted—deploying 1,500 troops to cordon off Kenema and Kailahun districts from the rest of country to prevent Ebola spreading to other parts of the country – were now working in reverse. In addition, perhaps, to keeping Ebola in, the cordon was keeping new cases out. As Chief Keili-Coomber explains: "There are some interesting ironies… The checkpoints manned by the police and army to quarantine our district, have indeed had a very bad effect on our local economies. However, these same checkpoints now serve to keep others from coming in from areas that are less resolute in fighting the disease."

Still, much remains to be done. A recent Yale study suggests that if transmission via burial practices were eliminated, the secondary infection rate would drop by close 70 percent. Burial practices in which mourners handle bodies, "are effectively serving as super-spreader events." Recent reports state that safe burials are now taking place in over 90% of Ebola deaths in Sierra Leone. And initiative like that shown in Kailahun and Kenema holds huge promise.

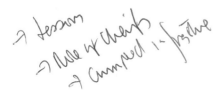

Part IX

Other Writings: People and Books

1.
Alfred Akiko-Betts: An Appreciation[69]

Alfred Abraham Akibo-Betts, who died in July 2006 in London, was an extraordinary politician – probably the most patriotic and committed figure in Sierra Leone's politics in the last twenty-seven years or so. Various commentators since his death have recalled – more in sadness than in anger – some unsavoury incidents in which Akibo (as everyone called him) got himself involved in his early forays into national politics. Everyone, however, agrees that Akibo soon after transcended those misjudgments, found immense gravitas, and was so successful as a public figure (first by unearthing massive corruption in his own government, and then by providing by far the most competent and effective leadership of the Freetown municipality in living memory) that many rue his failure (for he made an attempt) to become President of this badly mismanaged Republic.

I first met Akibo when he was Mayor of Freetown in 1993. In less than two years after becoming Mayor, Akibo had transformed the once shambolic City Hall (for many years a haven, like the crumbling City Hotel adjacent – famously Graham Greene's haunt – for prostitutes) into an elegant neo-Georgian edifice. It was an immensely delightful meeting: Akibo's sense of humour, his great ambition for his city, his deep concern (somewhat barely discernible among many in the capital then) for the war then ravaging parts of the country were striking. Months later, Akibo's City Council donated tens of millions of leones towards the government's – then the National Provisional Ruling Council, NPRC, junta – war effort. It was easy then to deride this gesture (wasn't the Mayor trying too hard to be in the good books of the junta? Surely the city itself badly needed those funds?), but one can now only be nostalgic about it: for the farthest that high-mindedness now go within City Hall is for the current Mayor to seek newspaper headlines by grumbling aloud about how paltry the sum is that the government allocates for the cleaning of the streets facing his own office.

---

[69] Concord Times (Freetown) 16 August 2006

Akibo's tenure at City Hall was memorable for two things: he was able to make Freetown reasonably clean and clear major thoroughfares and streets of clogging market stalls; and he was able to make the city solvent. Both of these achievements, taken for granted while Akibo's tenure lasted, can now seem like outlandish dreams.

The idea of the colourful, charismatic politician is not always reassuring; but Akibo was able to combine magnetism with great humility: a lover of the spotlight (he assiduously wooed the media), Akibo nevertheless was always self-deprecating. I don't remember him speaking out of turn: and this is remarkable for such an outspoken and articulate politician with such strong views. I think in the end he enraged the current government [of Tejan Kabbah's] by his well-timed, occasional criticism of the paralysis which has passed for government for some years now.

During the gruesome rebel attacks on Freetown in January 1999, Akibo's property in downtown Freetown was destroyed, and he was nearly killed. The war left him a broken man; but till the end he maintained a high spirit and a strong belief that some form of national resurgence was still possible. When I went to Freetown a few months after the attacks, I visited Akibo in his offices – or what passed for an office: a little cramped building with a large desk and several chairs, the only one surviving in the compound – on Bathurst Street in central Freetown. He had painted a sign in front of the building reading "Sierracratic Commonsense Salvation…" There was a touch of self-parody, never mind pathos, about it all; about this great man of grandeur reduced to affecting a sense of high-purpose and resurgence in this shrunken, blighted little edifice with no money and no following.

I spent an hour with him, for most of the time drinking beer and chatting about old days and the great tribulations that the country had gone through. Akibo's memorable old aphorisms enlivened the discussion: the slightly inapt ambience made them sound like some old recordings from a remote, more blissful past. "Our altitude is our attitude," he would say. I understood him to mean that Sierra Leone can aspire and reach any height once its citizens adopt the right attitude towards their nation. He spoke about his loss and personal suffering and humiliation with no bitterness, only sadness.

I next met Akibo a few years later, in his house on Spur Road, in the westend of Freetown. He had been partially paralyzed by stroke, and was confined home – a modest house which now seem near-derelict – in pain, overwhelmed by memories of loss and abandonment. He spoke – in sadness as well as in some bitterness – of his unrequited life-long sacrifice for the country. He had not made money in his long life in public office; he did not have money to be taken out of the country for treatment. The government, because Abiko was associated with the opposition All Peoples Congress (APC) and had been critical, did not care about him.

The public that he had served so selflessly did not appear to care either. He pointed this out to me as a lesson: this is a nation that does not reward honesty and selflessness; this is a nation that punishes its distinguished citizens. It is the prime problem of Sierra Leone, he said. He was being philosophical: the words, spoken deliberately, were a searing commentary and a warning. I was very touched. With me at the time were my good friends Kingsley Lington, David Tam-Baryoh, Isaac Massaquoi and Mohamed Swaray. After our meeting with Akibo, we made frantic efforts to enlist the help of a few highly-placed government officials, pleading on behalf of Akibo. We hit a wall. We felt helpless. Akibo showed us mementos of glorious days: medals and awards he had received from other Mayors and dignitaries abroad, invitations, pictures with other Mayors, pictures showing Akibo holding the key to a US city, mementos of Akibo's work to twin Freetown with cities like Hull (in the UK) and many others.

He had grand ideas and dreams for his historic city, thinking it comparable in grandeur, if not wealth, to any other historic city: Akibo towered above all the charming little local politicians whose idea of themselves as statesmen is their presumed ability to attract external assistance. Sometime later, I was on a Sierra Leone National Airlines flight from Freetown (going to London) when one of the air hostesses came over to me and told me somebody wanted to talk to me. I followed her to a corner where a man was crouched alone on a seat meant for two. It was Akibo. Some people of goodwill had volunteered to pay his way to London for medical treatment, after many months of suffering. We spoke for an hour or so. It was the last time we spoke. At Gatwick

Airport, as I was walking to catch the bus to Heathrow – to take a flight to Canada – I heard a quick announcement on the PA system calling on the people who had come to pick up Akibo at the airport to meet him at a counter...

I'll end where I began. Akibo was an extraordinary man, both as a politician and as a human being. I am singularly unsuited to writing an encomium, but I find that with someone who sacrificed so much for his country, and who was so wretchedly abandoned in the end, I can even find pleasure in being oleaginous. Few, if any, Sierra Leonean politicians in recent memory can claim the moral high-ground, the depth of patriotism and selflessness which Akibo exhibited. None identified as clearly with the idea – all-too-inchoate – that Sierra Leone can rise to become a self-sufficient, proud and honourable member of the community of nations. Certainly none embodied this aspiration as completely as Akibo did.

He lived all his life in Sierra Leone, rising from humble background to becoming a much-admired national figure. He was one of the few public figures in whom one cannot detect, however one is desperate to look, any trace of that old, if understated, national disease: sectarian or "tribal" alliance or consciousness. I see Akibo (along with Hinga Norman, another selfless patriot who has been abandoned and humiliated by the country) as a sterling national hero whose loss will be missed for decades to come.

2.
Sorious Samura: Commitment and Voyeurism[70]

On a trip to war-wracked Vietnam in the 1950s—the country was then enmeshed in a bloody anti-colonial war pitting patriotic Vietnamese against the French—the English writer Graham Greene had one of his moments of inner conflicts. Boarding a plane at the military airport at Hanoi for Dien Bien Phu (which would later be the scene of the most decisive battle of the war), Greene saw among the passengers two photographers in camouflage uniforms. These men, Greene wrote, "seem to me comparable to those men who go hunting big game with cameras alone." He continued: "I always have a sense of guilt when I am a civilian tourist in the regions of death: after all one does not visit a disaster except to give aid—one feels a voyeur of violence, as I felt during the attack two years ago on Phat Diem.I told myself then that I hated war, and yet here I was back—an old voyeur at his tricks again."□

We are happy that Greene returned to Vietnam again and again, for out of those trips—in addition to very incisive articles he published on the war in the London Times and the Spectator magazine—emerged the wonderfully prescient and delightful novel, A Quiet American, which so accurately predicted the foolish American takeover of the Vietnam War from the French.

I immediately thought of Greene's anguished reflections after watching Sorious Samura's recent documentary, "Living with Refugees," on BBC Channel Four in London in December 2004. Samura, a Sierra Leonean photo-journalist, is a famous man in London, where he lives. His debut documentary, Cry Freetown, won many prestigious awards, including the Rory Peck Award 1999. The documentary was memorable. It showed the Sierra Leone war (which began in 1991 and officially ended in 2002) in its

---

[70] Znet, 5 March 2005

lurid nastiness, not to say pointlessness. Samura had not gone there to see for himself: he was living in Freetown then, was caught up in the fighting, and bravely took the pictures while hiding. I had my criticism of "Cry Freetown" at the time it came out, but it would be completely foolish of anyone to deny its morbid power, as well as Samura's bravery and passion to tell a much neglected, but profoundly important, story. The documentary deserves all the praises and all the awards.

I met Samura not long after the documentary's release. He was then living in London. He had become so famous that a London publisher with whom I had lunch was desperate to have the two of us "connected" (his words). Apparently, both the publisher and Samura had read a short review of "Cry Freetown" I had written, in which I criticised aspects of the documentary. The publisher gave me Samura's number. I called Samura the next day. He sounded extremely friendly, and said he would immediately visit me. I was then living in a crummy apartment in Southeast London with a friend, but never mind. Samura came over, and, along with two of my friends (Isaac Massaquoi and Kingsley Lington), we drove in his car to town. He mentioned my review—which had criticised the documentary for not showing actual scenes of Revolutionary United Front (RUF) brutality, concentrating only on violence by ECOMOG. I had written that perhaps this indicated that Samura started taking the pictures after he was safely relocated in an area that ECOMOG had taken over from the RUF. But Samura told me that his editors at Insight, which produced the documentary, had excised some of the most ghastly pictures, and these were mainly those showing RUF handiwork. I felt privileged to be told this, even though Samura had said something similar on TV and elsewhere. It was all friendly chat, and we exchanged cards.

Samura next issued Exodus, which is a 45-minute documentary about Africans giving up all hopes, as the blurb on Insight's website puts it, "of their continent offering them a decent future – or indeed a future of any kind. These people head for the West with no proper documentation, with the worst means of transportation and are at best aiming for a bizarre and dangerous means of entry into an unknown land." I do not particularly like Exodus—it seems to me a little reductive, presenting the issue as though dangerous migration journeys are a distinctly African phenomenon, when in fact there are probably more Chinese illegally entering North America by boat across the Pacific than there are Africans entering the West, legally or illegally, every year—but the documentary has real value, and might have been an eye-opener for some people. "Return to Freetown," a sequel to "Cry Freetown," is far better. By simply tracing some of the child victims of the Sierra Leone war he highlights in "Cry Freetown," showing them gradually returning to the fold of normal society, Samura very effectively demonstrates the foolishness of the war that had ravaged his country, and indeed the cruelties and dementia of rebel warfare, particularly its sick methodology of child soldiery. Again, nothing particularly spectacular, but the documentary is satisfying in its own way.

In 2003, however, Samura began to experiment with a new, but not so new, form: he produced "Living with Hunger (Surviving Hunger)," in which he lived for a month in a hut in a remote Ethiopian village, sharing the meager food and bare living of the other villagers. I watched this documentary twice when it came out but still do not understand the point of it. It must have pleased some people, including Samura's producers at Insight, however, for the following year Samura was off to Chad, there to live for a month with refugees fleeing the depredations of the Janjawiid militia in Darfur. The result is Living with Refugees. This is how Insight describes it all on its website: "Award-winning journalist Sorious Samura is increasingly gaining a reputation for a new kind of journalism which not many others can do. It's 'real' reality TV stories that offer a unique perspective into the lives of people facing terrible situations. On this journey he set out to become, for all intents and purposes, a refugee. He traveled to Chad to live with a family in a refugee camp for one month. He lived under exactly the same conditions, eating what they ate, drinking what they drank. Sorious built close intimate relationships with the people in this situation sharing their hopes and fears. This film provides a unique insight into what life is really like for a refugee."

"A new kind of journalism": this is obviously misleading. The idea of living, or pretending to live, lives of people one is writing about or documenting—what the late Hunter Thompson called gonzo journalism—is an old eccentricity. Lawrence of Arabia did it to great effect, penetrating a culture that was then seen as mysterious to Westerners; Thompson as well did it very well. At best it can lead to effective ventriloquism, as in the case of some of Thompson's writing, in particular his book about the raucous bikers, Hell's Angels.

Samura, as well, is high-minded in his practice of the genre. He told a Time magazine writer—who wrote a laudatory piece on him recently—that what he is doing is representing 'the innocents: Who is telling their story? I want to represent them.'☐

I decided to write this piece immediately after reading this statement: It is all very well for an artist or writer to do his thing only to make money or to entertain: High-mindedness attracts suspicion and scrutiny. So, to return to my earlier difficulty: exactly what does "Living with Hunger" tell you about starving people? Or "Living with Refugees" about refugees living in an impoverished, bleak Sahelian nullity like the part of Chad that the Darfur refugees live almost abandoned?

The promotional blurb on Insight's website attempts to answer the second question: "Through Sorious video diaries and the filming of the crew who shadowed him throughout his experiences, we see the life of a refugee as it's never been seen before. It's a first, an exclusive and a must-see film for anyone wishing to truly understand what it is like to be a refugee." Really?

Self-denial has always had an obvious appeal: we admire Gandhi partly because of his principled renunciation. But there is something distinctly creepy about a famous man living in a rich country traveling to some backwoods place and pretending to share the miseries of the poorest of the poor, only to get richly rewarded for it. The sense of voyeur instantly suggests itself.

Am I reading too much into this matter? Perhaps; but I knew all along, thanks all the same, that to lack adequate food, going hungry, is a most excruciating experience; even without experiencing it, I know that to be driven from one's home into an arid land as a refugee is thoroughly hellish. Does one need to survive a tsunami to know it was a most horrendous disaster?

Yet "Living with Refugees" does reveal a few interesting facts: about the bureaucratic ineptitude of relief administration, in particular those of the UN; the corruption of local officials etc. Very well; but what exactly is the context of all of these? To watch only this documentary is to go away with the impression that the whole mess is a mysterious humanitarian disaster. We hear little about the war, the Janjawiid terror gangs, the demented regime in Khartoum, the efforts of the AU and the UN to end the fighting, and the various militia groups.

Indeed this kind of journalism is really not new. It is an idiosyncratic form perfected by the British. Jonathan Dimbleby became notorious for showing, on the BBC, the famine in Ethiopia under Haile Sellasie without showing the war fuelling that famine, thus succeeding in undermining the government so completely that it was soon after overthrown. The same was earlier done with respect to Biafra.

Samura is no Dimbleby, and his concern about the plight and dereliction of Africa and Africans is utterly genuine. Still, I wonder how these—his two latest, and least elegant, efforts—advance his determination to, as he puts it with no hint of irony, represent the innocents.

3.
On Eldred Jones' Freetown Bond[71]

Just down from university sometime in 1994, I went to interview Professor Eldred Jones at his home for a newspaper. A nasty bush war had been raging in the countryside, but Freetown was untouched. At Fourah Bay College (FBC), however, the war had some immediacy. Shortly after it started, several students from the university who had gone on holidays to their villages in the countryside had been abducted by the Revolutionary United Front (RUF) rebels, and those who escaped returned with graphic stories of atrocities. A coup had occurred, and the youthful soldiers who constituted what they were pleased to call National Provisional Ruling Council (NPRC) were in the habit of frequenting the college's campus, the appearance of support from the famous school adding some glamour to the "revolution." Jones, the universally venerated long-term principal of the university, was retired to his home at Leicester, at the tip of Mount Aureol, where the university is elegantly situated. Surely, I thought, the great man would have something to say about the war?

I had met him earlier at one of the cultural events at the home of Karl Prinz, the immensely well-respected German ambassador and patron of intellectuals and local artists, so he had agreed to the interview when I telephoned him. There wasn't much he would say about the war, however, since "it is very difficult to deal with some of these amorphous groups now emerging here and there in Africa," he said. Professor Jones had been blind for many years, and he wasn't known to express political opinions. Probably Sierra Leone's most admired academic, a much beloved lecturer and internationally famous literary critic, his great passion remained scholarship and the academia. He spoke with great fondness of his time as principal of FBC, and of his continuing work on African literature, editing the premier journal *African Literature Today*.

The profile-interview, bland and laudatory, ran a few days later. The following day, Professor Jones, as usual driven by his wife, came to our

---

[71] Vitabubooks, 19 July 2014.

office on Pademba Road in Freetown, and handed me a small envelope. The note enclosed thanked me for a well-written report, but there was a complaint. The mysterious woman I had referred to in the article wasn't his wife: his wife was called Marjorie not Margaret, as I had written. It was a devastating reproach; and, full of shame, I got my editors to run a correction in the next edition.

Freetown Bond: A Life Under Two Flags, Jones' luminous and delightful memoir adds, for me, an extra, retrospective, weight to my foolish mistake in misidentifying Mrs. Marjorie Jones. Perhaps conditioned by his almost-Victorian upbringing, Jones typically treats the issue with a (sort of) English reticence, never sentimentalising or romanticising it; but if it has any meaning, the phrase "better half," often bandied about carelessly, is a perfectly etched description of the relationship between Mrs. Jones and her husband. She has been Jones' friend, lover, partner and wife – as well as amanuensis and inseparable companion – for almost all his adult life. They had met at university during World War II, and got married in 1952. Marjorie and her husband co-founded *African Literature Today* in 1968 and co-edited it for decades. This memoir, and that admirable journal, would not have been brought to us without Marjorie.

The memoir has a little more to say about the war for which I had dashed to speak to Professor Jones, which would later engulf the entire country, including Freetown, and even Jones' once-cloistered neighbourhood of Leicester Peak was occupied by foraging thugs called "rebels." Jones found himself, against all his instinct, having to play a (sort of) political role, though even with this clearly traumatic experience, the recollection is made with mordant humour and self-deprecation.

Professor Jones is now almost 90; he turned 89 in January [2014]. The memoir shows what an interesting, rich, and immensely satisfactory life this very humane and civilised man, the nearest thing to the scholar par excellence that Sierra Leone has produced, has lived.

Two Flags

The title of the memoir refers both to Jones' dual heritage as Creole (culturally English as well as African) and one of his lifelong intellectual preoccupations: a very deep scholarly interest in this inheritance and the cultural stew of Freetown in which he grew. It also, more literally, refers to the fact that Jones was born in the British-ruled Sierra Leone, and rose to eminence, as one of Africa's foremost academics and cultural evangelisers, in independent Sierra Leone. Though very much English in his education, Jones remained firmly rooted in his Creole cultural heritage, which itself is a form of dualism, a condition of hybridity. Post-colonialist intellectuals of a quite different hue and capability, expressing new anxieties, long saw in the Creole evidence of rootlessness and schizophrenia. It is the kind of vanity that never appealed to Jones.

He has remained throughout his long and immensely successful academic career, though deeply appreciative of the new literature from Africa, unaffected by those wonderful fad theories of academe (post-colonialism, post-structuralism). One gets a clue from the memoir how this remarkable poise was achieved on page 45. Here Jones writes: "I have always been content to live and work in Sierra Leone. A reasonably happy childhood, an easy transition from school and college to work, further study, more work, travel, all was undertaken with Freetown as a tethering post. I was always attached." Academic success seems to have come to Jones easily: after Oxford, he rather effortlessly got hired as a lecturer at Fourah Bay College, and his rise in that institution was steady. His work on Elizabethan and Jacobean drama, and particularly his pioneering role in promoting the new African literature through his critical articles, mostly published in the exalted *African Literature Today*, made him an international academic star, coveted as a visiting professor in Europe, the US and Canada. "Everywhere I went," he writes, I received flattering offers to take on more permanent appointments…My standard response was a polite 'no' in view of my commitment to Fourah Bay College." The result of this is that Jones is unique among academics in lacking throughout his career the great anxiety to publish, to get tenure, to be invited to conferences, to be cited by peers. When he returned to FBC as a lecturer in 1953 armed with a BA honours from Oxford, Jones had no intention of pursuing a PhD, but a British colleague convinced him that a PhD was "fast becoming a union card" in academe, and so he went for it. He secured his PhD from Durham University in 1962; and he published his first book in 1965.

This memoir, like all of Jones' published work, is as a consequence completely free of the unpleasing asperity into which disagreements among academics often descend, to the negation of their cause.

Urbane and at home in Africa as in Europe, Jones very early took a deep interest in his native Krio language. It is of interest to learn from this memoir that the Krio language was the subject of Jones' dissertation for his diploma in education in 1949, after his BA from Fourah Bay College (part of University of Durham at the time). Jones would subsequently gain admission at Oxford's Corpus Christi College, where he earned an honours degree in English, pursuing his interest in Elizabethan literature, especially Shakespeare. He maintained these two interests – Krio and Shakespeare – throughout his career, publishing the award-winning *Othello's Countrymen* (an original study of the depiction of Africa in English renaissance literature) in 1965, and a shorter study, *The Elizabethan Image of Africa*, in 1971.

After these two books, Jones focused on the extraordinarily interesting literature pouring forth from Africa, and, of course, on his lifelong interest in the Krio language, co-authoring, with Clifford N. Fyle, *A Krio-English Dictionary* in 1980. He took a particular interest in Wole Soyinka, becoming the Nigerian writer's most exalted literary champion until Soyinka won the Nobel Prize in 1986. Jones wrote a book length study, *The Writing of Wole Soyinka*, published in 1988, and took to referring to Soyinka as "WS Our WS" (Wole Soyinka Our William Shakespeare). Soyinka's turgid and opaque prose in *The Interpreters* (his, thankfully, only novel) did indeed need a dedicated champion; and since the Nobel he has focused, in the tradition of creatively exhausted artists, on political pamphleteering, year after year issuing book after unreadable book about the horrors of his country's dysfunction. (I write as someone whose preference is Achebe, a finer much greater writer).

Fourah Bay College

Jones became a student at Fourah Bay Collge in 1944, and has remained committed, in different forms, to the university since then. The most valuable part of this memoir is Jones' reflections on his time as principal of the college; it is by far the best account I have read of the decline of the college as a centre of excellence. Jones was principal for eleven years (longer than any other principal before him except the African-American Edward Jones, 1840-1859) from the turbulent 1970s to the meltdown in the 1980s (he retired, almost completely blind, in 1985), by which time Fourah Bay College was now issuing its own, rather than Durham University's, degrees.

He gives three reasons for FBC's decline: the expansion of the student population without a corresponding increase in its financial and other resources; the frivolity and foolishness of students, and the depraved national politics of Siaka Stevens. The expansion of the student population caused, first and foremost, accommodation and related problems. A recurrent problem, Jones writes, was the administration of corporate student finances, followed by food and other conditions of residence. The shortage of campus accommodation for students led to enforced non-residence, and this in turn resulted in transport problems. The management of these problems was not helped by the irresponsibility of students. Jones writes: "During the 1950s and 1960s Sierra Leonean students who qualified for entry...got covered... with full board, a book allowance and other college fees. The book allowance was paid to the college, which issued vouchers exchangeable at the college bookshop – which was one of the finest bookshops in West Africa, managed by Hans Zell. Students in the 1970s started agitating that this allowance should be issued to them directly; the college submitted, since this had become a major source of friction." Now paid directly to the students, the allowance, as any minimally discerning person would have foreseen, was now no longer used to buy books, and the bookshop's capital base collapsed. It ceased to exist – a valuable intellectual and cultural resource lost forever.

Here's another: "A similar assertion of rights turned the dining halls into canteens with boarding grants going direct to students – making it easy for the scholarship to be eliminated altogether," Jones laments. Another primitive assertion of rights had to with the objection to the introduction of foundation year courses, which Jones promoted, incorporating courses in languages, literature, the sciences, history. Meeting strong resistance the programme became ineffective. Jones writes in rue: "Our societies in the developing world are still held back by strong residues of traditional thinking which impedes progressive approaches to problems. Logic is held back by belief in magical and occult manipulations which, in turn, perpetuate a reluctance or even inability to pursue truth in scientific as well as in more general matters. Unless we are able to induce a more enterprising, a more adventurous attitude in our educated citizens, we will be condemned to be mere imitators even in the solution of our own particular problems." (p.74)

I would add to this very wise observation that most of the students going to university were the first from their families to be so privileged, and that there was no culture of book reading in their homes, nothing to augment the courses they take at university. This lack of a broader pedagogical canvass was almost certainly one of the reasons for the persistent student nihilism that Jones had to deal with. A striking one had to do with one Ali Kabba.

Kabba was a student leader in the early 1980s driven by what Jones calls Gaddafi's "more exotic influence" in the form of the Green Book. Kabba's application of the confusions of the self-serving and almost illiterate ruminations of that book took the form of feverish juevenile outrages, including the flogging of other students. Jones writes that this "was not tolerated by the college and in due course, the Libyan Colonel's direct influence on student affairs faded." It didn't, really; it only took on a more covert and more sinister form -- it was the key element creating the civil war of the 1990s.

An earlier expression of student unrest, a more spontaneous rhetorical gesture, had also triggered an unhappy outcome: the 1977 students demonstration led directly first to the vandalisation of FBC and the beating up and alleged rape of students by President Siaka Stevens' thugs, and then to the imposition of a one-party state. Jones was principal during both these events, and he almost became a victim in the first. The students had rained insults on Stevens as began his speech as chancellor at convocation on campus but he calmly continued. When it came Jones' turn to speak, he began by apologising to Stevens for his students' rudeness. This later struck the wily Stevens as odd: Jones was apparently reading from a speech, which could only mean – Stevens thought – that he had known about the insults prior to the event. The following day, as thugs beat up students, a call came to Jones from the government demanding a copy of the speech. Of course, the apology was never there; it had been an off-the-cuff statement. But well-wishers, more politically attuned that Jones, had advised Jones to take cover, which he did just in time: there were APC thugs looking for him.

Could a good foundation course at FBC be instructive to the students to be better able to understand their options in their world than these futile gestures? If they had read Turgenev and Conrad and Shaw and Camus, they would have recognized worlds similar to theirs – corrupt, oppressive, dominated by a few – but also a warning about the simplicities of revolution and the futility of nihilistic gestures. Instead, on their own they read Fanon and Mao and Che and Gaddafi, and did not read those other writers: that added reading could have struck a note of balance between the tendency towards nihilism and a check on fatalism. Surely, if Kabba had had read Shaw, he would have been careful about recruiting someone like Foday Sankoh into a revolutionary project: he would have known that revolution attracts not just those to whom the world is not good enough but also those who are not good enough for the world.

The point is that university students – whose social positions are by definition transitory but very much aligned to those of the ruling classes – cannot lead revolutions; very likely they end up being "useful idiots" – the phrase is allegedly Lenin's – (or worse) of the ruthless sociopaths who ultimately wield control. Mengistu in Ethiopia physically eliminated most of the student leaders who had been his allies, and Sankoh, a homicidal voluptuary, wiped out, in one purge, the people that amounted to the intellectual driving force behind the RUF. They, like Sankoh, may not have been aware of this, but their approach to politics faithfully reflected those of their enemies. It was a version of the scum politics that Stevens had introduced: politics driven by the idea that the hoped-for change, the reality of political success, will come when one simply eliminates the "right" people. Without solid, well-worked out ideas and a concrete political programme, they target enemies, not people, for only they are real. That leads, of course, to purposeless violence and destruction driven purely by simple rejection and rage.

Jones' Legacy

Jones's legacy as a teacher will remain the gold standard in Sierra Leone: his former students universally revere him, and many of them are highly successful. But younger scholars more influenced by the academic fashions of the 1960s and 1970s have not shared his apparent over-reverence for the English renaissance classics and even Creole culture. Lemuel Johnson, a fellow Creole literary scholar and poet, may be one such. To begin with, Johnson's depiction of the Creole personality (in *The Devil, The Gargoyle, and The Buffoon: The Negro as Metaphor in Western Literature*, 1969) as "schizophrenic dualism" with "an exaggerated inability to develop a sense of equilibrium between [the] African and English experiences," is sharply at odds with Jones' views. Jones finely articulated his views on Creole identity in a 1968 essay: Those who are part of the Creole society, he wrote, "as they celebrate their weddings with gumbe music or dance in evening dress to the strains of western-style bands, or talk to their dead during an awujo feast, or sing Bach in the choir on Sundays, seem quite unaware of their 'rootlessness', and display a surprising self-confidence." The essay is found in *Freetown: A Symposium*, which Jones co-edited with the pioneering historian of Sierra Leone Christopher Fyfe).

In his *Shakespeare in Africa (and other Venues): Import and Appropriation of Culture* (1998), Johnson mocks that "rummaging among other people's marginalia and parentheses" to discover, for example, that Christopher Columbus actually mentioned Sierra Leone in his accounts of his journeys... Ah, he writes, "it is true that those among us who read long and irrelevantly in the endnotes and footnotes of our imperial curriculum did make a point of revealing that their excursions made for startling recognitions. They said, for example, that in those 'under-cellars' of our colonial library even Sierra Leone was now and then mentioned..." Though Johnson does not mention Jones or his book, the inference can be drawn.

What about the 418-page Krio-English dictionary? The tome claims that Krio is a West African language which has adapted "even its English and European borrowings into the mould of other West African languages, particularly the Kwa language group to which Yoruba belongs." The dictionary is a landmark cultural and intellectual achievement, but its argument is not settled; I myself remain a little unconvinced. In a 1962 paper entitled "Mid-Nineteenth Century Evidences of a Sierra Leone Patois," published in Sierra Leone Language Review, Jones demonstrated how the introduction of Yoruba-speaking Liberated Africans to the Sierra Leone colony in the nineteenth century may have significantly changed the early patois spoken in the colony, leading to the development of the Krio language as it is spoken today. But in this paper, as in the dictionary, one does not get a sense of process over time. The point is that Krio as a language in its early beginnings right into the twentieth century was not the language of the Creole elite; it was a subaltern language, purely oral and protean, and was therefore despised as patios or "broken English." In the nineteenth century it wasn't spoken, or it being spoken was actively discouraged, in educated Creole homes. (In contrast, Afrikaans, with origins very similar to Krio, was early embraced as a nationalist rallying point by the descendants of Dutch settlers in South Africa, helping it to develop an impressive literature and ensuring its primacy in the country for decades as the official language.). Edward Blyden, a refugee from Liberia, with his cultivated and alert foreign ears and eyes, first recognised its peculiar merit; and he described Krio in 1884 as the "speech of the Sierra Leone streets." The slightly revanchist celebration of Krio as indigenous is perhaps a welcome embrace of the majority poor, non-elite Creole culture; but this point ought to be made more clearly.

But this is merely carping. The achievement is marvellous, and it can be built upon. This will be a fitting tribute to a great man who dedicated his long life to the work. Salute Professor Jones!

4.
Mallam O: The Publisher as Writer[72]

The publishing industry is an arcane world, with its own rules and logic. Commercial consideration, of course, has always been paramount, but publishers who consider themselves serious - that is dealing in books with more exalted appeals: they all like to call this 'academic' these days - are careful not to sound or appear philistine, though philistine is exactly the word that has been hurled at book publishers throughout the ages, by outraged authors. The legendary Samuel Johnson had some unprintable things to say about them, as had, more recently, such famous names as VS Naipaul and Paul Theroux (who tend not to agree on much else).

Writing, for serious writers, is transcendent work; there is a spiritual quality to it. Great publishers share this commitment, but not always - at least in the view of writers. But what of publishers who are themselves writers, or who indeed started their careers as writers? A good number of publishers have issued excellent memoirs, but this is not what I am talking about. Politicians and thieves and monks also publish memoirs, but no one, therefore, considers them writers. My knowledge here is limited, but I can think of very few publishers who started as writers. Osman Sankoh (aka Mallam O), a Sierra Leonean biostatistician, epidemiologist, and environmental researcher (you read me right), is one such. Dr. Sankoh is the founding publisher of the Sierra Leonean Writers Series. The aspiration itself - setting out to publish books on Sierra Leone by mainly Sierra Leonean authors - demands a certain brio.

Books have to be sold and read and reviewed. They call for a certain industry and an associated culture: a reading, appreciative public; an economy that allows books to be bought, and a culture of universities and book reviewers and book stores. None of this is true of Sierra Leone

---

[72] *Patriotic Vanguard*, 18 March 2007.

at the moment. So why did a smart and successful young scientist think establishing a publishing series for Sierra Leone makes any sense? Why invite the pain?

"I find interesting parallels with the now defunct African Writers Series which got started with Chinua Achebe's *Things Fall Apart*," Sankoh tells me in his quiet but passionate way. "I started the Sierra Leonean Writers Series after the publication of my book, *Hybrid Eyes - An African in Europe*, and the overwhelmingly positive reaction to it. I wrote and published this book also in German as *Ein Vermittler zwischen zwei Welten - Afrika und Deutschland*." Sankoh was then a doctoral student in Germany, and the German edition gave him "a surprising exposure in Germany. I got invited by key newspapers to contribute articles; and by intercultural organisations to do readings and talk about the theme of the book. All this was unexpected. I only wanted to tell a story. I knew many Africans had had or were still having not-too-dissimilar experiences that had gone untold. I wanted to tell a credible story with me at the centre. I tried it; it worked. But it was not easy for me to find a publisher."

He eventually found one, but the publisher made it known that he was taking a "risk": it might not pay off in financial terms. The narrative is very familiar. In fact the publishers made a huge profit out of the book. It was then that "I realised that there were probably better writers of Sierra Leonean descent both at home and abroad who should be given an opportunity to publish their works. Many such works would be thrown aside because there are not many publishers willing to take the risk of publishing budding writers or those less well known. I wanted to do something to change that situation. Fortunately my family allowed me to use our meagre resources to establish the Sierra Leonean Writers Series, SLWS."

Sankoh is now based in Accra, Ghana. I read his *Hybrid Eyes* (and reviewed it) when it came out, and when I moved to Ghana in 2004, for a one-year stint, he was among the first people I wanted to meet. An hour or so after I phoned him, Sankoh came to my flat at Osu: a neat, semi-suburban part of Accra with a street called Oxford, where some of the city's best restaurants and bars and casinos are located. With his smooth, anodyne face, the goatee neatly trimmed, he looked less the academic than a mildly successful businessman. I was slightly taken aback. We instantly became friends, and he would drop by for a beer and bit after work almost every evening thereafter.

The publishing house he established after the success of *Hybrid Eyes* is called Africa Future Publishers, which was registered in Germany by his wife of many years, Jariatu, a wonderful hostess (as I, a frequent weekend visitor at their North Legon house, remember it). The couple are now working on moving Africa Future Publishers to Accra, and subsequently still, to Freetown, Sierra Leone.

Africa Future Publishers focuses on academic, fictional, and scientific writing that, Sankoh says, "will complement other relevant materials used in schools, colleges, universities and other tertiary institutions. The Sierra Leonean Writers Series aims to promote good quality books by Sierra Leoneans, writers of Sierra Leonean descent from around the world, and writers writing on or about Sierra Leone."

There is something deeply moving about Sankoh's efforts, the purity of his dedication. "Even if the initial readership [of SLWS books] is made up of people outside Sierra Leone, it is our hope that students and other readers in Sierra Leone will eventually be among the primary beneficiaries of these new works," Sankoh says. "Not only will people in Sierra Leone be able to read materials that relate to their own lives and experiences, budding writers will also be able to draw inspiration from the efforts of their compatriots and other established writers."

There is, of course, no money in it - yet. The SLWS has issued over a dozen titles, including memoirs, poetry anthologies, and a recent novel by Yemah Lucilda Hunter, author of the successful historical novel *Road to Freedom*. While these interesting titles have done well abroad, few in Sierra Leone, which does not have a serious bookstore, have heard about them. Sankoh makes his living as Deputy Executive Director of the scientific NGO INDEPTH Network, which he joined in 2002. The group recently won millions of dollars from the Bill and Melinda Gates Foundation, and it coordinates thirty-four health and demographic surveillance system (HDSS) sites in Africa, Asia, Central America and Oceania (see www.indepth-network.org).

Sankoh has continued to publish researched papers in a range of journals. His work on epidemiology and biostatistics has been published in *Tropical Medicine and International Health* and the *International Journal of Epidemiology*. He once dropped off a package of these publications at my Accra flat, recondite pieces beautifully jacketed, which I proudly placed on my book shelves, aside a half dozen or so Nkrumah hagiography (all published in Accra) and a valuable collection of essays on African security (an enduring interest of mine) edited by my good old friend Ismail Rashid (another academic). I included the Rashid collection in a review of books on Africa for the journal *African Affairs*, which is published by Oxford University Press. I regret to report that I have still not been able to read through Sankoh's papers, and I hope he understands. Still, I would proudly point at these collections to my visiting Ghanaian friends - academics, journalists and university students (not all female) - as the work of a distinguished compatriot.

I notice that I have mentioned the lack of a bookstore, which no doubt partly accounts for the sad contraction in the reading habit, in Sierra Leone twice. I understand that President Tejan Kabbah has finally noticed this. At the recent launch of the fascinating novel *The Wind Within* (by Sierra Leonean author Rachael Massaquoi), a government minister announced that the President plans to set up a decent bookstore in Freetown on his retirement. I know the President quite well (even before he became President). Doubtless he has been less than effective as a national leader, but he is refreshingly literate. He even has culture: he can lay claim to being responsible for the booming music industry in the country - by the singular act, at the launch of a new CD by Jimmy B, of calling on all radio stations in the country to give priority to Sierra Leonean music. That was, I think, in 2002. Now look at the result...

All of this came to me on learning that Sankoh's publishing house will be issuing a book by Joe A.D Alie, the head of the history department at Fourah Bay College (FBC) whose exalted teaching career spans several decades. Dr. Alie is already the author of an acclaimed history textbook (used in schools and colleges) as well as several 'pamphlets' (which surely should also have been published as textbooks). His forthcoming *Sierra Leone since Independence* is very much anticipated.

One hopes that President Kabbah will mark this on his calendar (the book appears before the July national elections)...and one hopes that the event finally gives a much-needed fillip to the Sierra Leonean Writers Series.

5.
Nelson Mandela's Struggle for Peace[73]

On 27 November 1995, a calm voice issued this jarring statement on the BBC: "Abacha is sitting on a volcano. And I am going to explode it underneath him." It belonged to Nelson Mandela. He was 77, and had already been president of South Africa for a year. Mandela was referring to Gen. Sani Abacha, an obdurate and corrupt dictator in Nigeria who, in addition to still holding the winner of his country's presidential election in solitary confinement, had just executed the writer and environmentalist Ken Saro-Wiwa and eight other activists from oil-blighted Ogoniland. The nine had been condemned by a military tribunal.

Mandela was angry; Abacha had rebuffed his studiously private and civilised appeal for the release of Saro-Wiwa and his fellow activists. By doing so, Abacha had drawn the battle line, stoking the fiery passion for justice still burning in the breast of the aged champion of freedom. To his end Mandela lived by the dictum, which he articulated with great eloquence at his trial at Rivonia in 1964, that though he abhorred violence, he was willing to employ it to fight "tyranny, exploitation, and oppression."

Mandela had to back down from his hard-line stance against Abacha amidst pressure from the "realists" in his government who were concerned that a newly liberated South Africa was on a collision course with some of those who had been among the staunchest backers of his African National Congress (ANC) during the terrible years of apartheid.

Appraisals and reminiscences of Mandela since he died on 5 December [2013] have justly stressed his great commitment to social justice, his largeness of spirit and towering humanism, his lack of saintly affectation (in sharp contrast to Mahatma Gandhi, with whom some have compared him) and his courage, dignity and political astuteness. What tends to be missing from most of the encomiums, perhaps because he has now been so warmly embraced by the world, is what Mandela himself always made

---

[73] *African Renewal*, 16 December 2013.

sure to emphasise at every opportunity, that he was first and foremost an African nationalist with a vision—shaped by his experience of raw racism and oppression perpetrated by a minority fascist regime—of commitment to the continent and all its people.

It was this vision that saw him in 1961 travel to almost all of independent Africa, drumming up support for his fledging armed struggle; it was out of this experience that he settled on his great legacy for the world: reconciliation and redistributive, rather than retributive, justice after the experience of tyranny and war—what has now (somewhat uneasily) become the sprawling and protean field of transitional justice. "I have done whatever I did, both as an individual and as a leader of my people," Mandela told the judges at his trial at Rivonia on 20 April 1964, "because of my experience in South Africa and my own proudly felt African background, and not because of what any outsider might have said."

He was not and never wanted to be seen as a pacifist: for him freedom and justice were worth fighting and dying for. His harsh journey from prison to the presidency enabled him to pursue his vision, which afterward needed to be broadly applied across Africa. The government of Abacha, secure in oil wealth and facing a fractured opposition whose leadership preferred comfortable exile to the necessary task of national leadership, was the first setback to Mandela's vision in 1995. The following year he was appointed chair of the Southern African Development Community (SADC), a regional economic bloc, and that brought him to confront an even more onerous problem: Zaire (now the Democratic Republic of Congo) was fast sliding into chaos under its long-term kleptocrat, Mobutu Sese Seko. Nothing could stop this slide, and the problems of that massive, unwieldy country still remain largely unresolved.

Such setbacks tested the nerve of the old warrior, so that when an electoral crisis in tiny Lesotho, which looks like a dot inside South Africa on a map, threatened to lead to a civil war in September 1998, Mandela quickly authorised military intervention. Though unpopular and messy— the South African forces, never completely weaned of the brutality of their past, sometimes carried out gratuitous attacks on civilians and local infrastructure—the intervention did succeed in preventing civil war.

It was, however, Mandela's work on Burundi that assures his legacy as a peacemaker in Africa. Aging and in poor health, Mandela took over in December 1999 the position of chief negotiator of the long-running conflict in Burundi, after the death of Julius Nyerere, the erstwhile holder of the position. He characteristically brought his passion and outspokenness, not to mention his enormous prestige and charisma, to the job. Less than a month after he took over the position, Mandela made clear what his conception of peace was. It is not possible, he told the UN Security Council on 19 January 2000, in an address on that blighted little central African state, "to establish regional peace unless component parts of this region establish domestic foundations for a stable democratic order."

Peace, like freedom, like democracy, in Mandela's clear-sighted and dignified vision, is a positive attribute: the conditions for its full enjoyment must be established before it is possible. This vision recalled his address to his judges at Rivonia in 1964: such was his principled consistency. "During my lifetime ...," he said, "I have fought against white domination, and I have fought against black domination. I have cherished the ideal of a democratic and free society in which all persons live together in harmony and with equal opportunities."

Burundi needed this breath of fresh air. Like its far more famous twin, neighbouring Rwanda, the country had been beset by ethnic conflict since gaining independence, first from Belgium as a United Nations Trust Territory on 1 July 1962, and then as a country on 1 July 1966. Communal fighting, mainly along Hutu-Tutsi lines, has led to the death of hundreds of thousands of people over the decades. When the plane carrying Burundi's President Cyprien Ntaryamira and Rwanda's President Juvénal Habyarimana (both of them Hutu) was shot down over Kigali on 6 April 1994, widespread ethnic violence exploded once again. It was this event that triggered the genocide in Rwanda. Mandela, not yet in power when the plane was shot down, must have been particularly horrified by the genocide, which tended, in some people's view, to undercut the great hopes that his election had unleashed for Africa.

The continuation of preventable suffering of people anywhere in the world, he said in that address on Burundi to the Security Council, "demeans all of us."

Starting soon after his appointment to the Burundi position, and determined that such horror would never again affect the region, Mandela helped hammer out the Arusha Accord that was signed on August 2000, and he caused to be deployed a large South African force to lead African Union peacekeepers in the country. (On 21 May 2004, by its resolution 1545, the UN Security Council established the UN Operation in Burundi (ONUB), which took over leadership of the African Union forces.) Upon Mandela's death, the government of Burundi released a statement acknowledging his role in the country's current peace: "Burundians will always remember that it is Nelson Mandela who brokered the peace deal that led to transitional power-sharing government after the achievement of the Arusha Agreement for Peace and Reconciliation in Burundi, paving the way for a new era of peace, security and democracy in Burundi."

There are some who continue to blame Mandela for an alleged reticence on Zimbabwe as his old comrade Robert Mugabe ran the country down. It is worth remembering, however, that Mugabe was a highly admirable leader when Mandela got out of prison and indeed throughout much of Mandela's time in office. Mandela did in fact speak out against Mugabe as the situation in Zimbabwe became more and more septic: in 2010, in a public address, Citizen Mandela condemned what he called "the tragic failure of leadership in our neighbouring Zimbabwe."

The African Renaissance, an idea popularised by Mandela's successor Thabo Mbeki and one that Mandela fully supported, has certainly not yet been realised. There are still petty wars and petty tyrannies, not to mention an unequal global economic and political system, holding the continent back. But Mandela's life and work for the continent suggested that it is possible.

6.
Liberia in New York City[74]

A few years ago I stayed at a friend's apartment in a Dickensian high-rise building on Bowen Street in Staten Island, New York, for a couple of days. The building was full of Liberians, many very young. There, my friend took me to a restaurant and bar in one of the cramped apartments. The booze was much cheaper than elsewhere, and the talk was all Liberian: it was an illegal business outfit, of course, since it wasn't registered, and was tax-free. I felt I was in a version of Monrovia, but with the money…

Liberians have been living in the US for decades; indeed, many of Liberia's ruling elite before the coup of 1980 had US citizenship: the father of President Tolbert, the last of the Americo-Liberian leaders, was actually born in the US, into an African American family. What I did not notice during my stay there was an inchoate animosity in the Liberian community deriving largely from the country's recent past of bloody coup and horrific civil war – and reflecting the deep divisions, political, social, and ethnic, in Liberia itself.

Jonny Steinberg's very interesting account of Liberia's New York community through the eyes of two of its protagonists lays bare the troubles of this immigrant community in a charming way. For two years, Steinberg, a South African writer and journalist, shadows the two men in the neighborhoods of Clifton and Stapleton in the Parkview area of Staten Island, New York, which hosts some 4000 Liberian refugees.

This methodology has its risk – prolonged intimacy of this sort can undermine objectivity and even sound judgement – but Steinberg balances the picture by talking to countless other Liberians and consulting more conventional sources. More importantly, he visits Liberia for a month, and travels around the country, including to the

---

[74] A review of Jonny Steinberg's *Little Liberia* (London: Jonathan Cape 2011), first published in *african.org* June-July 2011.

county where one of the protagonists, Jacob Massaquoi, hailed. The result is a nuanced and sympathetic account. (Here is the place for me to state, by way of full disclosure, that I know Steinberg, and I met him during his Liberia visit. I was then head of the Liberia Office of the New York-based International Center for Transitional Justice, ICTJ).

This book, in my view, is valuable for two reasons. Firstly, it serves as a very trenchant, though understated, criticism of the rather faddish approach to transitional justice – the knee-jerk idea that after atrocious wars as what Liberia experienced, and without a careful consideration of the history and socio-political configuration of the country, there is need to set up a South African-style truth commission as a way of accounting for the conflict and of fostering reconciliation. Steinberg followed the Liberian Truth and Reconciliation Commission (TRC), especially the Commission's – on the face of it – commendable attempts to collect civil war-related testimonies from diaspora Liberians in the US. In fact, discordant political and ethnic interests and the deep divisions in the Liberian community (epitomised by that between Massaquoi, who experienced the war and sustained a shrapnel wound to the leg, and the gregarious and charming Rufus Arkoi, who had arrived in Liberia before the war and had become a successful football coach training young Liberians in New York, among other valuable community work) seriously undermined this effort. Even within Liberia, as I saw for myself while working with the TRC, the process was wobbly and controversial from the start, and it was unable either to create "a clear picture of the past" nor "facilitate genuine healing and reconciliation" (the TRC's core mandate).

Steinberg is a lot more critical of Arkoi than of Massaquoi, which I find unfair. Arkoi is described as having "sat out the [Liberian] war in the US" and is accused of harboring designs to be President of Liberia. But Arkoi went to the US long before the war (like many thousands of Liberians), and, being neither a soldier nor in fact a politician, should not be reasonably expected to go back and experience the brutal, nihilistic conflict. As it happens, I find the admirable work that Arkoi has been doing in the US important enough to qualify him way over and above the countless number of other portfolio politicians in Liberia wanting to be president. Massaquoi, for his part, was a young student who got caught in it – he had not gone back to the country to see for himself. One admires his endurance, sympathises with his sufferings during the war, and wishes him well in his staunch ambition to be highly educated. One respects his community work, too. But one does not place him on a higher level than Arkoi.

Secondly, Steinberg's exploration of diaspora politics, and the travails of a transplanted community, is both subtle and immensely timely. He makes some play of the slight revulsion of older Liberians who were well-established in the US towards the newly-arrived, war-displaced and somewhat febrile young immigrants. But this is as old as immigration itself, and the literature on the Irish-Americans, Italian-Americans, and of Jewish Americans, shows the deep uneasiness bordering on neurosis among settled ethnic communities towards the influx of poorer, less educated members of their ethnicity in their neighbourhoods – the kind of pathology which indicates fear of one's middle class pretensions being exposed.

There are a number of repetitions in this book, and they are stylistically laboured. One thinks as well that some of the minor characters which Steinberg invests some efforts in sketching are extraneous. It certainly would have been very helpful if Steinberg had reflected more systematically on the issue of memory, the underlying – though unstated – theme of this book. We get a tantalizing glimpse of this in the final chapter. Steinberg gives a copy each of his manuscript to Arkoi and Massaquoi to read before publication. As one would expect, the busy Arkoi is uninterested, or is interested only in the promise that he will get a portion of the royalties from it. The more sophisticated Massaquoi, however, is appalled at the portrayal of him; he doesn't seem to recognize a lot of what he had told Steinberg in the course of a year and half. Or, rather, he wouldn't quite want to see that in print. The whole thing seems to him to have been a hoax, a set-up, by the writer to get materials out of him for the author's own purpose. He feels proprietorial, or at least this is Steinberg's impression.

I suspect that something more than this is at play in Massaquoi's subtle mind. Memory gets affected by time and distance, and what people share with strangers or others of their experiences is often mediated and abbreviated by this; often determined by circumstance. This is why truth commissions are a very tricky thing. In that process, truth itself is on trial. This is the principal lesson I get from Steinberg's book…

7.
In the Footsteps of Graham Greene[75]

In 1934 the English writer Graham Greene, only thirty-one and never been to Africa before, was cajoled by the Anti-Slavery Society to visit Liberia and follow-up on some awful findings made four years earlier. Liberia had been established as a settlement for freed American slaves with the motto 'The Love of Liberty brought us here." This was, of course, a hoax; and in 1930, a League of Nations report on the country found that "slavery as defined by the anti-slavery convention" existed in the country. The situation was so bad, the Commission opined, that "any hope of improvement" was futile "without the introduction of outside special assistance."

Trusteeship or colonisation was recommended but never carried out. Greene's romantic fascination for the exotic and his broad liberal views were already well known. He trekked through Liberia (accompanied by his young cousin Barbara) with the aid of twenty-six African porters and cooks: hardly any motor road was available in Liberia outside the capital. That epic journey is described in *Journey without Maps* (first published in 1936), a profoundly insightful, sympathetic and informative book.

Tim Butcher takes the book as his inspiration for his own *Chasing the Devil*. Unlike Greene, however, by the time Butcher set out for his trek through Liberia in 2008/09, he was already a grizzled Fleet Street veteran having reported from the region as the Telegraph's Africa correspondent, and having done a more challenging trek through the Congo (the result being his much-praised *Blood River*.)

He gives two reasons for doing this book. He had reported on Liberia when Charles Taylor, the country's former blood-drenched and utterly corrupt dictator, was engaged in fighting insurgents. In the Telegraph he had accused Taylor of practising ritual murder and cannibalism,

---

[75] Review of Tim Butcher, *Chasing the River: The Search for Africa's Fighting Spirit* (London: Chatto & Windus 2010), published in African.org (August-September 2011)

sensational charges but certainly not unfounded. Word got to Butcher that Taylor would kill him if he ever got hold of him, and so Butcher could not report from Liberia when Taylor was finally forced out of the country into self-exile. He now wanted to explore the country more. The more important reason Butcher gives is that as a reporter burdened by the daily deadline he was unable to study Africa more profoundly. He now thinks that his reports were superficial, and feels punished by a "stone in [his] shoes" for that. His return to Liberia through Sierra Leone following Greene's epic footsteps is his way of making up for that.

Though this ambition is not as elegant as Greene's purpose, it is all well and good. But Butcher, unlike Greene, had clearly already made up his mind about Liberia before he sets out (also with a companion, only in his case a young man just down from Oxford). It is entirely Butcher's choice to walk through the bush from the Sierra Leone border through Liberia, since there is a motor road from there to Monrovia (Liberia's capital) and vehicles are available, but he keeps mentioning the hardships of the trek, perhaps to underscore his own stamina and brio (the British press constantly describes him, quaintly, as an "explorer", though what this means is unclear).

Irritating though his grouses can be, Butcher's reporting through the trek is often good and accurate. It is his anachronistic insistence on seeing "devils" all through the way, engrafting arcane meanings onto mundane events, that makes one think that his journey is rather pointless. He obviously learns nothing he could not have read in a good anthropology or history book on the country in a library at Oxford. As he nears Monrovia – making sure he followed the exact route that Greene took: another constant source of irritation, that insistence on bettering the master in that one – Butcher apparently stumbles on an illumination, his Eureka moment.

The great enervating problem of Liberia and its proneness to violence result not from politics but from tradition, Butcher finds. The problem was Poro (the secret society for men widely practised in the region), something which Greene "had failed... to fully account for." "If you believe, as many in the Poro do, that a person does not exist fully as a human unless initiated, then the killing of a non-initiate for ritual reasons is… no worse than the killing of an animal for the pot." Killing "for the pot"… the image, of course, evokes cannibalism, the enduring trope of Butcher's anachronistic book.

In fact, many more discerning observers have applauded the very positive role that Poro played during the war. In his Beyond Anarchy (published in 2005, way before Butcher set out on his Liberia trip), Amos Sawyer notes that during Liberia's civil war, every town or village was occupied by rebel militia fighters, gangsters who exercised tomcatting powers over defenceless people. The state had imploded, and the only thing that kept the sense of community, of society, alive was Poro. Leaders mobilised community people to resist the nihilism of the youthful militia fighters, and that kept the sense of community alive in the face of state atrophy.

That Butcher misses this crucial point makes one to conclude that he has not quite succeeded in removing that stone from his shoes. He should try harder.

Lansana Gberie

8.

On J. Sorie Conteh's In Search of Sons[76]

A few years ago, J. Sorie Conteh, a Sierra Leonean writer of a learned disposition, published *The Diamonds*. The novel very successfully captures the social and environmental meltdown caused by the 1950s diamond rush in eastern and southern Sierra Leone. The hero is a peasant farmer, Gibao Semabu, who leaves his village and a well productive rice farm for the more interesting and promising diamond-mining town of Sewa. It is a totally graft-addled world, and Gibao quickly succumbs to the greed and corruption, and takes things a step further -- he commits ritual murder on the recommendation of a sorcerer who promised that the return will be vast diamond finds. He is arrested, tried and hanged for murder instead. The novel is a parable – in the manner of some of Thomas Hardy's stories (set in rural, rapidly industrialising England of the 18th century) – of the destruction of the bucolic and beautifully-ordered rural world by unregulated wealth-finding; and if Conteh's authorial voice concluding the novel appears a little fad-driven, it nevertheless is accurate: "What was to become a diamond boom became a curse on the nation. Herein lies the irony. The economic benefits of diamonds, which were meant to free people from the clutches of poverty, instead enslaved them in the clutches of greed."

Conteh has now published another novel, and this time he explores – in the manner of Chinua Achebe – some rather tragic aspects of our cultural heritage. The novel is entitled *In Search of Sons*, part of the Sierra Leonean Writers Series issued by Osman Sankoh's Africa Future Publishers. This very interesting enterprise merits a few sentences in this review.

---

[76] Published in Patriotic Vanguard on 11 February 2010

Sankoh started the Sierra Leonean Writers Series (SLWS) after the success of his first book, *Hybrid Eyes – An African in Europe* in late 1990s, while still a doctoral student in Germany. Realising that there "were probably better writers of Sierra Leonean descent both at home and abroad who should be given an opportunity to publish their works," Sankoh told me in an interview, he used his own money to set up the series. The publisher is now based in Accra, Ghana; and Africa Future Publishers, which was registered in Germany by his wife of many years, now operates from Accra. I had got to know Sankoh during a stint in Ghana (2004-2005), and we became close friends. He publishes academic, fictional, and scientific writing. The SLWS has issued more than a dozen titles, including memoirs, poetry anthologies, a novel by Yema Lucilda Hunter, author of the successful historical novel *Road to Freedom*, and *Sierra Leone since Independence* by the respected historian Joe A. D. Alie.

We are lucky that he has now published *In Search of Sons*. The publisher sent me an electronic copy of the novel early last year. I read it rather quickly, as I do most electronic materials (that old fashion part of me!); but until late last year when I received the hardcopy, I didn't savour its richness and complexity, its mordant and didactic tone, and its critical but affectionate treatment of a proud but rather flawed culture.

The story is set somewhere in Moyamba District among the Kpa-Mende, but it could be any other place in rural West Africa. It is pre-independent Sierra Leone, but of course there is nothing insular or 'tribal' about Talia, where the story actually unfolds. There is a school (run by Irish Catholic sisters), a church, and some people quote, somewhat improbably, Krio proverbs; alongside these, of course, are the River Mermaid, Sande Society, the chief who must be given a new wife each year, anxieties about witchcraft, the petty peasant gossips…

The opening is seductive but slightly misleading. It begins as reflection by a young medical doctor and nun, Kunaafoh, as she stands by her

351

residence "majestically facing the Atlantic Ocean" – so this is Freetown. The romance of the ocean is commented on – the "rhythm and dynamism of the oceanfront", we read, and then think immediately about those tourist manuals. But the story is no romance, or it is romance gone badly awry. For Kunaafoh, we learn, "was the only girl among three children. After her mother's third pregnancy, no other babies were born, much to the displeasure of their father, who wanted many more children, preferably sons, to pass on the family name and inherit the land." In fact there is another pregnancy, but a tragic one: now ageing and probably in ill-health (the inference can be easily drawn), Kunaafoh's mother badgers herself, to please her husband, to get pregnant –"in search of other sons." And she dies in labour. Conteh, like Joseph Conrad, has a tendency to leave nothing unsaid; and the moral tone is earnest: the story is explicitly cast as a commentary on a cruel barbaric side of a culture that has proven so resilient – and tragic.

This is, of course, barebones summary, omitting many interesting sidelights. One of them has to with attitudes towards accumulation of wealth. Here the setting moves to Ginger Hall in Freetown (there is an egalitarianism of sort in Talia: no one, not even the amorous chief, appears that rich). It concerns Hindowaa's brother, Fanday, who is helping educate Hindowaa's two sons in Freetown. Fanday had served in the Second World War – one of the hints that this is the late colonial period in Sierra Leone – and was living with his wife and two cousins in Ginger Hall. He was reputedly rich, and had his money stacked in a trunk in the house. No one knew where he got so much money from, though his wife is a trader, and they live frugally. So the rumour goes around that Fanday and his wife were devilish people with a large snake in their house guiding them and bringing them money. This must sound familiar: in Nostromo, a novel about an unstable and impoverished Third World country, Conrad spoke about "that obscure instinct of consolation" among the poor which associates wealth with evil.

It is a beguiling idea: the notion that those who are materially better off than us are really morally stained and repugnant people. This idea is, in fact, not African at all: it goes back to the early, "primitive," Christians, who, facing the might and fabulous wealth of Rome, contrived Hell in the Other World for those wicked Romans, and a shiny wonderful City of God somewhere in the after-world (this was St. Augustine's luminous contribution) for the disenfranchised and impoverished Christians...

There is a Conradian coincidence, too, at the end of the novel. Kunaafoh, who had been helped to flee Talia – she was to have been forced into a marriage with the aged Chief – by the Catholic Sisters (and had been given up as forever lost) just returned from Ireland, a medical doctor, in time to witness her mother's death. The poor woman is in labour in the secret society bush for women, and when Kunaafoh and a Catholic nun, Sister Kono, arrive, they ask to see her. But they were both non-initiates, and the request was summarily turned down: "How dare...a non-initiate, ask to enter the grove and in the process render it profane"? So the one chance of saving poor Giita (Kunaafoh's mother) by two Western-trained medics is squandered by "tradition." Giita dies.

This end, melodramatic and at the same time steeped in pathos, is the sum of Conteh's deeply moving story; a very fine delineation of a proud culture with its utterly cruel, irrational side. It is not a religious fable; this is the work of a novelist who is also a great cultural critic, an anthropologist.

9.
Between Prayers and Satan[77]

Over the past few years, an impressive body of work that can be loosely called war literature has emerged in Sierra Leone. It seems to be dominated by poetry; and though some of the poets did not experience the recent civil war in Sierra Leone directly (as combatants, say), their consciousness – and imagination – has been profoundly shaped by it. The outputs have become more and more assured, and more and more prolific. In last month alone two poetry collections were issued – *Manscape in Sierra*, by the well-known Elvis Hallowell, and *Of Flours and Tears*, by a striking new poetic voice, Ahmed Koroma. I have read Manscape, which collects Hallowell's poetry from 1991 to 2011, with great satisfaction: the 279 poems here are sophisticated, evocative, and immensely assured; and one hopes that Hallowell will now stop celebrating Syl Cheney-Coker's belittling comment about him as a "poet worth waiting for in future." The poet has arrived.

The name of Ahmed Koroma's debut poetry collection is taken from a poem with the anodyne title "Prayer," which languidly promotes the curiously persistent rumour about the phlegmatic nature of Sierra Leoneans:

"the saturated mixture of flour and tears/the expectation from all these years/did my people pray their lives away/while satan's maniacal laugh echoes/outside the minaret walls."

There is no question mark, suggesting that Prayer, much more than Satan, is the problem. And this Satan is persistently evoked, his presence – sometimes dominance – perhaps underlining the futility of Prayer and the helplessness of the confessional adherents. Koroma is a very political poet, and the acuity of his judgments is one of the pleasures of these poems. But in 'Of Flours [flour or flours?] and Tears," one suspects a mordant form of poetic license: one that appropriates, as I mentioned at

[77] A Review of Ahmed Koroma's *Of Flour and Tears first published on Leonenet10 July 2012*

the start, a curious belief that Sierra Leoneans can take anything in their slothful bliss.

The sense that Sierra Leoneans are laid-back, can suffer any indignity from their rulers in silence, persists even after a brutal civil war that should surely have convinced everyone otherwise. Or should it? In the first year of that war itself, a feverish American journalist passed through the country's capital and wrote an outrageously sarcastic piece for her paper entitled "Wake up, and it's still there." She commented on the sad state of dysfunction in the country, the usual atrocity journalism of poverty and filth and corruption and pointless suffering; she wrote apparently unaware that there was already a war in the southeastern part of the country. In Liberia, she sighed, a slight increase in the price of rice led to a coup and the bayoneting of the President by his own soldiers. In Sierra Leone, ah, there is still the slothful General Joe Momoh growing fatter each day as he daily exhorts his countrymen to "tighten their belts!" Momoh would very soon be overthrown, Sierra Leone itself would implode, the atrophied state and its helpless citizens only rescued by foreign forces. Supposing the journalist is to return to Sierra Leone today, would she still wish for a Samuel Doe-type intervention here? I truly doubt it.

The poems in Koroma's collection were written over nearly a decade, and they cover the war and the process of uncertain peace and democratisation that has followed. But they are organized loosely thematically, not chronologically, which poses some difficulty. Where, for example, could one place this powerful poem, "The Red Sun" (which is, of course, so much more than a mere metaphorical flourish):

"its redness penetrates the grayish clouds/with westerly wind racing toward the rocky hills/a hungry stomach, a duodenal bacterium, waiting out/a breakfast meal, a maggot feast the rays will bring/but we stay all night; witness the red anopheles' fl ight/with strained eyes we now see the tired moon/when the sun is awake we will play hide and seek/we will sing a song, we will fret no gloom/but the warning sign, we dare not look at him/lest the redness follows the eyes that never sleep/this sun blinds those that dare to dream/those with zest and fervor, those unafraid to speak."

The Sun, of course, is very much up, and has been for the past five years. And, of course, the "warning signs" have been there – retinas of eyes awake may well have been burnt, and in some of the policies of the bearer of the Sun's mantle – the name is also Koroma – some of those who've dared to dream have gotten badly burnt, have gotten blinded. I do not know when this poem was first published – all the poems in this collection have appeared on Leonenet, the internet forum – so one is not sure whether to call it alarmist or prescient. But it is very, very good.

The Sun, it seems, would burn and burn, and its victims suffer in enervating helplessness – or so it seems, as one must pick at random in the absence of a guiding chronology, we are told by "I Sit and Watch":

"I sit and watch
at mount olympus
when terror comes
to reign so long
I sit and watch
singing a sad song
when terror comes
and reigns so long"

The Terror, one suspects, is of a different hue and intensity from the Sun, but it is its distinctive product. Here the poet seems to be speaking about the so-called rebels of the Revolutionary United Front, the pillaging thugs whose depredations nearly destroyed Sierra Leone so thoroughly as to make the Sun, once again, palatable after a few years of hiatus. But here again the poet seems to forget the great resisters of that nihislistic force, the Kamajors and other civil defence forces.

Koroma is far from being a partisan poet: his vision is wider, his anxieties broader and deeper. He is concerned, above all, about the systemic being, about the nature of the postcolonial condition. What's this Independence, he asks in a poem that plays on that loaded word ("In-Dependence")?

"I ponder
what species eat their young at birth
and celebrate the birthdays of years to come
the jubilation last night
our deliberate mental block
of why we celebrate our independence
Is it the love for our motherland
our freedom from shackles
vise on our ankles
Is it our mind, being decolonised
our transient divorce overnight
what independence
but we celebrate."

African (or specifically Sierra Leonean) independence, in this stern, somewhat romantic, vision is anything but liberating; it is in fact so disabling as to be meaningless ("our freedom from shackles/vise on our ankles".) That idea of minds being "decolonised," however seductive, is a romantic one, and it can suggest either earnestness or special pleading.

The poet is on surer ground when he is nostalgic about his own corner of Sierra Leone, his Kaibara City and Sackville Street, which he celebrates in the poem with the title 'Nostalgia" ("Kaibara" has a poem with the name.) The language evokes grit and great dereliction ("Sackville Street is dark again/the kerosene lamps are out/and there's mourning... the kid in the gutter... is now an expert/ on kalashnikov and alphajets") but it is genuinely affectionate. Those who depart, the Roman poet Horace wrote, merely change their skies, and not their condition. Really? Koroma's alarming vision here is rooted in reality, but he is not there as witness – he has traveled. When he returns, he finds Sackville Street "bright again/the kerosene lamps are re-flaming/and yes the rain is gone/but can I still see my rainbow/after this bloody storm." The theme of going away and returning is again played on, very effectively, in the poem "'Exodus" – and here the poet tells us of a wonderful welcome of a returned son of Sackville Street "to this land of great drought" as "the water flows fast uphill gushing/and greeting those who dare to return." The law of gravity, for that moment, is suspended.

That tone of joy and celebration is affecting, and it rescues this collection from its otherwise period bleakness. The nation, after-all, survived the war, and would, can still recover the promise of independence of decades ago.

In *Of Flours and Tears* Koroma seeks to prepare our minds for the much-awaited process of genuine liberation which would lead us all to see our "rainbow/after [the] bloody storm."

10.
VS Naipaul and Africa[78]

Towards the end of his magisterial *Decline and Fall of the Roman Empire* (the final volume completed in 1776), Edward Gibbon pauses to reflect on how by the 15th century the Greeks – the creators of modern civilisation – began to take serious notice of the newer nations of northern Europe, which they "could no longer presumed to brand with the name of barbarians." Relying on their accounts, he sketches the "rude picture" of the "life and character" of Germany, France and England. Of particular interest to Gibbon, who was English, is the account of the Greek Byzantine writer, Demetrius Chalcondyles (1423-1511), of life in England during his time. What distinguished the English from other Europeans, Chalcondyles wrote, was their singular disregard for marital honour or female chastity. The English had the habit of throwing their wives and daughters on male visitors who would sleep with them as a sign of welcome; and among their friends, women are "lent and borrowed without shame." Gibbon affects to disbelieve this account, vainly protesting that "assured of the virtue of our mothers, we may smile at the credulity, or resent the injustice, of the Greek." Chalcondyles' account, he wrote, "may teach an important lesson, to distrust the accounts of foreign and remote nations, and to suspend our belief of every tale that deviates from the laws of nature and the character of man."

Gibbon's compatriots have never taken this lesson to heart. At the height of their imperial triumphalism only decades after Gibbon's death, the English virtually invented modern travel writing as a sort of forensic tourism. But the initial impulse was sometimes exalted, particularly in the 18th and early 19th centuries. Noteworthy in this regard was the body of work produced by the explorers dispatched to West Africa by the Association for Promoting the Discovery of the Interior of Africa(formed in London in 1788), of which the most luminous were the accounts of Mungo Park. Park's method – once arrived in West Africa, in the area where modern The Gambia occupies, he took time to learn

---

[78] Pambazuka, 8 January 2015.

the local Mandingo language, and showed appropriate respect for African sovereignty, showing deference to chiefs and local notables, and respecting even slaves as only less privileged human beings – was so exalted compared to what we are now all-too-familiar with that it is probably pointless to hold it as the gold standard. But it is worthy of note for that reason. Later in the 19th century came what Graham Greene has derided as "the white sneer," part of something quite new – British superiority: it was the period of what the historian Philip Curtin has called "pseudo-scientific racism." Exemplifying this was Richard Burton's *Wanderings in West Africa* (published in 1863) and W. Winwood Reade's *Savage Africa* (1864): vulgar and voyeuristic tracts that the Pan Africanist Edward Blyden acidly described in 1887 as the work of "brooding and irregular minds." They were period pieces; in the decade leading to World War II, a different kind of travel writing emerged: Graham Greene's *Journey without Maps* (1936), an account of his trek from Sierra Leone through Liberia, and Geoffrey Gorer's *African Dances* a year earlier, were rigorous and sensitive and honest accounts, unsentimental about empire, and illuminating Africa in profound new ways. These books remain important historical records.

By the time VS Naipaul, a hugely talented writer who won the Nobel Prize in 2001, made his forays into Africa, beginning in the late 1960s, much of what can be "discovered" in Africa had been written about; there was hardly anything exotic about the continent to "explore." Naipaul, born in Trinidad of Indian heritage, is himself a product of empire; but a long residence and success in England has transformed him, at least in his own eyes, to an Englishman of the Evelyn Waugh-type, sniffing at postcolonial countries with the kind of cultivated disdain that people less dark than himself would be shy of exhibiting lest they be accused of racism. Naipaul has, of course, faced this accusation, most prominently from his contemporary from the Caribbean, the great poet Derek Walcott. But since he is so clearly a "wog" himself, who surely must have faced racist slights in England, this kind of reproach has merely added to his myth as a supreme artist, beyond definition.

Naipaul was, however, rather careful during his first encounter with the continent: out of about nine months spent in East Africa, mainly in Uganda, in 1966, he allowed himself only a magazine article on Idi

Amin's coup and a section, albeit the longest, of his novella, *In a Free State* (1971).

I first read this book in the home of a Jamaican British lawyer who – like many other Caribbean intellectuals – disdained Naipaul but almost compulsively read his books anyway, in London in 1997. In that novella, like other colonial novels that preceded it (particularly Greene's *Heart of the Matter*, set in British-ruled Sierra Leone of the 1940s) Africa is only background; the key characters are European expatriates, actually a very odd English couple driving through a disrupted Uganda under curfew, facing violence, and then seeking refuge in a European compound. This was true to Naipaul's knowledge and rather wise of him. I was hypnotised by the writing at first: though I found the narrative inferior to Greene's, Naipaul's simple elegant sentences and brilliant scenes combined to produce supreme entertainment. Any time Naipaul lingers a little on an African character, however, humour shades into disgust. In a hotel scene, an African bartender leaves behind him "little disturbances of smell;" and about some well-dressed educated Africans – perhaps diplomats or politicians or civil servants – the narrator glibly says, "They hadn't paid for the suits they wore; in some cases they had had the drapers deported." This was at the time that Idi Amin had expelled Indians in Uganda and confiscated their businesses; and Naipaul, sympathetic to the Indians, now felt that all Africans in Uganda were complicit in the theft. This was a first glimpse into Naipaul's dark convoluted mind.

It was during his time in Uganda that Naipaul met the young American soon-to-be-writer, Paul Theroux, who in 1998 published an entertaining and blistering account of his long friendship with Naipaul, depicting him as a desperate sort of snob and misogynist who reserved a special kind of cruelty for weak and defenceless people, and Naipaul's attitude to Africans as racist. The book didn't shock anyone who had followed Naipaul's writings and pompous pronouncements over the decades, but Theroux was condemned all the same by many critics for back-stabbing – until, that is, the publication of Patrick French's authorised biography of Naipaul, *The World is What it is* in 2008, which fleshed out these charges in excruciating detail.

In 1975, on assignment for the *New York Review of Books*, Naipaul spent several weeks in Zaire (now the Democratic Republic of Congo), out of which emerged a long article, "A New King for the Congo", and a novel – said by some to be Naipaul's most accomplished – *A Bend in the River*. These two works best encapsulate Naipaul's attitude to Africa, and they deserve to be read closely. Both works are a rather tendentious tribute to Joseph Conrad, who set three important works – two stories, 'An Outpost of Progress' and the famous novella *The Heart of Darkness*; and *The Congo Journal* – in the country: Conrad's influence on Naipaul is like a millstone around Naipaul's neck where Africa is concerned; and this influence both fires and limits his vision of the continent. It was clearly from Conrad that Naipaul derived his interest especially in that Central African country.

Naipaul arrived in Zaire shortly after Mohamed Ali's famous rumble-in-the-jungle fight with Foreman: the place was still in the news for his mainly American readers. Naipaul's interest in politics and history here, as elsewhere in his many writings, is perfunctory and idiosyncratic; in fact he has very little political instinct, for which he is proud, and hardly any aptitude for serious historical inquiry, a judgment he may contest. He appeared curiously uneasy about educated Congolese he met, including university students who could talk intelligently about Stendhal. He detected among them a certain kind of 'rage' – a favourite word of his – the sort of 'resentment' which he felt will "at any time be converted into a wish to wipe out and undo, an African nihilism, the rage of primitive men coming to themselves and finding that they have been fooled and affronted." Pretentious, meaningless, pompous talk, of course; and over and over again he invokes Conrad, as in this defining paragraph: "To Joseph Conrad, Stanleyville…was the heart of darkness. It was there, in Conrad's story, that Kurtz reigned, the ivory agent degraded from idealism to savagery, taken back to the earliest ages of man, by wilderness, solitude and power, his house surrounded by impaled human heads. Seventy years later, at this *bend in the river* [my emphasis] something like Conrad's fantasy came to pass." He was referring to Mobutu, Zaire's then hopelessly corrupt leader, who – unlike Kurtz – had been "maddened not by contact with wilderness and primitivism, but with the civilization established" by the likes of Kurtz.

This theme – of an Africa of nihilism and lurking danger from which any sensible person should escape – is fleshed out in the novel that followed, *A Bend in the River*(1979) In it Naipaul, now more confident and certainly more arrogant than when he wrote *In a Free State*, is adventurous. The narrator is a dislocated Indian trader who is trying to find a fortune in a rapidly disintegrating Congo. The place had had its civil wars, and a strongman had emerged who uses European mercenaries and his own brutal troops to impose some kind of order. This order is wholly patrimonial, but the strongman has style: he even articulates an 'ideology', and publishes a book of his own saying, which he deems to as wise as Mao's. His vision is large: he is intent on creating a 'new man' in an Africa that can square up with the world. He creates a new city, the Domain: but this Domain is a hoax; it is the work of Europeans, and, once left to Africans, to whom it has no meaning, it will return to 'bush'. This is very obviously Naipaul's view of postcolonial Africa: Africa has gone to seeds after the European colonialist left, the villas they built – like the villas the Romans left in Britain – now turned into primitive camping sites. "The big lawns and gardens had returned to bush; the streets had disappeared; vines and creepers had grown over broken, bleached walls of concrete or hollow clay brick." In the end, there is the inevitable chaos and violence; and Salim barely escapes with his life – to Europe, that bastion of solidity, security and civilization, the place where Naipaul long called his home.

Since postcolonial Africa, then, is both a hoax and dismal failure, there must be an essential Africa that has survived all the great cruelties, the slave trade (about which the novel makes flippant references), the colonial intrusion, and the postcolonial meltdown. Naipaul gives a hint in the novel that this essence is religion, African spirituality: something that has survived the great foreign onslaughts; that has withstood even the two greatest imperial religions since antiquity, Christianity and Islam, which elsewhere had swept away all other religions they had encountered. Christianity destroyed the mighty state paganism of Rome and Islam overwhelmed the state Zoroastrianism of the great Persian Empire almost upon encounter. Have both failed in Africa? But this is not the question that interests Naipaul, who himself has professed to have no religion. "I suppose you can say," Indar, a character very much Naipaul's alter ego says in the novel, "that some people have been so depersonalised by those religions [Christianity and Islam] that they are out of touch with Africa." This, in fact, is an iteration of an old European pathology that modern Africans, unable to fully negotiate the foreign influences with their inherited cultures, are sucked into some kind of neurotic dualism and have lost touch with a romantic old Africa. Naipaul carried with him this dubious idea through his 'travel on a theme' in Africa for his *The Masque of Africa: Glimpses of African Belief* (2010), what might be said to be his crowning work on the continent.

He found full support for this idea from Susan, "a poet of merit and a literature teacher", in Uganda: eager perhaps to impress her famous visitor, a potential promoter, Susan tells Naipaul what he clearly wanted to hear: "My people had a civilisation... The missionaries ... brainwashed us ... When a person or race comes and imposes on you, it takes away everything, and it is a vicious thing to do." In Gabon, where Naipaul celebrates the lush rainforest (he finds African spirituality there) and then bemoans the fact that the Chinese (who he claims hate nature) will soon denude it, another star-struck intellectual tells Naipaul, "The new religions, Islam and Christianity, are just on the top. Inside us is the forest."

It is a theme that Naipaul has explored before, though tangentially, in an article on Ivory Coast that appeared in the New Yorker magazine in 1984. In the article, "The Crocodiles of Yamoussoukro", Naipaul appeared to admire the great achievements of that country under its veteran leader, *Houphouët-Boigny. They included Abidjan (the country's capital), which "begun unpromisingly on the bleak mud of a fetid lagoon" had become a great commercial and sophisticated city. So postcolonial Africa, after-all, is not all failure? Having made this allowance, however, Naipaul then* discovers a féticher who was famous with the locals; and then he lingers round the crocodiles in an artificial lake by the presidential palace in Yamoussoukro. Finally, Naipaul began to wonder whether Abidjan and Yamoussoukro weren't standing on sand, the perishable creation of magic.

African religion, in Naipaul's view, is a reckoning after magic; and Naipaul believes that such 'earth religions' send the mind back to the "beginning of things". No one, of course, will go to Naipaul for instruction on African religion, about which there are many excellent studies. One reads him for the beautiful sentences, and to get a taste of his latest prejudice.

In *The Masque of Africa* Naipaul records his impressions of the role of religion in Uganda, Ghana, Nigeria, Ivory Coast, Gabon, and South Africa in 2008–2009. He finds this role everywhere overwhelming. In a reminder of the parable that one should never go back in old age to a place where one had a good time in youth, Naipaul is appalled by Uganda, which he found overpopulated with cruel people who throw garbage all around their cities and eat cats. He seems to like West Africa, particularly Ghana, better: he finds Accra a city of municipal order, clean and well-maintained. His impression of Ghana is, of course, helped by the generosity of one of his Ghanaian hosts, who saves the stingy Naipaul the trouble of paying some bills, but he is right about Accra. In parts of Ghana, however, he is appalled by stories of people who eat cats. He warms up to JJ Rawlings, a former president of Ghana, partly because the cat in his house where Naipaul is entertained seems to be happy, and Rawlings' wife is a charming hostess. He collects horrible stories of "kitchen cruelty" in Ivory Coast: the locals, despite living in cities, kill cats in a particularly brutal way and eat them. In a previous visit, a member of the country's ruling elite had entertained Naipaul to dinner, and Naipaul accordingly makes admiring comments about the country's elegance (and makes scornful statements about Ghana). This time, the Ivorian elite, preoccupied with their political troubles, are not at hand to share Naipaul's luminous company at home, and Ivory Coast has become a land of cruelty and backwardness. He finds mounds of garbage everywhere he goes. From self-loathing Richmond, a servant of his Ghanaian host – these are the kinds of people Naipaul likes, his key sources for the book – Naipaul collects and foolishly relates a nasty rumour about Houphouët-Boigny indulging in human sacrifice as fetish practice. You will not know from this stupid account that Houphouët-Boigny was a life-long Catholic, was a member of the French parliament, and served with distinction in several ministerial positions in France before leading his country to independence in 1960 as its universally admired leader.

In Nigeria, he is at first almost overwhelmed by the energy and chaos of Lagos before admiring its entrepreneurial spirit. He is horrified by the garbage there, too. Miles away from Lagos, he gets undiluted pleasure from a pristine forest enclave the Yoruba use as religious sanctuary: here again he seems to find the essence of African spirituality in the forest. When he gets to Northern Nigeria, Naipaul's old antipathy towards Islam is on display: he starts seeing moraines of garbage right outside the small airport in the ancient city of Kano (which he ridicules for its pretention to antique greatness), and he bemoans the poverty and illiteracy presumably created by Islam in the area. He reports seeing "innumerable, thin-limbed" Muslim children "in dusty little gowns, the unfailing product of multiple marriages and many concubines." Though politics are very large in the Nigeria, and though Boko Haram was already active, you get no sense of that in Naipaul's fluent but idiotic account. You will not even know that the country produced the eminent writers Chinua Achebe and Wole Soyinka, both of whom have written with great penetration about politics and religion in Nigeria. Naipaul has made disdainful remarks about both writers, and Achebe long dismissed Naipaul as an absurd modern-day Conrad spouting "pompous rubbish" about Africa. The section on South Africa, the weakest in this very weak, perfunctory and pointless book, is second-handed: Naipaul relies on the guidance of controversial South African writer Rian Malan. Even amidst its great sophistication and complexity ("the skyscrapers of Johannesburg did not stand on sand", Naipaul says, sheepishly), Naipaul hears of fetish people dealing in human body parts in Johannesburg. He meets with Winnie Mandela, who expresses her disappointment with the new South Africa. Naipaul then indulges in his typical idiosyncratic reflection on the country's past, and he concludes: "after apartheid a resolution is not really possible until the people who wish to impose themselves on Africa violate some essential part of their being". This is, of course, awkwardly Conradian; and, of course, it is nonsense.

How, then, can one sum up Naipaul's long, almost obsessive, engagement with Africa, a continent he clearly does not like? Naipaul was in his 70s, an asthmatic and hefty old man struggling to walk, when he made the long trip for *The Masque of Anarchy*; frequently he grouses about inconveniences, little troubles, and about reasonable requests for money by seers, fétichers, fortune-tellers, and others for their time. He clearly felt that he had something new and important to say about Africa. In an interview after the book's publication, Naipaul spoke about a 'developing sympathy' for Africa that sent him back there in his old age, "to write of Africa in another way...I was looking for the human breakdown, as it were. I had to be very particular. I didn't want to write about politics, or local internal trouble. I just wanted to stay with fundamental beliefs, if I could find them."

Naipaul's idea of sympathy is as mysterious and meaningless as his Africa. And is the work of seers, fétichers, fortune-tellers an example of 'human breakdown'? Is it fundamental to African belief or is it a money-making endeavour which – though important in some settings – is actually tengential to African belief? Surely, Islam in Northern Nigeria is old enough to be considered indigenuous there? It is nonsensical to consider the two great religions, Islam and Christianity, with their large moral, philosophical and humanitarian claims, foreign in any country where they are widely practised. Only an ignorant bigot can make such claims; and though an accomplished and sometimes insightful writer, Naipaul has revealed himself, over and over again, as a bigot where Africa and its people are concerned. He has not evolved (a favourite word of his).

So *The Masque of Africa* fails, and fails resoundingly. Perhaps Africans should stop taking note of such blinkered travelers – they harp back to previous centuries, and Africa, despite its current troubles, has moved on.

11.
Amos Sawyer's *Beyond Plunder*[79]

In 1871, the famous Liberian patriot and Pan Africanist Edward Blyden, accused of bedding the wife of President Roye, fled the country. Blyden was born in the Virgin Islands in the West Indies in 1832, and had immigrated to Liberia in 1851. A highly gifted man, Blyden would remain there for thirty years, gradually rising to the highest levels of Liberian society: beginning as a Presbyterian minister, Blyden then became newspaper editor, professor of the classics, President of Liberia College, Ambassador to Britain, Minister of Interior, and Secretary of State. In exile in Sierra Leone, Blyden wrote a friend that Monrovia, the Liberian capital, was "in a state of constant commotion" when he left. "The postmaster had been shot on the streets two days before I left by a mob of some thirty men who pierced his body with numerous bullets," he wrote. "And mobs were the order of the day. Such a people as the unfortunate Liberians will do anything to destroy a man who they hate. May the Lord shield me from their malice."

I recently read this letter – which was sent to Henry Venn, of the Church Missionary Society (CMS), in London – at the CMS archives at the Birmingham University Library. Blyden returned again to Liberia after several years, contested presidential elections, and, losing, went back permanently to Sierra Leone, where he died in 1912. It is not difficult to imagine why the talented Blyden would have thought that gaining the presidency of a country he had come to fear would make all the difference in the world.

Liberia has always been the quintessential unitary state, with power almost exclusively confined to its small coastal capital. The Liberian political elite has always been very small – probably numbering a few dozen – and firmly in control of the political processes was the President

---

[79] Review of Amos Sawyer *Beyond Plunder: Towards Democratic Governance in Liberia*

(Boulder, Colo.: Lynne Rienner Publishers, 2005), Concord Times September 2008.

who, though chosen in a somewhat sham election, acted very much autocratically. To displease the President meant, as Blyden found out, exile or worse. Graham Greene, passing through Liberia in the 1930s, observed this shambolic situation with great acuity. "There was a kind of unwritten law that the President could take two terms of office and then he had to let another man in to pick the spoils," Greene noted in *Journey Without Maps*, his classic travelogue. "It was a question of letting... the newspapers were his; most important of all, he printed and distributed the ballot papers. When King returned in 1928 he had a majority over his opponent...of 600,000, although the whole electoral roll amounted to less than 15,000." When Greene encountered the President, "Africa, lovely, vivid and composed, slipped away, and one was left with... an affable manner and rhetoric, lots of rhetoric...'Once elected, [the President said], and in charge of the machine...why then, I'm boss of the whole show.'"

Amos Sawyer is, like Blyden, a Liberian intellectual and politician who has risen to the highest levels of the Liberian state and society, including university professor and dean, and then Interim President of the country for four years at the height of its civil war, 1990-1994. Sawyer has published a number of works on his country, most notably *The Emergence of Autocracy in Liberia* (1992), which details Liberia's trajectory from a mordantly corrupt settler oligarchy in most of the nineteenth and twentieth centuries to patrimonial autocracy and brutal military rule, arguing that the country's founding was "flawed in conception." The book connects Liberia's political culture and subsequent bloody conflict to its solely extractive and primary resource industry, which was made to benefit only its foreign exploiters and a few in the Monrovia charmed circle.

After leaving office as Interim President – appointed by West African and Liberian civil society leaders – following a markedly turbulent tenure, Sawyer founded the Center for Democratic Empowerment (CEDE), a non-governmental organisation which aimed to help push some of Sawyer's political ideas into the public consciousness. When Charles Taylor became President in 1997, he quickly found such ideas subversive. In November 2000, Taylor's thugs broke into and ransacked CEDE's Monrovia offices. Sawyer took the hint; he and Wesseh fled the country, and CEDE moved to neighbouring Ivory Coast. Sawyer later went back to the University of Indiana. *Beyond Plunder* was written while Sawyer was associate director and research scholar at the Workshop in Political Theory and Policy Analysis at the university.

The book draws both on his research as an academic and his experience as a politician, though the combination is not always a happy one. In fact the best parts of the book are the first three chapters, where Sawyer's academic eyes are most in evidence; when, in the subsequent chapters, he attempts to combine theory and practice, as he puts it, the effect is often tedious. At that point one wishes that Sawyer had written a straightforward memoir.

Beyond Plunder recounts what Sawyer calls the "tragic period of pillage, plunder, and carnage" which led to the complete collapse of Liberia's governing institutions, the emergence of Taylor at the helm of the state, and the subsequent occupation of the country by thousands of UN troops. While Sawyer notes the "destructive consequences of individual agency," in particular the roles of figures like Samuel Doe (the Master-Sergeant who ruled the country from 1980 until his murder and mutilation in 1990) and Taylor), he focuses on the serious institutional problems which characterised the Liberian state throughout its existence.

Liberia had been established in 1822 by American blacks – some of them just freed from slavery – in an experimental process of colonisation sponsored by the American Colonization Society (ASC). The country became a republic in 1847, the first in Africa. But whatever glamour this bestowed was undercut by the fact that this independent republic really concerned only a few thousand Americo-Liberians (as the freed blacks were called); at the end of the nineteenth century the settlers, now formally governing the geographical space of modern Liberia, numbered only 25,000. When in 1874 the Liberian government decided that other groups adjacent to Monrovia would be allowed representation in the national legislature as "referees and advisers," their advice was restricted to matters involving their own ethnic groups, and they were denied the vote.[80]

---

[80] Yekutiel Gershoni, "Minority Rule and Political Trade-In, *"Liberian Studies Journal* xxvii I (2001), 63-81.

Very little attempt was made to open up political space for the indigenous Liberians; as Yekutiel Gershoni has noted, even the perceptive Blyden looked beyond them to encourage more immigration from American blacks.[81] The overriding goal of the settler elite society, Sawyer notes, was to "maintain its cohesion and dominance" in the country. State capacity was, in consequence, severely limited; even by 1930 when Graham Greene visited, he reported that beyond Monrovia, Liberian government officials were little more than desultory exiles stealing what they can from the impoverished indigenes. In fact, it was only as a result of pressure from the encroaching French and British empires that the Liberian government attempted to set up formal governing institutions, however feeble, across parts of the country. This exogenous pressure, writes Sawyer, "thrust upon" Liberia the requirement of "strong centralized control." The US government refused to adopt Liberia as a colony or to acknowledge its independence until Abraham Lincoln did so in 1862 (Liberia declared itself an independent republic in 1847). Only the paternal support of Britain, whose anti-slavery colony in Sierra Leone was something of an inspiration to Liberia, ensured Liberia's survival in its early stages. The British helped set up a Liberia Frontier Force (LFF), with a British officer, the opportunistic Major Robert Mackay, as commander; a few years later, in February 1909, Mackay attempted to overthrow the Liberian government and failed.

Liberia's fortune changed forever when in 1926 President Charles Dunbar Burgess King signed an agreement with the American Firestone Company to invest $20 million in rubber plantation; the company also gave a loan of $5 million to the government, and then took the management of the country's customs to ensure the loan was paid back. Firestone fueled both a measure of economic growth and an extreme form of patrimonialism, with receipts from its taxes and royalties being controlled directly by the Presidency. This ensured that the Liberian government had enough resources to ignore the overall socio-economic development of the country, as well make the Presidency a very potent and overwhelming force. In the mid 1950s, William Tubman, the

---

[81] See Gershoni, "Minority Rule and Political Trade-In."

embodiment of this new patrimonialism, had made the presidency utterly personalised: without attempting to make serious, inclusive reforms, he simply created "a new political base of settlers of low status, indigenous chiefs, and members of the Monrovia elite who had become disaffected with their own inner circle." Tubman "doled out public money to buy loyalty, established an elaborate and greatly feared security network, crushed those members of the opposition whose loyalty he could not buy, and rammed through legislation and constitutional amendment removing presidential term limits." This presidency, more a personal cult than anything else, was what William Tolbert inherited in 1971. The humourless and uncharismatic Tolbert made only feeble attempts to respond to the growing demand by the indigenous population and radical intellectuals in Monrovia for greater inclusion and openness of the democratic space. He was murdered in his bedroom by Doe in 1980.

In power, Doe replicated the cruel dialectics of settler rule by substituting his largely illiterate Krahn ethnic group as the new masters of Liberia, and himself the new, very violent dictator. He had no time or comprehension for the settler pretense to refinement and high ideals; his was raw, unmediated power. It was this regime that Taylor, a former Doe employee, took on in 1989. When he became President, he proved even worse than Doe: Taylor's regime was almost entirely destructive; he failed to build (or rebuild) a single school or hospital; and even the Robertsfield Terminal building his forces destroyed long ago still remained a shell. More violence followed, and the UN intervened. After a successful process of disarmament of the warring militias, Liberia's war, which claimed the lives of thousands of civilians, and led to the almost complete destruction of the country's already limited infrastructure, was declared over. The country had an election in late 2005, which Ellen Johnson-Sirleaf, a former UN employee, won. Taylor is now in the detention of the UN-Sierra Leone Special Court, facing crimes against humanity for his role in the war in neighbouring Sierra Leone.

The question is: What next? Sawyer advocates "a serious and systematic effort to reconstruct institutions differently," and he calls for the convening of a "sovereign national conference" to chart out a future for the country. (Sawyer wanted this conference to have been held before the elections, but it wasn't. In a correspondence with me, he insists that there is still a need for it). Sawyer wants in particular reforming and limiting the awesome powers of the presidency, since he himself, as President, saw how "presidential approbation was the single most valuable asset sought after in Liberian society, and how laws and norms reinforced each other to uphold its value." To an extent this is true of most African states, but as we have seen, Liberia's historical experience shows that this is perniciously true of the country. The problem is that in the current reality of the complete neutering of all institutions of state, the President, even an enlightened and apparently progressive figure like Johnson-Sirleaf, will not particularly welcome the diffusion of her authority, which such a reform will surely lead to.

One of the more hopeful (and in a sense surprising) aspects of the Liberian reality is that the old elite, the Americo-Liberians – who still constitute a highly influential class – see themselves, and are seen by others, as integrally a welcome part of Liberian society, and are indeed among the most active advocates of comprehensive reform. As Stephen Ellis has shown in his study of the Liberian civil war, *The Mask of Anarchy* (Hurst 1999), the Americo-Liberians were not particularly targeted by any of the factions in the Liberian war.[82] The only community among Liberia's sixteen ethnic groups that proved somewhat problematic was the Mandingos, and that is because many of them seem to look to Guinea as their homeland. Johnson-Sirleaf, who understands this problem very well, has been actively trying to co-opt them in the political process, and this seems to be working.

Sawyer, however, is looking beyond what a President, however progressive, can do to address deeper institutional problems that can be addressed by reforms, and for strengths that can be built upon. He discusses in detail most of these – mainly traditional and embedded institutions – but this is difficult to follow. (Sawyer warns in the Preface that some practitioners may find the book "not sufficiently prescriptive; some scholars may find it not sufficiently analytical or theoretical; and many Liberians may find it jargon-laden," and one has to admit to a tinge of frustration at having to constantly engage with too many esoteric concepts and terms which sometimes look contradictory). The salutary

---

[82] Stephen Ellis, *The Mask of Anarchy: The Destruction of Liberia and the Religious Dimension of an African Civil War* (London: Hurst, 1999), 192.

work of Poro and traditional chiefs are all very well, but one has either to build a modern democratic state or not at all; and some traditional institutions simply have to be downgraded or entirely superseded. Sawyer writes that he seeks a transformation of Liberia "from a highly centralized governmental arrangement to a system of multiple centers of limited authority". This task, he writes, should better be decided by a national consultative conference. Consultative conferences, however, by their nature must have a more limited mandate to be effective; their agendas in any case are often controlled by the people who organize them, and in this case, it will have to be the government of Liberia, which no doubt will have a slightly different view of what reconstituting the political order should be.

An underlying theme throughout *Beyond Plunder* – and a very serious one – is that the recent experience of war and predation shows clearly that the fortunes of the three countries of the Mano River basin – Liberia, Sierra Leone and Guinea – are intimately linked, and any lasting solution must involve intimate cooperation and coordination among the states. Sawyer even suggests that a form of federation or confederation is highly desirable, a point which certainly reflects the reality of artificial borders dividing the peoples of the sub-region. I think this is a very important point, for as we saw during the more than a decade of conflict in the region, the attempts to treat each country in isolation only helped to complicate the crises. It is to be hoped that Sawyer's views will be taken seriously by the leaders and peoples of the region.